Organizational Justice and Human Resource Management

FOUNDATIONS FOR ORGANIZATIONAL SCIENCE

A Sage Publications Series

Series Editor

David Whetten, *Brigham Young University*

Editors

Peter J. Frost, *University of British Columbia*
Anne S. Huff, *University of Colorado and Cranfield University (UK)*
Benjamin Schneider, *University of Maryland*
M. Susan Taylor, *University of Maryland*
Andrew Van de Ven, *University of Minnesota*

The FOUNDATIONS FOR ORGANIZATIONAL SCIENCE series supports the development of students, faculty, and prospective organizational science professionals through the publication of texts authored by leading organizational scientists. Each volume provides a highly personal, hands-on introduction to a core topic or theory and challenges the reader to explore promising avenues for future theory development and empirical application.

Books in This Series

PUBLISHING IN THE ORGANIZATIONAL SCIENCES, 2nd Edition
Edited by L. L. Cummings and Peter J. Frost

SENSEMAKING IN ORGANIZATIONS
Karl E. Weick

INSTITUTIONS AND ORGANIZATIONS
W. Richard Scott

RHYTHMS OF ACADEMIC LIFE
Peter J. Frost and M. Susan Taylor

RESEARCHERS HOOKED ON TEACHING:
Noted Scholars Discuss the Synergies of Teaching and Research
Rae André and Peter J. Frost

THE PSYCHOLOGY OF DECISION MAKING: People in Organizations
Lee Roy Beach

ORGANIZATIONAL JUSTICE AND HUMAN RESOURCE MANAGEMENT
Robert Folger and Russell Cropanzano

RECRUITING EMPLOYEES: Individual and Organizational Perspectives
Alison E. Barber

Robert Folger
Russell Cropanzano

Organizational Justice and Human Resource Management

Foundations for
Organizational
Science
A Sage Publications Series

SAGE Publications
International Educational and Professional Publisher
Thousand Oaks   London   New Delhi

For information:

 SAGE Publications, Inc.
2455 Teller Road
Thousand Oaks, California 91320
E-mail: order@sagepub.com

SAGE Publications Ltd.
6 Bonhill Street
London EC2A 4PU
United Kingdom

SAGE Publications India Pvt. Ltd.
M-32 Market
Greater Kailash I
New Delhi 110 048 India

Printed in the United States of America

Library of Congress Cataloging-in-Publication Data

Folger, Robert
    Organizational justice and human resource management/
by Robert Folger and Russell Cropanzano.
        p. cm.—(Foundations for organizational science)
    Includes bibliographical references and index.
    ISBN 0-8039-5686-X (cloth: acid-free paper)
    ISBN 0-8039-5687-8 (pbk.: acid-free paper)
    1. Organizational behavior—Moral and ethical aspects. 2. Personnel
management—Moral and ethical aspects. 3. Distributive justice.
I. Cropanzano, Russell. II. Title. III. Series.
HD58.7 .F65 1998
658.3—dc21   98-8895

    99 00 01 02 03 04 10 9 8 7 6 5 4 3 2

Acquiring Editor:	Marquita Flemming
Editorial Assistant:	Frances Borghi
Production Editor:	Astrid Virding/Wendy Westgate
Production Assistant:	Karen Wiley
Typesetter:	Marion Warren
Print Buyer:	Anna Chin

To my parents on their 50th wedding anniversary.
—R.F.

To my wife, Carol.
—R.C.

Contents

Introduction to the Series

The title of this series, **Foundations for Organizational Science** (FOS), denotes a distinctive focus. FOS books are educational aids for mastering the core theories, essential tools, and emerging perspectives that constitute the field of organizational science (broadly defined to include organizational behavior, organizational theory, human resource management, and business strategy). The primary objective of this series is to support ongoing professional development among established scholars.

The series was born out of many long conversations among several colleagues, including Peter Frost, Anne Huff, Rick Mowday, Ben Schneider, Susan Taylor, and Andy Van de Ven, over a number of years. From those discussions, we concluded that there has been a major gap in our professional literature, as characterized by the following comment: "If I, or one of my students, want to learn about population ecology, diversification strategies, group dynamics, or personnel selection, we are pretty much limited to academic journal articles or books that are written either for content experts or practitioners. Wouldn't it be wonderful to have access to the teaching notes from a course taught by a master teacher of this topic?"

The plans for compiling a set of learning materials focusing on professional development emerged from our extended discussions of common experiences and observations, including the following:

1. While serving as editors of journals, program organizers for professional association meetings, and mentors for new faculty members, we have observed wide variance in theoretical knowledge and tool proficiency in our field. To the extent that this outcome reflects available learning opportunities, we hope that this series will help "level the playing field."

2. We have all "taught" in doctoral and junior faculty consortia prior to our professional meetings and have been struck by how often the participants comment, "I wish that the rest of the meetings [paper sessions and symposia] were as informative." Such observations got us thinking—Are our doctoral courses more like paper sessions or doctoral consortia? What type of course would constitute a learning experience analogous to attending a doctoral consortium? What materials would we need to teach such a course? We hope that the books in this series have the "touch and feel" of a doctoral consortium workshop.

3. We all have had some exposure to the emerging "virtual university" in which faculty and students in major doctoral programs share their distinctive competencies, either through periodic jointly sponsored seminars or through distance learning technology, and we would like to see these opportunities diffused more broadly. We hope that reading our authors' accounts will be the next best thing to observing them in action.

4. We see some of the master scholars in our field reaching the later stages of their careers, and we would like to "bottle" their experience and insight for future generations. Therefore, this series is an attempt to disseminate "best practices" across space and time.

To address these objectives, we ask authors in this series to pass along their "craft knowledge" to students and faculty beyond the boundaries of their local institutions by writing from the perspective of seasoned teachers and mentors. Specifically, we encourage them to invite readers into their classrooms (to gain an understanding of the past, present, and future of scholarship in particular areas from the perspective of their firsthand experience), as well as into their offices and hallway conversations (to gain insights into the subtleties and nuances of exemplary professional practice).

By explicitly focusing on an introductory doctoral seminar setting, we encourage our authors to address the interests and needs of nonexpert students and colleagues who are looking for answers to questions such as the following: Why is this topic important? How did it originate and how has it evolved? How is it different from related topics? What do we actually know about this topic? How does one effectively communicate this information to students and practitioners? What are the methodological pitfalls and conceptual dead ends that should be avoided? What are the most/least promising opportunities for theory development and empirical study in this area? What questions/situations/phenomena are not well suited for this theory or tool?

What is the most interesting work in progress? What are the most critical gaps in our current understanding that need to be addressed during the next 5 years?

We are pleased to share our dream with you, and we encourage your suggestions for how these books can better satisfy your learning needs—as a newcomer to the field preparing for prelims or developing a research proposal, or as an established scholar seeking to broaden your knowledge and proficiency.

DAVID A. WHETTEN
SERIES EDITOR

Preface

The What and the Why of Social Justice

This is a book about organizational justice. In particular, it is about the conditions of employment that lead individuals to believe they are being treated fairly or unfairly. In the course of writing this book, we have reviewed a vast body of literature indicating that justice is an important motivator for working people. We will show that when individuals perceive a lack of fairness, their morale declines, they become more likely to leave their jobs, and they may even retaliate against the organization. Fair treatment, by contrast, breeds commitment, intentions to remain on the job, and helpful citizenship behaviors that go beyond the call of formal job duties. In short, justice holds people together, whereas injustice can pull them apart.

As a prelude to our book, this preface is organized around two broad questions: What is justice and why does it matter? We take up this issue in three sections. First, we define organizational fairness in a general way, distinguishing it from related philosophical ideas. Second, we examine why justice matters in human societies. We argue that fairness concerns arise out of a predicament faced by many social animals: How can one pursue individual goals in the context of a social group? Fairness provides a means for resolving this dilemma. Finally, we conclude by again asking the question: What is justice? This time our answer will be more specific, focusing on the different varieties of fairness that influence work life.

What Is Justice? Social Science and Philosophical Definitions

For a scientific investigation to go forward, it must define—in even a cursory sense—the object of inquiry. Social justice researchers have succeeded in that task, but their definition has had trouble competing with more popular conceptions. The term *justice* has a colloquial meaning that is very close to its philosophical origins. It is social scientists who employ peculiar terminology. In this section, we try to illustrate how researchers have approached these definitional matters. We discuss and define the meaning of social justice, both as understood by philosophers and as understood by social scientists.

Let us start by considering where scholars concur. Social scientists and philosophers would agree that a "just" act is one that is perceived to be good or righteous. Similarly, both groups of scholars would also suggest that an act can be good without being fair (or unfair). For example, Aristotle believed that a good person should live a life of temperance or moderation. By that view, a drunkard or hedonist is not a righteous person. People who consider excessive drinking to be bad, however, probably would not say that it is "unfair." Fairness and unfairness seem irrelevant concepts for imprudent behavior harming no one else.

On the other hand, suppose the drunkard begins to inconvenience his or her coworkers. Harm to coworkers by a drunkard, when the coworkers did nothing to deserve being harmed, seems to qualify as an injustice. Why? The answer is that judgments about justice usually involve a social context and unwarranted actions by one party that harm or threaten other parties (such as by imposing consequences that they consider to be undeserved). If a person drinks and harms no one else, then although this behavior might be wrong-headed, stupid, and even sinful, it is neither fair nor unfair. On the other hand, once that individual begins to affect the lives of others, then fairness can become an issue. We can describe the selfish alcoholic—willing to ignore the prospects of imposing undue harm on others—as unfair.

In organizations, justice is about the rules and social norms governing how outcomes (e.g., rewards and punishments) should be distributed, the procedures used for making such distribution decisions (as well as other types of decisions), and how people are treated interpersonally (Bies & Tripp, 1995a, 1995b). When no outcomes are being assigned and when there are no processes for assigning them (i.e., no one is interacting), then justice becomes moot. When people interact, however, they begin to treat one another in certain ways. They might, for example, derogate each other (i.e., take away someone's social status or self-respect) or they might treat each other respect-fully (i.e., assign each other positive status). Some transactions and other types of interactions are judged to be virtuous or fair, whereas others are not "proper" and are unfair. When we say that someone has treated us "unfairly," we mean that he or she has violated some ethical standard(s) regarding moral behavior. That person has not treated us as we believe people "should" be treated.

From this introduction, it is probably clear where philosophers and social scientists diverge. Ethical philosophers are interested in providing *prescriptive* or *normative* definitions of justice. Loosely, we can say that they give us guidance as to how we should behave (Donaldson & Dunfee, 1994; Waterman, 1988). Philosophers attempt to develop standards and "first principles" that allow us to make ethical decisions. Of course, this enterprise defines *justice* with respect to some philosophical system. The same act can be seen as more or less fair, depending on which philosophical system one utilizes. For this reason, people vary in what they see as ethical behavior (Hosmer, 1995; Jones, 1991). For example, Rokeach (1973) argued that individuals who value both equality and freedom tend to view wide gaps between the rich and the poor as unfair. They do not like it when a relatively small number of people control a disproportionate amount of the available wealth. These individuals often prefer democratic socialism as a means of rectifying what they see as an "unfair" income distribution. On the other hand, those who have strong values for freedom but less for equality are more oriented toward free-market capitalism. Wide variability in incomes is not unfair in this philosophical world view because equality is a secondary value. For people with this orien-tation, a lack of justice can result from government restrictions and "confis-cation" of their wealth through taxes. Justice, in this philosophical sense, refers to the extent to which a given action, outcome, or circumstance is in alignment with a certain ethical paradigm (Hosmer, 1995).

If this book were about philosophical views on justice, the content would focus on applied ethical principles, perhaps even a touch of theology. It would probably not be empirical, although it might be informed by data (cf. Don-aldson & Dunfee, 1994; Randall & Gibson, 1990). However, we have offered the reader this definition of justice only by way of contrast. For social and organizational scientists, justice is defined phenomenologically. That is, an act is "just" because someone thinks it is just and responds accordingly. This definition is subjective and socially constructed. As one might imagine, two or more people can disagree. Justice, then, is a perceptual cognition. People perceive a certain event. They then make judgments regarding that event and store them in memory. Justice is a means by which individuals make sense out of their social worlds. We can see from this analysis that justice perceptions share much in common with stereotypes, schemas, heuristics, and attitudes.

The distinction between the philosophical and the social scientific view of justice is important for understanding terminology. Suppose there was a moderately sized family business. On retirement, the owner of the firm gave his inexperienced son the job of president, thereby passing over employees with greater seniority, more experience, and better performance records. Was this promotion unfair? A philosopher might say *yes* or *no,* depending on his or her ethical inclinations. For example, the individual who strongly believed in the doctrine of employment at will would see the company as the personal property of the owner. Although the owner's decision may have been foolhardy, it is not unfair. The owner can do whatever he wants with his property. One might debate this conclusion (most philosophers probably would), but the resolution ultimately depends on one's values. Depending on one's point of view, the act could be seen as fair.

A social scientist has a narrower question. In this case, the act is unfair when observers judge it to be unfair. The social scientist assesses perceived fairness by collecting data. If most people perceive the act as an injustice, then it is an injustice—as far as the social scientist is concerned. Another investigator disagreeing with that appraisal would probably refer to the quality of the data rather than to some abstract ethical system.

In this book, of course, we will be using the social scientific definition. Justice is about how rewards and punishments are distributed by and within social collectives, and it is also about how people govern relations with one another. It is about who gets what and whether the participants in (and observers of) these transactions believe them to be righteous. It is also about the reactions of participants and observers to the righteousness of other kinds of human interactions—those that seem to lie beyond material transaction and distribution. Once we understand what justice is, we can easily comprehend why it is so central to human affairs: People care deeply about how they are treated by others.

It should come as no surprise to learn that scholars of all stripes and eras have been concerned with social justice. Many of the earliest human writings, such as Hammurabi's Code and the Bible, showed an interest in social justice. These writings discussed how people should treat other people and how resources should be allocated. The myths and folklore of every culture also contain at least some tales designed to teach moral and ethical lessons. Likewise, in the Western philosophical tradition, philosophers since Plato and Aristotle have wrestled with issues of fairness. Indeed, it seems natural for human beings to worry about justice. Children show a concern for fairness at a very early age (see Wilson, 1993, for a review). Research reviewed by de Waal (1996) indicates that nonhuman primates show a rudimentary sense of justice; they practice reciprocity and punish those members who have the temerity to harm the group, displaying what ethologists call moralistic aggression. Despite differing norms, all human groups show at least some concern with fairness (Wilson, 1993), if this is understood to mean playing by the rules and abiding by ethical standards.

Although anyone can easily imagine unfair situations, it is difficult to envision a social world in which justice would not even be a consideration. We know unfairness because it violates our sense of what is fair. Anything else would require us to imagine a world in which no one cared about who got what, or in which there were no rules governing the allocation of benefits and punishments. This is not easy for us to contemplate. Indeed, when we meet people with absolutely no sense of justice we label them *psychopaths* or *narcissists* and assume that they are mentally ill (Wilson, 1993). Some might even suggest that a person who does not consider fairness should be separated from the rest of us by means of incarceration.

Why Justice?

All of these observations point to the pervasiveness of justice considerations in human endeavors. However, none of them specifies why this is so. We are much like the proverbial fish who, having never been anywhere else, fails to see that it is in the water. Because we often think in fairness terms, we have difficulty imagining how it could be otherwise. We can understand why justice is important by remembering that fairness concerns itself with what things get allocated and how these allocations take place. Thus, to say that justice matters is more or less synonymous with maintaining that people care about how they are treated by others. The roots of justice can be found in our inclination to affiliate with other people.

With these observations in mind, we are now ready to answer the "why" question. This preface will approach the matter broadly, dividing our argument into four sections. First, we discuss why people live and work in groups. We emphasize that social collectives, in the broadest sense of that term, provide *Homo sapiens* with a variety of advantages. Second, given the advantages of group living, it seems likely that gregariousness had clear survival value. On the basis of this, we will argue that sociability is built into the human psyche. Nature has endowed humans with a set of inclinations or needs that other people are helpful in fulfilling. Third, we will examine human needs in more detail. Generally speaking, human needs can be organized into two broad categories. One set of needs is economic or quasi-economic. For example, people require shelter, food, and so on. Another set is socioemotional. For example, people tend to be desirous of status and a sense of dignity. Such needs draw us to others. Fourth, we discuss how individual inclinations tug people into social groups as a means of fulfilling their needs. Consequently, most of us seek out others, but we tend to do so to fulfill our own objectives. As such, outcomes in the group need to be negotiated. Justice provides the vehicle by which these negotiations can occur.[1]

Why People Need Other People

The bottom line in species survival is the reproduction of viable offspring (Wright, 1994). Of course, to reach this goal one needs to stay alive long enough to mate. This requires obtaining adequate food and escaping predators, among other things. Human beings are especially vulnerable as infants. As Gould (1981) observed, humans are born relatively immature, as not much more than embryos. In addition, the large size of infant heads makes deliveries difficult and dangerous for mothers (Diamond, 1992). Fortunately, humans and related species can pool their otherwise modest physical resources by forming social groups. For most of evolutionary history, these groups consisted of small clans composed mostly of blood relations who made their living as hunter-gatherers (Diamond, 1992). Once groups are organized, all sorts of advantages begin to accrue. People can gather themselves into hunting parties (or, perhaps more accurately, scavenging parties; see Lewin, 1988), fight as a team, and share the all-important chores of child rearing and education.

Given these considerations, we might suspect that people would work together on the basis of nothing more than straightforward, rational considerations. This idea is no doubt largely true, as reason allows people to select among a plethora of alternative groups. For instance, we pick and choose among potential employers by taking our self-interest into account. A job applicant might accept the position that offers the highest pay (although he or she weighs other things as well; see Chapter 4 in this volume). In addition, we can also choose to modify the collectives of which we are already a part. For example, the size of a corporation might be expanded in order to boost manufacturing efficiency (Fukuyama, 1995).

Despite the strength of these arguments, they tell only part of the story. Purely rational considerations require a reasonably good intellect. Neither the cheetah nor the gray wolf sits down and reasons through the best hunting strategy—much less conducts an empirical study. Rather, the cheetah evolved as a solitary stalker and the gray wolf as a pack hunter. Within each species, style shows little variance. By extension, rational considerations cannot account for a key aspect of human life: People (or the ancestors of people) were affiliating in collectives before modern brain capacities had evolved (de Waal, 1996; Lewin, 1988). Undoubtedly, reason influences the mechanisms by which we select our comrades and friends. It also provides us with innovations and ideas for how these groups can be changed and adjusted. Our orientation toward others in general, however, predates sophisticated cognitive and linguistic capabilities. It is a more basic inclination, in the narrow sense that our thinking capacities developed within the context of our social natures, not the reverse.

We need to be extremely careful not to overstate this point. We are not arguing for biological determinism. A large brain provides humans with tremendous flexibility for engaging in innovative planning. Likewise, we do not intend to understate the role of culture. Obviously these influences are very important. It is also clear, however, that the vast majority of people, from all walks of life, eschew a solitary existence. Most of us seek some contact with others, although we vary widely in whom we choose and how much contact we prefer. With these caveats in mind, let us now take up the matter in greater detail.

How Nature Built Humans to Work
With Others: Evolution Within a Social Setting

Most anthropologists agree that humans share at least two attributes: big brains and a tendency to affiliate in social groups. These characteristics are, of course, related. Big brains allow us to keep track of who is in our in-groups and who else, conversely, is not (Bigelow, 1972). Moreover, they help us to remember the dominance hierarchies under which we all live, and they guide us in crafting the necessary political tactics to compete within that hierarchy (de Waal, 1996; Lewin, 1988). Using our intelligence, humans can also distinguish those among us who are honest and worthy of our trust from those who are selfish "free-riders" (Cosmides, 1989).

There is a subtle theme running through all of these examples. Human beings were probably organizing themselves into social groups when they were still *Australopithecus afarensis*. In other words, we were living in clans before we were humans or even hominids (Lewin, 1988; Wilson, 1978; Wright, 1994). Additionally, our big brains—the hallmark of humanity—did not condition us to this gregarious lifestyle; rather, the gregarious lifestyle helped lead to the evolution of the brain. Keep in mind that evolution is a response to environmental pressures. For our ancestors, that environment was largely a social environment. To state the matter loosely: We became human because we were social animals. Our evolutionary history has built us so that we need things that are best fulfilled by others.

Two Sets of Needs

Loosely speaking, people can be said to have two broad sets of needs. On the one hand, of course, are the basic needs that are requisite for individual survival: These are demands for concrete material things, such as food and shelter. This would also include legal tender (i.e., money) that can be readily exchanged for goods. These material needs can be said to have "a consummatory facet . . . [and] can be enjoyed immediately" (Lind, 1995, p. 96). Personality theorists (see Campbell & Pritchard, 1976; Cropanzano, James, & Citera, 1993; Murray, 1938) have given a great deal of attention to concrete, material cravings. In fact, this family of needs has been studied under a variety of names, such as physiological needs (Maslow, 1954) and existence needs (Alderfer, 1969, 1972). In the present discussion, we are not attempting to invoke a specific need theory. The only issue here is that a variety of human desires can be subsumed under this general family. To separate our thinking from the personality literature, we shall refer to these simply as *economic needs* (in keeping with Cropanzano & Schminke, in press).

The second class of needs is more directly tied to our social natures. To a greater or lesser extent, people desire to be valued and esteemed by others. As Lind (1995) remarked succinctly, some things are desired "because they have greater implications for feelings of inclusion and social identity" (p. 96). Among other things, this would include a sense of dignity and the respect of one's peers (cf. "belongingness needs," Maslow, 1954; "relatedness needs," Alderfer, 1969, 1972). In this discussion, we shall refer to them simply as *socioemotional needs* (Cropanzano & Schminke, in press). These socioemotional needs drive home the reason that humans feel compelled to affiliate with other people, because there is no way for us as humans to fulfill these desires completely by ourselves. To some extent, people must look to other humans for status and esteem.

The Predicament: Trying to Meet Personal Needs in the Context of a Social Group

Group cooperation often enhances the ability to provide for economic needs. For this reason, a general tendency to seek out others has evolved (Simon, 1983). In addition, this tendency manifests itself as a set of socioemotional needs that go unfulfilled unless peers act in ways that meet those needs. For such reasons, people choose to affiliate with others. People hope that ultimately their comrades will help them attain their goals.[2] Unfortunately, those comrades have many of the same objectives for themselves. They seek collaboration in order to achieve their goals, which might be incompatible with the goals of those seeking their help.

The situation can be understood thus: If our comrades are not helpful to us, then we are more likely to seek a new set of associates. Likewise, if we are not helpful to our comrades, then they will be motivated to abandon us. They depend on us to give them respect. For this reason, each person cannot be overly demanding of others. Everyone should show at least a modicum of concern for the needs of his or her peers. Ultimately, successful collectives are based on a grand compromise—everyone agrees to keep his/her personal self-interest partially in check so that something is left for other members of the group.

Justice norms develop as guidelines for fair interaction and rules by which exchanges are made. In the act of framing norms, social groups decide what is "right" and "ethical." These norms help us to regulate both our own behavior and the behavior of others. For example, we know that if we take too big a portion of the profits for ourselves, we risk the disdain of our coworkers. Justice makes us aware of those boundaries. Furthermore, justice affords us a sense of predictability. When we have clear rules, we know how decisions are made and what outcomes we are apt to receive in the long run. In a fair system, for example, we are likely to be less upset when a particular transaction does not go our way. This affords us more confidence that outcomes will be distributed adequately in the future.

Of course, it is difficult to monitor some transactions, and it is not always easy to know whether you are being treated fairly. Added to these concerns is another important fact: Members of a group have an incentive to cheat. This is because "free riding," if undetected, allows the cheater to maximize his or her benefits without endangering his or her future. Justice norms offer a partial solution. Sound fairness principles can provide clearer standards by which a peer's behavior can be evaluated. This could make it easier to detect free riders.

In sum, other people are the avenue by which individuals fulfill many of their needs. Justice provides us with a system for getting our needs met in an orderly and fair way. Once group members agree on the rules of fairness (no mean task), then everyone need only abide by them. Doing so means that you can address the needs of others while others are addressing your personal interests. We shall demonstrate this matter more explicitly in our next section.

What Is Justice (Revisited)? Distributive and Procedural Justice in Work Organizations

At this point, it might be useful to consider the social scientific approach in more detail. As we have seen, philosophical theories of social justice are intimately concerned with how people relate to one another in exchange situations. Any outcome assigned by a group or individual, be it money or status, can be judged with respect to fairness. Because these are important reasons that people are driven to affiliate, justice is critical for understanding interpersonal relationships and group processes (Greenberg, 1988a). We can say, therefore, that justice involves at least two or more actors and some category of resource. We can define these terms broadly. The actors need not be individual people but can be social units, such as organizations or even nations. Likewise, the resources can be economic or socioemotional. The interactions that take place are governed by some rules or procedures, formal and explicit as well as informal and tacit. For example, an organization selects among job applicants on the basis of interviews. In this case, the two actors are the organization and the individual who has applied for a new job. The outcome is whether or not the job was obtained. The process refers, in part, to the manner in which the interviews were conducted.

This example underscores an important aspect of contemporary justice theories. The person who is seeking a job actually has to make multiple fairness judgments. He or she can evaluate the fairness of the outcome (Was it right that I did not get this new job?) and the fairness of the process (Were interviews conducted in the right manner to render a decision?). The first judgment refers to distributive justice, whereas the second refers to procedural justice. In addition to procedural and distributive justice, there is a third category or form of fairness—interactional justice—that refers to interpersonal treatment received at the hands of others (Bies, 1987b; Bies & Moag, 1986; Greenberg, 1988c). It is often identified with, or seen as closely related to, procedural justice (e.g., Greenberg, 1990c; Tyler & Bies, 1990).

Distributive Justice

Distributive justice is the perceived fairness of the outcomes or allocations that an individual receives. It can cause workers to lower their job performance (Greenberg, 1988b; Pfeffer & Langton, 1993), engage in withdrawal behaviors (Pfeffer & Davis-Blake, 1992; Schwarzwald, Koslowsky, & Shalit, 1992), cooperate less with their coworkers (Pfeffer & Langton, 1993), reduce work quality (Cowherd & Levine, 1992), steal (Greenberg, 1990c), and experience stress (Zohar, 1995). To state the matter starkly, distributive injustice causes about every pernicious criterion ever chronicled by organizational scientists!

When people render a distributive justice judgment, they are evaluating whether an outcome is appropriate, moral, or ethical. Making this decision is trickier than it may appear, for there is seldom an objective standard of righteousness. To decide if something is fair, people must generate a benchmark or frame of reference. We call this standard a *referent*. Although a variety of referents are possible (Kulik & Ambrose, 1992), social comparisons have received the most attention. For example, if a person needs to decide whether or not his or her pay is fair, he or she can simply find someone in a similar job and compare their compensation levels. If the two salaries are equal, then there is no inequity. If one discovers that one is being "overpaid" (again, this is relative to a given referent), one is likely to experience guilt (Greenberg, 1982; 1988a); however, it should be noted that people tend to get less upset when an inequity is in their favor (Hegtvedt, 1993). On the other hand, being "underpaid" is more troublesome. Individuals are likely to react negatively when their rewards are substantially less than those of a comparison person.

Distributive fairness is judged by referent standards. What a person receives cannot determine outcome justice without considering the outcome relative to some standard of comparison. Sweeney, McFarlin, and Inderrieden (1990), for example, predicted pay satisfaction from actual salaries and self-reported referents. Salary was an important predictor, but including the referent accounted for additional variance in pay satisfaction. Thus, two people with the same outcomes may perceive different levels of justice if they are not using the same referent. In a related vein, Stepina and Perrewe (1991) obtained longitudinal data from discontented individuals who improved their satisfaction by changing their referent standards (e.g., enhanced sense of accomplishment from comparing with the less accomplished).

Procedural Justice

When social scientists refer to procedural justice, they are still indicating an evaluation or subjective judgment. However, in this case it is an appraisal of the process by which an allocation decision is (or was) made. As an area of inquiry, procedural justice emerged on the scene more recently than distributive justice, although it has now been studied for some time. Folger and Greenberg (1985) were the first major researchers to apply procedural fairness to work settings. Since that time, there has been a veritable flood of procedural justice research. This work has had important practical implications. Evidence now shows that when people believe that decision-making processes are unjust, they show less commitment to their employers, more theft, higher turnover intentions, lower performance, and fewer helpful citizenship behaviors (for recent reviews, see Cropanzano & Greenberg, 1997; Tyler & Smith, in press). People care about how they are treated, and these procedural justice perceptions do much to shape their relationships with their employers. For this reason it is important for us to articulate more clearly the attributes of fair decision procedures.

The "Voice" Tradition of Thibaut and Walker (1975)

The study of procedural justice grew out of Thibaut and Walker's (1975) work in the mid-1970s. Thibaut and Walker were interested in understanding disputants' reactions to various forms of legal proceedings. They divided dispute resolution into two stages: a process stage in which evidence was presented and a decision stage in which a third party rendered a verdict. Thibaut and Walker were interested in a circumstance involving three individuals: two disputants and a third-party decision maker such as a judge. Generally speaking, the disputants were willing to forgo decision control if they were allowed to retain process control. In other words, participants saw the resolution process as fair and were contented with the results if they were given a sufficient chance to present their cases. This was termed *voice* (Folger, 1977). We should not understate the importance of voice in the study of procedural justice. Thibaut and Walker (1975) launched an area of inquiry that continues to the present day (e.g., Shapiro & Brett, 1993).

Leventhal's Six Attributes of Fair Procedures

In their early work, Thibaut and Walker (1975) virtually equated voice with procedural fairness. However, in later research, Leventhal (1976, 1980) expanded the list of process characteristics that could increase perceptions of procedural justice. Leventhal's list of six attributes is now famous. To be considered fair, a procedure should be (a) consistent, (b) bias free, (c) accurate, (d) correctable in case of an error, (e) representative of all concerned (a feature related to voice), and (f) based on prevailing ethical standards. For the most part, Leventhal's early thinking has proven to have been astute. Research generally attests to the importance of these six attributes (Lind & Tyler, 1988). One of the prevailing trends in recent organizational justice research is found in the application of Leventhal's six characteristics to various practical situations. For example, Alder and Ambrose (1996) used Leventhal's list to devise standards for building fair computer-based performance monitors. Likewise, Gilliland (1993) adapted the Leventhal attributes to workplace selection. In doing so, he provided guidelines for fairer assessment systems. Although this new work adjusts Leventhal's (1976, 1980) original model to fit the needs at hand, his basic six criteria seem to have withstood the test of time.

Interactional Justice

Interactional justice refers to the quality of the interpersonal treatment received by an individual. Certain kinds of treatment are likely to be perceived as fair, whereas others are seen as unfair. Interactional justice was introduced as an independent, third type of fairness contrasted with both procedural and distributive justice (Bies, 1987b; Bies & Moag, 1986). Nowadays, interactional justice is frequently treated as an aspect or component of procedural justice (e.g., Cropanzano & Greenberg, 1997; Greenberg, 1990c; Tyler & Bies, 1990), although some have called this scheme into question (Greenberg, 1993a). It is a straightforward matter to conceptualize interactional justice as an aspect of process if decision-making processes are conceptualized to include processes of implementation and communication (e.g., how the decision is explained). Also, at least some research has found that ratings of procedural and interactional fairness are highly correlated (e.g., Konovsky & Cropanzano, 1991). In such a classification scheme, procedural justice has two aspects: a structural or formal component (represented by Leventhal's six attributes and related work) and a social component (represented by interactional justice).

Whether considered independently or as part of the procedures, interactional justice itself can be thought of as having at least two components (Brockner & Wiesenfeld, 1996; Cropanzano & Greenberg, 1997). The first subpart is *interpersonal sensitivity.* Fair treatment should be polite and respectful. The recipients of insensitive treatment are prone to poor attitudes, conflict, and low performance (e.g., Baron, 1993; Bies & Moag, 1986). The second subpart of interactional justice includes *explanations* or *social accounts.* Explanations tell the recipient why something unfortunate or untoward occurred. They provide a rationale. Individuals are much more tolerant of an unfavorable outcome when an adequate justification is provided (Bies & Shapiro, 1988; Shapiro, 1991; Shapiro, Buttner, & Barry, 1994).

Plan of This Book

We have covered a lot of ground without yet leaving the preface! Let us, therefore, summarize the major points. In colloquial language, justice is usually thought of from a more or less philosophical perspective—a fair act is one that seems righteous. Often, justice refers to situations in which some transaction is involved, such as an exchange of goods or services. Although the social science definition of justice shares much in common with its philosophical counterpart, there is one major difference. Within the social sciences, an act is just because some observer or observers judge it to be so. In this case, fairness is subjectively defined. The social science literature concerns itself with why some acts, but not others, are perceived to be fair. It also examines the results of making such an evaluation. This definition constitutes the subject matter for this book.

Considerable interest has been paid to justice by both philosophers and social scientists. This, along with some of the research reviewed previously, indicates that fairness is of great concern to people. In this preface, we have suggested that people's interest in justice results from a fundamental natural dilemma: We have individual needs that can best be satisfied through interaction with others. These needs include relatively concrete economic needs, such as money, and relatively abstract socioemotional needs, such as a concern with personal dignity. The dictates of fairness provide people with standards for assessing whether these needs are met within the context of social settings, which often can become complex.

Finally, we introduced the idea of distributive and procedural justice in work settings. We noted that distributive justice refers to the perceived fairness of the outcomes assigned during a transaction. Procedural justice, on the other hand, refers to the process or means by which outcome assignments are made. We indicated that the distribution-process dichotomy is fairly central to the modern understanding of social justice, although some additional distinctions involving interactional justice suggest that it can also make sense to distinguish between (a) structural features designed for procedures (e.g., formal mechanisms for meeting Leventhal's procedural criteria, such as an institutionalized appeals board) and (b) behavioral features of implementation revealed in the conduct of people who administer procedures (interactional justice elements such as efforts to provide sincere, adequate explanations and to treat those affected by decisions with the dignity and respect owed human beings).

The rest of the book will build on the ideas outlined in this preface. It may be helpful to think of this volume as two books in one. The first "book" is a theoretical review of the justice literature. This can be found in the three opening chapters. Chapter 1 examines distributive justice, and Chapter 2 examines procedural justice. Chapter 3 not only introduces interactional justice but also tries to provide a preliminary conceptual synthesis for interpreting how the various forms of justice relate to one another. The second "book" can be found in Chapters 4, 5, and 6. In those three chapters, we apply research on justice to various topics in organizational behavior. Chapter 4 reviews the literature concerning social justice and selection systems. Chapter 5 turns its attention to performance appraisal. Finally, Chapter 6 considers the role of (un)fairness as both a contributor to and a means of resolving workplace conflict. We close the book, in Chapter 7 and Chapter 8, with a new theory of fairness and a discussion of emerging directions for future theory and research.

Notes

1. In this section, we do not intend to imply that human biology does or should determine the content of human ethical systems. Although such a position was suggested by Wilson (1978), it has the disadvantage of confusing what *is* with what *should be.* That is, it conflates the descriptive with the prescriptive (Singer, 1981). This has been termed the "naturalistic fallacy" (Donaldson & Dunfee, 1994; Wright, 1994). Our point is far more modest. We maintain only that our biological nature provides us with a broad set of potentialities and problems. Some of these problems are addressed by human ethical systems.

2. Much has been written about the human penchant for selfishness. Is this all there really is to us? The answer is difficult because we are actually asking at least two questions at one time. Whether we answer this question *yes* or *no* depends on how we define our terms. When one thinks of selfishness, one usually means a willful decision to pursue one's own good at the expense of others. We shall term this *moral* self-interest. On the other hand, there is also *genetic* self-interest. For instance, certain behaviors make it more or less likely that, on average, one's genes will be passed on to the next generation. The two are not the same. Consider the case of a father who risks his life to save a child. (Such things are not rare.) This father is manifesting a trait we might call *familial love.* In our ancestral environment, familial love was no doubt adaptive, in that it allowed us to pass on our genes. In this narrow sense, we might say the father is motivated by self-interest or even (were we to push the matter) a sort of "genetic selfishness." However, this does not make the father any less altruistic, for there is no willful decision to pursue his own ends to the neglect of another person. From the perspective of our species, the act might be selfish, but from the perspective of the father and child it is an act of pristine altruism.

1   Equity and Distributive Justice as Outcome Fairness

What do employees consider unfair? How do they react to perceived injustice? A growing literature on organizational justice (e.g., Greenberg, 1990a) deals with such questions. We begin our introduction to that literature by focusing on a single topic in this chapter, the fairness of outcomes. Human resources management has administrative responsibility for a number of outcomes that employees receive as part of their exchange relationship with employers. For example, human resources managers commonly have some oversight in employee outcome areas such as wage and salary administration. Supervisors also play a role in determining many employee outcomes (e.g., promotions, work assignments, disciplinary actions), of course, but human resources managers frequently review supervisors' decisions about such outcomes, provide relevant guidance as well as training, and contribute to discussions about overall policy in those areas. Obviously human resources managers have a major stake in employees' perceived fairness of outcomes.

Our discussion begins with an example of a salary increase and how reactions to it changed dramatically in a very short time. We will refer back to that example in presenting the conceptual framework about outcome fairness that is the focal point of this chapter—the theory of inequity in social exchange (Adams, 1965).

1

An Example of Reactions to Pay

Imagine the scene at an office in London when a 26-year-old bond trader, Michael Lewis, finds out his salary package for the coming year at Salomon Brothers' British offices. Lewis, the author of *Liar's Poker* (1989), described the salary announcement and his initial reactions to it in the following terms:

> The managing director shuffled some papers in front of him, then began. "I have seen a lot of people come through here and shoot the lights out in their first year," he said, then named a few young managing directors as examples. "But I have never seen anyone have the kind of year that you have had . . . "
>
> "What can I say," he said, "but congratulations?" He spoke for about five minutes and achieved the desired effect. When he finished, I was prepared to pay him for the privilege of working at Salomon Brothers . . .
>
> The money always came as an afterthought and in a knot you had to disentangle. "Last year you made ninety thousand dollars," he said.
>
> Forty-five was salary. So forty-five was bonus.
>
> "Next year your salary will be sixty thousand dollars. Now let me explain those numbers."
>
> While he was explaining that I was paid more than anyone else in my training class (I later learned that three others were paid as much), I was converting ninety thousand dollars into British pounds (fifty-six thousand) and putting that into perspective. It was certainly more than I was worth in the abstract. It was more than I had contributed to society. . . . It was more than my father had made when he was twenty-six, even factoring in inflation, which I did. It was more than anyone else my age I knew made. Ha! I was rich. I loved my employer. My employer loved me. I was happy. Then the meeting ended.
>
> And I thought again . . . I decided, in the end, I had been taken for a ride, a view I still think is strictly correct. (pp. 201-203)

We will use Adams's (1965) theory of inequity to explore both Lewis's initial and later reactions to his pay.

Some Basics of Inequity Theory

Adams (1965) couched his theory of inequity in the broader context of social exchange—that is, two-way transactions in which each side provides something to the other and, therefore, also receives something in return. Employees, for example, have an exchange relationship with employers. Employees expend time and effort in working for employers; in the language of equity, those are some of the contributions that employees make as their inputs to the exchange. In return, employers provide wages and other forms of compensation as some of the outcomes employees receive for working. Adams wanted to understand (a) when and why such exchanges might seem fair or unfair to employees (the antecedents of perceived inequity) and (b) what employees who felt unfairly treated might do (the consequences of perceived inequity).

Antecedents of Perceived Inequity

Discussion of inequity's antecedents calls for a slightly enlarged description of inputs. Despite sexist language, Adams's (1965) description still serves well:

> On the man's side of the exchange are his education, intelligence, experience, training, skill, seniority, age, sex, ethnic background, social status, and, of course, the effort he expends on the job. Under special circumstances other attributes will be relevant. These may be personal appearance or attractiveness, health, possession of certain tools, the characteristics of one's spouse, and so on. They are what a man perceives as his contributions to the exchange, for which he expects a just return. (p. 277)

Adams also stressed subjective perception in a subsequent passage:

> Whether or not an attribute having the potential of being an input is in fact an input is contingent upon the possessor's perception of its relevance to the exchange. If he perceives it to be relevant, if he expects a just return for it, it is an input. (p. 277)

The subjectivity of inputs is one reason for the subjectivity of fairness itself; employees might think that seniority should count toward higher wages, for example, whereas management might contend that nothing other than performance ought to count. As has often been said, equity—like beauty—is in the eye of the beholder.

Consider some of the inputs that occurred to Michael Lewis as he began evaluating his pay increase. In initially concluding that his new salary "was certainly more than I was worth in the abstract," he assessed his "worth" in terms of possible criteria such as what he "had contributed to society." He also considered age as a potentially relevant input. Because the money was more than his father had made at Michael's age, and because it was more than anyone else his age he knew made, he at first considered himself "rich" with respect to the rate of return on such inputs (the ratio of outcomes to inputs that, as we will describe, is at the heart of inequity theory's understanding of reactions to outcomes). Estimates of coworkers' performance constitute another source of information about potentially relevant inputs. The managing director supplied such information in commenting that he had never seen anyone else have as productive a first year as Michael did.

Adams's list of employees' potential outcomes also bears quoting:

> Pay, rewards intrinsic to the job, satisfying supervision, seniority benefits, fringe benefits, job status and status symbols, and a variety of formally and informally sanctioned perquisites, such as the right of a higher-status person to park his [*sic*] car in a privileged location. (p. 278)

Outcomes need not be positive. Negative outcomes include working conditions that employees would rather avoid (e.g., boring tasks, harsh supervision). Note that because the nature of an unpleasant experience is essentially the same whether it is classified as a costly input (forgoing an enjoyable leisure activity) or as a negative outcome (enduring a boring work activity), some confusion might exist regarding whether to classify a negative experience at work as part of one's inputs or outcomes. Addressing that issue, Adams indicated that the distinction between inputs and outcomes is useful conceptually but need not become a sticking point:

> In classifying some variables as inputs and others as outcomes, it is not implied that they are independent, except conceptually. Inputs and outcomes are, in fact, inter-correlated, but imperfectly so. Indeed, it is because they are imperfectly correlated that there need be concern with inequity. There exist normative expectations of what constitute "fair" correlations between inputs and outcomes. The expectations are formed—learned—during the process of socialization, at home, at school, at work. They are based by observation of the correlations obtaining for a reference person or group—a co-worker or a colleague, a relative or a neighbor, a group of co-workers, a craft group, an industry-wide pattern. (p. 279)

For example, Michael Lewis might have been encouraged to treat 1st-year traders and salespeople at Salomon Brothers as a reference group because of the managing director's comment that Lewis had outperformed all others (past and present) during their 1st year.

Adams's comment about "normative expectations . . . based by observation of . . . a reference person or group" suggests that people's perceptions about the fairness of a social exchange are influenced by what they consider to be the normatively appropriate rate of return for that type of exchange. That normative rate becomes the criterion used for judging the fairness of a person's outcome-input relation (i.e., outcomes in return for having contributed certain inputs valued by the person with whom the exchange is conducted).

The normative rate is usually a matter for conjecture and interpretation rather than a matter that can be verified directly in some objective sense. That is, the "going rate" of fair return is not always identified so explicitly as in such statements as "This is a minimum-wage job, so you know exactly what the rate-per-hour is." Instead, the normative rate is often inferred from other information. Adams assumed that employees often use social-comparison information—especially outcome-per-input information about the return rate of "a reference person or group"—as the basis for drawing conclusions about exchange norms.

For example, the Salomon managing director said that Michael Lewis was paid more than anyone else in the same training class. Adams (1965) "assumed that the reference person or group will be one comparable to the comparer on one or more attributes" (p. 280); in this case, the other trainees are a relevant comparison group because they had all started work in the same Salomon job as Lewis at the same time as he did. When the managing director referred to Lewis's 1st year as better than anyone else's, that statement implied differential inputs between Lewis and other trainees. Using arbitrarily as-signed numbers as an illustration, let's say that Lewis then believes he pro-duced twice as much revenue for Salomon as the average of all other trainees (i.e., two input units for Lewis, an average of one for others). Suppose he also believes there is a going rate for pay (outcomes) based on revenues produced (inputs). Whatever amount others in the same training class receive indicates the going rate on a per-unit basis, because we have assigned a value of one for their inputs. Lewis uses this per-unit rate as a normative standard and doubles the outcome amount to estimate what he should expect to get if Salomon pays him fairly. If paid less than twice what someone else in the same class is paid, therefore, Lewis will perceive that he was treated inequitably. The next section formalizes this type of illustration algebraically as an equation.

An Equation for Inequity

Labor's longstanding cry for justice in the workplace has a familiar ring: "A fair day's pay for a fair day's work." In presenting his theory of inequity, Adams (1965) used an algebraic expression to indicate how someone might evaluate the fairness of pay, benefits, promotions, and the like. Any compensation for labor represents something provided to an employee in exchange for contrib-uting toward an employer's opportunity for profit. Adams used the term *outcomes* as a generic label for any and all types of returns from an exchange. The nature of exchange is the source for two aspects of Adams's algebraic formula for fairness perceptions (the equity equation): (a) his use of Person and Other as labels; and (b) his use of two ratios—for Person, on one side of the equation, and for Other, on the other side. Person and Other come from modeling exchange as a transaction between two parties. The Person ratio and the Other ratio express the amount each receives on a per-unit-given basis (i.e., outcomes or inputs as received or given). Thus, "a fair day's pay for a fair day's work" reflects the ratio of pay:day. In that expression, pay is the employee's outcome. Days represent one way to count units of labor—an example of the more general term, inputs, that Adams used in referring to the contributions that each party makes when participating with another in an exchange (e.g., an employee working for an employer on a daily basis).

Adams (1965) conceived of fairness as the giving and receiving of equivalent value—much like the concept of reciprocity that Gouldner (1960) called a universal norm of fairness. Where P stands for Person and O for Other, the formula for equivalent ratios is $O_P{:}I_P = O_O{:}I_O$. An inequality sign between the two ratios would represent the unfairness of one person's being inequitably advantaged and the other's being inequitably disadvantaged. Adams thought that either version of unfairness would be disturbing but that they would be accompanied by qualitatively different emotions. According to Adams, the overbenefited party tends to feel guilty, whereas the underbenefited party tends to feel angry. We will comment further on such feelings, along with other possible reactions discussed by Adams, in the subsequent section on the consequences of perceived inequity.

Before addressing reactions to inequity, however, we want to make two points that are sometimes overlooked about the term *Other* in the equity equation. First, note that although the general reference to social comparison has connotations about Other as a person or group distinct from Person, Adams (1965) himself did not insist that the comparison had to be social in a literal sense. That is, the comparison could either be interpersonal (a social comparison, between or across individuals) or intrapersonal (a within-individual comparison, perhaps over time), as the following passage clarifies:

> Other is usually a different individual, but may be Person in another job or in another social role. Thus, Other might be Person in a job he held previously, in which case he might compare his present and past outcomes and inputs and determine whether or not the exchange with his employer, present or past, was equitable. (p. 280)

At one point, for example, Michael Lewis described an intrapersonal comparison that even goes beyond the range of illustrations Adams mentioned. Lewis (1989) described a comparison between pay announced at the time of his conversation with the managing director and an imaginary amount in the future. "Salomon Brothers people in 1986 wanted their money *now* because it looked as if the firm were heading for disaster. Who knew what 1987 would bring?" (p. 203). In effect, he referred to a purely hypothetical comparison of an intrapersonal type.

Second, when referring to social comparisons that do involve some reference person or group as Other (the truly interpersonal case), theorists and researchers sometimes allude to Person and Other in relation to one another—as if the two were in direct exchange. Strictly speaking, however, Other need not be in a direct exchange relationship with Person, as the following passage from Adams (1965) notes:

> *Other* is any individual with whom Person *is in an exchange relationship* [italics added], or with whom Person compares himself *when both he and Other are in an exchange relationship with a third party, such as an employer* [italics added], or with third parties who are considered by Person as being comparable, such as employers in a particular industry or geographic location. (p. 280)

We will note a few implications now about two-party, direct exchange versus direct exchange with an employer as third party and Other as a second party used for comparison purposes (to determine normative rate). In later sections on consequences, we will return to a further discussion about these implications.

If Person and Other always referred to two parties in direct exchange with one another, then inevitable constraints on available resources would dictate that whatever Person gained would be Other's loss, and vice versa (i.e., exchange of tangible, material goods entails a zero-sum game in an objective sense, although subjectively each party might feel benefited). In Michael Lewis's case, for example, his direct exchange took place with Salomon Brothers as his employer: The more they paid him, the less the firm kept toward net profit. As an illustration of an alternative arrangement, one possible three-party example could involve the previously mentioned comparison with other trainees. There, too, more for Lewis would mean less for them as Other. But that is not true in other possible three-party situations such as, for example, the comparison Lewis made with his father at the same age.

At age 26, his father obviously worked for a different employer than Michael did, which makes this example most comparable to the third type of Other mentioned in the Adams passage quoted previously: an Other used for comparison purposes by Person when each of them is in an exchange relationship with a different third party, and those third parties are considered comparable. Although Adams (1965) referred to employers in a particular industry or geographic location (e.g., Salomon Brothers and another Wall Street firm), analogous three-party situations would involve any Other who worked for a different employer than Person, which obviously was the case with Michael and his father. Note what happens either when Michael compares himself with his father at the same age, or when he compares himself with 1st-year trainees at other firms. On the one hand, Michael would not feel so favorably treated by Salomon if his father had made even more money than himself at the same age, nor would he feel good if he learned that trainees at other firms made more than he did. On the other hand, Michael himself would not have made any less money (in an objective sense) regardless of whether his father were to have made more money at age 26, and regardless of how much money other firms paid their trainees. This lack of a zero-sum relationship with Other is always the consequence when Other works for a different third-party employer than Person. Again, the point is that just because Other is used for the comparative purpose of estimating the normative exchange rate does not mean that Person and Other are themselves in a direct exchange with one another. The same thing can be said of the Person-with-Other comparison when Other is Person at another point in time; clearly it makes no sense to describe Person as in direct exchange with himself or herself.

Consequences of Inequity

Recall that Adams (1965) referred to anger as a possible consequence of inequity when people feel underbenefited, and that he referred to guilt as a possible consequence in the case of overbenefit. We will focus primarily on anger and other reactions to underpayment (disadvantageous inequity) to simplify the illustrations; for a discussion of guilt as a reaction to overpayment, see Mowday (1996). There are several reasons for this restricted focus, which also helps make for a briefer presentation of the theory. First, as noted, other sources address advantageous or overbenefited inequity. Second, Adams (1965) himself (also citing Homans, 1961) argued that the threshold for experiencing overpayment and feeling guilty has less likelihood of being exceeded in comparison to the greater ease with which the threshold for underpayment and anger are exceeded. As he put it, "The threshold would be higher presumably in cases of overreward, for a certain amount of incongruity in these cases can be acceptably rationalized as 'good fortune' without attendant discomfort" (p. 282). Third, some of the evidence supporting predictions about guilt has been challenged, and this topic continues to suffer (although not necessarily justifiably) from the aura of controversy. Because we do not want to take space in discussing a controversy no longer of great interest, we essentially ignore the topic of overpayment and reactions related to guilt.

Instead, we will use the twin themes of anger and aggression as a bridge from the single type of justice discussed in this chapter to the two other types discussed in the next. We see anger and aggression as themes that can integrate the psychology of outcome-centered perceptions (distributive justice) with the psychology of perceptions centered on process issues (procedural and interactional justice, topics covered in the next chapter). We will argue in the next chapter that issues related to process determine whether people are merely angry about the consequences of an exchange (e.g., outcomes such as pay) or also become angry at the exchange partner. In other words, process-related issues determine the targets of aggression—the direction in which aggressive actions and hostile reactions are pointed. Our conclusion differentiates between two types of subsequent reactions that can emerge from the initial perception of disadvantaged inequity: (a) anger aimed at other people and social institutions associated with the state of disadvantage (e.g., the employer or the organization) and (b) situations in which no other party is targeted for punishment or retribution (in which case some self-directed anger might occur). Those two types of reactions ultimately receive the majority of our attention, although the following section discusses the wider range of additional reactions also considered by Adams.

Alternative Ways to Alleviate the Distress of Disadvantageous Inequity

Adams (1965) theorized that perceived inequity feels unpleasant and motivates people to reduce those unpleasant feelings. Someone dealing with the unpleasantness of inequity might use any of a variety of methods, which Adams called means of inequity reduction. One way to deny the existence of an inequity, for example, would be to deny the relevance of the ratios that revealed the inequity and caused the initial discomfort; this tactic involves what Adams called changing the object of comparison.

Note that changing the object of comparison refers only to the outcome-input ratio of a reference person or group Other (e.g., coworkers' pay rates). That comparison rate shapes normative beliefs about fair pay from the employer with whom Person is in direct exchange, but Person is not in direct exchange with comparison Others such as coworkers. For that reason, it is possible to mentally switch from one reference person or group to another, while still remaining physically in the same primary (direct) exchange relationship. (A physical change to a different exchange relationship, rather than a psychological change that entails considering some other person or group more relevant for comparison than the one originally considered, involves a different reduction method discussed next—leaving the field). Michael Lewis remained employed by Salomon Brothers the entire time that he considered different reference standards such as his father's pay at age 26 and the pay of peers his age who did not work for Salomon Brothers. In fact, he rapidly considered several such possibilities all in the space of a few moments, which illustrates how easily this tactic might be used in the service of reducing perceived inequity. If Lewis had at first felt underpaid and then these same thoughts had flooded his brain, that sequence would be an example of changing the comparison object to reduce inequity. Because the sequence actually occurred in the reverse manner (his initial happiness turned to bitterness), we note that changing the object of comparison can also lead to perceptions of increased rather than decreased inequity.

The inequity-reduction method called *leaving the field* can also be illustrated using Lewis's situation. Suppose Lewis begins to feel underpaid, either initially or after further reflection. When those feelings become intense enough to motivate action, he might consider changing jobs (e.g., to take a higher paying job at Goldman Sachs or some other Wall Street firm). This method allows the employee to eliminate a perceived inequity from the present employer by going to work for another—one perceived to pay employees more equitably.

The remaining methods of inequity reduction relate directly to each of the four terms in the equity equation: (a) Person's outcomes, (b) Person's inputs, (c) Other's outcomes, and (d) Other's inputs. Adams in effect used these four terms to generate eight possible methods for reducing inequity, because he also distinguished between (a) altering outcomes or inputs and (b) cognitively distorting them. First, we will address each of the four equation terms by illustrating the resolutions that Adams called *altering*. In trying to alter one's own outcomes or inputs, or in trying to alter Other's, such efforts represent an attempt to change actual conditions from inequitable to equitable. After illustrating the four altering methods, we will turn to what Adams called the method of *cognitive distortion*. That method allows a parallel set of four possibilities (one for each equation term); they occur when a person's perceptions about one or more of those terms changes, even though all of them have remained objectively the same as prior to that cognitive distortion (i.e., the changed perceptions have a psychological source rather than a source that involves any actual changes in the work environment's circumstances or conditions).

Altering the Outcomes or
Inputs of Person or Other

Our four examples of altering address first the case of Other as another person or group working for the same employer as Person—a common social comparison—and then the case of employer as Other (in direct exchange with Person). Each of the four principal methods of inequity reduction is numbered, and we illustrate each of those two varieties under the same numbered heading:

1. *Person's outcomes.* This method of altering focuses on reducing or eliminating the perceived disadvantage by increasing one's own outcomes. At one point in his description of why he eventually became angry about the size of his raise and the amount of the bonus for his previous year's work, for example, Michael Lewis (1989) wrote the following: "I looked around me and saw people getting more when they hadn't generated a penny of the revenues themselves" (p. 203). Suppose he then argued with the managing director for an increase to his bonus. Note that in the case of a comparison Other such as another Salomon employee or group of employees, this method might alter only the single term—Person's outcomes—in this version of the equity equation so long as the Other's pay remained the same (e.g., the managing director adds to Lewis's bonus but keeps all other bonuses to 1st-year trainees the same as before). If a limited budget for compensating employees meant that increasing the amount for one person meant decreasing the amount for another, however, then two terms would be changed simultaneously (Person's outcomes go up and Other's outcomes go down), which would mean algebraically that less of a boost to Person's outcomes would be necessary to restore equity. The greater algebraic ease of change does not mean greater feasibility, though, as one of Lewis's comments about his managing director makes clear: "Money out of my pocket was money in the pocket of the man who has sung my praises. He knew that better than I" (p. 203).

Meanwhile, consider the implications for altering Other's outcomes if Person is instead focusing exclusively on the direct exchange with the employer (i.e., the employer's outcomes and inputs become the numerator and denominator of the ratio for Other). For example, consider the following additional comment by Lewis (1989): "I wasn't sure how many millions of dollars I had made for Salomon Brothers, but by any fair measure I deserved much more than ninety thousand dollars" (p. 203). If Lewis could get an increment to his raise (or a larger bonus), the firm might simply transfer some portion of those millions of sales back in his direction. This change would affect two terms in the equation simultaneously: Lewis's outcomes increase, and Salomon's decrease. Embezzlement would similarly involve a doubly efficacious means of reducing inequity.

2. *Other's outcomes.* Reducing the outcome term in the comparison ratio would also reduce inequity. We've already given some examples in which Other's outcomes changed simultaneously along with Person's outcomes. The following comment by Lewis, however, provides the basis for discussing a further possibility that changes only the single term of Other's outcomes: "[H]e was explaining that I was paid more than anyone else in my training class (I later learned that three others were paid as much)" (p. 202). As the basis for a hypothetical illustration of altering only Other's outcomes, suppose

Lewis confronts the managing director with this discovery. He argues success-fully that those three others should have their pay reduced in light of the director's own claim that Lewis's performance had been far superior to anyone else's.

If Person's attention instead focuses exclusively on direct exchange and the discrepancy with the employer's outcomes, then this method of altering would center on reduced revenues for the firm. Earlier, we noted that getting in-creased compensation might dip into the firm's coffers if management did not reduce some other employee's compensation instead. Other ways of reducing the employer's overall profit picture do not have to involve a direct increase to the employee's compensation (Person's outcomes) at the same time. Sabotage such as arson, for example, might wreak havoc on profits without benefiting Person as employee directly. Embezzling, on the other hand, would literally remove some of those revenues but would simultaneously increase Person's outcomes. Employee theft might do either of the following: (a) If the employee steals something of value and can sell it for profit or benefit directly by using it, Person's outcomes increase and Other's outcomes decrease simultaneously; or (b) if the employee steals something of no value to him- or herself or anyone else (e.g., bond certificates that cannot be traded privately because no black market for them exists), then he or she harms the firm's profits without personally benefiting and thereby decreases Other's outcomes without in-creasing Person's.

3. *Person's inputs.* Another altering method centers on lowering one's own inputs. Relevant actions might involve various forms of reduced effort, such as coming in late, leaving early, not working as hard while on the job, and so on. Consider that (a) the managing director said Lewis's performance far outshone anyone else's in memory, yet (b) three others in his training class received the same compensation as he did. Based on such evidence, he might conclude that some of his efforts were wasted: Less effort (with less to show for it) had still been adequate for others to receive compensation just as high as his. The flip side implies that reducing his efforts would have no harmful effects on his level of compensation (i.e., inputs could be reduced without adversely influencing outcomes). Indeed, one feature of the Salomon pay system contributed to exactly those sorts of consequences. "By edict from Gutfreund [head of Salomon at the time], a floor and a ceiling were set each year around the bonuses of 1st- and 2nd-year employees irrespective of their achievements" (p. 200).

A related effect involves the difference between hourly versus piece-rate pay for nonexempt employees: Once the rate of outcome per input (pay per piece of goods produced) has been fixed, a piece-rate worker cannot slacken effort substantially without simultaneously diminishing his or her outcomes, whereas someone paid hourly for the same work might easily find ways of reducing effort that do not get noticed and hence do not threaten the chances of being fully paid for each hour of clocked time on the job. Note, however, that piece-rate workers have been known to withhold effort as a way of preventing one potential source of reductions to the piece rate, namely, dropping it because analysis by industrial engineering found examples of some workers completing each piece much more rapidly than others. Such "rate busters" rarely go unpunished by coworkers in some way (by social ostracism if not in such physical forms as "binging," in which a worker's hard hat is suddenly struck with a metal object that causes a loud vibration).

Such examples involve a complex mix of three parties in the employment exchange (Person, a coworker Other, and the employer as Other). Even limited exclusively to the direct exchange of employee and employer, again, a given action can accomplish more than one method of inequity reduction simultaneously. For example, reducing effort might lower the employee's inputs while at the same time lowering profits as the employer's outcomes. Lewis probably would not have such an option because his sales-based compensation is like piece-rate pay in that it requires effortful inputs on his part to sustain or increase his outcomes, but an hourly paid employee could restore equity or at least reduce the amount of inequity even more effectively, when reducing his or her effort did not cause a reduction to his or her own outcomes but did reduce the employer's profits (outcomes).

4. *Other's inputs.* Michael Lewis, in noting the relation between his compensation and that of the managing director, had said that "Money out of my pocket was money in the pocket of the man who has sung my praises"; he also mentioned having noticed "people getting much more when they hadn't generated a penny of the revenues themselves" (p. 203). Presumably, because Lewis was in sales and the director was in management, the director was one of those people. If Lewis tried to more equitably balance his outcome-input ratio and the manager's by altering the director's inputs, that method in this case would mean finding a way to make the director have to expend more time, energy, or effort in his own job. Perhaps Lewis might be motivated, therefore, to create extra work for the director—so long as the means for doing that would not reflect poorly on this own performance (e.g., turn in reports with exactly the right amount of detail, but organized in legitimate ways that would require more effort for the director to read and comprehend).

Examples of ways to increase an employer's inputs include forms of sabotage and reduced quality. Money spent to repair sabotaged machines, for example, represents an increment to those inputs, as does rework and expenditures for additional checks on quality. Again, such efforts might effect another term in the equation simultaneously—such as reduced revenues (employer outcomes) when reduced-quality products do not sell as well. If insurance covered arson (including monetary supplements to cover downtime until damage is repaired) and thus meant no reduction in the employer's outcomes, but the aggravation and stress of dealing with insurance forms and delays represent an additional investment of effort, then such an example more closely approximates the pure case of altering only the employer's inputs. Perhaps a relatively pure illustration involving Michael Lewis would be selling the same volume but in ways that would require increased investments by Salomon for additional personnel (e.g., having to hire extra part-time help because the nature of some of the sale agreements requires more paperwork than usual).

Cognitively Distorting the Outcomes and Inputs of Person and Other

Four other tactics illustrate that the terms in the equity equation can also be changed psychologically and perceptually rather than actually being altered in any objective sense. Sometimes these responses are merely rationalizations; in fact, Adams (1965) noted that the perceptual modes of inequity resolution often operate like cognitive dissonance reduction.

1. *Person's outcomes.* Altering actual monetary outcomes requires an objective change in the situation, but cognitive distortion can change the perception of work-related outcomes that have some less tangible and material properties (i.e., where subjective interpretation plays a large part in determining their relative value). In feeling less adequately paid than some other Salomon employees, for example, Michael Lewis might shift his attention to nonmonetary outcomes for the sake of distortions to restore equity. Illustrations might include coming to believe that his secretary gave him more helpful assistance than other people received, or that his desk was located in a more comfortable area.

Other examples can illustrate how Lewis might use perceptual changes to restore equity with the employer as Other. One illustration of outcomes with psychologically enhanced value comes from how Lewis (1989) reacted just before he had learned the dollar amount of his compensation (but after hearing his performance praised by the managing director). "I felt deeply reverent about the firm, my numerous bosses, John Gutfreund, . . . and everybody who had ever had anything to do with Salomon Brothers. . . . I didn't care about money. I just wanted this man to approve of my performance" (p. 202). Someone who says "My employer has to pay a less-than-fair wage because profits are down, but at least here I am given complete autonomy and can work on the projects I enjoy most" also has used the tactic of distortion by finding a source of additional positive value on a nonmonetary dimension. Weick (1964), who confirmed the existence of such reactions empirically, called them examples of *task enhancement* (see also Greenberg, 1989); typically, this refers to an enhancement of the intrinsic value obtained from doing a certain type of work, which means an increase in intrinsic motivation. As Lewis put it after receiving lavish praise from his boss, "I was prepared to pay him for the privilege of working at Salomon Brothers" (p. 202).

2. *Other's outcomes.* In the case of Other as a coworker, a cognitive distortion might make that employee's work area seem like an unpleasant place to work or make that person's tasks seem more onerous than one's own. Michael Lewis, for example, might initially feel inequitably paid because he supposedly performed better than all of his classmates, yet three of them received as much pay as he did. To reduce inequity by means of cognitive distortion, Lewis might subsequently remember the terrible clients those classmates encountered when pursuing sales—which made his classmates hate their jobs (and have to work harder, which would explain and help to justify why their sales were not on the same level as his).

Reducing an employer's outcomes psychologically might be accomplished by distorting the utility of those outcomes for the employer—also like changing the comparison standard that Other might use, so as to think of the Other (from his or her perspective) not as overbenefited but actually as deprived in some relative sense. Although the dollar amount received by Person or Other would be hard to distort, the subjective value of that amount *to the respective individuals* will certainly be a function of each individual's perspective. In a conversation with a colleague at Salomon Brothers that Lewis reports, for example, a colleague was discussing John Gutfreund—head of Salomon Brothers. The colleague made the following remarks that illustrate how even the wealthy can be thought of as feeling that their outcomes are low: "You don't get rich in this business.... You only attain new levels of relative poverty. You think Gutfreund feels rich? I'll bet not" (p. 203). Similarly, directors of a firm might not perceive that the company had made sufficient profit to cover the substantial reinvestments needed within an intensely competitive market (e.g., additional costs for renovation, or for research and development). An employee at a pharmaceutical company who felt shortchanged, for example, might reevaluate his or her compensation (in the direction of perceiving it to be fair) in the light of cognitive distortions about how badly the company needed to pour money into research on potential new drugs—in other words, coming to convince himself or herself that more money for paying employees simply was not available.

3. *Person's inputs.* An altered perception of one's own outcomes often has a parallel effect on the perception of one's own inputs. The same reevaluated

conditions that might make Lewis come to perceive his area as a more enjoyable place to work in comparison with a colleague's, for example, might also make his task assignments seem less like drudgery. In other words, the inputs are perceptually altered to seem less aversive and effortful than before. Such changes are again an implication of coming to find the work more intrinsically valuable and motivating; when a task enhancement effect occurs, the increased intrinsic interest in the work makes it not only seem more beneficial (an added outcome), but also less burdensome (a decreased input).

As a means of restoring equity with his employer as Other, Lewis might shift attention away from his effort and instead focus on some other inputs subject to cognitive distortion. Recall, for example, his having said that "it was more than anyone else my age I knew made" (p. 202). By focusing on his very young age, he could come to see his employer as generous (willing to pay even an inexperienced junior person quite handsomely).

4. *Other's inputs.* The coworker in a noisier, dirtier, more crowded area might also be perceived as having to exert more effort (e.g., to concentrate harder, given the distractions). Once the detrimental conditions have been perceived as the basis for Other's lower outcomes, they might also be perceived as the basis for Other's higher inputs. In other words, the cognitive reevaluation causes the peer's job to be seen as entailing harder work or more work. Similarly, a person might suddenly recall a coworker's additional work assignments previously not considered as part of Other's inputs. The compensable qualities of Other's job could also be reevaluated, as is the case when an assignment considered routine now looks as if it involves an extraordinary amount of responsibility. Adams (1965), for example, told of participants in an experiment whose own work was actually more difficult and time consuming than the work of a coworker using a simple adding machine, who was paid one-third more money. The participants, rather than thinking of themselves as having higher inputs and lower outcomes, distorted their perceptions about the sophistication of the coworker's assignment, referring to it as a task that demanded mathematical skill. As Adams put it, "Simple *adding* on a machine became *mathematics*" (p. 293).

Contradictory Predictions About
Angry Reactions to Adverse Inequity

Equity theory describes antecedents and consequences of perceived unfairness but does not link antecedents and consequences in a predictable manner. Stated differently, the same antecedent conditions can create tendencies antithetical to one another—and the theory provides little guidance regarding when either tendency might predominate. This theoretical dilemma arises because the implications of some altering methods run in the opposite direction from the implications of some cognitive distortion methods that would operate on the same term in the equity equation. Indeed, someone who initially feels underpaid might either work less hard as a means of altering Person's inputs to reduce inequity or might work harder than ever—if that individual instead cognitively distorts the amount of Person's current inputs (reducing the perceived value of his or her contribution to the exchange). The theory does not have a definitive answer regarding when one of these two diametrically opposed responses will occur rather than the other.

Recall that Adams had identified anger as a major emotional response to underpayment inequity, in contrast with guilt about overpayment. Anger certainly seems consistent with the altering methods used for reducing inequity with the employer as Other (e.g., theft, sabotage, reduced work effort). On the other hand, anger does not seem to describe the emotion felt when someone reevaluates his or her job more favorably by using cognitive distortion as the means of inequity reduction. Indeed, "this is fun—not work" sounds like a perception that would enhance effort rather than reduce it.

As mentioned earlier, Weick (1964) obtained evidence for exactly such an enhancement effect—one involving a positive reevaluation in cognitive terms that also triggered a positive (increased effort) behavioral response rather than negative, angry behaviors (reduced effort). Task enhancement reflects rationalization or dissonance reduction that occurs as the second of two stages. At the first stage, a person agrees to perform a task even though the work seems as if it might be unenjoyable, and the pay seems low. The magnitude of the dissonance experienced initially (before dissonance reduction begins) is larger the more onerous the task and the less extrinsic compensation provided for performing the task (e.g., inequitably low pay). When the second-stage process of dissonance reduction occurs, however, attitudes align with behavior via rationalization and self-justification. Having agreed to work on the task for an insufficiently rewarding amount of pay, the person can justify his or her choice by perceiving enhanced rewards from doing the work itself: "Maybe it's not so bad after all. It might even turn out to be interesting and enjoyable—more fun than work." With such an attitude in place, the employee relishes working on this assignment and pursues it with new eagerness and enthusiasm.

The feeling of being unfairly underpaid goes away if, for example, Person inputs once characterized as costly suffering (task-related effort as "hard labor") now seem much less onerous ("This hardly seems like work at all"). Essentially the same task-enhancement effect occurs if the distortion focuses on the Person-outcomes term of the equation ("In fact, this is actually a lot of fun; the more I do, the more satisfaction I get from the experience."). Reviews of equity theory (e.g., Vroom, 1969; Zajonc, 1968) pointed out something odd about such task-enhancement effects. People should enjoy their work if their dissonance-reducing rationalizations create such enhanced perceptions of a task, which should result in enhanced performance and productivity. Yet that seems incompatible with the idea of unfair underpayment producing anger and corresponding examples of reduced productivity (shirking, "goldbricking," etc.).

Michael Lewis's description of his own reactions shows that the same person can actually react quite differently to his or her situation within a short time frame. Recall that Lewis was initially elated ("I was rich . . . I was happy") but that those feelings hardly lasted at all ("Then the meeting ended. And I thought again. . . . I decided, in the end, I had been taken for a ride"). Lewis also indicated that others at Salomon showed signs of mixed reactions:

> People responded in one of three ways when they heard how much richer they were: with relief, with joy, and with anger. Most felt some blend of the three. A few felt all three distinctly: relief when told, joy when it occurred to them what to buy, and anger when they heard that others of their level had been paid much more. (p. 201)

The potential for such widely varying reactions—within and across people— makes equity theory of little value without the basis for predicting when each of those reactions is most likely to occur.

Anger as Socially Targeted Resentment: Toward a Solution for Inequity's Predictive Dilemma

It turns out that considering the fairness of social processes and social conduct eliminates this theoretical dilemma and reconciles otherwise apparently contradictory findings. By social processes and social conduct, we refer to topics addressed in Chapter 2 on procedural justice and interactional justice. In that chapter, we will connect processes and conduct with issues such as blame and accountability.

Here, however, we merely preview those conclusions with a preliminary, intuition-based approach. We approach equity's predictive dilemma by first clarifying the nature of anger as the emotion that Adams (1965) associated with adverse (disadvantageous) inequity. Next we link that reconceptualized view of anger with issues of blame and accountability for wrongdoing. We then illustrate implications of blame for procedures with and without choice, which lead to task-enhancement versus anger-related tendencies, respectively.

Anger as Resentment Against Social Targets

What is the nature of anger about inequities? We think the answer to that question should take into account the nature of the behavioral tendencies fostered by such feelings. We think the question ought to be reworded, for example, as follows: What distinguishing features of anger can account for feelings motivating a desire for revenge, retaliation, and punishment (behaviors accompanying the emotion called *resentment*)?

Thus, the first key to resolving equity's predictive dilemma involves conceptualizing injustice-provoked anger as an emotion generating hostile, punitive action tendencies directed toward a social target—another person or a social institution such as a business organization. This emotional hostility can produce retaliation against people in positions of authority—such as those at the top of the organizational pyramid who are ultimately responsible for both its strategic direction and its day-to-day operations. Hostility might also generalize to the organization as a whole and hence invite retaliation against anything or anyone symbolically associated with the organization. The latter, generalized reaction illustrates what it means to say that anger can be directed against an institution as well as against an individual.

Equity theory overlooked the necessity of clarifying anger in this fashion and hence never overcame the predictive dilemma. Note that actions such as sabotage take aim at Other, reducing Other's advantages and increasing Other's burdens (whether Other is a lone supervisor, a top management team, or the organization as a whole—a generalized target for retaliation). The distinguishing feature of anger in response to injustice, therefore, is that it constitutes a focused reaction rather than merely a diffuse emotional state of distress. Feeling unfairly treated by someone or some institution gives anger a direction, a target—namely, a person or organization held accountable for the perceived injustice.

When accountable persons or organizations fail to mitigate injustice, alleviate its consequences, or make the injustice more palatable or the accused wrongdoer more forgivable, they become targets of anger aroused to motivate punishment for those failures. An employee can become angrily motivated to punish unfair management practices, for example, when he or she holds management responsible for carrying out those practices without due regard for employee welfare—or to put it another way, when management's actions seem to consider only the best interests of management and no one else's. Justice, understood properly, addresses constraints on social behavior that a moral community considers appropriate as a balancing force to offset unmitigated pursuit of self-interest. Anger, as a response to social injustice, arouses the urge to punish those who do not adhere sufficiently to the accepted codes of conduct governing self-interest.

Social Targets as Accountable and
Blameworthy for Wrongdoing

When A forces B's input investments up and returns-as-outcomes down, that tends to invite hostility from B—as revenge and retaliation, or punishment so that A "doesn't get away with it." Clearly, Adams (1965) had such hostility in mind when he mentioned anger as an emotion accompanying disadvantageous inequity. And, just as clearly, this emotion implies an increased tendency to respond toward another person in a negative manner. The anger Adams was talking about, therefore, is an outwardly directed, socially targeted response tendency. In everyday speech, people describe this tendency as feeling resentment toward another person or some social institution (e.g., an organization) because that person or institution acted unfairly. To put it another way, we hold the person or institution accountable (blameworthy, liable for damages) and hence perceive ourselves as justified in at least expressing reproach—and perhaps in seeking revenge. Our anger thus constitutes an implicit charge of wrongdoing, and retaliation as punishment seems an appropriate response.

Viewed in that way, an angry, hostile response to inequitable adversity hinges on perceptions of blame and the accountability of conduct. Think about various experiences of adversity. Some seem unfair in that a person's best, most conscientious efforts go insufficiently rewarded. When you have that kind of experience, you might say that you do not get what you deserve, and the outcome seems unfair in that sense. Note, however, the important difference between not getting what you deserve and being unfairly treated by someone else. The former might occur with or without actions by other people, whereas the latter occurs because of someone else's unjust actions.

Suppose a farmer carefully nurtures acres of crops, for example, only to lose the farm to creditors when a tornado destroys the crops and any chance for recouping investments. Is the farmer treated fairly in terms of receiving what he or she deserves? One argument suggests that people get what they deserve automatically—whatever the result—when they place their property at risk by subjecting ownership to the whims of nature and uncertain weather conditions. Many people, however, would feel uncomfortable about such an argument. Intuitively, something seems amiss when extreme efforts go completely uncompensated. Such results seem unfair because the person does not appear to receive what he or she deserves. But in those cases we do not necessarily feel that another social actor has behaved unfairly; instead, if no one else's misconduct was involved, we are more likely to say something along the lines of "life is not always fair." If we want to personalize impersonal forces or speak in more anthropormophic terms, we might refer to "God" or

"Mother Nature" as having been responsible. Sometimes such patterns of thought do, therefore, imply a personalized, targeted form of anger directed toward a "higher power"—such as in the biblical account of Job, whose friends urged him to curse God for devastations brought into Job's life. Often, however, a depersonalized source is emphasized (e.g., fate, Kismet), and onlookers advise the suffering victim to become resigned, to learn to live with misfortune. Thus, we can speak of someone's not receiving what he or she deserves and refer to that as being unfair in one sense; but in the sense of unfairness as social injustice, it makes more sense to distinguish personalized and depersonalized cases.

In contrast to the loss of the crops, which results only from the uncertainties of natural disasters, the action of lenders who foreclose on a person's property raises issues of accountability and hence possible blameworthiness, misconduct, liability, and culpability. Natural disasters are amoral; human conduct, on the other hand, occurs in the context of moral norms. These norms allow the degree of regularity, stability, and predictability that makes social life possible. Violated norms of fair conduct invite reprobation, rebuke, and reproach at the very least (i.e., verbal censure as a form of punishment, aimed at the violator's loss of face and diminished reputation). Flagrant violations, especially those associated with severe harm, often elicit much stronger reactions of hostility and punitive retaliation. Suppose, for example, the banker who foreclosed on the farm had capitalized on a legal loophole as a way of seizing the farmer's land and making an exorbitant profit by reselling it—not coincidentally, to a mall developer whose loan the same bank had approved only the day before. If seen as unfair and improper exploitation, trampling on another person's rights and violating expectations about treatment in a civil society, then the banker's actions might well prompt a desire for revenge from the farmer. Indeed, the farmer might be encouraged in such action by the belief that others in town would at least covertly approve (and might even overtly join in acts of punishment such as a boycott of the bank).

Illustrating a Solution for Equity's Dilemma of Prediction—The Role of Choice

We have not yet indicated how to predict when such hostility might result from underpayment, and when cognitive rationalization ("I love my work") might result instead. At this point, we will simply illustrate one way of making the relevant predictions; in our next chapter we expand on it. Our illustration stems from a suggestion first made by Deci (1975) and subsequently confirmed in several investigations. The Deci hypothesis and the subsequent research involved adding an independent variable to the context of inequitable pay—choice. In turn, choice is but one example of a much broader category—aspects of *procedures*—that also includes other methods for determining outcomes (e.g., decision-making and conflict-resolution procedures). Reactions to different aspects of procedures constitute the broader topic of procedural justice that we address in Chapter 2.

Deci examined studies showing reduced work inputs (representing the angry response to underpayment); he compared them with the design conditions of studies such as Weick's (1964) that showed task enhancement and increased work inputs instead. He identified several relevant differences. Among them was the procedural element of choice.

Three sets of data later confirmed Deci's hunch about procedural choice as a way to solve the puzzle. Two of them (Folger, Rosenfield, Hays, & Grove, 1978; Folger, Rosenfield, & Hays, 1978) looked at motivation (task interest) and performance, whereas the third (Cropanzano & Folger, 1989) assessed reproach-related attitudes directly by asking about the perceived fairness of treatment. In addition, the first two experiments manipulated choice as the presence or absence of an option to reject the low compensation and refuse the work, whereas the third varied whether the participants got to choose which of two performance tasks would determine compensation. Undercompensation conditions produced a similar pattern of results as a function of choice in all three studies. Unfavorable outcomes in the absence of choice produced reproachful, angry responses (e.g., low performance, perceived unfairness). These did not occur when the procedures allowed participants some form of choice. Here, then, is one resolution of equity theory's predictive dilemma, based on the results from these studies of choice: (a) The altering response of decreased effort due to anger occurs when people have no choice but to receive disadvantageous outcomes such as underpayment; decisions that led to that inequity were entirely under the control of other social agents (people other than the individual who gets shortchanged). (b) The cognitive-distortion response of task enhancement and hence enhanced effort occurs when people are freely offered the opportunity to accept or reject an offer involving disadvantageous outcomes. Recall that outcomes from a task are multidimensional; beyond the compensation offered, the work experience itself provides intrinsic outcomes. Sometimes people choose to accept an offer that undercompensates them for work on the task because the official compensation is only part of what they hope to receive; it provides certain tangible benefits, but the work itself has sources of satisfaction that offset the lack of tangible reward in the compensation. In such cases, the act of committing oneself engenders a dissonance-like process of self-justification, and the intrinsically rewarding features of performing the task capture enough attention to inspire particularly dedicated work.

Although the situation of choosing versus not choosing to work for insufficient compensation (i.e., making the decision to be inequitably underpaid, or someone else's making that decision) can account for the two differing reactions to inequity, such situations do not exhaust the range of events people face when feeling inequitably treated. In fact, being allowed to make such a choice comes rather infrequently (e.g., when considering different job offers). As we try to show in the following chapter, however, choice provides but one example of how to solve inequity's predictive dilemma based on aspects of procedure. If being given a choice is but one potential aspect of procedures, and if procedural differences are associated with different perceptions of fair treatment, then other aspects of procedure might also function like choice in steering responses toward task enhancement or instead toward resentment.

Note that Michael Lewis eventually became angry in a situation hard to classify in terms of choice. On the one hand, his greatest degree of choice (voluntary acceptance of an offered pay level) occurred in initially agreeing to work for Salomon Brothers. By the time he learned about his 1st-year bonus and next-year salary, he was already somewhat committed to working for that firm and could be considered "stuck" to a degree; that is, the various financial costs of changing jobs (e.g., relocation costs) and related inconveniences (e.g., psychological stresses related to being uprooted) served as a deterrent. Relative to the situation of full choice when joining a firm (especially if choosing among various attractive offers at the time), the situation in which employees find themselves when learning about their annual salary adjustments represents more of a "no-choice" condition. That makes Lewis's anger understandable from the perspective we have offered.

On the other hand, explaining his eventual hostility as a function of choice versus no-choice situations does not fully model the most likely psychological dynamics. In Chapter 2 we not only argue that choice is but one potential cue for making judgments about procedural fairness, as suggested earlier; we also argue that procedural variations such as choice represent but one of several types of cues used to make another, related judgment: the degree to which social agents seem blameworthy (warranting accusations of wrongdoing for unjust treatment of other people). If you make a choice of your own free will, and subsequent events create negative consequences that affect you unfavorably (including those that seem inequitable, at least initially), then you have no one but yourself to blame. If you have no choice, and others impose negative (inequitably low) outcomes on you, they are to blame. Having a basis for blaming others is consistent with feeling anger, hostility, and resentment toward them; having only yourself to blame is consistent with dissonance-reducing rationalizations (e.g., task-enhancement effects). In the next chapter, we explore several additional procedural variations beyond choice—as well as the broader context of interpersonal conduct in general—as further grounds

for assigning blame and hence for determining whether resentment or ratio-
nalizing task enhancement is more likely to occur.

Human resources management touches on a number of issues regarding
workplace motivation and labor-management relations. In order for organizational justice frameworks to fulfill their promise for improving the practice
of human resources management, they should offer guidance regarding when
employees will view management actions in an unfavorable light (see our
example of the farmer who suspects a bank lender of unscrupulous, exploita-
tive conduct). In this chapter, we have tried to show that equity theory alone
has not lived up to that promise. In the next, we consider how subsequent
developments have moved beyond equity theory and have provided some of
the additional tools needed for theories of organizational justice to contribute
to the practice of human resources management. Following that account,
subsequent chapters will illustrate some of the numerous applications of
justice concepts that have appeared in the organizational literature.

2 Process as Procedural and Interactional Justice

In Chapter 1, we referred to the presence versus absence of choice as a procedural variation that determines whether adverse inequity leads to anger or to task enhancement; high choice about the inequity produces a task-enhancement reaction (e.g., job satisfaction and intrinsic motivation), whereas low choice—or no choice—produces anger. Choice is one of many possible variations in procedural arrangements used for decision making, and so we indicated that our discussion of choice was a prelude to the broader topic of procedural justice. We also noted that procedures, in turn, represent but one example of several dimensions of situational variables that can all affect thoughts about where to place blame (e.g., on oneself vs. on another person). Among those situational variables, the general manner in which one person treats another (e.g., with sensitivity and consideration vs. with callous contempt) is related to a further subdistinction among categories of justice—interactional justice. This chapter addresses procedural and interactional justice as related topics that are nonetheless useful to differentiate for some purposes.

To preview those topics, we return to the example of Michael Lewis at Salomon Brothers that we began in Chapter 1. There we focused on his outcomes (salary and bonus) and frames of reference he used for comparative purposes of evaluating those outcomes—in effect, considerations about his own outcome and the outcome-input ratios of others (the topics of distributive justice and the distributive norm of equity). Here we can add examples to illustrate procedural and interactional justice considerations at Salomon Brothers.

A Preview of Procedural Justice

Procedural justice refers to fairness issues concerning the methods, mechanisms, and processes used to determine outcomes. For example, these issues might involve considerations about the proper way to conduct a decision-making process, a dispute-resolution process, or an allocation process in an organization. Political science often touches on such issues as they pertain to the larger society and formal, institutionalized procedures. What is the proper form of a constitution, for example, and what methods of voting and citizen representation ought to be implemented (e.g., autocratic rule; an oligarchy; a pure democracy in which all vote and the majority rules; a representative form of government in which people vote for legislators, who in turn determine tax rates and other matters affecting the entire citizenry)?

Lewis's description implies that the management of Salomon Brothers used relatively autocratic (nonparticipatory) procedures for determining salaries. For example, he never mentioned any chance to present his own arguments regarding compensation (offering interpretive comments about his performance in light of constraints, making his best-case arguments for the level of compensation he felt he deserved); any such opportunities seem to have been absent prior to the notification about what his bonus and next year's salary would be. That lack of participatory input to decision making stands in contrast to methods that our research review will show have enhanced perceptions of procedural justice—namely, the form of participation called *process control* (Thibaut & Walker, 1975) or *voice* (Folger, 1977).

Although we illustrate the central thrust of procedural justice by focusing on voice as an additional aspect of process beyond choice, clearly numerous other characteristics of procedures can also influence their perceived fairness. At Salomon Brothers, for example, the managers who made autocratic decisions about their subordinates' pay were themselves constrained by a prior autocratic decision made above them in the corporate hierarchy: "By edict from Gutfreund [Salomon's CEO], a floor and a ceiling were set each year around the bonuses of first- and second-year employees irrespective of their achievements" (Lewis, 1989, p. 200). Note, therefore, one reason that the structural features of a decision-making process can blur the conceptual distinction between procedural and distributive justice: Because certain structural constraints limit the range and types of possible outcomes, those aspects of the decision-making process make some forms of distributive consequences impossible to achieve (i.e., "irrespective of their achievements"). Lewis's comment implies that an equitable correspondence between employees' achievements and their pay could, because of the ceiling that capped potential bonuses, only extend up to a certain level of achievement; beyond that level, all would receive the same maximum bonus, even if some of those exceptional employees had vastly outperformed others also receiving that top bonus.

Such procedures prevent equity, thereby confounding procedural and distributive injustice. For that reason, our discussion focuses on structural elements of procedures that do not impose automatic constraints on outcomes and do not automatically dictate the amounts of outcomes going to various people. A decision-making process that allows voice as the opportunity for all affected parties to express their views, for example, does not predetermine which party's arguments will be most persuasive in influencing a decision maker. In contrast, other features of procedures sometimes do predetermine the nature of the outcome distribution, such as by assigning certain types of outcomes to certain types of people as a function of incorporating that procedural feature into the decision-making process. When part of the "procedures" for determining raises involves stipulating that salaries will vary according to seniority, for example, then the procedure is no longer "pure process" that can always be implemented in the same fashion yet generate different outcomes (cf. Folger, in press; Rawls, 1971); rather, each time the organization uses this procedure for determining salaries, the most senior employee will always get the highest salary. In theory, procedural justice and distributive justice have independent conceptual status as two distinct theoretical constructs; but in practice, process and outcome no longer have independent status when procedural constraints entail predetermined implications for outcome distributions.

A Preview of Interactional Justice

In contrast with formally institutionalized structures regarding a decision-making process, such as rules about outcome ranges (confounding distribution and procedure) or rules about who participates in decision making and how (a structural element of pure process, unconfounded with outcomes), other aspects of interactions between outcome receivers and outcome givers do not involve formally imposed constraints on roles and behavior. These less formalized aspects of interaction—pertaining to the topic of interactional justice—can also influence perceptions of fairness, however, and ignoring their impact would leave a significant gap in understanding how people feel about the way they are treated.

Consider what must have transpired during the conversation Michael Lewis (1989) had with his boss, for example, in light of the following description:

> "What can I say," he said, "but congratulations?" He spoke for about five minutes and achieved the desired effect. When he finished, I was prepared to pay him for the privilege of working at Salomon Brothers. . . . I began to understand why they give you a talk before they give you the money. (p. 202)

On the one hand, institutionalized rules or guidelines at Salomon probably dictated this "talk-before-money" sequence as part of the decision-making process's formal structure (i.e., part of the boss's prescribed role as evaluator and raise setter). Many companies, for example, require that such conversations take place; to ensure adherence to that structural feature of the decision-making process, such companies often ask their employees to sign a statement affirming that the conversation took place (a signature explicitly said not to have any implications as to whether the employee agreed or disagreed with the manager's judgments).

On the other hand, the actual content of such conversations inevitably has a more spontaneous character; rarely, if ever, can a preordained set of procedural rules dictate every word of that conversation, much less nuances of style (e.g., aspects of nonverbal communication such as body language and stylistic features of expression). Consider the following comment by Lewis (1989) referring to the content of the message delivered by his boss: "And I thought I knew how to sell. The boss put my small abilities to shame. He pushed all the right buttons" (p. 202). To push the right buttons and thereby get Lewis to react to his raise in the manner the boss wanted, this savvy member of Salomon's management probably drew more from personal experience than from formal guidelines for the procedure of conducting a salary review session. "Pushing all the right buttons" even suggests that this boss might have personalized some of his message in ways he knew would appeal to Lewis. Note also the use of the word *sell*. A formal procedural guideline or rule can dictate that a "tell-and-sell" conversation take place during a salary review session, but the exact *content* of that conversation (and its trappings, such as stylistic features that add persuasive context to persuasive content) can affect perceptions of fairness at least as much if not more so. Does a procedure, for example, include the requirement that bosses explain to subordinates the reasons for the latter's compensation? The presence versus absence of that requirement might be seen as an aspect of procedural justice, and perceptions about the fairness of the procedure would probably be more favorable when that requirement is included rather than excluded. The content of the explanation, however, can influence perceptions of fairness in ways that go beyond the mere existence of an explanation per se.

It makes sense to differentiate such aspects of the content of the explanation from procedural justice; yet they also seem to be conceptually independent from the fairness of the outcomes (although they obviously might also influence the perceived fairness of outcomes, which is what explanations designed to "sell" the fairness of outcomes hope to accomplish). One reason for referring separately to procedural and interactional justice, therefore, is to have the latter as a separate construct in order to include nonprocedurally dictated aspects of interaction such as explanation content and the persuasive features of communication efforts.

Other aspects of interactions, in addition to the content of explanations, can also have an impact on fairness perceptions, independent of contributions made by outcome or procedural considerations. Here, for example, is Michael Lewis's (1989) description of the interpersonal nature of the salary discussions (i.e., how employees were made to feel in that setting), which we will use to illustrate further connotations of interactional justice:

> Being paid was sheer misery for many. On January 1, 1987, 1986 would be erased from memory except for a single number: the amount of money you were paid. That number was the final summing-up. Imagine being told you will meet with the divine Creator in a year's time to be told your worth as a human being. You'd be a little edgy about the whole thing, too, wouldn't you? That's roughly what we endured. (p. 201)

Note such expressions as *misery, edgy, endured,* and *your worth as a human being.* Envision being called on the carpet or being sent to the principal's office as a schoolchild. Implicitly, a great deal of potential exists for people to feel demeaned by having to endure such an event and its reinforcement of the one-up–one-down nature of hierarchy ("Remember, I'm the boss and you're not"). Such situations are probably not calculated to reassure people in advance that they are human beings of ultimate worth, likely to be treated with dignity and respect. Indeed, a key feature of the experience was that it made employees feel as if they had been reduced to "a single number" in the eyes of their employer.

Interactional justice, therefore, has also been used in referring to aspects of social conduct with implications for other people's dignity. Willfully acting toward another person with callous disregard for his or her feelings—in demeaning, rude, or insulting ways, for example—does not betoken a strong interest in seeing that both parties meet on a level field and equally embrace a spirit of fair play. Fairness dictates that concern about others' well-being plays some role in governing actions (social conduct). Acting with blatant disregard for others' feelings, therefore, implies so much unfettered self-interest as to interfere with due consideration of opposing interests and others' well-being. Someone who thereby reveals intentions more malevolent than benevolent cannot epitomize the essence of justice, even if he or she does not deny others an exchanged outcome of fair value and does not violate any formal requirements of decision-making procedures. The category of interactional justice, therefore, serves to cover these additional sources of perceived unfairness that do not fit conveniently under the headings of distributive and procedural justice.

Having conveyed a preliminary sense of procedural and interactional justice by example, we now turn to illustrating those concepts in concrete terms. In the following sections, we first address procedural justice, then interactional justice, by discussing only a limited number of principles that apply to each term. There is a great deal of room for ambiguity and confusion with regard to the distinctiveness of procedural and interactional justice and their overlap. In order to distinguish them as separate concepts first, before subsequently turning to subtle nuances about their overlap and shared functional character, we limit the following section on procedural justice to an examination of voice. Similarly, we also limit the next section on interactional justice to an examination of excuses and justifications as two examples of explanation content. In addition, we try to keep the discussion as concrete as possible by illustrating these concepts with operational definitions used in experiments that manipulated a given concept as an independent variable.

Procedural Structure: Choice and Decision Control, Voice and Process Control

Although experiments with choice (discussed in Chapter 1) confirmed Deci's (1975) speculation and hence resolved equity's apparently contradictory predictions, choice is only one potential procedural element—too specific for broad statements about reactions to perceived injustice in general. There are practical limitations on how much choice people have as ordinary citizens, much less as employees. And from a theoretical perspective, some instances of positive reactions to choice can be trivial or difficult to interpret with much confidence, because the freedom to choose introduces the potential for confounding choice with outcome favorability. People who are free to choose usually choose more favorable outcomes; seeing that they are happy afterward, you might either conclude that the favorable outcome made them happy (trivial) or realize that it will be hard to tell how much of the happiness came from the outcome and how much from the choice (ambiguous). (Incidentally, the experiments described in Chapter 1 avoided that confounding.)

Work by Thibaut and Walker (1975, 1978), however, had already paved the way for an expanded perspective on procedural fairness—one that analyzed the structure of decision-making procedures for resolving disputes. Their analysis treated choice (which they called "decision control") as only one structural component of such procedures and initiated the study of other process-related elements by drawing attention to one in particular (which they called "process control"). Essentially, they looked for aspects of procedures that might make up for not giving a disputant total freedom of choice about how to control the dispute (and not giving even the minimal control over decisions that comes from having a veto).

Illustratively, suppose you and someone else cannot agree about the proper division of some valuable assets regarding which you both claim to have legitimate rights. To avoid endless haggling (not to mention possible bloodshed), you both agree to have the matter settled by someone else. Despite thinking that you have the right to a certain portion of the assets, granting someone else the unilateral authority to impose a solution will deny you any opportunity to choose some portion as yours. Choice is now in that third party's hands alone. Thibaut and Walker described such a situation as not unlike arbitration or a formal hearing in civil court. (We ignore at this point the possibility of arrangements such as mediation, in which disputing parties do retain some freedom of choice—namely, the freedom to veto proposed suggestions, because mediators act in an advisory capacity only).

What might substitute for freedom of choice when someone else makes the final decision? Thibaut and Walker (1975, 1978) answered this question by first noting the simple, logically derivable distinction between two parts of decision making: (a) getting ready to decide and (b) deciding. The unilateral authority to make a decision is exercised at the latter point by the third party, and they called it *decision control*. Binding arbitration, for example, gives the third party total control over the final decision. But what should the third party be doing before making a decision? What should you and the person with whom you have been arguing do during that time? Is there anything the two of you should be allowed to do that might make up for losing direct decision control (i.e., choice)? Could some form of indirect control be granted to you as a substitute for direct control? Wouldn't that depend on what governs (e.g., controls, constrains, influences) the third party's actions prior to decision making? How should the decision maker's actions be governed prior to that time? Are there certain forms of procedural regulations it makes sense to apply?

Anyone who has ever experienced a formal or informal hearing can probably realize how many options and variations might become relevant considerations once such a series of questions is raised. In fact, Gerald Leventhal performed just such an exercise once, introspecting about aspects of process and the elements that might be vital to each aspect (Leventhal, Karuza, & Fry, 1980). We will return to his laundry list of considerations later. For now, however, we note that Thibaut and Walker (1975, 1978) opted for a much simpler strategy and came up with an elegant, extraordinarily influential, all-purpose answer capable of shaping the form of any response to such questions. By saying that all preparations prior to a final decision involve the process stage of decision making, they noted a process-stage form of indirect control that parallels the third party's direct control (decision control) exercised at the decision stage. They referred to this indirect control—the opportunity for disputing parties to attempt to influence the decision maker—as being *process control*. If the third party has total decision-control power, an all-purpose answer to perceived procedural fairness is to give the disputing parties as much process control as possible, consistent with the constraint that neither disputant has more of such power than the other. Of course, it is an easy matter to imagine many different ways in which disputing parties can control what goes on prior to a decision (e.g., gathering evidence, presenting evidence and information, questioning one another, making arguments, and offering interpretations about evidence, information, and the other party's statements). The chance to exercise such opportunities is what Thibaut and Walker meant by a high amount of process control for the disputing parties.

One of the major conclusions about providing people with process control, amply documented by Lind and Tyler's (1988) comprehensive review, constitutes what has been called the *fair-process effect* (Folger, Rosenfield, Grove, & Corkran, 1979). That is, the more someone considers a process to be fair, the more tolerant that person is about the consequences of the process, such as adversely unfair outcomes that a decision-making process creates when it governs the distribution of outcomes. For example, employees who feel that their supervisor has conducted performance appraisals in a fair manner (compared with those who do not feel that way) tend to give more positive ratings of pay satisfaction, their loyalty to the organization, and their trust in the supervisor—independently of pay amount and perceived fairness of pay (Folger & Konovsky, 1989). This means that in the case of pay perceived to be unfairly low, the fairness of the process kept reactions to low pay from being as negative as they would have been otherwise. Of course, another example of this very general effect is for fair processes to influence the perceived fairness of outcomes directly; the same low amount is considered less fair as an outcome when produced by an unfair process than when produced by a fair process (Lind & Tyler, 1988). These findings, however, should also be considered in the larger context of some potential for raised hopes (from fair processes) to be dashed (by unfair outcomes)—an opposite tendency known as a *frustration effect* (Folger et al., 1979).

For now we will ignore that possibility of backlash and concentrate exclusively on the more salutary effects of voice and other ingredients of decision-making methods that make subsequent decisions palatable. We can summarize extensive evidence (for details, see Lind & Tyler, 1988; Tyler & Smith, in press) and a variety of conceptual issues in terms of the following specific points:

1. Thibaut and Walker (1975, 1978) used the concept of process control in a particular context—deliberations during conflict-resolution proceedings, especially those conducted in courts of law (e.g., civil hearings). In addition, that term also has a somewhat narrow connotation because it presupposes that a particular psychological mechanism—perceived control—is responsible for enabling fair-process effects.

Hirschman's *Exit, Voice and Loyalty* (1970), on the other hand, used the term *voice* as a dependent variable rather than as an independent variable and also cast in much more general terms a description of actions relevant to the notion of process control. In the courtroom context, process control refers to actions that an attorney representing a disputant can take, such as presenting evidence and offering rebutting arguments to challenge the other party's evidence. Hirschman referred to voice more generally in terms of "the political process, par excellence" (p. 16); that is, the process of trying to exercise influence on behalf of one's own interests and causes.

In turn, Folger (1977) borrowed Hirschman's concept of voice and suggested that it serve as a more general substitute for the concept of process control. Moreover, by operationalizing it experimentally as an independent variable, Folger showed that voice operated in a nonlegal context to produce fair-process effects similar to the process-control effects found by Thibaut, Walker (1975, 1978), and their colleagues in studies that operationalized it with procedural variations drawn from analogous aspects of the legal context. (Incidentally, the alternative context involved pay as compensation for work on a task, the first use of procedural justice concepts in an organizationally relevant scenario.) Folger operationalized voice in a way that illustrates the underlying construct readily: The research participants either had no way of communicating their interests to a decision maker (a "mute" condition), or they had their opinions transmitted (the operationalization of voice).

2. In principle, the concept of voice can refer to any manner of communicating with a decision maker (e.g., conveying opinions); operationally, the Folger (1977) experiment involved a written statement restricted to indicating what the worker thought was fair pay for the task being done. Subsequently, based on evidence by Tyler (1994), it has become necessary to note the importance of distinguishing between voice as a formalized, structural aspect of procedures and voice as it pertains to events that actually transpire when

voice is exercised. The following descriptions characterize those two distinct usages of the term:

   a. As a structural property of the procedural arrangements for making a decision, the presence versus absence of voice indicates one way that those procedures formally prescribe and constrain the role opportunities for affected parties who do not exercise unilateral control over the decision. Although they cannot exercise final authority autonomously, the procedural provision of voice means they can exercise an *opportunity* to convey a message about their interests to the relevant decision maker (the chance to "have a say" in what should be done).

   b. In contrast, events that transpire along with the exercise of voice represent implications related to taking advantage of a procedural opportunity (and observing the consequences) rather than the implications of that opportunity's mere existence. On the one hand, the mere existence of the opportunity for voice (as a structural feature) might imply that whoever designed and implemented those procedural arrangements did so with principles of fairness in mind (which could contribute to a fair-process effect). On the other hand, psychologically meaningful perceptions that relate to fairness can also depend on the impact of voice as exercised, particularly with respect to the reactions of the decision maker (indicating whether or not the voiced opinions were "heard," depending on whether the decision maker really seemed to be "listening").

Please note that we are referring to a subtle variation in the efficacy of voice: not whether it is efficacious in actually influencing the decision maker to rule in favor of the opinion expressed, but whether it is efficacious in being taken seriously (i.e., whether the decision maker seems to have given the expressed views their due consideration, regardless of whether the final decision imposes consequences consistent with favoring those views). Tyler's (1994) study showed that under some circumstances, a fair-process effect will result from the presence of voice as a structural component of procedures only when the more subtle "fair hearing, considered judgment" aspect of enacted procedures accompanies it (cf. Folger, Konovsky, & Cropanzano, 1992). As we will subsequently discuss, impressions of how a procedure has been enacted can depend on relatively stylistic aspects of the decision maker's interpersonal conduct— the dimension of fairness now commonly known as interactional justice. For this reason among others, therefore, these subtleties of determinants of reactions to voice indicate why lines between procedural and interactional justice can blur in practice even though they make conceptual sense in principle.

   3. Folger (1977) did not assume that perceived control accounted for voice's effects; in fact, he chose Hirschman's (1970) concept of voice precisely

because it has no specific connotations with respect to any assumed causal mechanisms responsible for fair-process effects (in contrast with the psychology-of-control connotations associated with the Thibaut and Walker process-control terminology). Specifically, referring to voice rather than to process control leaves issues about the psychological mediator open for empirical investigation, rather than imposing any particular form of explanation (e.g., mediation by perceptions of control, or by the perceived fairness of someone's having provided a form of indirect control—the opportunity to try to exert influence—as a substitute that compensates for the lack of direct control). Current evidence and thinking, in fact, implies that perceptions of control might not be crucial. Rather, the crucial mediator of fair-process effects might be the perception that someone else "did the right thing" (provided voice; listened attentively and treated a request seriously, despite then having to deny it in light of other legitimate considerations).

4. Another distinction roughly parallels the structure versus enactment distinction discussed previously: the instrumental and noninstrumental (sometimes called "expressive") effects of voice (cf. Lind & Tyler, 1988; Tyler, Rasinski, & Spodick, 1985). Phrased differently, is voice important only as the means to an end, or does it have value as an end in itself? As means, voice can prove instrumental to obtaining desired outcomes; that view of voice emphasizes people's concerns about the outcomes they receive and relegates voice to a more subsidiary role (as an indirect substitute for outcomes). As an end in itself, being given an opportunity to express one's own opinion becomes a valuable outcome (e.g., reflecting a certain amount of esteem that the other person implicitly acknowledges; obtaining access to rights that, if denied, would indicate being held in low esteem). Ultimately, empirical evidence might establish that either the instrumental role of voice exclusively, the noninstrumental role exclusively, or both, contribute to the impact that voice has on perceived procedural justice and on the related phenomenon of fair-process effects (for a discussion and an indication of some controversy about interpretations of current evidence, see Shapiro, 1993).

Summary Statement on Voice
and Procedural Justice

A variety of measures in a variety of studies have shown that participants denied voice respond more negatively than those who exercise meaningful voice. We can tie this statement back to the discussion in Chapter 1 of anger and resentment. When low outcomes indicate the possibility of distributive injustice, aspects of procedural justice—such as the presence or absence of voice—can help determine whether the potential victim of inequity responds with hostility toward an alleged perpetrator of injustice. In fact, providing voice versus excluding it structurally (or functionally) can in itself determine whether the decision maker gets tagged with the label of wrongdoer. Some evidence exists, therefore, that voice affects reactions toward decision makers independently of the level of outcomes that their decisions provide to others (e.g., main effects for manipulations of voice).

We can relate this influence of voice back to the previous chapter's discussion of blame: Decision makers who provide meaningful forms of voice and allow participants to exercise voice in a meaningful fashion (e.g., by giving serious consideration to the opinions expressed) can avoid one source of charges of wrongdoing. They are, in a word, less likely to be considered blameworthy and to be reproached accordingly. Moreover, they are less likely to become the targets of punishment that often accompanies reproach. The research evidence thus indicates that voice is another procedural element, along with choice, whose presence tends to constrain reproach and whose absence removes a constraint against reproach. To put it yet another way, unfavorable outcomes from decisions can encourage reproaching the decision maker and others psychologically associated with adverse consequences (e.g., someone who fails to mitigate suffering despite a low-cost opportunity to do so). Without choice, voice, or some other procedural element to act as a restraint, the extent of reproach is limited only by the extent to which outcomes do not seem unfavorable (or by conditions that make people reluctant to indicate how unfavorable they think the outcomes are, such as fear of retaliation).

Beyond Choice and Voice: Prelude to Interactional Justice in Studies of Explanation Content

Subsequent research has added to the list of process-related features that can alter perceptions of fairness independently from outcome qualities—the types of things lumped together under the common heading of "procedure" in this discussion so far, but that include some prospects currently referenced in the literature with the use of other terms as well (e.g., interactional justice, interpersonal sensitivity). Again, it can be useful for concrete illustration to describe these as factors manipulated experimentally. Such illustrations also potentially add the clarity that can come from focusing on operationalizations rather than on terms perhaps laden with excess theoretical baggage. The next section describes experimental manipulations of perceived fairness in terms of explanation content, thereby illustrating the concepts of *excuses* and *justi-*

fications that made an early appearance in leading toward writings on the construct of interactional justice.

We must first issue some caveats about our own theoretical baggage in advance, however, to make explicit some of the biases that have already played a role in how we organized our discussion of fairness and the distinctions among distributive, procedural, or interactional justice as labels for variations on themes of fairness. Two points are relevant:

1. We sometimes refer to procedural and interactional justice as variations on a common theme of process-related factors. That deliberate conflation of constructs reflects our bias toward viewing both as factors relevant to assigning someone blame—making that person a target for anger and resentment, warranting punishment. At the same time, we will also discuss independent reasons for separating the two constructs. Indeed, they might implicate blame in different fashions and perhaps to different degrees. Perceptions of interactional justice, such as those based on the degree to which one person shows interpersonal sensitivity toward another, might implicate blame and wrongdoing more directly than aspects of procedural arrangements, which are perhaps more ambiguous in terms of whether they are attributable to someone's intended stance toward the well-being of others.

2. We believe that everyday perceptions of fairness are fundamentally grounded in two issues—social consequences and social conduct. On the one hand, these are distinct; for example, they can be conceptualized and manipulated experimentally as independent factors. On the other hand, they are also inextricably interwoven in their joint impact; for example, they interact statistically, so that the impact of one depends on the relevant level of the other. In more commonly used terms, *social consequences* has a meaning roughly similar to that of outcome-related factors (i.e., those related to distributive justice and equity); *social conduct* has a meaning roughly similar to that of process-related factors (i.e., those related to procedural and interactional justice). For that reason, we also refer to an Outcome × Process interaction as shorthand for the joint impact of social consequences and social conduct.

By social consequences we mean a category closely related to, but broader than and somewhat distinctively conceptualized from, those outcome-related events traditionally associated with equity and distributive justice. As one norm of distributive justice, for example, equity is perhaps most applicable to the tangible products of an explicit exchange—such as the return on investment from an economic transaction. Our construct of social consequences refers instead to the psychological impact of exchanged outcomes and other events with impact on a person's well-being, whether resulting from one-way transfers or other socially mediated processes beyond exchange. Moreover, it refers to the socially relevant consequences of such events. Socially relevant consequences involve benefit or harm done to the well-being of one or more members of a social order. The nature of benefit and harm refers to that social order's understanding of well-being; in turn, judgments about benefit and harm are grounded in evaluative criteria potentially unique to it, such as the social norms it routinely sanctions.

By social conduct, the second factor in a two-factor approach that we elaborate more comprehensively in Chapter 3, we mean human behavior in a social context—actions that have relevance not just for a single person, but for a wider community of persons (in particular, the relevant moral community). When someone designs and implements procedures with one set of structural features rather than another, that is social conduct. When one person insults another, that is social conduct. More generally, social conduct is behavior with moral overtones. Social conduct is behavior that a moral community has a stake in evaluating and sanctioning (negatively or positively). Individual and collective interests teeter around a delicate balance point. Individual interests cannot be pursued in a totally unfettered fashion without some degree of potential threat to collective interests, yet total devotion to the other's good ultimately has no practical value if lack of attention to self-interest makes one incapable of helping others (e.g., through neglect of one's own physical well-being, leading to starvation and death rather than effectively sustained altruism). That balance is always in danger and is never achieved to perfection. Nonetheless, it is not simply a theoretical ideal without practical consequences. Rather, its pursuit must be sustained to at least some degree in order for acceptable social relations to survive—for life among human beings to be at least minimally stable and secure. By social conduct, we refer to actions judged in light of criteria relevant to such desiderata of life among human beings. In particular, our construct of social conduct relates directly to the notion of blame that has been an underlying theme running throughout these two chapters—a theme we explore even more explicitly and comprehensively in Chapter 3. Communications loom large among morally relevant aspects of human interaction. Our next topic focuses on the content of communications—and, in particular, on the information contained in messages designed to explain reasons for actions taken. It should be obvious that moral evaluations of conduct will vary according to the acceptability of such explanations. Inadequate, unacceptable explanations make a person more susceptible to being punished for wrongdoing. In fact, the two broad categories of explanations we review in the next section—excuses and justifications—can work to deflect charges of wrongdoing and to insulate someone initially suspected of wrongdoing from suffering punishment. Note, however, that we also discuss these in a fashion designed to integrate social consequences and social conduct because of our assumption that the two combine jointly in judgments relevant to fairness. That is, we discuss excuses and justifications as factors related to social conduct, but we present them in the context of experiments demonstrating an Outcome × Process interaction, where the Outcome factors have a bearing on social consequences.

Interactional Justice From Explanation Content (Excuses and Justifications)

Our examples of excuses and justifications, as experimentally operationalized, come from studies showing statistical interactions between process and outcome factors. Bies (1987b) subsequently pointed out that these two studies help illustrate how two different types of communicated explanations—each a different type of "account" given by Agent (the Other in a direct exchange) as an interpretation of harm to a Victim (Person, again translating to the terminology of inequity)—can restrain reproach and retaliatory feelings toward harmdoers. The distinction is even implicit in the concept of harmdoing itself; the account can focus on the harm (reinterpreting the damage done— the social consequences) or the doing of it (reinterpreting implications for revenge-relevant concepts such as culpability, accountability, liability, and the like—the key aspects of social conduct). Originally introduced by Austin (1961), these two categories have been called *justifications* and *excuses,* respectively.

Excuses

Imagine being in one of the following conditions of an experiment (Folger & Martin, 1986): (1) You think you have virtually shoe-in chances of getting a very desirable prize, a bonus for your being able to help with a project; or (2) you think you might be allowed to participate and thus to get the bonus, but that a prescreening has made that possibility extremely remote. In either case, you later receive a note from the experimenter canceling the project. It contains one of the following messages: The cancellation has occurred because of an equipment failure (in Conditions 1-A and 2-A); or the experimenter who originally offered the bonus has written that "I've decided" not to continue (in 1-B and 2-B).

This process-related manipulation thus varied the information content of an excuse (cf. Greenberg, 1993a) and hence its implications for blaming Agent (the experimenter): either in a manner sufficient to count as mitigating circumstances that absolved Agent of responsibility (1-A and 2-A) or in a manner insufficient to count as mitigating (1-B and 2-B). This design tested directly whether or not such a procedural element can influence the extent to which reactions toward an outcome provider (Agent) become more negative as the outcomes themselves become more negative (the general hypothesis in this line of studies). Notice that the outcome itself, in this case, is always exactly the same (no award given), which helps control for a host of alternative possible explanations otherwise not ruled out when outcomes vary. Variations in reactions, that is, are based entirely on factors influencing perceptions of an objectively identical situation (from the standpoint of the award not received). Thus, because Victim's prior expectations about the probability of obtaining the award were manipulated, the experiment created a situation in which 1-A and 1-B Victims were exposed to a substantial loss compared with their high expectations (anticipating virtually shoe-in odds), whereas 2-A and 2-B Victims were exposed to a much more trivial experience in relation to their already low expectations. If nothing else matters other than outcome-related considerations, negative reactions toward Agent should be much stronger from either set of Condition 1 (high-expectation) Victims than from either set of Condition 2 (low-expectation) Victims.

Yet, that difference in reactions based on differences in expectations was nowhere to be found when the results from the highly expectant 1-B Victims were compared with the results from the unexpectant 2-B Victims. Even though the 1-B group suffered a much greater loss in expectancy-relevant terms, they showed no greater reproach toward the Agent who withheld the award than did the 2-B group. From the standpoint not of the harm's magnitude, but of the context in which it was done, however, both of these "B" conditions put Victim participants in the role of reacting to someone whose excuse for causing harm had a special character: Mitigating circumstances, beyond that person's control, made it impossible for the person to prevent the harm.

The absence of any explanation at all, other than an arbitrary and capricious attitude ("I've decided"), represents the opposite end of the fair-explanation continuum. Note that communicating an explanation might not seem "procedural" enough to put in the same category as choice and voice. For that reason, some writers prefer another label (such as accounts or interactional justice). From another perspective, however, there is a rather striking functional parallel among the effects produced by voice, choice, and excuses: All three types of manipulations interact with outcome favorability in the same fashion. Thus, the egregiously unfair "I've decided" note produced greater venom toward the note's writer the greater the outcome expectations had been. Consistent with the predicted Outcome × Process interaction, that is, the highly expectant 1-A participants were angrier than the unexpectant 2-A participants. (In fact, one of the former actually took a swing at the award withholder—a very deserving coauthor of that article—before the debriefing could begin. We have always viewed this reaction as an indication that experiments can have much more realism and impact than their critics realize. Our attempts at creating resentment and retaliation in the lab have at such times been almost dangerously successful.)

Justifications

Another study (Folger, Rosenfield, & Robinson, 1983) illustrates a manipulation of justification and shows how the same type of Outcome × Process interaction also results from this second category of communicated explanations. Again, a negative outcome stayed the same in its objective characteristics throughout all conditions of the experiment: All the research participants thought that they had lost in a competition for a desirable prize. And once again, the general psychological principle of relative-deprivation research (Stouffer et al., 1949) suggested a way to vary perceptions of loss despite keeping the objective amount of loss identical. This outcome manipulation created two levels for the magnitude of perceived loss (severe vs. mild), analogous with the manipulation of past expectations in the Excuses study (more extreme vs. less extreme violation of expectations). Severe-loss participants learned that they would have won if the experimenters running the competition had not changed the competition's scoring rules. Mild-loss participants also learned about the change of rules, but they thought they would have lost even by the original scoring procedure.

The fairness of the process was manipulated by varying the type of justification for the change in rules. In the poor-justification conditions, the rule change was made to appear rather arbitrary and capricious (somewhat like the "I've decided" change in the Excuses experiment): The change was described as based on the personal opinion of one of two experimenters. In the good-justification conditions, however, logically reasoned arguments were given to legitimate the change as essential for a fair competition. The results showed that with this legitimate justification, the outcome manipulation had no effect on reactions; that is, severe-loss participants did not exhibit a greater tendency to reproach than mild-loss participants. Reproach and resentment tendencies were much greater for a severe loss than for a mild loss, however, when a weak justification robbed the process of its legitimacy.

Notes on the Procedural-Interactional Distinction: Social Conduct as "System Throughput"

Choice and voice relate to procedural justice, whereas excuses and justification relate to interactional justice in the sense of that term amplified by its relation to account giving and explanation content (Bies, 1986; Bies & Moag, 1986). Yet all four types of manipulations have produced the same form of Outcome × Process interaction in the studies described earlier. The following discussion uses the notion of "system throughput" to explain both (a) one basis for distinguishing between procedural and interactional justice and (b) one type of reason why they nonetheless can (and often do) function in the same way, yielding similar effects.

Two terms from equity theory correspond with two concepts from the general theory of systems: inputs and outputs. In systems-theory terms, the neglect of process amounts to overlooking "throughput" as a series of transforming events that help generate a final product. The terms of the equity equation—inputs and outcomes—do not totally ignore the history of events leading up to outcomes, of course, but they provide incomplete information about that history by indicating only its starting point. The equation shows a static snapshot of that starting point: the quantities entered as input terms. It neglects all of the history and potentially important social context between the time inputs were put in (e.g., labor was exerted) and the time outcomes came out (e.g., wages were paid). Some of those in-between-times or throughput events involve the full span of decision-making activities, such as collecting information, clarifying and interpreting the information, evaluating the information in terms of criteria established by objectives and priorities, and so on. Human resources managers are well aware of how such events can influence fairness perceptions.

Events at either of two points in time can influence perceptions of the throughput process of decision making, which explains why both types of events can influence fairness impressions. First, consider events that take place prior to the point at which a decision gets made. During the time before the decision is made, do the people whom the decision will effect have a role in that process, and do they feel that the role has a legitimate set of constraints and opportunities? Thibaut and Walker (1975) emphasized process control as a concept for describing role opportunities, namely the extent of opportunity for trying to influence a decision maker. Choice obviously represents another important form of opportunity. Such role characteristics govern behavior during the time when a decision is being made; they pertain to the structure of the decision-making process, the features useful for describing the decision architecture (e.g., roles of organizational participants).

It should not surprise human resource managers that the structural design of work arrangements can affect employee perceptions and motivations. Hackman and Oldham's (1980) Job Characteristics Model of work design, for example, described ways of structuring jobs to enhance intrinsic motivation. Notably, their element of task autonomy (being granted decision-making authority over some aspect of work, thereby enhancing intrinsic motivation by increasing a sense of responsibility) has a parallel with the structural element of choice (Cropanzano & Folger, 1989). Deming's (1968) writings on total quality provide an analogous illustration about structure as the degree of constraint versus opportunity in a system. He noted that technical aspects of the production process (e.g., machine technology, sequential assembly of parts by different workers on a production line) or features of the environment (e.g., market fluctuations) can constrain a worker's output (Peters, O'Connor, & Eulberg, 1985). You might feel unfairly paid if your piece-rate productivity was limited by a poorly designed machine or a slow predecessor on the assembly line, for example, and likewise if your sales commission were adversely affected by your having been assigned a poor territory. Deming (1968) used the existence of such imposed constraints as an argument against merit-based pay, claiming that many problems of low productivity were the fault of management decisions (e.g., about machinery, work design, territory, product strategy). It is easy to see how the presence of constraints on work can raise issues of fairness.

Now consider a second category of events that influence fairness perceptions, namely events occurring after decisions have been made. The excuse study (Folger & Martin, 1986) and the justification study (Folger, Rosenfield, & Robinson, 1983) illustrated such events as examples of communications about the decisions. These explanation events, which give the reasons for a decision after the decision has occurred, are not the same as the structural elements of the decision-making process itself. The throughput metaphor emphasizes similarities rather than differences between the two types of events, however, even though they occur at two points in time. The differences indicate grounds for the distinction between the first set of events as related to procedural justice and the second set of events as related to interactional justice. The similarities help show why procedural and interactional justice nonetheless share at least some commonalities as nonoutcome- or process-related aspects of organizational justice.

A close look at the content of some communicated explanations reveals a key source of similarity and shared features: Explanations often contain details about the decision-making process. The content of excuses and justifications often describes aspects of throughput pertaining to the role-governed, structural features of the decision-making process. Excuses of mitigating circumstances such as an equipment failure, for example, claim that the decision maker's "hands were tied"—his or her role was structurally constrained. Relatedly, notice that the opposite of the excuse or justification was an "I've decided" example of unconstrained authority. In the studies described previously, the interactional justice component of an excuse or justification influenced fairness perceptions because of the content of the explanations. That content described what happened while the decision-making process was taking place. Therefore, even though the event of communication occurred after the event of deciding, the communication affected perceptions about how the decision-making process had transpired. On that score, the functional effects of procedural justice structural elements (e.g., voice or choice) or interactional justice communication content (e.g., explanatory excuses or justifications) look the same.

A human resources manager might wonder why organizational justice theorists make the distinction between procedural and interactional justice. In fact, if the two simply reflect alternate routes to the same goal (viz., influencing fairness perceptions), this distinction seems somewhat arbitrary. On the one hand, the distinction emphasizes that there are two different ways to influence fairness perceptions other than by characteristics of the outcome distribution itself. These can (but need not) apply at two different points in time, which helps expand the repertoire of the human resources manager. On the other hand, ignoring the distinction or combining the two categories for some purposes helps emphasize that either set of events can accomplish the same objective from the manager's perspective—constructing a defense against reproach for wrongdoing and against possible retaliatory or punitive attack.

In the studies reviewed, excuses and justifications mitigated reproach about outcome adversity—just as voice or choice had done. In other words, excuses or justifications acted as stand-ins for choice or voice. One organizational implication is that when managers make decisions without allowing an employee any voice or choice, they can then be held severely accountable (the more severe the outcome) if the explanation for the decision does not provide a good excuse or justification. Giving prior choice or voice to Victim might make Victim at least partially accountable for the consequences of the decision-making process. Withholding choice or voice tends to leave Agent fully accountable, which makes the content of explanations crucial as the "account" of what happened (Bies, 1987b).

Beyond Explanatory Content:
Interactional Justice as Interpersonal Sensitivity

Up to this point, we have described interactional justice in a roundabout fashion, using examples (excuse and justification manipulations) rather than a conceptual definition. In fact, one potential element of a formal definition— the time difference between events involved in making a decision and enacting or implementing one (when communications about the decision can occur and explanations might be given)—fails to provide sufficiently solid grounds for emphasizing such a distinction. Now we want to pave the way both for a more extensive treatment of interactional justice and a possible conceptualization of it. An extended treatment is needed because we have allowed excuses and justifications to stand as the only examples of interactional justice. In fact, examples of interactional justice go far beyond those two types of accounts and even beyond the area of postdecisional explanations or communications—so much so that identifying new instances that might qualify as interactional justice seems to be a growth industry in the field of organizational justice! Our discussion in this section is meant to foreshadow such developments.

Several reviews of interactional justice have been written (e.g., Folger & Bies, 1989; Greenberg, 1990a; Tyler & Bies, 1990). Again, it is not our intention to be comprehensive in coverage. Here, we only touch on some isolated illustrations mentioned in those reviews. We begin by elaborating somewhat our earlier discussion about communicated explanations, which only touched on excuses and justifications. We do so, however, not only by placing communication within the broader context of things done when implementing a decision, but also by placing such implementation in the broader context of Agent conduct (hence tying these points back to attributions about the intentions behind someone's conduct).

The following quote from the Tyler and Bies (1990) review provides a starting point:

> Recent research has found that people's procedural fairness judgments are influenced by (a) interpersonal treatment they receive from the decision maker, which may have little or nothing to do with the formal procedure, and (b) whether the formal decision-making procedure is properly enacted by the decision maker. (p. 81)

Note that although interpersonal treatment and decision enactment constitute topics distinct from formal procedure per se (i.e., they are interactional justice topics), they influence perceptions of procedural fairness. That statement fits with the earlier discussion on parallels between procedural and interactional justice. Note that although we also frame our discussion of interactional justice in terms of the two subcategories of enactment and interpersonal treatment, we want readers to be aware of the considerable overlap between the two.

Enactment

Explanations. Tyler and Bies (1990) called "providing an account of (or explanation for) the decision" an aspect of making sure that the formal decision-making procedure has been enacted properly. Clearly, what counts as proper can depend on local norms of propriety; some decisions might seem so routine that no explanation is required, and some Agents might not be expected to give explanations because no one believes that their authority should be questioned. Often, however, people affected by a decision feel entitled to hear why it was made (Bies, 1987a; Greenberg, 1990a; Milkovich & Newman, 1987). Theory and research by Bies and his colleagues (e.g., Bies, 1987a, 1987b, 1989; Bies & Moag, 1986; Bies & Shapiro, 1987, 1988; Bies, Shapiro, & Cummings, 1988; Shapiro, 1991; Shapiro, Buttner, & Barry, 1994) have broadened the study of accounts, as has Greenberg's related work on impression management (e.g., Greenberg, 1988a, 1990c). For example, Bies (1987b) offered a much-expanded categorization about various types of accounts (see also Greenberg, 1990b). Also, research has documented the fact that voice and explanations can have independent impact on fairness judgments. Finally, certain stylistic or qualitative aspects of an explanation seem to be at least potentially as important as some features pertaining to the content of an explanation. The distinction between excuses and justifications refers to explanation content, but only to a difference in the focus of the content (viz., on responsibility for the harm vs. on the harm itself). Apart from whether the content of the explanation is designed to excuse or to justify, such messages can vary in the quality of the reasoning that is used. In order for a procedure to be perceived as having been enacted fairly, the explanations given should contain reasoning that adequately supports the claim and that conveys sincerity on the part of the person giving the explanation (Bies et al., 1988).

Other Features of Proper Enactment. Again noting that proper enactment varies with the circumstances and the eye of the beholder, we can nonetheless summarize those features commonly contributing to perceived procedural fairness (drawing from sources such as Folger & Bies, 1989; Leventhal, 1980; Tyler & Bies, 1990). For example, we have already discussed one common norm for the proper enactment of procedures with voice: People want to believe not only that voice was granted, but that it was adequately considered (Tyler, 1987). Leventhal's (1980) procedural-justice criterion of representativeness also suggests that the expression of interests can be accomplished by other people on one's own behalf. Combined, these imply that people want to be sure their views are considered, and having those views considered might be as important (under some, as yet unknown or unspecified, circumstances) as how the views get expressed in the first place. Of course, people sometimes seem to place great value on the sheer opportunity to express their views personally, such as the value alleged for catharsis as the purging of emotions ("I just want a chance to get it off my chest"). As a speculation, however, we conjecture that some independent value also exists in demonstrating that certain interests were taken into account, regardless of how such interests became known (i.e., whether they were expressed by the person or interest group in question). It is a challenge of management to persuade employees that their interests were considered when no formal or informal mechanism has been used for ascertaining what those interests are.

Aside from hoping that a decision maker takes the interests of relevant constituencies into account, people also look for indications that Agent has not allowed his or her own personal biases to affect the decision. Relatedly, people want to see that the criteria for decision making are applied uniformly across all instances in which decisions are made (e.g., using selection criteria evenhandedly and consistently with respect to every applicant in a hiring pool). Finally, people's sense of propriety and fairness is affected by the timeliness with which the consequences of a decision are made known to those affected.

In addition to general norms of propriety, specific norms may apply to a given situation. This would be the case for specific areas of human resources management practice. A human resources function such as testing might have certain norms of propriety regarding confidentiality and privacy, for example, whose impact on perceived fairness is greater than the impact of those issues regarding other aspects of work (e.g., random searches for weapons). Subsequent chapters of this book treat in more detail the fairness norms of interactional justice specific to various areas of human resources management.

Interpersonal Treatment. Being fairly treated goes beyond receiving fair outcomes, as the work on procedural justice has suggested. In turn, the work on interactional justice has suggested that being fairly treated goes beyond the formal characteristics of procedures. Some origins of the interactional justice concept, however, come from early work on procedural justice that constitutes an alternative to Thibaut and Walker's (1975, 1978) orientation. In particular, Leventhal (1980) extended procedural justice beyond process control by citing the following criteria: consistency (applying standards uniformly over time and across persons), bias suppression (minimizing personal self-interest and narrow preconceptions), accuracy (relying on high-quality information and well-informed opinion), correctability (allowing decisions to be reviewed and revised or reversed), representativeness (taking into account various interests), and ethicality (taking into account prevalent standards of moral conduct). Several of those have been incorporated into the reviews of procedural enactment summarized earlier. The ethicality criterion and its emphasis on moral conduct, however, seem to stand apart from the rest. Even though the two interactional justice subcategories of enactment and interpersonal treatment overlap considerably, the general concept of treating people ethically and responsibly appears to have opened the door for organizational justice scholars to write about a wide-ranging set of standards for moral conduct. Their underlying theme is probably best captured by Greenberg's (1993a, 1993b) term, *interpersonal sensitivity.*

In writing survey items to capture different aspects of Leventhal's procedural criteria, Tyler (1988; Barrett-Howard & Tyler, 1986) was one of the first to recognize the importance of ethicality and its implications for fair treatment as interpersonal sensitivity. Indeed, an even earlier survey (Tyler & Folger, 1980) had noted such issues in describing the basis of citizens' reactions toward their encounters with the police. The perceived procedural fairness of those encounters was affected by aspects of police conduct such as politeness, courtesy, showing respect for citizens' rights, and displaying other forms of behavior seen as appropriate for public officials. In his 1988 survey, Tyler also operationalized ethicality as being polite and showing concern for respondents' rights. Being polite and respecting people's rights expresses one way of thinking about interactional justice as interpersonal sensitivity. Similarly, two studies by Bies (1986) identified the following criteria: honesty, courtesy, timely feedback, and respect for rights. Timely feedback was mentioned previously as an aspect of proper enactment, but it is easy to see how it also displays a sensitivity to another person's feelings and hence counts as an aspect of moral conduct (treating another person fairly according to prevailing norms of decency).

An experiment by Greenberg (1993b) showed the impact of sensitivity to others' feelings as an aspect of moral conduct. Note that apologies are often classified as a category in typologies of accounts (cf. "penitential accounts," Bies, 1987a). To express remorse about a decision does not necessarily convey any explanatory, informative content about the decision-making process, however, which led Greenberg to distinguish between the information content of an explanation and the sensitivity shown by a postdecision communication. Those were manipulated independently (e.g., sensitivity conveyed by "I'm sorry" communications) and showed independent impact. Similarly, the act of providing a sincere, adequate explanation (see the earlier discussion of proper enactment of formal procedures) might also be taken as an expression of sensitivity about another's feelings—showing that Agent can empathize enough with Victim to recognize that Victim wants to know "why?" rather than to be treated like a nonhuman entity or an object of contempt not entitled to an explanation.

Properly enacted procedures and interpersonally sensitive treatment of Victim coalesce under the general rubric of morally appropriate conduct by Agent. Thus, although Leventhal identified ethicality as a separate criterion of procedural fairness, it might be considered a catchall heading he added for *other* aspects of moral conduct not already included in his categories, such as bias-suppression, consistency, or accuracy. Indeed, an early draft of a related monograph subsequently published by Leventhal et al. (1980) did not have the category of ethicality. Being biased, inaccurate, and inconsistent clearly seems less ethical than being unbiased, accurate, and consistent. To put it another way, morally appropriate conduct reflects well-meaning intentions, those that have other people's well-being in mind. Moral conduct takes into account other people's interests and well-being rather than operating only on the basis of self-interest. The search for justice in society or its institutions (e.g., organizations) is a search for actions and consequences reflecting one primary feature of underlying intentions—the intended support of a moral code that sustains cooperativeness sufficient for an inevitably interdependent human existence. In the next chapter, we highlight the significance of morally irresponsible intentions as a cornerstone principle for understanding reactions to perceived unfair treatment and the interrelations among distributive, procedural, and interactional justice. Chapter 3 describes two theoretical frameworks that provide slightly different perspectives on these interrelations.

3 Two Theoretical Syntheses

A familiar theme of organizational science is that employees are not power-less, despite the subordinate status of labor relative to management. Revenge for perceived injustice can take a variety of forms that even the most powerful management cannot eliminate entirely. The British labor movement, for example, is famous for having turned "work to rule" into a tactic of subtle sabotage difficult to condemn: Workers decrease the organization's profits by scrupulously following every management policy and dictum to the letter, which inevitably makes the organization run less efficiently due to bureaucratically created bottlenecks. Employee theft is common enough to have earned an industry label of *shrinkage*; other terms include *pilferage* and, in England, *the fiddle* (Mars, 1973). Greenberg (1997) showed that employee theft occurs in response to both outcome and process factors, yet management seems powerless to prevent 100% of such theft. Relatedly, disgruntled employees would not be expected to deliver "service with a smile" as often as employees who feel fairly treated. The extent of goodwill that a company has among its customers is hard to trace to individual employees, yet those employees can act toward customers out of such embitterment (about organizational injustice) that the company's reputation suffers immeasurably.

At Salomon Brothers, Michael Lewis (1989) witnessed some of the effects that can occur when employees do not think kindly about their employer:

The head trader of British government bonds . . . had quit. The managing directors of the London office fell to their knees (figuratively speaking) and pleaded with him to stay. He was the backbone of a new and fragile enterprise, they said. Screw backbones, he said, he had been offered much money by Goldman Sachs, and he was going to get while the getting was still good. He was, after all, merely a trader trading his services. What did they expect? They expected, they said, for him to forget about trading for a moment and consider the importance of loyalty to the firm.

And you know what he said to that? He said, "You want loyalty, hire a cocker spaniel." (p. 205)

This passage illustrates another potential behavioral response to perceived underpayment—turnover. But more than that, it also explicitly reveals the absence of organizational commitment as a cause of turnover and implicitly connotes a reproach directed against the (soon to be former) employer. The black humor of the last comment—a parting shot about management's being hoisted on its own petard—subtly implies that although the switch to a new employer certainly made economic sense from the standpoint of the head bond trader's financial condition, he might not have so readily considered changing jobs if loyalty to Salomon Brothers had been an issue. But it was not.

Why not? In this chapter, we consider two possible answers to that question as a way of integrating the themes of distributive, procedural, and interactional justice. One way of answering questions about reactions to perceived injustice comes from Referent Cognitions Theory (Folger, 1987b) and its subsequent modification (Folger, 1993); for both of these we use the acronym RCT. Another set of answers comes from Group Value Theory (Lind & Tyler, 1988) and its subsequent modification as a Relational Model of Authority in Groups (Tyler & Lind, 1992); we refer to these collectively as the Lind-Tyler or L-T program.

The word *group* in both the L-T labels indicates one difference between the two perspectives reviewed in this chapter; RCT has less group emphasis. An additional difference in emphasis, however, is more central: The L-T program uses a positively framed approach to address issues such as employee loyalty toward organizations (or groups, more generally) and their authorities (i.e., leaders); the RCT program, in contrast, uses a negatively framed approach—attending to "the dark side" of reactions to perceived unfairness (e.g., theft, sabotage, and workplace violence by disgruntled employees). After reviewing both approaches, we will conclude by commenting about possible implications of that difference in perspective.

Reproach and Negatively Toned
Emotions as a Unifying Theme: A Prelude to RCT

We deliberately slanted the tone of our first two chapters in the negatively framed direction as a way of leading up to the RCT description. In particular, a phrase such as *the determinants of reproach* captures an underlying theme we used to guide our review of justice concepts and reactions to perceived unfairness. Such a phrase implies that when employees react to perceived unfair treatment by management, they do not simply calculate a cost-benefit or outcome-input ratio and act on self-interest modified by fairness norms (i.e., maximizing personal benefit within the constraints of overall fairness that takes others' outcome-input ratios into account). Rather, they display behaviors that can best be understood only by considering the types of negatively toned emotions most likely to operate at the motivational core of those responses. This approach is consistent with viewing motivation as discrepancy reduction; in other words, striving to eliminate or reduce a gap between a desired state and an actual state that is negatively discrepant from it.

Instead of looking at discrepancy reduction dispassionately (cf. versions of control theory with machine analogies such as adjustments by a thermostat), however, we argue for an emotional emphasis consistent with expressions such as *righteous indignation* and *moral outrage*. Michael Lewis (1989), for example, hardly seemed neutral and dispassionate in his own feelings about money matters at Salomon; indeed, his reactions were emotionally toned ("I felt cheated, genuinely indignant," p. 203), and his descriptions of other Salomon employees likewise expressed venom. Thus, in using the word *reproach,* we mean to imply not only an implicit accusation of wrongdoing (a belief, or cognitive component, as one antecedent or concomitant of reactions) and an action tendency or motivational urge consistent with attempting to administer punishment for wrongdoing (the behavioral component), but also certain emotionally toned aspects associated with the antecedents and concomitants of reactions to injustice (the affective component). When research participants receive an insultingly low offer from an exchange partner in an experimental paradigm known as the Ultimatum Bargaining Game, for example, they often veto the offer even though it means losing money and thus acting against economic self-interest (for a review, see Murnighan & Pillutla, 1995). One explanation for such effects is that participants feel emotionally invested in punishing others who seek to act without regard for principles of fair conduct in social relations.

We think an approach to injustice based on negative emotions has especially fruitful heuristic prospects because it can unite developments in procedural and interactional justice with the original project of understanding distributive justice undertaken by Adams (1965) in developing his theory about inequity—a term itself framed negatively (as *inequity* rather than *equity*). Note, for example, that in conceptualizing equity as a state of balanced or appropriately equivalent outcome-input ratios, Adams said virtually nothing about how it felt to experience such a state or what it might motivate people to do. Rather, he focused almost entirely on discrepancies from that neutral reference point of "deservingness" for the justice of an exchange—receiving either more or less than prescribed by that standard for a fair rate of return. His theoretical program emphasized the consequences of felt injustice. His own research primarily investigated behavioral implications of guilt as a reaction to overpayment, but he also sought to identify various consequences of underpayment as variations on the theme of anger.

Some of Adams's (1965) own words indicate most clearly both the scope of what we want to accomplish and how it relates to his original objectives. Consider, for example, the following passages:

> What are the consequences of outcomes being perceived as meeting or not meeting the norms of justice? Nearly all the attention given to this question has been to establish a relationship between perceived injustice and dissatisfaction. . . . Does a man treated unfairly simply express dissatisfaction? Are there not other consequences of unfair exchanges? (p. 268)

> Relative deprivation [cf. Stouffer et al., 1949] and distributive justice [referring to work by Homans, 1961], as theoretical concepts, specify some of the conditions that arouse perceptions of injustice and, complementarily, the conditions that lead men to feel that their relations with others are just. But they fail to specify theoretically what are the consequences of felt injustice, other than dissatisfaction. (p. 275)

> Men [*sic*] do not simply become dissatisfied with conditions they perceive to be unjust. They usually do something about them. (p. 276)

The topics of human resources management covered in the remaining chapters of this book, for example, represent areas in which a variety of programs and policies can affect employees' outcomes for good or ill. Managers would surely hope that those programs will not fail because of resistance and that those policies will not be ineffective because employees ignore or contravene them out of spite. Hence, we think theory and research on reactions to perceived injustice have a special role to play when "do something" means being motivated by righteous indignation to act punitively toward management.

Since Adams's time, attention has shifted dramatically away from inequity and toward topics associated with procedural and interactional justice. We think the prospects for an integrated, synthetic view of justice phenomena would improve by seeking a single, common concern as the root of the three slightly different terms for fairness. To anticipate one way of characterizing our general conclusion, we call that concern the interest in seeing wrongdoers punished (for the related theme of "look for cheaters" as a "Darwinian algorithm" stressed by a biopsychological evolutionary perspective, see Cosmides, 1989). Our review of RCT presents it as the major theoretical approach that addresses that concern directly, whereas the L-T approach adopts a relatively positive orientation and addresses a slightly different set of issues. The theme of punishment for wrongdoing has a more negative tone consistent with hostility about resentment, which characterizes both the original and modified versions of RCT. That theme not only unifies the three terms for injustice, but also helps show how the original and modified versions of RCT are related. In particular, the emergence of developments in interactional justice helps explain why modifications were necessary—namely, because the original version of RCT was conceptualized in relation to procedural justice as an instrumental means to achieving the ends of distributive justice (i.e., promoting equity and preventing inequity), whereas interactional justice has relatively noninstrumental connotations and implications.

RCT and Culpable Intentions: How Conduct and Consequences Signify Reproachable Motives

Intentions help define what people mean by hostility and aggressiveness. An accident that causes harm unintentionally is not considered an act of aggression, for example, whereas an assassin's bullet that misses—causing no harm—is considered aggression. RCT runs closely parallel to classic positions about anger and aggression (see Folger, 1987b, for a summary of the original version and Folger, 1993, for a summary of the modified version).[1] In Chapter 1 we noted that Adams identified anger as a possible reaction to adverse inequity and that he had been unable to predict when anger-related responses occur. Beginning in Chapter 1 with our treatment of choice as a second-factor independent variable (i.e., in addition to first-factor variables responsible for perceptions of adverse inequity) and continuing in Chapter 2, we then showed how procedural justice (i.e., voice and other variables) and interactional justice manipulations (i.e., excuses, justifications, and variations related to interpersonal sensitivity) helped predict such responses. RCT is an overarching theoretical framework that helps explain one basis for those predictions.

Wanting to punish a culpable offense is like wanting to vent one's anger aroused as moral outrage. Inequity as distributive injustice signifies that something worthy of outrage has occurred: Victim's suffering is undeserved, because it does not match some standard for a fair return of outcomes from Victim's inputs. The magnitude of inequity affects the perceived severity of the harm and also identifies one basis (although most often only a partial basis) for the charge of wrongdoing: The lack of equivalence across two outcome-input ratios implies undue influence by an irrelevant distortion—an error (mistake, wrong) whose correction would restore the meaning implied by representing such proportions algebraically as an "equation" (equivalence relation) in the first place.

Thus, Adams's (1965) theory of inequity starts by referring to situations in which Person has already identified a means of determining or estimating the fair rate of return from an exchange—namely, the outcome-input ratio of Other (representing either the exchange partner's return rate or the return rate used by the same exchange partner in allocations to someone else, such as one of Person's coworkers). RCT refers to the fair-return standard, however, as only one of various comparative standards that might influence reactions to the outcomes actually received from an exchange (or, for that matter, outcomes received by whatever means). That is, RCT treats the Other outcome-input ratio, which Person uses to determine a fair-return rate, as only one of several possible sources for thinking about outcome levels differing from those that Person possesses by virtue of the exchange.

We can illustrate this difference between RCT and Adams's inequity theory, which has not been discussed in either version of the former but is relevant to both, by referring again to Michael Lewis at Salomon Brothers. When Lewis (1989) received news about his annual raise and bonus, some of his reactions centered on thoughts about standards of fair pay; for example,

> "I have never seen anyone have the kind of year that you have had . . ." He [the managing director giving Lewis the news] was explaining that I was paid more than anyone else in my training class (I later learned that three others were paid as much). (pp. 201-202)

This "later" news about peers' pay made Lewis's pay no longer seem fair, and the basis for perceived injustice was an outcome-input comparison of the following sort: Person (Lewis) = $90,000 as outcome, performance better than "anyone" as input, versus Other (three classmates) = $90,000 as outcome, performance below Lewis's level as input. On the other hand, Lewis's impressions and feelings about his pay were also influenced by other comparative standards not linked explicitly to fairness; for example, "By the standards of our monopoly money business, ninety grand was like being on welfare" (p. 203). RCT considers either type of comparative standard, whether used to assess fairness or not, as examples of a more general category termed *referent outcomes.* This concept simply signifies that a person reacts to any given outcome in the context of others salient at the time; it is a shorthand expression for the general process of relativity in judgment that has been treated more extensively by literature on that subject (e.g., Folger, 1984; Helson, 1954; Kahneman & Miller, 1986; Parducci, 1965; Thibaut & Kelley, 1959). In particular, referent outcomes influence the perceived satisfactoriness of a person's outcomes—the extent to which the latter are seen as having favorable or unfavorable consequences for the person.

How do referent outcomes influence Victim's perceptions about Agent's intentions? On the one hand, some outcomes received in exchange seem so egregiously unfair (in comparison to referent outcomes used as fairness standards) that the exchange partner seems prima facie culpable (i.e., the equivalent of being presumed guilty unless circumstances indicating innocence are forthcoming as contrary evidence). Such an inequity can make it hard not to hold the exchange partner (Agent) at least partly accountable for the harm done in shortchanging others (Victim). It prevents Victims from receiving what they should have earned to compensate them for giving up their inputs (e.g., time sacrificed, effort exerted) as contributions to the exchange.

But the outrageousness or offensiveness of an adverse inequity does not always, in and of itself, fully establish culpability for the offense. Where does blame lie; whose fault is the inequity; who should be answerable, held accountable, or liable? The information needed to address such questions comes from details about procedures used, the propriety with which they are enacted, the sensitivity toward Victims shown by Agents in positions of authority, and morally responsive conduct in general by agents. In turn, such details are most informative about culpability when they have implications about the kinds of motives and intentions attributable to Agent. Evaluative standards for procedures, the propriety with which Agents enact procedures, and other aspects of morally responsible conduct by Agents (e.g., appropriate indications of sensitivity to Victim suffering) can influence perceptions of both the extent of wrongdoing and the extent of Agent's culpability as a wrongdoer—a person whose apparent intentions do not match key obligations assigned to people in roles of authority, members of society, and human beings in general. Because procedures impose constraints on roles and their enactment, Agent's use and proper enactment of procedurally fair practices (e.g., choice, voice) tend to imply that Agent lived up to such obligations and hence acted consistently with the intention of trying to be fair. Someone who meets all legitimate obligations tends to be exonerated from wrongdoing rather than being censured. The proper implementation of fair procedural practices, therefore, shifts culpability away from Agent.

Excuses and justifications perform a similar function. To be worthy of rebuke and hence potentially punishable, Agent aggressiveness (offensive, culpable conduct) must be wrong in the sense of being illegitimately prompted. Illegitimate aggressiveness is prompted by motives that cannot be excused (e.g., as coerced or understandable in light of mitigating circumstances) or whose intended consequences cannot be justified (in light of some overriding moral purpose or value, superordinate goal, or an acceptable cost-benefit calculus with regard to all morally relevant interests). Intentional aggressiveness causes or threatens to impose unjustified consequences; that is, the intended consequences threaten to impose burdens on harmed Victim(s) that outweigh the moral value of offsetting benefits to the Victim(s), others in society, or the long-term well-being of society in general.

When does management conduct seem sufficiently unjust, at least in the eyes of employees, to warrant rebuke—including forms of rebuke that act as punishment directed against management? Following from the line of reasoning we have pursued, the answer requires an attribution about the motives and intentions of management with respect to their obligations toward employees. The shape of this answer can follow from the general guidelines provided by work on distributive, procedural, and interactional justice, but what seems like a reproachable intention will also depend on circumstances. The literature we review on each of several topics throughout the remainder of this book helps reveal how such circumstances influence fairness perceptions and reactions. Always, however, those circumstances exert influence by coloring perceptions of intent. And always, the information used to make inferences about intent is information about Agent conduct in the following forms: (a) acts by Agent; and (b) consequences (or presumed consequences) of those acts or consequences for which Agent is otherwise held accountable, even if they do not follow directly—in a cause-and-effect sense—from Agent's actions. The standards for evaluating the fairness of consequences are those associated most closely with the concepts of distributive justice such as equity (although we address some major alternative concepts of distributive justice—notably equality and need—in the final chapter of this book). The standards for evaluating the fairness of actions themselves, whether instrumental to consequences or assessed for their intrinsic morality as actions per se, are standards most closely associated with the concepts of procedural justice and interactional justice.

A Prelude to Two Recent Theories About the Impact of Agent Intentions

Our own theoretical perspective was embedded in the structure of Chapter 1 and in our interpretation of the concepts we reviewed there. Nonetheless, we tried to write that chapter in a fashion consistent with an eclectic viewpoint rather than in terms specific to any particular theory. Next, we expose the underlying theoretical superstructure by describing it in more formal terms. Then, for the sake of introducing at least some balance, we describe an alternative theoretical perspective.

Referent Cognitions Theory and Beyond

The experiment on excuses (Folger & Martin, 1986) and the experiment on justifications (Folger, Rosenfield, & Robinson, 1983) were designed as tests of the RCT conceptual framework. Another study (Folger, Rosenfield, Rheaume, & Martin, 1983) was actually the first study explicitly based on RCT. Several comprehensive treatments of RCT have appeared (Folger, 1986a, 1986b, 1986c, 1987b); one of those (Folger, 1986a) reinterpreted the experiment on voice and improvement (Folger, 1977) in RCT terms. A study by Cropanzano and Folger (1989), cited in the Chapter 1 discussion of choice, followed from RCT reasoning as well. The same reasoning was used as the basis for a chapter that reviewed the motivational implications of procedural justice (Cropanzano & Folger, 1991), and the RCT approach has also been incorporated into a general framework of justice (Sheppard, Lewicki, & Minton, 1992).

An Initial Version of RCT: Referent Outcomes and Referent Instrumentalities

RCT used the cause-and-effect logic of procedures as means and outcomes as ends that flow from those means (i.e., *throughput*). Although means and ends are instrumentally related in cause-effect fashion, RCT nonetheless separated standards for evaluating the justice of means from standards for evaluating the justice of end results. Analogously, organizational effectiveness criteria are different, depending on whether they apply to attaining resources as inputs, operating smoothly as throughput, or making high-quality products and providing customer-pleasing services as outputs, even though the input-throughput-output sequence represents a series of causally instrumental events (each influencing the next).

Referent Outcomes: Standards for Evaluating Obtained Outcomes. The sources of standards for evaluating end results (outcomes and consequences) can never be fully identified. The perception of being relatively deprived (suffering harm based on outcome shortcomings) might vary from moment to moment, depending on which unattained outcomes vie for attention with the outcomes made available to the perceiver. Research on relative deprivation initiated an unfinished search for the determinants of reference groups and membership groups as sources of comparative judgments. Similarly, Adams's (1965) reference to relative deprivation and social comparison spawned several attempts to describe what determines the "choice" of a comparison standard, but no such attempt has gained universal acceptance as a definitive answer to this age-old question. The research on perceptual judgments in general reveals that they can be affected in complex ways by numerous contextual factors (Helson, 1954; Parducci, 1965). In addition, events have the capacity to "recruit" their own "norms" (Kahneman & Miller, 1986). Finally, political themes and other ideological grounds for envisioning utopian communities—or simply "a better world"—suggest that the capacity for dissatisfaction with current outcomes is limited only by the capacity to imagine a better outcome. Because no limits need exist on sources of imagined alternatives, the frame of reference used for evaluative purposes is potentially unbounded at the "better" end of the evaluative continuum.

RCT proposed a new solution to this issue, the problem of referent outcomes as evaluative standards for obtained outcomes. Working out the details of this solution is an ongoing effort contingent on developments in a separate body of theory and research—the psychological literature on imagined "counterfactual" alternatives to a given representation of reality (Kahneman & Miller, 1986; Kahneman & Tversky, 1982). A rapidly growing literature has made considerable progress in identifying what brings to mind one alternative rather than another (e.g., Kahneman & Miller, 1986; Roese & Olson, 1995), and dissatisfaction has been shown to vary as a function of such counterfactual thinking. The general approach centers on concepts such as "mutability"—the extent to which events can be made subject to a mental process of "undoing," which changes certain features of events and substitutes them with alternatives. Norm theory (Kahneman & Miller, 1986) has guided much of this research. Its central tenet is that undoing proceeds from abnormal to normal. Events tend to elicit a normatively acceptable frame of reference. If some feature of experienced events seems abnormal within that evoked frame, the abnormality is restored to normality by the mental process of undoing. A better (closer to normatively appropriate) alternative is thereby imagined. Exposure to a salient social comparison (e.g., someone else's outcomes or outcome-input ratio) is but one example of how such a process might be triggered, and outcome-input ratios are but one potential source of imaginable alternatives that can serve as comparison standards for evaluative purposes—a person's referent outcomes within a given situation. Thus, RCT drew attention to certain types of cognitive mechanisms whereby obtained outcomes elicit referent outcomes for comparison, with the result being dissatisfaction that varies according to the size of the discrepancy between a given outcome and its referent alternative.

Referent Instrumentalities: Turning Dissatisfaction Into Resentment. Sources of dissatisfaction about outcomes constitute the first factor in RCT's dual-factored approach; the second factor addresses what turns dissatisfaction into resentment. In Chapter 1, we used *reproach* as a synonym for *resentment* that more closely approximates its intended meaning from an RCT perspective. Feeling resentment toward another person means that person's actions warrant reproach because they reflect wrongdoing or at least some culpability based on morally problematic (and perhaps reprehensible) intent. The consequences of actions might be harmful and yet not constitute wrongful harm or wrongdoing. Dissatisfaction or frustration about a harmful (relatively depriving) outcome might not entail resentment toward the source of the outcome, just as the pain from being poked by a sharp umbrella need not lead to attacking the umbrella's owner (who might happen to be your mother or spouse, innocently moving other objects that accidentally cause the umbrella to fall on you). Unfortunately for the sake of clarity, everyday language use also contains examples such as "I resent this bad weather because it's ruined my weekend, the only chance I've had to relax in the last 5 years." Here, the emotional terminology of resentment is invoked even though we do not imagine any feelings of ill-will being directed toward another person as a result. For that reason, the present chapter has referred to reproach for the sake of a different connotation—one closer to the image of someone who warrants being charged with wrongful misconduct.

How does wrongful misconduct turn outcome dissatisfaction, based on thoughts of a referent alternative, into resentment as an inclination to rebuke another person? Here RCT proposed a form of counterfactual logic that related ends and means in a causally instrumental fashion—the source of another term, *referent instrumentalities,* as the second factor in this two-factored approach. Just as the first (outcome-related) factor acts as a determinant of dissatisfaction about outcomes, the second (process- or conduct-related) factor acts as a determinant of culpability that turns dissatisfaction into resentment and a reproachful inclination. Just as referent outcomes entail mutability, the mental undoing of actual events, and an imagined substitution of normatively appropriate features in place of abnormalities, referent instrumentalities function as the normatively appropriate substitutes for events that precede outcomes.

Thus, for example, a dissatisfying (and possibly adversely inequitable) pay raise might be cause for ruminating about events that occurred prior to your having learned about the pay raise. Which ones were instrumental to your receiving the pay raise you did? Of those, which seem abnormal? When you recall their occurrence, which ones cause you to react with thoughts such as "It should never have happened" or "She had no right to do that" or "They promised not to use that method of evaluation"? Did people in positions of responsibility contribute to such events or fail to exercise their authority in sufficiently attentive ways, allowing improprieties to go uncorrected?

RCT used labels such as *unjustified* to describe thoughts like those (although labels such as *counternormative* or *illegitimate* might be better to avoid confusing *unjustified* with the distinction between justifications and excuses). The key point is simply that people can imagine alternative, more normatively appropriate ways for events to have taken place. Theory and research about the determinants of perceived procedural injustice, therefore, helps indicate why someone would come to think about the events that preceded an outcome as abnormal: The use of unfair procedures would tend to elicit thoughts about fair procedures as a referent instrumentality. Similarly, a perfect excuse makes it difficult to imagine how someone could have acted any other way. When someone could and should have acted differently, however, and the actions they did take led to unfavorable outcomes for another person, then the latter has reason to feel resentful toward the former. Here is another way to put it: "If only the agent had acted as he or she *should* have, then I *would* have received a better outcome" (Folger, 1993, p. 164).

An Updating of RCT: From Causal to Deontic (Moral) Logic

More recently, a somewhat revised version of RCT (Folger, 1993) incorporated the results from field surveys (Brockner et al., 1994). Other nonlaboratory data have also appeared whose configuration fits the outcome × process interaction predicted by RCT (e.g., Greenberg, 1994; McFarlin & Sweeney, 1992; Sweeney & McFarlin, 1993). The revision stemmed in part from developments related to interactional justice, particularly those pertaining to interpersonal sensitivity shown after a decision.

Originally, RCT focused on procedures and on explanations (excuses and justifications) as they related to causal responsibility, which highlights the instrumental, means-ends connection between procedures and outcomes (as had Thibaut & Walker's, 1978, account of process control). As we have tried to emphasize throughout the preceding chapter and in the introductory remarks of this one, however, the Agent role—and the inference regarding whether Agent intentions match a commitment to moral obligations—entails more than mere cause-effect considerations. Causal responsibility by Agent is neither necessary nor sufficient to warrant reproach; rather, the key issues of intent pertain to moral accountability and the intended meaning of Agent's actions.

The interpersonal sensitivity shown by Agent after a decision (sensitivity about the consequences of the decision for Victim) has logically independent status from causal responsibility as a concept. Although in a position of responsibility vis-à-vis Victim, Agent's personal role in causing Victim harm can be less important than the manner in which Agent's subsequent actions portray his or her general intentions. The same comment applies to actions by Agent throughout the time before, during, and after a decision-making event such as a conflict-resolving judgment or a pay allocation.

We have stressed the central concept of inferred intent by Agent regarding obligations toward Victim (e.g., management obligations toward employees). Similarly, Folger (1993) described this modified version of RCT as an effort "toward a dual-obligations model":

> The revision of RCT identifies things being exchanged as the first (outcome-related) factor of a two-factor model. The second (process-related) factor—the agent's role—requires greater attention in an expanded approach that focuses on the obligations of that role. I contend that in the context of employment, the agent's moral obligations toward the employee entail more than fair treatment with respect to the wages and benefits given in exchange for labor, and more than fair treatment with respect to the implementation of policies and procedures that determine those levels of compensation. In addition, a moral obligation exists to treat the employee with sufficient dignity as a person; doing so entails numerous aspects of conduct beyond those regarding compensation as ends or decision-making procedures as means to those ends. Rather, all aspects of the agent's conduct, whether or not they have a direct bearing on employee compensation or the means for determining compensation, can carry implicit messages about whether the agent views the employee as someone worthy of that minimal level of respect to which all humans should be entitled. (pp. 174-175)

Philosophers speak of moral obligations as entailing a particular way to think about people and their relations with others—a so-called deontic logic, based on the same Greek root (*deon,* duty or obligation) used in referring to Kantian and related moral philosophies as deontological. Notably, such moral postures make central the regard that people should have for their fellow human beings. The concept of human dignity plays a key role in helping to specify the types of obligations that ought to guide interpersonal behavior, and hence the types of evaluative standards applied when deciding whether another person's actions seem censurable, reproachable, and the like.

This reorientation of RCT, therefore, reflects the influence of the concept of interactional justice (especially as ethicality and interpersonal sensitivity) on the field of organizational justice. Even though it shares an extremely close conceptual kinship with procedural justice (a term most closely identified with Thibaut and Walker's (1975) notion of process control) or process fairness (Leventhal's term, a more encompassing phrase consistent with incorporating not only all of his procedural criteria but also related procedural features such as voice and choice), the concept of interactional justice has done more to encourage a deontological orientation and a consideration of moral obligations involving all aspects of human conduct.

This moral tone seems extremely important, whether or not consensus has yet emerged about the precise conceptual or operational definition of interactional justice. The deontological language of moral obligations makes clear that Agent's motives and intentions matter. As the concept of interactional justice has evolved, the attention to issues of interpersonal sensitivity has grown, and these imply a broadened scope of moral obligations for Agent. The revision of RCT tries to make explicit some of the implications of those developments.

Rethinking Agent's Moral Obligations. Previously, the RCT concept of instrumentalities limited the Agent's moral obligations by focusing exclusively on the Agent's role as an administrator of procedures that precede and determine outcomes. Procedural justice concepts such as voice or choice apply directly to that role, implying that Agent has an obligation to use these and related methods because of their perceived fairness. Whether they represent means to fair ends such as an equitable distribution of outcomes, or fair means as ends in themselves (e.g., granting inviolate rights), the common perception of their relevance to fairness makes Agent accountable for their use. Their absence is counternormative, invoking counterfactual ruminations. To put it another way, their absence calls for explanation. Further obligations of Agent apply to the content of that explanation: In the presence of unfair outcomes and the absence of fair procedures, Agent should supply a good excuse or an account that adequately justifies either the means or end results. Meeting all such requirements does not exhaust Agent's obligations as implied by the remaining aspect of interactional justice—interpersonal sensitivity *after* the consequences of a decision have been decided, not just enactment propriety and sensitivity *before* a decision.

A Research Example: Helping Employees Cope With a Ban on Cigarettes at Work

A recent study by Greenberg (1994) helps illustrate our point and, relatedly, the reason why he has emphasized this type of difference between the information content of explanations ("informational justice") and the interpersonal sensitivity toward Victims ("interpersonal justice," pp. 288-289). Greenberg surveyed employee responses to the announcement of a work site smoking ban that was scheduled to take effect 5 days later. Survey questionnaires were completed immediately after the announcement. Unknown to them, the respondents heard one of four different announcements that varied both information and sensitivity on a randomly assigned basis.

The minimal information conditions included a cursory explanation that briefly mentioned the following reasons for the smoking ban: health dangers, both to those smoking and to nonsmokers near coworkers who smoked, and "costs of smoking to our company" in terms of "increased insurance expenses and workplace dangers" (p. 290). One of the two minimal information conditions included further remarks scripted by Greenberg (1994) to minimize the sensitivity shown smokers as Victims. Note that this text also identifies Agent intentions (management's motives for the smoking ban) in organizational efficiency, business-related, cost-cutting terms:

> I realize that it's tough to stop smoking, but it's in the best interest of our business to implement the smoking ban. And, of course, business must come first. To help you continue to work effectively while adjusting to the new policy, we will be making a smoking cessation program available to you. It will be free of charge to you and conducted during your regular working hours while you are receiving full pay. We'll be giving you more information about this program later on. For now, though, we want you to understand that our goal is to minimize disruption of the work flow while you adjust to this new policy. (p. 291)

In sum, the combination of low information and low sensitivity addressed Agent obligations in only the most minimal fashion. Note that although the company offered to help smokers cope with their loss by providing a free cessation program, the explicitly stated intent referred to ensuring that work effectiveness did not suffer.

Greenberg (1994) scripted the contrasting high-sensitivity condition to vary only in the "degree of concern and social sensitivity demonstrated over the outcomes received" (p. 289) by adding remarks that included the following:

> Smoking is an addiction, and it's very tough to stop. We are quite aware of this, and we do not want you to suffer . . . we have your long-term interest at heart in implementing this policy . . . we don't want you to suffer or resign. . . . To show you that we mean it, and that we really care, we are prepared to help you [cessation program mentioned, as in low-sensitivity condition]. . . . As you can see, we really do care. (p. 291)

Greenberg also used RCT as a basis for predicting that this sensitivity manipulation would interact with outcome severity in affecting the reactions of smokers to their loss. Obviously, the loss would be greater for heavy smokers than for light smokers, and Greenberg reported the effects of the sensitivity manipulation on reactions by those above and below the median self-reported number of cigarettes smoked daily.

Consistent with other RCT studies, Greenberg (1994) found an outcome ×
process (severity × sensitivity) interaction on a general index of smoker
reactions that included affective, cognitive, and behavioral components. Notably, the behavioral component included items on intention to quit, which
correlated .93 with a scale of affective commitment (reduced emotional
attachment to the company associated with reduced inclination to work
there). The cognitive component contained fairness-related items that included phrases such as "believe it is fair for the company to impose a smoking
ban" and "believe the company did the right thing" (p. 292). We interpret the
general index, therefore, as a proxy variable for our reproach construct.

To contrast RCT's previous causal-instrumentality orientation with the
moral-obligations revision, we compare two effects from Greenberg's (1994)
study and a separate explanation for each one. The first involves his manipulation of information content, which also produced an outcome × process
(severity × information thoroughness) interaction consistent with previous
RCT findings. We describe that effect in terms of counterfactual reasoning
about the cause of the ban. We then indicate why such causally counterfactual
reasoning would not be sufficient to account for the second effect, involving
the outcome × process interaction from the sensitivity manipulation as a
process (interactional) variable. The latter point suggests that it would be
more parsimonious to interpret both effects by considering moral obligations
and the intentions of Agent.

Consider first the contrast between the previously described, minimal
information about costs and the following high-information, additional information Greenberg's (1994) script included in that contrasting condition:

> Smokers . . . cause twice as many job-related accidents, and an unsafe work force
> endangers us all. For example, cigarette smoking is a frequent source of fires on the
> job. Other kinds of accidents are also caused by smoking on the job as workers
> fumbling with cigarettes often divert their attention from what they're supposed to
> be doing. Our insurance company estimated that last year alone, we lost over
> $300,000 due to smoking-related accidents. We lost about the same amount from
> computer terminals that went down due to smoke in the air. (p. 291)

According to a view of procedures as causally instrumental means to producing equitably justifiable ends, how would such information affect counterfactual reasoning in a fashion different from the effect of the explanation for the
smoking-ban decision given in the low-information condition?

RCT was originally based on such a view that indicated how alternatively
imaginable processes (as causally related sequences of events) encouraged
resentment about deprivation relative to alternatively imaginable outcomes.
Note that heavy smokers would have a much more favorable referent outcome,

as an alternative to the ban, than would light smokers; relative to the conditions of the ban, the former would (in the imagined alternative of no-ban conditions) be enjoying the desired outcome of a cigarette more often. The counterfactual cognitions of heavy and light smokers have greatly differing consequences as end results in the world imagined "if only this ban weren't in effect." Compared to that imagined no-ban world, heavy smokers suffer more in the actual, ban-imposed world. Their greater suffering gives them more to complain about, more harm for which management as Agent might be held accountable. Because heavy smokers suffer greater harm for which they might blame management, their reactions tend to differ (more than the reactions of light smokers) depending on whether or not they do find management to blame.

If reactions to present consequences can thus be affected by imagining alternative consequences as a possibility, then the strength of negative reactions toward management and against management actions will depend on the ease of imagining how management could have acted otherwise and why management should have acted otherwise. With only a minimum of detail about the costs that smoking imposes, a workplace that permits smoking tends not to seem as unreasonable as one where smoking is banned. Only when definitive, large costs get cited does it become harder to view management as having viable alternatives to the ban. Hence, the more detailed set of explanations tends to prevent light and heavy smokers from differing so much in their reactions as they would if alternatives to the ban do seem viable. This example of a causal reasoning approach to RCT predictions, therefore, implies that the effect of a more informative explanation is to prevent the mental "undoing" of causally instrumental events. An argument about high costs, made convincing with details, undercuts the counterfactual argument that management could and should have been able to act in a causally different manner, thereby bringing about very different effects.

For all we know, the counterfactual reasoning of smokers might follow the phenomenological paths just described—especially if inadequate explanations do a poor job of cognitively blocking the "downhill" path (more easily traveled during mental ruminations) from the "abnormal" state of a ban back to the more "normal" conditions of a ban-free world. The phenomenology and counterfactual reasoning that applies to differentially sensitive messages about management concern for smokers (e.g., grounds for the cessation program), however, has nothing to do with the causes of the ban. An Agent who says, "I'm sorry for this harm, I understand how hard on you it must be, and I'll do everything I can to help you cope with your suffering" does nothing to change thoughts about the causes of the ban in the first place (or its reasonableness). Detailed, thorough, compelling reasons for having a smoking-banned workplace versus a ban-free workplace should decrease the ease with which smokers can continue to think that a ban-free site should never have been abolished. When a message from management expresses concern for smokers whose cigarettes have been banned, that information does not bear on a ban-free site as a counterfactual option because it assumes the problem of coping with a smoking-banned workplace at the outset.

To put it another way, the two types of information (differences in the thoroughness of details about high costs vs. differences in indications regarding management concern for smokers) involve two different sets of comparisons about consequences: (a) working under smoking-banned conditions versus working under ban-free conditions and (b) working under smoking-banned conditions for a management that seems to care a great deal about the stress thereby imposed on workers versus working under smoking-banned conditions for a management that has taken fewer pains to demonstrate such concern. Such a difference can help explain why Greenberg (1994) found evidence for two main effects (i.e., effects showing independent, incremental impact from two separate factors) in both this study and a previous lab study (Greenberg, 1993b) that manipulated sensitivity as well as information thoroughness. This suggests that sensitivity and explanatory content such as excuses or justifications can have similar functional effects but for slightly different reasons—that is, on the basis of mechanisms that can operate independently of one another.

We suggest that these mechanisms might not be as different as they seem from RCT's original counterfactual analysis. Agent's power over Victim enables Agent to impose harmful conditions on Victim; management can impose smoking bans. The capability of imposing harm or hardship, however, brings with it certain types of obligations—which, unmet, bring greater wrath the more harm or hardship imposed. Some of those obligations are like the physicians' credo: First, do no harm. Explanations and justifications for causing harm help to determine whether best-intentioned efforts were exercised in attempting to live up to that obligation. An Agent in the position to impose harm, however, cannot blithely ignore the amount of harm imposed just because it could not have been prevented or it appears to have been well justified. An Agent's obligations to Victim do not cease just because Victim's status as Victim seems immutably determined. The effectiveness of Victim's attempts to cope with hardship might well depend on Agent's meeting those additional obligations, which in turn depends on Agent's intention to exercise significant regard for Victim's well-being. Different degrees of successful future coping, therefore, loom as mental alternatives for comparison (counterfactual alternatives) based on different intentions inferred about Agent's motives and sense of obligation about caring for Victim.

Greenberg's (1994) manipulation of sensitivity shows how a very subtle basis for inferring slightly different motives can have a powerful and profound effect. Both the low-sensitivity and the high-sensitivity communications indicated that management had chosen to provide a free smoke-cessation program. The messages differed only in the stated reason that such a program had been provided. The low-sensitivity message told smokers that management offered the program "to help you continue to work effectively while adjusting to the new policy," and the message subsequently reiterated this business-oriented motivation quite explicitly in the following terms: "We want you to understand that our goal is to minimize disruption of the work flow while you adjust to this new policy" (p. 291). The high-sensitivity message reiterated a different theme: "We do not want you to suffer . . . we don't want you to suffer . . . we really care . . . we really do care" (p. 291). Indeed, the announcement of the cessation program was prefaced with a clear reference to those intentions: "To show you that we mean it, and that we really care, we are prepared to help you" (p. 291).

A free smoke-cessation program clearly benefits heavy smokers more than light smokers, so it is understandable that reactions to the smoking ban would vary directly with the desire for smoking frequently. It is not so readily apparent why two groups of heavy smokers would react very differently to management's having provided such a program, based only on management's self-professed reasons for offering the program. Yet the reactions did indeed differ, and quite dramatically. On the 7-point index that Greenberg (1994) calculated, heavy smokers who heard the high-sensitivity message responded with a level of acceptance above the midpoint ($M = 4.35$), whereas those who had heard the low-sensitivity message reacted in a significantly more negative fashion ($M = 2.44$).

We argue that such a difference becomes more understandable if employees do, in fact, care about management's intentions to meet certain types of obligations with regard to hardships imposed on employees. Employees look to see whether management finds ways to express its concern about employee well-being. When insufficient concern has been shown, employees respond according to the extent of hardship imposed. On questionnaires measuring expressions about the extent of unfairness or lack of acceptance of a policy, they will express their own concerns more vociferously the greater the hardship endured. In a related study of pilferage tendencies that varied according to the sensitivity of a message communicating a temporary wage reduction (Greenberg, 1990a), the data suggest that employees can also become inclined to manifest their displeasure behaviorally.

In short, employees' motivational inclinations can vary as a function of the motives they infer on management's part. Management has two sets of obligations when it comes to hardships imposed on employees. In the first place, imposing hardships should be avoided if possible. Employees' inferences about management motives will determine whether a hardship seems as if it might have been avoided. The corresponding counterfactual can be described in causally instrumental terms, which had been the original emphasis in RCT terms: This hardship *would* not have occurred if management cared enough about its employees—cared as much as it *should* have, that is, when it comes to the obligation of seeking to avoid hardship in the first place.

Suppose, however, management explanations indicate that the hardship could not have been avoided (an excuse) or should not have been avoided (a justification). The results of various studies about effects from interpersonal sensitivity suggest that employees perceive an extension to management obligations: the obligation to *alleviate* suffering from hardship that cannot be avoided or that has been justified on sufficiently compelling grounds. Questions about management motives and intentions will influence whether the extent of the efforts to alleviate suffering from hardship seems adequate or not. Here, the counterfactual takes a different shape: Would suffering be alleviated more if management cared more about the hardships it imposes— that is, cared as much as it should about the obligation to alleviate suffering as much as possible?

Ultimately, therefore, both types of counterfactual reasoning reduce to a similar logic of inference about obligations and intentions. One, which focuses on the causes of hardships imposed, raises questions about causal contingency: Would I (as Victim) be better off now, if only Agent had acted with greater concern for moral obligations about imposing hardship on me? The other focuses on the consequences of hardships imposed and raises questions about their continued (potentially severe) impact versus possible alleviation: Is the extent of my capacity to endure hardship placed in jeopardy; that is, would my coping be in less jeopardy if only Agent cared more about how much I might end up suffering? Both forms of counterfactual, "if only," reasoning indicate a concern about Agent's capacity for ill will—the willingness to exploit a relationship for one's own purposes.

We think Greenberg's (1994) study reveals an impressively subtle sophistication about the nature of moral obligations and the nature of concern for self-interest versus an interest in others' well-being. Although we perhaps stretch the interpretation, we argue that the separate manipulations of explanatory content and sensitivity can help illustrate—at least by analogy—a continuum of moral obligation anchored by self-interest on one end and concern for Victim suffering on the other. The least adequate (and also insensitive) forms of accounts fail to indicate a sense of moral obligation toward others, as if only one's own self-interest matters. The explanation that emphasized the costs of smoking in the workplace, on the other hand, implied a concern for some workers—especially nonsmokers harmed by sidestream smoke. The addition of a high-sensitivity message extended the expression of concern to the remaining category of employees—smokers—by emphasizing how much management cared about their well-being (adjustment) as well.

Relational Concerns Expressed
by Authorities in Groups

Obviously we think the counterfactual reasoning schema of RCT has value for predicting reactions that vary according to the reference standards used for evaluation. For that reason, we have tried to show how the same form of reasoning can be extended from the causal to the moral (deontic) realms. We also think this extension is consistent with trends in justice theorizing and research about organizational justice, especially as the result of demonstrations about the potential impact of interpersonal sensitivity. We hasten to add, however, that our preferred interpretive stance is not the only one that can be used to derive an emphasis on moral obligations. Indeed, Tom Tyler and Alan Lind have consistently argued for that position as an alternative to what they see as an overemphasis on self-interest within the procedural tradition established by Thibaut and Walker (1975; see Lind & Tyler, 1988).

This alternative model has taken two forms. Initially Lind and Tyler (1988) referred to the Group Value Model; more recently they referred to a revised version as a Relational Model of Authority in Groups (Tyler & Lind, 1992). In connection with the developments leading to a revision, Tyler (1989) identified three primary considerations relevant to perceptions of justice—trust, neutrality, and standing. Our review touches only lightly on the general approach. We concentrate more heavily on the three components, which we relate to ideas about moral obligations and the intentions of Agent.

As a general approach, the reasoning used by Tyler and Lind (1992) has emphasized the importance of identifying with groups for the sake of sustaining a meaningful self-identity. We think the emphasis on groups is misplaced but that the core logic is unaffected whether or not a group context is evoked as the basis for that logic. Lind and Tyler (1988) seemed primarily concerned to find a "model of procedural justice that does not depend on self-interest calculations" (p. 230). They argued that "individuals in groups are more likely to put aside their own self-interest" (as evidenced by effects found in research on social dilemmas) and also cited an interpretation of such effects as particularly germane: "Dawes (1986) has argued that some social dilemma effects are such that they cannot be explained by reference to expectations of personal gain" (p. 230).

The emphasis on groups tends to give a long-term time perspective a central role. For example, Lind and Tyler (1988) pointed to group procedures as internal features of a group that give it a distinctive identity because such procedures "specify the authority relations and the formal and informal social processes that regulate much of the group's activity" (p. 231). Although informal processes were mentioned, they generally seem of secondary importance relative to more enduring formalized and institutionalized characteristics of procedures. Thus,

> Perceptions of procedures have greater impact on evaluations of groups than do perceptions of outcomes, because attitudes are generally viewed as one-time responses to particular situations whereas procedures have an enduring quality; this makes an unfair procedure much more threatening than a single unfair outcome. (Tyler & Lind, 1992, p. 135)

A cornerstone assumption, therefore, is "that in reacting to procedures people are primarily concerned about their long-term relationship to the authorities or institutions that employ the procedures" (1992, p. 140). As Tyler (1989) put it, the reasoning "assumes that people are concerned about their long-term social relationship with the authorities or institutions acting as third parties and do not view their relationship with third parties as a one-shot deal" (p. 831).

We argue that motives and intentions with respect to moral obligations are of central importance even in short-term relationships or "one-shot," single-occasion encounters. Thus we seek to emphasize a common logic shared with Tyler and Lind's (1992) relational approach, yet nonetheless extending to any type of social interaction. We do not think that concerns about morality, justice, and fairness require a group context to be activated. Note, for example, Tyler's (1989) reference to "third parties" and the emphasis on a relational model of authority. Such language implies that justice concepts apply only when a formal decision maker with allocative authority has charge over the distribution of scarce resources or the resolution of a conflict between two disputing parties. We used the term *Agent* instead to indicate another person whose actions have a bearing on outcomes and consequences, but clearly Agent can mean an exchange partner in a two-person transaction (e.g., seller and customer). Such a transaction surely epitomizes a common, everyday experience; concerns about fairness in exchange need not entail a group context, a hierarchy of decision making, or a formal authority.

For such reasons, we focus exclusively on what Tyler and Lind (1992) called the "three relational factors" of trust, standing, and neutrality, and try to separate the meaning of those terms from the context of groups and formal authority. We think these factors can be reinterpreted in a fashion consistent with themes we have emphasized throughout these first two chapters: that Agent's actions should imply intentions consistent with sufficient regard for general moral obligations transcending self-interest by giving some weight to the interests of others.

Reinterpreting Trust, Neutrality, and Standing

Our interpretation of the three relational factors seeks to build on the following theme mentioned by Tyler and Lind (1992): "The procedures used by an authority to reach a decision might be seen as an expression of the authority's values" (p. 135). We call these values intentions with regard to moral obligations, but the reasoning is similar. Indeed, Tyler (1989) made intentions central to his concept of trust; we simply seek to extend similar reasoning to the other two relational concepts as well. Thus we start with trust, sketch an interpretation in terms of intentions, then extend that reasoning to reinterpret neutrality and standing along similar lines.

Trust. Tyler (1989) introduced the concept of trust in arguing that "the long-term nature of group membership leads people to focus on the intentions of third parties" (p. 831). Being able to trust the intentions of third-party authorities is quite significant in dealings with such authorities, Tyler maintained, because they often have a considerably broad latitude of discretion available in exercising their authority (e.g., the manner in which procedures are enacted and consequences implemented). But the same can be said about the discretion that an exchange partner might exercise during a two-person transaction. Tyler (1989) also emphasized that "the intentions of authorities are especially important because current interactions allow people to predict the future" (p. 831). We suspect that intentions are equally important in one-shot encounters.

Tyler defined trust as "the belief that the intentions of third parties are benevolent, that they desire to treat people in a fair and reasonable way" (p. 831). Similarly, Tyler and Lind (1992) referred to the belief "that the authority can be trusted to try to behave fairly" (p. 142). Additional indications about the meaning of this concept come from their discussion of empirical findings and the operational definition supplied by questionnaire items in that survey research (a discussion of "factors . . . most closely related to the judgment that an authority is trustworthy," p. 156). Tyler and Lind suggested that authority competence would constitute an aspect of trustworthiness, as would ethicality. Both sets of items tapped intentions via a stem worded to ask how hard an authority tried to do each of several things. A survey of perceived management intentions indicated the largest correlation from an item on the attempt to find satisfactory solutions, and a survey about the intentions of legal authorities to solve problems. In general, however, Tyler and Lind argued that judgments of ethicality were more central. The relevant questions after the "How hard did authority try to . . . " stem were as follows: "Consider your views?" "Explain decision?" "Be fair to you?" "Take account of your needs?" (p. 156).

If trying hard refers to intentions, we suggest that managers, legal authorities, and anyone as Agent (including both exchange partners in a transaction) can also try hard to display the other two relational qualities of neutrality and attention to the other party's standing or dignity. Thus, the intentional aspect of trust hardly seems central as a defining feature. Moreover, the effort to be fair also seems as if it should apply generically as a concern about justice. What, then, remains to distinguish trust from neutrality, standing, or a general concern about fairness?

In reinterpreting the construct, we take our clue from some of the language Tyler and Lind (1992) used to express their ideas. We think the underlying themes involve language about benevolence, empathy, and attention to the personal needs of a particular person as a recipient of outcomes. In general terms, therefore, we link trust to the concerns of interpersonal sensitivity illustrated by the importance of motives inferred for management's granting smokers free use of a cessation program (viz., to alleviate the suffering from an imposed hardship). Tyler (1989), for example, referred to "belief that . . . intentions . . . are benevolent" (p. 831), and Tyler and Lind (1992) referred to "trust in . . . benevolence" (p. 156).

Tyler and Lind also cited, as relevant to the concept of trust, a finding about the correlation between fairness perceptions and perceptions of empathy. Note that empathy implies a willingness to identify with the concerns of a particular individual. In addition, we note the personal reference within survey items to "your views," "fair to you," and "your needs" as representing the inference that Agent is disposed kindly to the respondent in particular. Thus, although Tyler and Lind's most general description of their model identifies "concern for needs" and "consideration of views" as separable aspects within the construct of trust (p. 159), we see both as related to the notion of a *particularistic* orientation of good will toward a specific person whose views, concerns, and interests are taken into account. We elaborate further on this idea in the last two chapters of the book.

Neutrality. The notion of neutrality or impartiality refers as much to the absence of certain kinds of intention as it does to the presence of others. On the side of undesirable intentions to avoid for the sake of fairness, Tyler and Lind (1992) mentioned "bias or discrimination," "fundamental dishonesty or incompetence," and "inconsistency"; they summarized these in positive terms as "absence of bias or prejudice," "honesty," and "fact-based decision making" (pp. 158-159). Similarly, Tyler (1989) mentioned the importance of a "neutral arena" or "level playing field" (p. 831).

Again, we think fair conduct involves intending to observe moral obligations. To distinguish neutrality intentions from trustworthiness, we distinguish the latter as particularistically oriented sensitivity from the former as a disengagement from self-interest or favoritism toward others identified with one's self-interests. Indeed, neutrality might be conceived as a necessary but insufficient precursor to trustworthiness as empathy, in that neutrality entails denying or curbing self-interest whereas trustworthiness involves identifying with the interests of a particular other. The necessary-but-not-sufficient relation would help account for the commonality of "competence" (e.g., the intention to act with competent attention to detailed fact-finding) in the two constructs as described by Tyler and Lind (1992).

The prevalence of reference to "honesty" also warrants comment (e.g., "having an unbiased decision maker who is honest and uses appropriate factual information to make decisions," Tyler, 1989, p. 831). There is some ambiguity and possible confusion in the relational approach that this emphasis on honesty might help resolve. On the one hand, Tyler and Lind (1992) were seeking to distinguish their relational approach from the self-interest orientation that focuses exclusively on outcomes. On the other hand, the emphasis on long-term consequences within an ongoing group tends to bring self-interest about outcomes right back into the picture (viz., one's long-term expected-value outcome as the average to be expected from extended interaction within the group). Thus, for example, Tyler (1989) introduced his discussion of neutrality with the following comments: "People must think about their outcomes over time. Given that people cannot easily focus on short-term outcome favorability, how can they evaluate whether their outcomes from the group are reasonable?" (p. 831). His answer was that "over time, all will benefit fairly from the application of fair procedures for decision making" (p. 831) and that fair procedures entail neutrality. The concept of honesty, however, represents a moral value considered desirable regardless of implications for outcomes—short or long term.

Indeed, the notion of being honest—the intentional refraining from deceit—is a quintessential marker distinguishing deontological reasoning about moral obligations from outcome-based or consequentialist reasoning that addresses only the more utilitarian concerns common to economic models. Pushed to the extreme as an imperative or absolute command—which Kant called categorical because it is meant to apply universally under all circumstances rather than to apply contingently, conditioned on a given set of circumstances—the injunction "do not lie" actually threatens to impose harmful outcomes on many people. Moral philosophers questioning Kant's position (e.g., Bok, 1978) thus note that the obligation never to lie would cause unacceptable harm if you would have to hide the truth in order to prevent a killer from finding his or her intended victim. This dilemma helps show that an intention to honor a moral obligation (not to lie) can, indeed, interfere with both short- and long-term desirable outcomes, rather than consistently acting in an instrumental fashion as a means to attaining those ends more often (i.e., on the average, over time).

Notions such as honesty, therefore, help show that the intention to abide by moral obligations can have instrumental as well as noninstrumental value (which Tyler has sometimes termed a *value-expressive* function; e.g., Tyler & Caine, 1981). When making the effort to be honest and impartial entails an unbiased attention to gathering and using relevant facts, the intention to observe those standards of moral conduct should help promote outcomes that are as fair as possible to the majority of people the majority of the time (or at least on the average, over time). Yet, it is also true that being honest seems moral in and of itself; it is the right thing to do, whereas dishonesty is wrong. This also helps show that concepts such as Leventhal's (1980) notion of ethicality need not be identified exclusively with interpersonal sensitivity.

Standing. We view the concept of standing as a reference to another moral obligation—exercising intentional regard for the rights of others and privileges of others as members of human society, so that they are treated with due respect for their dignity as human beings (cf. Bies, 1989; Folger, 1988; Lane, 1988; Lind & Tyler, 1988; Tyler & Folger, 1980). In fact, Tyler and Lind's (1992) discussion of standing mentioned references (Lind et al., 1989; MacCoun, Lind, Hensler, Bryant, & Ebener, 1988) that described this aspect of their relational model as involving issues of "dignitary concerns" (Tyler & Lind, 1992, p. 141). Our emphasis differs from theirs primarily in focusing on a person's membership in the larger society of all human beings, rather than on the membership in a specific group, institution, organization, society, or state.

For example, Lind and Tyler (1988) argued as follows (in a passage from which we have omitted the references they cited):

> In particular, when one is treated politely and with dignity and when respect is shown for one's rights and opinions, feelings of positive social standing are enhanced. . . . On the other hand, undignified, disrespectful, or impolite treatment by an authority carries the implication that one is not a full member of the group, and this is very threatening indeed. (p. 141)

We assert that any person should be so obligated as to intend treating any other person in a fashion consistent with such ideals, independently from the presence or absence of a group or authority context. The same description would apply, only with reference to terminology about groups and authorities deleted. In that sense, "social standing" need not refer to one's relative standing in a specific group; rather, it can refer to a person's social significance as a human being.

This is not to deny that either a particular society's culture or the subculture within a specific group is irrelevant. Norms such as politeness are quite culturally unique, and concepts of rights vary widely according to the context of membership in a given group (e.g., the rights and privileges of belonging to a particular country club vs. rights guaranteed by the U.S. Constitution to all U.S. citizens). Again, that point underscores why we have begun this book with three chapters on generic justice issues and followed it with applications to a number of very specific functions of human resources management. Each of these topic areas might evoke idiosyncratic norms of justice, including those that influence whether employees feel they have been treated politely, with dignity, and with proper regard for their rights (as employees, as citizens, and as human beings). Employee conceptions of fairness and justice will vary from organization to organization, from nation to nation, from subculture to subculture—and the relevant aspects of standing will vary as a result.

A Look Ahead: Toward a General Fairness Theory

With a bow to the seminal contributions made by Lind, Tyler, and their collaborators on the relational approach to fairness, we can say that this chapter has addressed justice as a fundamentally relational topic. Central concerns about justice focus on inferences regarding whether people have honored their relational (social) obligations. We call that a relational perspective even though we do not see it as embedded in the context of a particular group. Rather, that type of concern about injustice and violations of fairness norms has roots in the normative order of a moral community. It is a universal concern, apposite to all human endeavors.

Justice is an aspect of morality involving social relations. The gluttony of a lone individual might be considered immoral, for example, but not an illustration of unjust behavior so long as it did no harm to anyone else (e.g., did not prevent other people from sufficient access to scarce resources; done in private so as not to offend). Being fair to other people means not allowing one's own unbridled pursuit of self-interest to become so excessive that it disregards consequences for the self-interest of others. A collection of people not intending to honor the social obligations of justice would soon find themselves living the existence Hobbes described as "solitary, poor, nasty, brutish, and short." No society could exist indefinitely in such a state, nor can any organization. Good practices of human resource management thus require attention to general concepts of justice as much as to the specific findings we describe in subsequent chapters.

We close this three-chapter opening to our book with a brief word about what lies ahead in a penultimate chapter on our own perspective, which we term Fairness Theory. In the present chapter, we have tried to show that several current models of organizational justice converge on a common orientation stressing perceived intentions to uphold moral obligations. We showed parallels between a revised conception of RCT and the relational orientation adopted by Tyler and Lind. Because Sheppard et al. (1992) also adopted the RCT perspective, the emphasis we chose seems broadly inclusive. In addition, we have tried to incorporate related points from Leventhal's (1980) listing of procedural considerations, from the work of Bies (1987) and his colleagues on interactional justice, and from Greenberg's (1990b) work on impression management and interpersonal sensitivity.

Two expressions seem to capture the flavor of this convergence and, at the same time, to foreshadow some missing aspects that future developments must address—the theme to which we return in our penultimate chapter. We have already commented on the significance of the first expression—relational obligations—as a summary expression that reflects many current developments in organizational justice. We propose a second—deonance—as a related expression that might promise to encompass some aspects of the latent potential not yet realized in this field.

In line with our emphasis on moral obligations about relationships among people in general, not only those in groups or subject to hierarchical authority, we chose *deonance* as a term for the sense of injustice experienced when someone egregiously offends the social mores that dictate condemning harm intended without sufficient regard for interests other than one's own. This experience ought to motivate behavioral inclinations, such as the tendency to express condemnation and perhaps to pursue retaliation or punishment, or else human society would be ill served. The willingness to exploit relationships, unchecked as an intention, deserves censure. Indeed, Cosmides (1989) obtained evidence she interpreted as being consistent with "look for cheaters" as a "Darwinian algorithm"; that is, the tendency to censure unbridled exploitation as a capacity so evolved as a consequence of conditions for human existence that it operates much like a mental heuristic, perhaps functioning with the characteristics of automaticity. Similarly, Wilson (1993) reviewed evidence from across the social sciences consistent with asserting the existence of a "moral sense" in which justice plays a primary role.

Motivational concepts have often been individualistic and hence focused exclusively on self-interest. Dissonance and reactance come to mind, the former motivated by psychological incongruence threatening self conceptions

(Aronson, 1969; Brown, 1965), the latter motivated by threats to individual autonomy and personal freedoms. Why not a psychological state of deonance as a basis for reacting against threats to social stability? True, the experience of deonance might tie together self-identity and group identity, as Lind and Tyler (1988) argued or as would be implied from Cosmides's (1989) emphasis on Darwinian selection for intentions consistent with survival during the eons of years when humans lived together as groups of hunter-gatherers. But if that sense now operates at the level of automaticity, as Wilson (1993) suggested and as Lind, Kulik, Ambrose, and de Vera-Park (1993) implied in referring to justice heuristics, it can also operate quite apart from a group-based, hierarchical context.

Moreover, the inclination to censure or punish wrongful intentions should not depend on having experienced harm directly—either because of immediate consequences to self or because of anticipated consequences over some long-term set of expectations relevant to self and one's own group. Rather, social living provides benefits on a constant basis to all human beings, who gain more from this interdependent existence than they would if forced to live in isolation from one another. A display of the intention to disregard obligations toward others, therefore, warrants censure regardless of future consequences. A person exhibiting such intentions has already benefited from life in society, and the display of a willingness to engage in unbridled exploitation of others amounts to indicating that the cooperation of others will not be returned in kind (violating the universal norm of reciprocity).

Here, then, are some implications about a future theory of deonance, whose themes we will pick up again in the penultimate chapter. First, such a theory should explain the sense of moral outrage and righteous indignation that can sweep emotionally over people even when their own self-interest does not seem to be directly involved. Why, for example, do many people all over the globe react with repugnance to violent "ethnic cleansing" slaughters, even when those who commit the violence surely constitute only the remotest probability of harm to the people elsewhere who experience that emotional reaction?

Only by understanding why people are held accountable for wrongful intentions (and actions) such as those will organizational justice scholars be able to speak with credibility to managers about social outrage over "unjust" management practice. Why, for example, has U.S. society seen a steady erosion of the once-dominant doctrine of employment at will, which essentially allowed employers to dismiss employees without cause? Why did public outcry and congressional testimony lead to plant-closing legislation? That legislation now mandates advance notice of layoffs. Prior to its enactment, justice research had already been undertaken to determine how variations in the extent of advance notice influenced the attitudes of laid-off employees (e.g., Brockner et al., 1994; Konovsky & Folger, 1991).

The capacity of general concepts of justice to anticipate future impact on management practice, including practice by changes in government legislation, is illustrated by that example in two respects. First, the investigation of advance notice sprang from the conception of timeliness as an interactional justice consideration (much as the original notion of interactional justice had come from investigations showing that MBAs felt unjustly treated by recruiters who failed to notify students promptly about the consequences of hiring decisions; Bies & Moag, 1986). Second, the measure of those former employees' reactions was ironically prescient: The respondents indicated the extent to which they might favor government action to limit organizational prerogatives exercised unilaterally by management. Here, too, is another example of how the experience of injustice has implications for behavioral intentions that might not immediately affect productivity or profit, but that nonetheless threaten the sustainability of a corporation. For that reason, we have consistently oriented our discussion toward the attitude of reproach.

Finally, we think notions such as deonance and relational obligations can forge much-needed links among the rapidly expanding plethora of concepts in the field of organizational justice. It seems to us that too much separation still exists across conceptually distinct categories of justice. True, the distinction between means and ends has profound implications, and hence a parallel distinction between procedural and distributive justice will always have useful implications. Similarly, extending beyond formal procedures to broader interactional considerations and interpersonal sensitivity highlights some topics that might otherwise be neglected. The downside of emphasizing the bases for distinguishing among concepts, however, can create an equally detrimental oversight—neglecting to specify how various perceptions about justice combine to influence reactions. For that reason, we have consistently emphasized an approach that shows how process-related concerns (whether derived from procedural or interactional justice concepts) can influence how people react to outcome discrepancies.

Summary

We think that employees who find management guilty of censurable offenses—perceived injustices of management wrongdoing—also have a desire to reproach the wrongdoers. Punishment does not inevitably follow the urge to reproach, but it can remain a latent possibility. Bies (1987a) summarized that idea nicely in his chapter on the "predicament" of injustice; essentially he noted that harmdoers are vulnerable to a variety of actions prompted by other people's moral outrage and sense of righteous indignation (acts of revenge, retaliation, retribution). Managers occupy the role of Agent—a position of accountability, with implied obligations concerning the proper way to conduct that role without inflicting undue harm. Agents who conduct roles improperly, who inadequately attend to their roles' obligations, are subject to reproach.

Reproach amounts to an accusation of wrongdoing, a charge that standards of moral conduct have been violated, a reminder that standards of accountability have not been met or obligations not honored. The inclination to reproach is consistent with the urge not only to reprimand but also to punish. Punishment is justified harm, imposed so that wrongdoers suffer for their misdeeds. The desire to punish tends to increase with the severity of harm experienced (Walster, Walster, & Berscheid, 1978). When Agent's perceived intentions seem consistent with a willingness to violate obligations about not allowing undue harm, the inclination to reproach grows with the perceived severity of Victim suffering or jeopardy; at work, that inclination can prompt employees to retaliate aggressively for unjust intentions in ways such as those mentioned above. This chapter has examined the nature of those intentions and their significance for two recent theoretical approaches to organizational justice.

Note

1. For example, RCT is consistent with the general relation between relative deprivation, equity, and the frustration-aggression hypothesis discussed by Brown (1965; Brown & Herrnstein, 1975). Brown referred to the general underlying principle as the "illegitimate disappointment of legitimate expectations" (Brown & Herrnstein, 1975, p. 274). *Illegitimate violation* refers to the modification of the original frustration-aggression hypothesis (Dollard, Doob, Miller, Mowrer, & Sears, 1939) by subsequent research, which showed that simple frustration does not evoke aggression as reliably as does frustration under circumstances termed arbitrary, illegitimate, capricious, unjustified, and so on (see Burnstein & Worchel 1962; Kulik & Brown, 1979; Pastore, 1950). This modification is similar in spirit to the instrumentality component of RCT focused on procedural justifications in the original version and to the referent conduct component in the modified version (broadened to include interactional as well as procedural aspects of Agent's conduct). The other part of Brown's expression, *legitimate expectations,* refers to a standard for evaluating outcomes or consequences. Hence, it is similar in spirit to the referent outcomes RCT component in the original version or the referent consequences component in the modified version.

4 Organizational Justice and Staffing Decisions

ON THE HORNS OF A JUSTICE DILEMMA?

Historically, organizations have approached staffing from what could be called a "prediction paradigm" (de Wolff, 1993). Under this approach, the human resource practitioner (e.g., an industrial/organizational [I/O] psychologist or a personnel officer) is primarily responsible for administering a valid test. Validity, of course, is seen as the extent to which a test correlates with some relevant criterion, usually job performance. As Arvey (1992) noted, a test is often considered fair if it more or less accurately predicts performance and does not differentially predict the performance of protected subgroups, such as women, minorities, and the disabled. "Fairness," therefore, reduces to "statistical fairness," and the justice of the instrument is assessed by a series of equations relating the predictor to some criterion. At other times, selection fairness is limited to the fairness of the outcomes or, more properly, the configuration of outcomes produced by the test. Thus, an instrument that disproportionately denies opportunities to a protected group might be opprobrious to some (Arvey & Sackett, 1993). In either case, the perceived fairness of the procedures and judgments used to render a decision are typically left unexamined (Arvey, 1991; Cropanzano, 1996; Gilliland, 1993; Schmitt & Gilliland, 1992; Singer, 1993).

The prediction paradigm also tends to deemphasize the relationship between the applicant and the organization. Indeed, the purpose of preemployment screening is to ascertain whether or not the applicant should be allowed to enter into a formal relationship. Selection, therefore, is seen as a boundary or gateway through which individuals must pass. Prior to entry, organizations often see themselves as having a particularly circumscribed set of responsibilities or obligations to the applicant. These felt responsibilities tend to broaden once an individual actually joins a firm. For example, mandatory urinalysis is seen as more acceptable when it is performed on applicants and less acceptable when it is performed on job incumbents (see Konovsky & Cropanzano, 1993, for a review).

An alternative to the prediction paradigm is to note that the applicant and the organization begin to form a relationship from the moment they make contact. The nature of this first contact can have profound implications for the relationship's future progress (see Gilliland, 1993; Herriot, 1989; Schuler, 1993b; Singer, 1993; Stone & Stone, 1990). For example, an applicant who is displeased with the selection apparatus may be less likely to accept a job offer and more likely to criticize the organization to outsiders. Therefore, all other things being equal, it behooves the organization to pay special attention to the needs and concerns of their applicant pool. Schuler (1993b) put it more directly, arguing that organizations need to pay as much attention to a test's social validity, or the extent to which it is seen as fair and acceptable, as they now pay to a test's statistical validity.

This chapter examines these issues in more detail. First, we will review several common selection procedures. In doing so, we will pay special attention to instruments that show impressive statistical validity, while simultaneously manifesting lower social validity. That is, the most valid tests are not necessarily perceived to be the most fair. This will underscore the need for employers to attend to selection fairness. From this review, we will then derive a set of general guidelines that seek to achieve social validity without compromising validity. Third, we will apply these guidelines to a series of commonly used tests, illustrating ways that some techniques can be improved without changing their essential form.

The Justice Dilemma in Action

Selection is something that I/O psychologists do quite well. In the past several years, researchers have validated a variety of different techniques. For example, procedures such as cognitive abilities testing (Hunter & Hunter, 1984), biographical inventories (Schmitt, Gooding, Noe, & Kirsch, 1984), and assessments centers (Gaugler, Rosenthal, Thornton, & Bentson, 1987) all show strong evidence of validity and utility. We also have a better idea of what does not work. For example, despite their wide use, unstructured preemployment interviews show low validity (Arvey & Campion, 1982). Similarly, graphology, or handwriting analysis, has been widely used on the European continent (Robertson & Makin, 1986) despite its dubious utility (Neter & Ben-Shakhar, 1989). Thus, from an exclusively statistical point of view we know what works and what does not, and we are in a seemingly excellent position for giving advice.

Although relevant data are limited, it seems to be the case that our advice is often heeded, but sometimes it is not. For example, in a study of American corporations, Harris, Dworkin, and Park (1990) examined the usage rates of 14 common selection systems. References and unstructured interviews were the two most widely utilized techniques, being used by 97.3% and 87.6%, respectively, of the responding companies. Although better than selecting individuals at random, neither of these techniques has particularly high validity (Reilly & Chao, 1982). Tests that are known to have higher validity, such as cognitive-abilities tests (Hunter & Hunter, 1984), personality tests (Tett, Jackson, & Rothstein, 1991), and honesty tests (O'Bannon, Goldringer, & Appleby, 1989), received considerably less use. In this same study, Harris et al. (1990) found that one of the major reasons given for not using certain techniques was the perceived offensiveness of these instruments. Procedures that caused uneasiness were less likely to be used, even when these techniques were considered valid. Consequently, as a practical matter, personnel officers already take into account social validity—even if academic researchers have been slower to see its relevance.

These results do not seem limited to the United States. In a British survey, Robertson and Makin (1986) also found that managers were usually selected on the basis of interviews (of a variety of different types) and reference checks. Personality and cognitive-abilities tests, although valid, were used somewhat less. At the time of this particular survey, biodata and assessment centers, both valid techniques, were hardly used at all. Indeed, only astrology and handwriting analysis were used less often!

Of course, neither of the surveys just cited can be taken as conclusive evidence that a lack of social validity causes organizations to avoid otherwise useful techniques. There can be other causes of low usage rates. Robertson and Makin (1986), for example, attributed some of it to misinformation among British organizations. Some employers may simply not realize that biodata and assessment centers make valid predictions. Nonetheless, the relatively limited use of certain instruments is suggestive, and, in any case, we will later review more direct evidence pertaining to each of these selection procedures. For now it seems useful to investigate the negative consequences that can accrue from using an unfair selection device.

Consequences of Unfairness

Treating applicants unfairly has some particularly pernicious consequences for organizations (Arvey, 1991, 1992; Gilliland, 1993). A partial list of these deleterious outcomes could include such things as negative attitudes toward the selection system and toward the company, a decreased likelihood of accepting a job offer, a greater likelihood of legal action, and, among those hired, poorer work attitudes and performance. We will discuss the evidence for each of these outcomes next.

Poorer Attitudes Toward
the Selection Technique

The cycle of injustice begins with the selection tool. Some of them are evaluated positively, whereas others are not. Once this initial decision is made, subsequent responses are set in motion. For this reason, it seems suitable that we open this review by briefly examining individual responses to various commonly used selection techniques.

Assessment Centers. Assessment centers are sophisticated tools for selecting and developing organizational talent. Although assessment centers can be used for a variety of positions, so far their greatest utility has been in selecting managers (for excellent reviews of this literature, see Thornton, 1992; Thornton & Byham, 1982). Assessment centers consist of a set of structured exercises, such as an in-basket, group business problem, and a leaderless group discussion. Job applicants participate in these exercises and are graded by a set of trained raters. These raters then meet to provide a summary score. Assessment center participants may also complete various other psychological tests, such as measures of cognitive ability. When properly designed and administered, assessment centers have proven to be valid predictors of job performance (Gaugler et al., 1987).

Besides their statistical validity, assessment centers have social validity as well. Several studies have found that assessment centers are well received by applicants (Bourgeois, Leim, Slivinski, & Grant, 1975; Davis, 1993; Kravitz, Stinson, & Chavez, 1996; Macan, Avedon, Paese, & Smith, 1994; Noe & Steffy, 1987; Robertson, Iles, Gratton, & Shapley, 1991; Schuler, 1993b; Schuler &

Fruhner, 1993). In addition, when compared to cognitive-abilities tests, assessment centers show much smaller ethnic differences (Schmitt, 1993).

Of course, there are always some exceptions. For example, Dodd (1977) surveyed a group of people who participated in an assessment center. Although the reactions to the center were generally positive, Dodd did find that between 10% and 30% of the participants did not believe the center provided an adequate appraisal of their work. Moreover, both Teel and Dubois (1983) and Noe and Steffy (1987) found that individuals who received favorable evaluations were more likely to prefer assessment centers than those who received negative evaluations. Overall, however, assessment centers are assessment techniques that maximize two important goals: high validity and high perceived fairness.

Biographical Inventories. Biographical inventories, more commonly known as *biodata,* can be understood as extremely elaborate application forms. The job seeker is required to complete a long series of questions about his or her life experiences. In and of itself, this seems innocuous enough. The problem for biodata, however, seems to be job relevance. These particular pencil-and-paper measures simply are not transparent to the applicant. As such, they are often viewed as unfair (for evidence, see Smither, Reilly, Millsap, Pearlman, & Stoffey, 1993; Stoffey, Millsap, Smither, & Reilly, 1991). Of course, this is not to say that biodata should never be used. In one study, Steiner and Gilliland (1996) found that neither American nor French respondents were especially negative toward biographical inventories, although other instruments received more positive ratings.

Biodata scales were originally developed using a purely inductive methodology (England, 1961; Owens 1976). Items were retained in these scales because they predicted work outcomes, not because they were intuitively or conceptually related to job behavior. To demonstrate this, let us consider some example items presented by Owens (1976, p. 613); for convenience, we have renumbered them. Keep in mind that these are actual items:

1. What is your weight?
   a. Under 135 pounds
   b. 136 to 155 pounds
   c. 156 to 175 pounds
   d. 176 to 195 pounds
   e. Over 195 pounds
2. What was your marital status at college graduation?
   a. Single
   b. Married, no children

    c. Married, one or more children

    d. Widowed

    e. Separated or divorced

3. When are you most likely to have a headache?

    a. When I strain my eyes

    b. When I don't eat on schedule

    c. When I am under tension

    d. January first

    e. Never had headaches

I suspect that the reader can see why applicants might be angry about losing a job because of when they have headaches. One can almost hear the wheels of litigation turning! Nevertheless, and this must be emphasized, biodata works. It is clearly a valid predictor of job performance (Hunter & Hunter, 1984; Schmitt et al., 1984). The problem is that some of the particular questions simply do not look as if they should work.

Cognitive-Abilities Tests. Cognitive abilities, or "intelligence tests, are plagued by one of the same concerns that haunt biodata. Simply put, examinees have trouble ascertaining how the ability to rotate objects in space, recall the definition of obscure words, or solve abstract analogies is related to job behavior. As Huffcutt (1990), Barrett and Depinet (1991), and Schmidt (1988) all noted, even in the face of overwhelming evidence for their validity, both the popular press and psychological writers alike continue to derogate the use of cognitive-abilities tests.

But for all of this controversy, the average American is less negative toward cognitive-abilities tests than one might think. Perhaps the best available data on this issue are the 10 national surveys reviewed by Lerner (1981). Lerner found that the vast majority of Americans were neutral to favorable in their attitudes toward standardized testing. Although encouraging, Lerner's data are limited in that they are not particular to work settings. In fact, Lerner's respondents were evaluating standardized testing for educational purposes. Additionally, these surveys did not compare cognitive abilities testing to other widely used assessment devices.

Fortunately, other studies help address these concerns. Surveys by Kravitz et al. (1996) and Rynes and Connerley (1993) had individuals compare cognitive abilities to other instruments. In general, these tests received a moderate ranking near the middle of the set. These respondents did not seem to love cognitive-abilities tests, but they did not seem to hate them either, and this conclusion seems to hold in both the United States and France (Steiner & Gilliland, 1996). Field studies by Smither et al. (1993) and Macan et al.

(1994), along with two experiments by Kluger and Rothstein (1993), also suggest that abilities testing is less acceptable than other assessment devices. On the other hand, one survey by Hayes, Citera, Brady, and Jenkins (1995) found positive reactions to cognitive-abilities tests.

At least some of the existing discontent about intelligence testing concerns the lack of apparent job relevance. For example, Smither et al. (1993) found that job applicants reacted negatively to cognitive-abilities tests containing abstract items. However, when more concrete items were utilized, respondents perceived the tests to be fairer. Consistent with this, Rynes and Connerley (1993) stated that cognitive-abilities tests are perceived as fairer to the extent that they contain items that are obviously work related. One solution seems clear. Employers can exchange general tests containing abstract items for more concrete tests that are explicitly related to work. We shall return to this issue in more detail later.

Interviews. Interviews are among the most commonly used of all staffing techniques (Harris et al., 1990). Although maligned in the past, recent work does suggest that interviews can be valid predictors of job performance—provided they have enough structure. Unstructured interviews are less valid (Huffcutt & Arthur, 1994; Motowidlo et al., 1992).

A great deal of empirical research has examined the perceived fairness of selection interviews. These data indicate that interviews are generally perceived to be fair (Kravitz et al., 1996; Latham & Finnegan, 1993; Rynes & Connerley, 1993; Smither et al., 1993; but see Hayes et al., 1995, for a noteworthy caveat). One informative field experiment was carried out by Harland and Biasotto (1993). These researchers found that when compared to an interview-only group, applicants who were subjected to both an interview and a personality test reacted more negatively. Adding a second predictor actually reduced perceived fairness. These findings are not limited to the United States. Singer (1993) conducted surveys of working people in Australia (Study 3) and New Zealand (Study 4). In both cases, staffing procedures were seen as fairer to the extent that they included an interview. Likewise, Steiner and Gilliland (1996) determined that interviews are seen as fair in both France and the United States. Of course, this is not to say that all interviews are conducted in a just manner. Bies and Moag (1986) found that when interviewers treated individuals with rudeness and disrespect, applicants formed more negative attitudes toward the selection process and the organization. Similar evidence was reviewed by Rynes (1993) and Thornton (1993). We will have more to say about interpersonal effectiveness later in this chapter.

Pencil-and-Paper Honesty Tests. Honesty tests are self-report inventories that attempt to predict theft and other troublesome behaviors in potential employees. Research suggests that honesty tests are effective in that they yield substantial validity coefficients (Ones, Viswesvaran, & Schmidt, 1993; Sackett, Burris, & Callahan, 1989), although questions about their usage remain (Guastello & Rieke, 1991; Lilienfeld, 1993; Moore & Stewart, 1989).

Other work has assessed the perceived fairness of honesty tests. Generally speaking, applicants seem to have fairly neutral opinions toward these instruments, neither particularly positive nor particularly negative. For example, Ryan and Sackett (1987) did not find appreciable amounts of ill will as a result of honesty testing. Likewise, in the previously mentioned surveys by Rynes and Connerley (1993) and Kravitz et al. (1996), pencil-and-paper honesty tests were given somewhat moderate ratings—neither especially low nor especially high. Interesting findings were also reported by Rosse, Ringer, and Miller (1996). Rosse and his colleagues (1996) found that honesty tests were seen as more fair than personality inventories, but less fair than taking no test at all. Steiner and Gilliland (1996) reported that both French and American respondents tend to be fairly cool toward honesty tests.

Personality Tests. Personality tests can be valid indexes of job performance. Although, of course, only certain traits, such as conscientiousness and agreeableness, are useful predictors (Barrick & Mount, 1991; Tett, Jackson, & Rothstein, 1991). Despite this favorable evidence, study after study has found that personality tests are seen as unfair (Ambrose & Rosse, 1993; Harland & Biasotto, 1993; Hayes et al., 1995; Kravitz et al., 1996; Rosse, Miller, & Stecher, 1994; Smither et al., 1993; Steiner & Gilliland, 1996; Stoffey et al., 1991). Moreover, a survey conducted by Westin (1978) found that a full 44% of respondents wanted to ban the use of personality tests. Among blue-collar workers, this percentage jumped to 69%. Rosse, Ringer, et al. (1996) found that job applicants would rather submit to urinalysis then complete a personality inventory. Why all the anxiety?

Some personality tests ask probing questions about one's personal life and mental health. These questions are often judged by applicants to be improper. Fortunately, these concerns over impropriety do not seem to extend to all personality instruments. For example, Rosse, Miller, and Ringer (1996) found that potential job applicants reacted much more positively to a vocational interest inventory. Such inventories (besides being more job related) do not contain the offensive sorts of questions found in more clinically oriented tests. Rosse and his colleagues proposed a readily available solution to the problem of personality screening. These ideas were directly tested by Jones (1991). Jones found that job-relevant personality items did not engender the negative responses usually associated with personality testing. This suggests that alternative instruments can be devised to maintain validity without being offensive.

Reference Checks. Although reference checks are widely used, they have been subjected to surprisingly little empirical research. The validation evidence that does exist is not especially encouraging. Reference checks tend to be poor predictors of job performance (Hunter & Hunter, 1984; Muchinsky, 1979; Reilly & Chao, 1982). On the other hand, applicants do see them as reasonably fair (Kravitz et al., 1996; Rynes & Connerley, 1993; Steiner & Gilliland, 1996).

Work Samples. When using a work sample, the testing organization has the applicant perform some task that is a component of the job. For example, a secretary might take a typing test. Work samples are excellent predictors of job performance (Robertson & Kandola, 1982; Thornton & Cleveland, 1990) and trainability (Robertson & Downs, 1989).

It has long been known that work-sample tests engender positive attitudes in job applicants (Cascio & Phillips, 1979; Kluger & Rothstein, 1993; Kravitz et al., 1996; Rynes & Connerley, 1993; Schmidt, Greenthal, Hunter, Berner, & Seaton, 1977; Schmitt, Gilliland, Landis, & Devine, 1993; Steel, Balinsky, & Lang, 1945; Steiner & Gilliland, 1996; Stone, Stone, & Hyatt, 1989). The job relevance of these work simulations is readily apparent to applicants. As is the case with assessment centers, work samples seem to show ethnic differences that are smaller than those exhibited by cognitive-abilities tests (Robertson & Kandola, 1982; Schmidt et al., 1977).

Workplace Drug Screening. Another hotly debated selection technique is employee drug testing (for reviews, see Crant & Bateman, 1989; Cropanzano & Konovsky, 1993; Konovsky & Cropanzano, 1993). Several observers have discussed the legal and scientific assumptions that underlie screening (Crowne & Rosse, 1988; Greenfield, Karren, & Giacobbe, 1989; Hoffman & Silvers, 1987). Drug testing can be a valid technique for identifying unproductive employees (Normand, Salyards, & Mahoney, 1990; Zwerling, Ryan, & Orav, 1990). However, role-playing experiments by Crant and Bateman (1990, 1993), Cropanzano and Konovsky (1992), and Stone and Kotch (1989) demonstrated that unfair drug testing procedures lead individuals to formulate more negative attitudes toward the testing organization. The oft-observed conclusion is that individuals often report that drug testing is an invasion of privacy (Stone et al., 1989) and that it can contribute to poor work attitudes (Stone et al., 1989; Stone & Stone, 1990; Crant & Bateman, 1993; Konovsky & Cropanzano, 1991).

Despite all this, it is perhaps safer to say that individuals are highly variable in their responses to drug testing. Some people object strenuously, whereas others are quite supportive (Murphy, Thornton, & Prue, 1991; Murphy, Thornton, & Reynolds, 1990). For example, in a survey of railroad workers conducted by Hanson (1990), 63% of respondents reported that drug testing was justifiable, whereas 33% said that it was useful. Likewise, in a random survey of Georgia residents, 37% reported approval of drug testing and another 13% strongly approved. It would therefore be a bit inaccurate, or at least premature, to say that drug testing is associated with negative attitudes for most people. In fact, the worst attitudes may come from drug users (Garland, Giacobbe, & French, 1989; Murphy et al., 1990; Rosse et al., 1996), although this finding is not universal (Stone & Bowden, 1989).

One can certainly think of various reasons why individuals might react differently to drug testing. However, one reason seems to be the manner in which drug tests are conducted. When drug screening utilizes procedurally fair techniques, individuals tend to react much more positively (Konovsky & Cropanzano, 1991). This general observation has been supported in a variety of studies, offering employers several options for increasing drug testing fairness.

At the most basic level, the drug screen should be accurate. Field studies by Cropanzano and Konovsky (1995), Gomez-Mejia and Balkin (1987), Kravitz and Brock (1997), and Tepper and Braun (1995) showed that individuals have little tolerance for inaccurate drug tests. This should come as no surprise.

Organizations should also explain why drug testing is important. People will accept screening if they have a good reason to do so. For example, employees who do not use drugs are more supportive of testing if they are forced to work with drug users (Farabee & Lehman, 1991). Consistent with this, a role-playing study by Crant and Bateman (1989) found that individuals were likely to support drug screening if there was a clear justification as to why it was needed. Similar findings were obtained in field studies by Stone and Bommer (1990) and Konovsky and Cropanzano (1991).

To increase the fairness of drug testing, employers should also take care to examine how individuals are chosen for screening. In a field study by Stone and Bowden (1989), respondents indicated that testing "for cause" was more acceptable than random screening. Cropanzano and Konovsky (1995) obtained similar results in a field study, although the effect sizes here were larger when a positive drug test led to harsh consequences and smaller when the consequences were more benign. Similarly, Stone and Kotch (1989), Stone, O'Brien, and Bommer (1989), and Cropanzano and Konovsky (1995) all found that testing was preferred when advance notice was offered to participants (see Cropanzano & Randall, 1995, for related evidence). Labig (1992) suggested that this finding must be qualified somewhat. His research suggests that some occupational groups value advance notice more than others.

It is also important to give people some voice or a sense of control. In a multiorganizational survey by Gomez-Mejia and Balkin (1987), managers reported that drug-testing programs were more effective to the extent that they included union participation (a form of employee voice). This finding was qualified somewhat by Cropanzano and Konovsky (1995). These latter authors found that voice was more important to the extent that the drug-testing program was being used to administer very negative outcomes, such as termination. If less negative outcomes were administered (such as counseling or treatment), employees were more tolerant of drug screening—even when voice was absent.

Although false positives are rare in a properly conducted drug screen (Cropanzano & Konovsky, 1993), it still behooves employers to construct some backup system for correcting mistakes. Research has shown that both managers (Gomez-Mejia & Balkin, 1987) and subordinates (Cropanzano & Konovsky, 1995) prefer a program that contains some type of grievance or appeals system.

Finally, individuals are also more tolerant of drug testing if a positive test leads to rehabilitation rather than termination. Generally speaking, employees prefer at least of modicum of leniency following a positive test (Abdenour, Miner, & Weir, 1987; Cropanzano & Konovsky, 1995; Gomez-Mejia & Balkin, 1987; Kravitz & Brock, 1997; Murphy et al., 1990; Stone & Kotch, 1989; Tepper & Braun, 1995). In this context, at least, a little compassion can go a long way. However, it should be noted that the staunchest supports of drug testing are also the ones who are the most willing to use heavy-handed punishment, whereas their more skeptical counterparts prefer greater leniency (Labig, 1992).

Summary. Our brief review of different selection procedures points to an interesting phenomenon. It is true that certain techniques, such as assessment centers and work samples, have high statistical validity and are seen as fair. These instruments should be recommended. It is also true that certain other procedures have low validity (e.g., unstructured interviews and reference checks). These should probably be avoided even if they are seen as fair. The problem for organizations is that certain other techniques are apt to arouse at least some discontent. This includes the statistically valid techniques of personality assessment and biodata. This may also include, although to a lesser extent, cognitive-abilities tests, honesty tests, and drug screening. Obviously, few firms will want to abandon all of these valid options. We will return to this matter after we have discussed the consequences of using fair and unfair selection devices.

Poorer Attitudes Toward the Testing Organization

Often people who feel they were unfairly treated are likely to form negative attitudes toward the hiring organization. This discontent can lead to a loss of public goodwill and may discourage other individuals from applying for positions or purchasing the firm's goods or services. Several studies have demonstrated that selection procedures impact the reactions of job applicants (e.g., Ambrose & Rosse, 1993; Crant & Bateman, 1990; Crant & Bateman, 1993; Gilliland & Honig, 1994b; Kluger & Rothstein, 1993; Macan et al., 1994; Noe & Steffy, 1987; Robertson et al., 1991; Rosse, Miller, et al., 1996; Rosse, Ringer, et al., 1996). We need consider but two examples here. Stoffey et al. (1991) showed that "unfair" staffing practices (such as abstract cognitive-abilities tests and biographical inventories) are associated with negative attitudes about the testing organization. Likewise, Smither et al. (1993) found that job applicants had more positive attitudes toward employers who used work simulations and unstructured interviews, and less positive attitudes toward employers who used abstract cognitive-abilities tests, biodata, and personality inventories.

Job incumbents seem to react about the same as job applicants. When tested by means that they consider unfair, incumbents also report poorer work attitudes, such as lowered job satisfaction and organizational commitment (Konovsky & Cropanzano, 1991). For example, considerable research suggests that when promotion procedures are viewed as unfair, employee ill will results (Beehr & Taber, 1993; Beehr, Taber, & Walsh, 1980; Bobocel & Farrell, 1996).

One might hope that giving a person a desired job (a favorable outcome) will mitigate the ill will resulting from an unfair selection practice. Although an advantageous selection decision might do some good, it does not completely solve the problem. For example, in one mail survey conducted by Singer (1993, Study 4), it was found that even after accepting a job with an organization, individuals who believed that the selection process had been unfair had lower organizational commitment, lower job satisfaction, and felt that they were working for a less effective organization. Likewise, a field study by Gilliland (1995) found that individuals selected on the basis of questionable selection practices reported lower organizational commitment and a decreased likelihood of recommending the organization to another person. These findings were also obtained in a field experiment by Gilliland (1994). A positive outcome may not always be enough to remove the ill effects of procedural injustice.

Decreased Likelihood of Accepting a Job Offer

Earlier, we noted the economic utility of a valid selection program. However, as Boudreau and Rynes (1985) emphasized, all such benefits are contingent on quality applicants accepting the job offers. Murphy (1986) showed that if top candidates turn down offers, the utility of a valid selection system is appreciably lower. This underscores how crucial it is for organizations to attract and retain the best applicants. Otherwise, the benefits of a valid selection program could be squandered.

Many factors go into job choices, and it would be a mistake to single out any one thing, including injustice, as the key determinant. However, as we have already seen, applicants form more negative impressions of organizations following treatment that is perceived to be unfair. It should come as no surprise to realize that applicants are less predisposed to accept a job with an organization they dislike (Cropanzano, 1996). "Unfair" selection procedures cause poorer attitudes toward the company (as we discussed earlier). These poor attitudes, in turn, cause lowered job pursuit intentions. This relation between selection fairness and intention to apply for or accept a job has been demonstrated time and time again (e.g., Gilliland, 1995; Macan et al., 1994; Noe & Steffy, 1987). One way to demonstrate this finding is to tie job choice back to the testing procedures we discussed previously.

Let us begin with cognitive-abilities tests. Kluger and Rothstein (1993) found that a low score on (what was perceived to be) an unfair cognitive abilities test was more likely to cause participants to give up their job search than was a low score on a work-sample test. Similarly, Stoffey et al. (1991) found that "unfair" cognitive-abilities tests and biographical inventories were more likely to lower job pursuit intentions than were "fairer" work samples (see also Cascio & Phillips, 1979; Stone et al., 1989).

Another controversial technique is drug testing. As we have seen, at least some individuals find drug screening objectionable. In a series of role-playing experiments, Crant and Bateman (1990, 1993) and Stone and Bowden (1989) found that individuals were less likely to accept a job at an organization that had an unfair drug screening policy. Similarly, in a survey by Karren (1989), it was found that about 20% of the respondents were less prone to work at an organization that engaged in drug testing.

Still other research has examined preemployment interviews. Although generally seen as fair, Thornton (1993) found that when interviews were not conducted in an interpersonally fair manner, the likelihood of accepting a job offer dropped precipitously. This effect was most pronounced when the interviewer was perceived as the company's representative (Harn & Thornton, 1985).

Personality tests seem to be particularly problematic. Rosse, Ringer, and Miller (1996) compared applicant reactions to urinalysis, two pencil-and-paper honesty tests, a personality inventory, and a no-testing control group. They found that applicants were most likely to accept a job when they were not tested by any of these techniques. This is no surprise given the questionable nature of these screening procedures. However, individuals were least likely to pursue a job when the organization administered a personality inventory. Indeed, even urinalysis was preferred to a personality inventory.

Increased Likelihood of Legal Action

Arvey (1991, 1992) observed that the legal definition of *fairness* has been expanding steadily. This more expansive definition opens up new avenues for legal action. In fact, legal scholars are already beginning to question the use of many personnel practices (Arvey, 1992; Seymour, 1988; Westin, 1978). Thus, organizations are going to have to survive in an increasingly litigious environment. Unfairness may increase the likelihood of a lawsuit (Bies & Tyler, 1993; Sitkin & Bies, 1993a).

Although limited, some supportive data do exist. Taylor, Moghaddam, Gamble, and Zellerer (1987) found that individuals who were denied entry into a desirable group for unfair reasons were more eager to appeal the outcome. Moreover, individuals who were denied entry for fair reasons were much more accepting of the results. Likewise, in a more recent experiment, Olson-Buchanan (1996a) found that undergraduate participants were more willing to file a grievance when they believed that a simulated selection system was unfair. Latham and Finnegan (1993) had managers, applicants, and attorneys compare unstructured, panel, and structured selection interviews. Whereas applicants showed a slight preference for the unstructured variety, managers and lawyers preferred structured interviews. In part, this was because the haphazard questioning in unstructured interviews could be grounds for a lawsuit.

Poor Job Performance Among Those Hired

Although the selection system may increase or decrease the likelihood of accepting a job, it is clearly only one of many determinants. Therefore, individuals will often find themselves working for organizations even if they believe they were selected unfairly. This may create performance problems. For instance, Konovsky and Cropanzano (1991) found that job incumbents who judged a drug-screening program to be unfair had lower job performance than their coworkers who evaluated the policy more favorably. Similarly, an experiment by Gilliland (1994) found that individuals who reported being hired by a fair selection system showed higher work performance. Note again that these effects were observed among job incumbents. Thus, even bringing a person into an organization may not fully mitigate the ill effects of unfair selection. However, more research on this topic is needed before firm conclusions can be drawn.

Summary and Conclusions

What have we learned from this? Very generally speaking, applicants are suspicious of cognitive-abilities tests, personality tests, drug screens, and biographical inventories. Applicants may also dislike honesty tests, but the data here are meager. Conversely, applicants like unstructured interviews, reference checks, and various forms of work simulations (such as job samples and assessment centers). With the noteworthy exception of simulations, organizations are in a bit of a quandary. Reference checks and interviews have somewhat poor statistical validity (Hunter & Hunter, 1984; Reilly & Chao, 1982; Schmitt et al., 1984) but are seen as fairer. Cognitive-abilities tests, drug screens, biodata, and personality tests have acceptable validity but are seen as less fair. Cropanzano (1994) and Cropanzano and Konovsky (1995) termed this conundrum the "justice dilemma." A test with high validity may also be one that gives rise to a sense of injustice.

Fortunately, there are ways to resolve the justice dilemma. To understand how this is accomplished, we will next discuss some general principles of selection fairness. Based on these principles, we will see that many of the seemingly unfair testing procedures can be redesigned to engender justice and thereby avoid the ill effects of injustice.

What Makes Selection Fair?

It is instructive to consider what selection would look like in an ideal world. Schuler, Farr, and Smith (1993) described such idyllic conditions. Under such conditions the employer would openly share all of the advantages and disadvantages of working in his or her company. Moreover, each selection technique would be plainly described and carefully explained. Job applicants, for their part, would honestly describe their own strengths and weaknesses, including reasons that they should and should not be hired. Indeed, under these conditions the selection process would appear more like career counseling and less like testing.

As Schuler et al. (1993) pointed out, such a vision is "pie in the sky." Organizations and applicants have different agendas and, as such, some lack of candor is inevitable. Nevertheless, the fact that such procedures may not be fully realized should not imply that some elements of this ideal cannot be obtained. Exhibiting these positive qualities could help organizations avoid some of the negative consequences that result from perceptions of unfairness. Consistent with this, various authors have suggested ways in which justice can be added to employee selection.

Gilliland's (1993) Model

Probably the most comprehensive model is offered by Gilliland (1993; see also Schmitt & Gilliland, 1992). This model is summarized in Table 4.1. Generally speaking, Gilliland (1993) maintained that there are three sets of attributes that are essential to fair personnel selection: the formal characteristics of the personnel system, the interpersonal treatment received by the applicant, and the explanations provided regarding the system.

As shown in Table 4.1, however, each of these three major attributes is further subdivided. There are four important formal characteristics. In particular, a fair selection system should be job related, it should provide the applicant with the opportunity to perform well, it should allow for reconsideration in the case of failure, and the procedures should be consistent across all applicants. There are four important aspects of interpersonal treatment. The assessment should be conducted by an effective administrator, the system should allow for two-way communication, the questions should be appropriate to the situation at hand, and information should be provided regarding the organization. (Actually, only the first three interpersonal treatment attributes are from Gilliland. We added the fourth ourselves.) Finally, there are three aspects of proper explanations. The applicant should receive timely feedback, selection information should be provided, and honesty should be maintained.

We will consider each of these attributes below. Keep in mind, however, that Gilliland's model is relatively new, and there is more evidence for some of these procedural rules than for others. Nonetheless, the available research is supportive. Gilliland (1995) conducted a content analysis of individuals' open-ended responses regarding their experiences as job applicants. He found that these responses sorted nicely into the various procedural justice categories. In fact, Gilliland and Honig (1994a) devised a reliable self-report instrument based on this model. Moreover, the Gilliland framework is highly consistent with similar work by Schuler (1993b), Thornton (1993), and Bies and Moag (1986). The difference, however, is that Gilliland's model is more comprehensive and subsumes much of the earlier research. Given this evidence, we will review the existing evidence and indicate areas where additional research is needed.

Job Relatedness. The first characteristic of a fair selection system is that it should assess criteria that are related to the job in question. That is, the candidate should be able to clearly deduce what characteristics are being assessed and why. Schuler (1993b) called this attribute "transparency." Considerable research has demonstrated that work simulations, such as job samples and assessment centers, are very transparent and, therefore, are also

Table 4.1   Methods of Increasing the Social Justice of Selection Procedures

---

I. Formal Characteristics of the Selection Procedures
   A. Job Relatedness
   B. Opportunity to Perform
   C. Reconsideration Opportunity
   D. Consistency of Administration
II. Interpersonal Treatment During the Selection Process
   A. Interpersonal Effectiveness of the Administrator
   B. Two-Way Communication
   C. Propriety of Questions
   D. Provide Information Regarding the Organization
III. Providing Explanations Regarding the Selection System
   A. Feedback
   B. Selection Information
   C. Honesty

SOURCE: Adapted from Gilliland (1993, p. 700).

considered fair (Bourgeois et al., 1975; Dodd, 1977; Robertson & Kandola, 1982; Schmitt et al., 1993; Schuler & Fruhner, 1993). Biographical inventories and some personality tests, on the other hand, are less transparent and are therefore considered less fair (Ambrose & Rosse, 1993; Kluger & Rothstein, 1993; Rosse, Miller, & Stecher, 1994; Rosse, Ringer, et al., 1996; Smither et al., 1993).

When a test is "transparent," its job relevance is readily apparent to the applicant. For less transparent tests, the job relevance is further removed. Research has shown that job relevance is one of the most important factors in determining selection fairness (Gilliland, 1995; Nevo, 1993; Rosse, Ringer, et al., 1996; Rynes & Connerley, 1993; Singer, 1993, Studies 1 - 3; Smither et al., 1993; Stoffey et al., 1991). For example, it is obvious to all that typing is an important secretarial skill and, therefore, to become a secretary one should pass a typing test. However, it is less clear why a secretary needs to be able to rotate abstract figures in his or her head and, therefore, a spatial-abilities test would seem less job relevant and less fair. An even stronger version of this was demonstrated in a study by Schmidt et al. (1977). Schmidt and his colleagues had job candidates complete a written test of mechanical ability and also an actual work sample. Both of these tests were assessing more or less the same psychological construct. Nonetheless, applicants greatly preferred the work sample and tended to dislike the paper-and-pencil test.

Opportunity to Perform. Applicants prefer selection procedures that allow them to "show their stuff" by demonstrating appropriate job-relevant competencies. One interesting investigation of this phenomenon was conducted by Hayes et al. (1995). Generally speaking, previous work has shown that applicants like structured interview techniques (Latham & Finnegan, 1993), although they seem to prefer the unstructured variety (Schuler, 1993a). Despite this, Hayes and his colleagues (1995) offered an important caveat. Able-bodied applicants preferred the technique more strongly than their disabled counterparts. Why? According to Hayes and associates, structured interviews contain a well-defined set of questions that may be circumscribed by a formal job analysis. This job analysis is likely to have been based on an examination of able-bodied job incumbents. As such, disabled applicants may perceive that they lack a suitable opportunity to explore their unique competencies and to explain their own nontraditional performance strategies.

Much of the concern over performance opportunities seems to be based on applicants' sense of personal control. According to Schuler (1993b) and Thornton (1993), certain techniques, especially those that the applicant does not or cannot understand, compromise this feeling of personal agency. For example, one study by Kluger and Rothstein (1993) found that individuals perceived that they had little control over their scores on cognitive-abilities tests. As such, these tests were perceived to be unfair. On the other hand, Kluger and Rothstein also found that applicants perceived greater control over their scores on biographical inventories. Thus, biodata was seen as more fair.

Reconsideration Opportunity. Gilliland (1993) suggested that staffing procedures are fairer to the extent that the individual is given a second chance to do well on the test. Although the proposition is reasonable, as yet there is little supportive empirical evidence, at least insofar as selection is concerned. In fact, in one field study, Gilliland (1995) found that reconsideration opportunity was not a particularly important factor in determining the fairness of selection decisions.

However, there are other staffing decisions besides selection, and it is here that reconsideration opportunities may become more salient. For example, incumbents are also assessed. One noteworthy example of this is the case of employee drug screening. Individuals who test positive for illicit substances may be subjected to some kind of punitive action. Field research shows that drug testing is more acceptable when it allows for some type of follow-up test (Murphy et al., 1990) or grievance procedure (Cropanzano & Konovsky, 1995; Gomez-Mejia & Balkin, 1987). Organizations also assess individuals in order to ascertain their suitability for promotion. Generally speaking, promotion activities are considered to be far more fair when they allow for future reconsideration (McEnrue, 1989).

Consistency of Administration. Another characteristic of fair selection procedures is that they are consistently administered (Van den Bos, 1996). Sloppy procedures that allow for favoritism and racial bias, for example, are very much disliked. One good example of this comes in research reported by Singer (1993). In a series of studies, Singer (1993, Studies 1-3) found that more justice was perceived when the organization used the same selection procedures for every applicant. It is also instructive to examine the types of inconsistencies that make staffing techniques unfair. Singer reported less perceived fairness when selection decisions were based on such considerations as nepotism, sex, age, or race.

Interpersonal Effectiveness of the Administrator. Fundamentally, selection procedures are operated by people. Some people are better at this than others. Research by Liden and Parsons (1986) and Schmitt and Coyle (1976) found that individuals preferred interviewers who were of an affable disposition. Similarly, Schmitt and Coyle reported that interviewer warmth and thoughtfulness were strongly related to positive perceptions of the organization and applicant intent to accept a job offer. Further supportive results were obtained in field studies by Iles and Robertson (1989) and Singer (1993, Studies 1-3).

Bies and Moag (1986) also found that individuals preferred being treated with courtesy. Rudeness, interruptions, and harassment were all seen as unacceptable. As commonsensical as this advice appears, a full 23% of the Bies and Moag sample mentioned it as a concern. Hence, this problem seems to be reasonably widespread.

The interpersonal effectiveness dimension is quite important but fairly broad. As such, it is extremely difficult to pin down the specific behaviors that convey a sense of interpersonal dignity. To alleviate this ambiguity, Harn and Thornton (1985) conducted a survey of 105 graduating college seniors who were currently experiencing recruitment interviews. Their findings are especially important because they allow us to identify the particular behaviors indicative of interpersonal effectiveness.

Interestingly enough, Harn and Thornton (1985) showed that a good recruiter acts like a good counselor. Three behavioral dimensions, in particular, were related to applicant outcomes. The first dimension was nondirective counseling behavior. Applicants preferred interviewers who made reference to the job candidate's feelings, summarized their statements, and made interesting comments. The second dimension was listening skills. Interviewers were preferred to the extent that they talked less, nodded when the candidate spoke, and set aside time for questions. The third dimension was the amount of information provided. Applicants want an open and honest exchange (Bies & Moag, 1986; Schuler, 1993b; Wanous, 1993). So respect and truthfulness are clearly related. The importance of providing honest information is discussed in more detail later.

Two-Way Communication. According to Gilliland (1993), two-way communication is an advantageous characteristic of the interpersonal interaction.

Effective two-way communication allows the applicant a sense of voice regarding the selection decision. Schuler (1993b) referred to this as "participation." In the simplest and most straightforward sense, participation exists when a job candidate can insert a reasonable amount of interpersonal input into the selection situation. This requires little more than allowing people their "say." For example, Smither et al. (1993), Schuler (1993b), and Thornton (1993) all maintained that individuals prefer unstructured interviews because in such a context, the applicants have a clear opportunity to "speak their piece" and present information they feel is relevant. Moreover, a series of three surveys by Singer (1993, Studies 1-3) also attested to the importance of open communication.

Participation can be conceptualized more broadly than this, however. In particular, fairness might be enhanced if organizations involve employees in policy formulation. Once more, available evidence supports this proposition. For example, in a field study by Gomez-Mejia and Balkin (1987), managers rated drug testing programs as more effective to the extent that subordinates were involved in their design and implementation. Similar findings were obtained in a field study reported by Cropanzano and Konovsky (1995).

Propriety of Questions. Another aspect of selection fairness is the propriety of the questions. In one field study, for example, Bies and Moag (1986) found that many interviewers simply behaved inappropriately. Some of their questions were seen as invasive and improper, and applicants therefore reacted negatively toward the organization. In another study, Rynes and Connerley (1993) also found that the content of the questions was a major determinant of interview satisfaction. This concern over propriety is not limited only to interviews. For example, research by Rosse, Ringer, et al. (1996) and Smither et al. (1993) suggested that personality and biodata items can sometimes be quite personal. As such, people often react negatively to them.

Propriety has a second manifestation. In the Bies and Moag (1986) sample, about 10% of the applicants expressed concerns over prejudicial statements. Again, as obvious as it may seem, some interviewers were unable to avoid overtly sexist or racist language.

Information Regarding the Job and the Organization. Although not explicitly mentioned by Gilliland (1993), other research suggests that selection systems are considered fairer to the extent that the employer explains the job requirements and the organization itself (Singer, 1993, Studies 1-3). Other evidence relevant to this point has been collected in investigations of Realistic Job Previews (RJPs). When conducting an RJP, the organization provides the applicant with an honest assessment of the pertinent tasks and the organization in general, even when such information does not reflect well on the company.

Considerable research has shown that the provision of this candid and honest information can enhance attitudes toward the organization (Liden & Parsons, 1986; Schmitt & Coyle, 1976; Singer, 1993, Study 4; Wanous, 1993) and reduce subsequent turnover (McEvoy & Cascio, 1985; Premack & Wanous, 1985). Some research also suggests that RJPs are especially effective when they are tailored to the particular needs and concerns of each individual job applicant (Thornton, 1993). In general, this work suggests that organizations should be candid and open about both their strengths and weaknesses.

Feedback. Schuler (1993b), Gilliland (1993), and Iles and Robertson (1989) also recommended that organizations offer applicants timely and useful feedback. Applicants especially prefer selection systems that provide them with feedback concerning their own performance. When such information is lacking, the system is seen as less acceptable (Liden & Parsons, 1986; Lounsbury, Bobrow, & Jensen, 1989; Schmitt & Coyle, 1976). This effect is not limited to the United States. Schuler (1993b) reviewed several German studies demonstrating that applicants respond more favorably to selection procedures that offer them candid information.

Besides containing performance information, Rynes (1993) noted that the feedback should have some other characteristics as well. Applicants also want information that is detailed and specific (Schmitt & Coyle, 1976). Cryptic platitudes are of little use. For example, Rynes (1993) presented evidence indicating that candidates prefer feedback that allows them to focus their search. No one wants to waste valuable time and energy on an organization where they have no realistic chance of being hired. Those energies could better be directed toward those employers with whom one still has a reasonable chance. Moreover, this specific information should have the added benefit of differentiating one organization from another. If all employers look the same, then the individual has little basis for making an informed decision.

Fair feedback is also given as swiftly as possible. For example, Rynes, Bretz, and Gerhart (1991) found that when feedback was delayed, job applicants tended to dislike an organization and became more likely to decline job offers. Similar findings were obtained by Arvey, Gordon, Massengill, & Mussio (1975).

Selection Information. According to Gilliland (1993), individuals react more positively when a selection procedure has been explained to them (see also, Gilliland, 1994). For example, in one study by Bies and Moag (1986), applicants preferred interviewers who provided adequate justifications when something negative occurred. When something went wrong, the applicant received an explanation. Similar results were also obtained in a role-playing experiment conducted by Bies and Shapiro (1988). Consistent with this, Crant and Bateman (1990), Konovsky and Cropanzano (1991), Stone and Bommer (1990), and Stone, Stone, and Pollack (1990) all found that drug screening programs were perceived to be fairer to the extent that they were adequately justified. Justifications also matter in the case of promotions. In two studies, Bobocel and Farrell (1996) found that white males were more accepting of a disadvantageous promotion decision if a decent justification was provided.

For an explanation to work, it should be seen as adequate (Bobocel & Farrell, 1996; Shapiro et al., 1994). Simply acknowledging the problem without providing an explanation seems to actually heighten resentment (Ambrose & Rosse, 1993). This consideration led Shapiro and her colleagues (1994) to examine the qualities that make a justification effective. In a series of studies, these researchers found that the reasonableness and specificity of the provided information was the most important determinant of explanation adequacy. Interpersonal sensitivity was somewhat less important. Shapiro and her colleagues found something else as well. When a rejection was very severe—that is, when an applicant wanted the job a great deal—even adequate explanations were of limited utility in reducing ill will. Explanations seem to work best when the damage is minimal.

There is another downside to supplying justifications. If not provided judiciously, they can have ill effects on the organization. For example, Crant and Bateman (1990) found that research participants were more accepting of a drug-testing program if the firm in question was having a substance abuse problem. In this case, screening seemed appropriate. On the other hand, those same participants reported not wanting to work at such a firm. All things being equal, wouldn't you prefer to work in an organization where substance abuse was not an issue? Companies need to use care in providing their accounts.

Honesty. Organizations should avoid deception (Schuler, 1993b). Lying gets job applicants very angry. In fact, in one study by Bies and Moag (1986), lying was the most commonly mentioned reason for a sense of injustice. Americans do not seem to be the only people who react negatively to dishonesty. Singer (1993) found that New Zealand students (Study 1), New Zealand managers (Study 2), and Australian managers (Study 3) also react negatively to dishonest selection procedures. Field studies in the United States by Liden and Parsons (1986) and Schmitt and Coyle (1976) also attest to the importance of sincere interviewers.

Summary

So far, this chapter has attempted to address two objectives. First, we reviewed a variety of commonly used assessment techniques from the perspective of organizational justice. In doing so, we observed that a justice dilemma often exists, whereby the most valid tests are not necessarily the ones that are considered to be the most fair. We next explored different characteristics that a fair staffing system should have, such as job relevance and interpersonal sensitivity. Now we want to return to the particular selection techniques that we discussed earlier. In light of our fairness attributes, we will consider how organizations can design fairer staffing procedures.

How Employers Can Make
Their Staffing Practices Fairer

So far in this chapter, we have seen that test fairness is important. We have also seen that many organizations are not using fair selection procedures. Consequently, they risk various negative consequences as a result of their assessment techniques. To help address this concern, this section will examine three ways in which organizations can improve their selection procedures without compromising validity.

Substitute Unfair Tests With Fair Tests

One easy solution to the justice dilemma is to understand that it does not always, or even usually, exist. Despite the troubling exceptions we have already discussed, valid tests are generally seen as fairer than their less valid counterparts (Harris et al., 1990; Rynes & Connerley, 1993; Smither et al., 1993). As a result, there are some assessment techniques that rate high on both validity and fairness. Thus, organizations have the opportunity to substitute an "unfair" assessment technique for a "fair" one.

Substitution requires an understanding of which tests are considered the most acceptable. We can gain some guidance from our earlier review. First, we know which procedures are most likely to be found in need of substitution: cognitive-abilities tests, personality tests, biographical inventories, and drug screens. However, we also have an idea of which procedures we can use as substitutes. Some consistently safe techniques include interviews, work samples, and assessment centers. Let us omit interviews for the time being because of their spotty validation record (Huffcutt & Woehr, 1992) and focus instead on work samples and assessment centers. When compared to cognitive-abilities tests, both of these tools yield comparable validity coefficients, smaller ethnic differences, and more positive perceptions of fairness. As such, work samples and assessment centers should be seriously considered as alternatives to other instruments.

However, many potential substitutes will not be as valid as work simulations. For example, in order to increase perceptions of justice, one could exchange an "unfair" biodata survey for a "fair" unstructured interview. This would probably have the desirable effect of increased social justice but would also have the negative side effect of compromised selection validity. If organizations do choose a substitution approach, they should be careful to select a valid alternative. This is not always done. Take, for example, the case of the General Aptitude Test Battery (GATB). Among other things, the GATB measures cognitive ability. As one might expect, the GATB is a valid predictor of performance across a wide variety of jobs (Hartigan & Wigdor, 1989; Hunter & Hunter, 1984). As a result of this evidence, the Public Employment Service once planned to screen all job applicants using the GATB. However, as Wigdor and Sackett (1993) discussed, the GATB is in abeyance as a result of competing fairness concerns. On the one hand, the GATB shows large differences between blacks at one extreme versus whites and Asians at the other. As the actual job performance differences are smaller than the test score differences, many are concerned that the test would treat blacks unfairly. On the other hand, because the GATB is equally valid for all ethnic groups, others have argued that score adjustments are unfair to white and Asian applicants. Thus, a valid test is not currently in use. Instead, the Public Employment Service is using an unstructured interview; a procedure with much lower validity.

Even if the substitution is done in a reasonable way, it still remains only a limited solution. For example, work simulations can be quite expensive relative to pencil-and-paper inventories (Thornton & Byham, 1982; Thornton & Cleveland, 1990). Moreover, although simulations are valid across a wide variety of jobs, the same simulation is not. That is, a simulation used to select managers will be somewhat different than one used to select pipe fitters. Thus, many simulations would be needed, and this may not be economically feasible when filling many different positions.

There is a broader issue as well. Simulations clearly measure job relevant traits. However, it is not clear that they measure all job relevant traits. For example, drug screens and personality tests may assess some additional dimensions not measured in work simulations. The choice of a selection instrument should not be "either-or." Rather, it would be preferable if organizations could use the techniques that add a useful increment to the validity coefficient. Strict substitution, which would preclude the use of a variety of procedures, would limit the employer's ability to tailor an optimal selection program. To address these concerns, it would be helpful to provide guidelines for redesigning unacceptable selection tests to make them fairer. It is to this suggestion that we now turn.

Modifying Existing Instruments

Rather than substituting current techniques with new ones, employers may wish to modify existing techniques. Certain selection techniques appear unfair because they do not seem job relevant (i.e., they lack transparency) or because they ask personal and invasive questions (i.e., question propriety does not exist). For instruments of this kind, modifications can sometimes be made in order to produce fairness. We have already alluded to examples of this. For example, Jones (1991) found that if the invasive and nonjob-related items were dropped, personality tests were seen as fairer.

Similar conclusions were reached from research on cognitive-abilities tests. As mentioned earlier, Smither and his colleagues (1993) found that when cognitive-abilities tests used items that were concrete rather than abstract, more positive reactions were engendered. One potential problem with this, however, was raised by Rynes and Connerley (1993): These authors cautioned that specific tests may fail to capture the general abilities necessary for adequate job performance. Currently, there is little evidence available to assess this issue. However, the data that exist show that this may not be a major problem. Research by Hattrup, Schmitt, and Landis (1992) found that various commercially available tests of job-specific skills actually captured broad cognitive abilities such as verbal reasoning and numerical ability. Thus, it should be possible to make tests more transparent without losing the essential constructs of interest. Nevertheless, Rynes and Connerley's (1993) caveat remains an important one.

Limits of the Modification Approach. Personnel assessment techniques can be modified and improved in a variety of ways. Changing an existing system is a common and viable option. However, like substitution, the modification approach will not work in all situations. Modifications can be costly. For example, an organization may have to develop job-specific cognitive-abilities tests for several different positions. Certain modifications may also compromise the test's validity. Advance notice, for example, seems to be a modification that improves the perceived fairness of drug testing. However, it also offers drug users an easy opportunity to temporarily abstain and thereby test negative. We can see that modifying existing procedures is an important tool. However, it is one that must be used judiciously.

Decreasing Outcome Negativity

In an earlier chapter, we noted that individuals are most likely to feel unfairly treated when they are assigned a negative outcome by an unfair procedure. When the procedure is fair, therefore, individuals report more justice—even when the outcome is negative. Under certain conditions, the reverse of this may also be true. Even when the procedures are unfair, individuals perceive relative fairness so long as the outcome is not particularly negative (Gilliland, 1993; Schmitt & Gilliland, 1992).

This fact suggests another way of mitigating the ill effects of an unfair staffing procedure. Under certain conditions, it may be possible to reduce outcome negativity. When this is done, even some "unfair" procedures may fail to produce a sense of injustice. In one field study, Cropanzano and Konovsky (1995) tested this possibility in the context of workplace drug screening. These researchers found that if the organization did not take a punitive approach to drug testing (i.e., outcome negativity was perceived to be low), individuals rated the drug screening program as fair even if it did not entail advance notice, lacked adequate justification, and lacked employee participation. In this instance, we can see that the organization was allowed a questionable screening procedure so long as it did not use this procedure to inflict serious harm.

However, a few caveats deserve mention. For one thing, some procedures were always desired, even when outcomes were not negative. For example, workers always expected a procedure that was accurate and that offered an opportunity for appeal. There is another problem as well. Clearly, it is not always possible to reduce outcome negativity. For example, selection typically involves a hire-don't hire decision. In this case, it is difficult to reduce the impact of an unsuccessful job attempt. These are two important limitations. It seems, therefore, that reducing outcome negativity can complement substitution and modification, but it is unlikely to replace either of the other two approaches.

Conclusions

In this chapter, we reviewed several staffing procedures from the perspective of organizational justice. We saw how some procedures are widely desired whereas others are widely disliked. Unfortunately, some "unfair" techniques are also those with the highest validity. Further, using a staffing method that is seen as unfair can cause a variety of negative outcomes such as lower morale, fewer applicants accepting jobs, and the threat of litigation. We, therefore, examined various methods of improving staffing fairness without compromising test validity. Whereas each technique is individually limited, taken together they offer an arsenal of alternatives.

There is a bottom line to all of this. Injustice is destructive to both job candidates and to the organization. It is best for all involved to eliminate unfairness by using socially valid selection techniques. But concerns about justice should not stop after a person has accepted a job. Once an individual is hired by an organization, his or her relationship has only begun. Employers need to produce fairness in the way they treat people on the job. We will begin to examine this treatment in our next chapter.

5 Organizational Justice and Performance Evaluation

TEST AND TRIAL METAPHORS

In Chapter 4, we discussed how people enter into an organization. We noted that some selection procedures were perceived by applicants as fair, whereas others were perceived to be unfair. In many respects, organizations benefit from using fair procedures and avoiding unfair ones. As important as this initial staffing appears, however, it should be obvious that selection is only the initial stage in an individual's relationship with an organization. Other events and incidents follow, and these build on the seminal staffing episode. People's relationships with their employers are constantly being shaped, cut, and reshaped over a series of events. We can think of these events as "justice episodes," because individuals try to judge the fairness of each incident. In this chapter, we will discuss a different justice episode or, rather, a recurring family of episodes. Our concern in Chapter 5 is with performance appraisal (PA).

That justice is important in PA we can have little doubt (e.g., Alexander & Ruderman, 1987; Folger et al., 1992; Greenberg, 1986; Korsgaard, Roberson, & Rymph, 1996; Taylor, Tracy, Renard, Harrison, & Carroll, 1995). However, we came to this realization quite recently. This is somewhat surprising because

PA research had an auspicious enough start. Thorndike (1949), for example, declared that "practicality" is a central concern for any performance evaluation instrument. It is clear from Thorndike's discussion of this issue that an important component of practicality was the response of the raters and ratees who give life to a PA tool. These responses, in turn, are at least partially determined by justice. However, for the next couple of decades, social responses to formal PA programs were shunted into the sidelines of academic research. With some important exceptions that we will review later, Thorndike's "practicality" was not a central research focus.

Academics instead turned their attention to the psychometric aspects of performance ratings (for reviews, see Folger et al., 1992; Ilgen, 1993; Latham, 1986). As Ilgen (1993) noted, this development was not altogether a bad one. After all, it is not unreasonable to see if something *can* be done before asking if it *should* be done. Or, to state the matter differently, if it is impossible to obtain reasonably accurate performance ratings, then individuals' reactions are somewhat moot. Furthermore, there has always been a strong quantitative tradition within Industrial and Organizational Psychology (see Katzell & Austin, 1992, for an interesting discussion of this and related issues). So all in all, it made good sense that a measurement perspective would come to preeminence in PA research. We call this quantitative orientation the *test metaphor.*

How PA Should Be Done: The Test Metaphor as an Academic Ideal

What Is the Test Metaphor?

The test metaphor is so named because it views PA simply as another type of psychological test. PA is "fair" to the extent that it accurately assesses performance. A good PA instrument is a good test in that it offers a valid representation of how a person is actually behaving. Banks and Roberson (1985) summed up the matter explicitly by stating that "accurate appraisers may well be those who become expert at applying principles of test development" (p. 129). DeVries, Morrison, Shullman, and Gerlach (1981) added that "today's reality makes psychometric issues surrounding performance measurement more relevant than ever" (p. 28). Issues of psychometric quality are of paramount importance. The test metaphor has therefore resulted in a great deal of research targeted at reducing sundry measurement errors, such as leniency and halo.

Historically, these measurement concerns have manifested themselves in two ways. The older tradition focuses on the psychometric quality of various PA formats. Although a variety of formats have been tried (e.g., Behaviorally Anchored Rating Scales, Management by Objectives, Behavioral Expectation Scales, etc.), no one format has yielded consistently higher validity than any other (for reviews, see DeVries et al., 1981; Kane & Lawler, 1979; Landy & Farr, 1980). When format research failed to produce sufficient quantitative purity, academic work turned inward and examined the rater as a new kind of psychometric tool. As a result, more recent attention has shifted from aspects of the format to the cognitive processes of the rater. This second tradition examined the rater's cognitive structures to determine the source of PA bias (for reviews, see DeNisi & Williams, 1988; Ilgen & Feldman, 1983). A detailed review of these two measurement traditions is beyond the scope of this book (but for a comparable discussion of these issues, see Dipboye, 1995; Folger et al., 1992, Ilgen, 1993). Besides, as we noted earlier, several excellent reviews already exist. For now, it should suffice to note that although the format and cognitive approaches have slightly different emphases, they share a common (and reasonable) concern with the accuracy of the ratings and are somewhat less focused on the social context in which these ratings occur.

Limitations of the Test Metaphor

Advocates of the test metaphor tacitly assume that organizations are more or less rational. Specifically, organizations decide to pursue certain goals, such as to manufacture a particular product line or offer a certain service. These general goals require that the work be divided up among various individuals and work teams. Consequently, everyone is given some smaller subgoal, the completion of which will help contribute to the overall organizational objective. From such a rational task allocation, it follows that each individual can be appraised according to what he or she has accomplished with respect to these rational standards.

Within this kind of intellectual system it makes perfectly good sense to deemphasize personal responses, interpersonal relationships, and other social considerations. If some rational and scientific standard of truth is assumed to exist, then all other considerations simply introduce test bias. Thus, social considerations are at best irrelevant and at worst, bothersome. A good example of how this perspective can manifest itself was provided by Folger and Lewis (1993). Folger and Lewis put forward evidence indicating that employee self-appraisals are seen as fair by participants. However, self-appraisals are also more lenient than supervisory and peer ratings (Campbell & Lee, 1988). Thus, self-appraisals are further away from the rational standards (i.e., they are less valid) and are not recommended for administrative decisions.

Once again, let us reemphasize that the test metaphor makes sense if one thinks of PA as a special type of psychological assessment. After all, is there any reader who prefers inaccurate evaluations (despite Ilgen's, 1993, insightful demonstration that we sometimes should be so disposed)? The devil, however, is in the details, or in this particular case, in the assumptions. As we shall see, certain tacit assumptions weaken the test metaphor and send us searching for a complementary perspective (for a more detailed discussion of these issues, the reader is referred to Folger et al., 1992, pp. 130-137).

Assumption 1: Work Arrangements Allow for Reliable and Valid Performance Assessment. For any psychological test to work, respondents must begin with a reasonably valid knowledge base. Their ratings are then based on this expertise. In PA terms, a valid knowledge base would suggest that the rater both understands and has had the opportunity to observe either task-related behaviors (i.e., the means by which the job is done), job outputs (i.e., the ends that are achieved), or both (Kane & Lawler, 1979).

Unfortunately, as Lee (1985) noted, many jobs are not constituted in a way that allows enough valid observational opportunities. For example, many service jobs do not yield a tangible output (e.g., therapy) and are difficult to evaluate critically. Also, more and more people work off-site, even at home, where they cannot be directly observed. Further, in order to respond more adaptively to a dynamic environment, many manufacturing jobs have lower levels of standardization. The manufacturing process itself can change rapidly (Jaikumar, 1986). This makes it difficult for managers to know, much less observe, the critical worker behaviors.

Of course, this does not mean that all, or even most, jobs cannot be reliably observed. In many cases, supervisors do have access to either outputs or processes. Under these circumstances, this first assumption can be reasonably met. However, for many other jobs, this is not the case. One central foundation of traditional PA is absent.

Assumption 2: Raters Can Assess Performance Accurately. Human beings have been described as "cognitive misers" (Fiske & Taylor, 1984), because when we make social judgments we tend to trade quality for quantity. That is, we have so many judgments to make that our cognitive apparatus is built for speed. Essentially, we make inferences about people by putting them into categories (e.g., good vs. bad performer). This process works well most of the time, but it can still serve to diminish the accuracy of performance ratings. In fact, considerable research has shown that this is, in fact, the case (DeNisi, Cafferty, & Meglino, 1984; DeNisi & Williams, 1988; Feldman, 1981; Ilgen & Feldman, 1983; Lord & Foti, 1986).

It is not that performance judgments are useless. Rather, human informa-
tion-processing strategies seem to put an upper limit on our accuracy. For
example, in one study, Borman (1978) videotaped a simulation of managers
handling a problem subordinate. This paradigm allowed Borman to construct
"true scores" of effective and ineffective performance. Borman then trained
raters and had them view the tapes. He even went so far as to reduce memory
effects by allowing people to view the tape repeatedly. The results were
intriguing. Raters did show solid levels of validity. Thus, in an actual organization, their ratings would probably have been useful. However, even under
these ideal conditions, raters still showed some marked disagreement. Our
rating skills are good (under optimal conditions), but they are nowhere near
perfect. Borman's findings were replicated in a field study by Wexley and Gier
(1989) that examined trained judges who were rating the performance of
participants in an amateur ski competition. Wexley and Gier found that even
the ratings of these experts, who had no other task but to observe the skiers,
still showed considerable disagreement.

We can see from this research that decent levels of psychometric quality can
be achieved if the ratings are made under appropriate circumstances. The test
metaphor is useful for helping practitioners to understand these conditions.
However, our accuracy is far from perfect. Thus, it would be helpful to
supplement the test metaphor with an additional framework for understanding the social context in which these imperfect ratings are made. Put
differently, the test metaphor is useful insofar as it goes, but it does not go far
enough.

Assumption 3: A Rational, Unitary Criterion Exists. Science can do a good job
of telling us how to measure something. It cannot, however, tell us *what* we
should be measuring. This "what" question can only be answered with respect
to someone's values (Keeley, 1983; Perelman, 1967; Simon, 1983). Thorndike
(1949), for example, explicitly noted that this "ultimate criterion" is a theoretical construct about which two reasonable people can differ. Whenever we
assign someone a performance rating, we are making a value judgment that
certain kinds of behaviors are more laudable than others. There are competing
values and perspectives about what should be assessed (Austin & Villanova,
1992). The upshot of all of this is that, even if we possessed a PA instrument
that was 100% accurate, someone might still believe it best not to use it, or to
measure something else, or to measure nothing at all. This is all a question of
values and there are many views about what is important.

If one value is, existentially speaking, as good as any other, then how do
organizations select certain things to measure. As discussed by Pfeffer (1981)
and Folger et al. (1992), the most powerful constituency (usually upper
management) simply imposes their values on everyone else. Thus, what gets
assessed is not scientific truth, but rather the things that are valued by the

powers that be. Unfortunately, as noted by Folger and Lewis (1993), these things will not necessarily make for the most effective organization. A performance evaluation system that does not take into account these competing perspectives and multiple values may be scientifically precise but socially unrealistic.

How PA Is Really Done: The
Political Metaphor as an Organizational Reality

As the previous description illustrates, academics have proposed a clear and more or less straightforward solution to the problems of performance evaluation: Take out the error and keep the truth. Let PA be guided by a cold but balanced scientific objectivity. We have also seen, however, that the image of the rater as a scientist-test developer is somewhat incomplete due to three tacit assumptions.

If PA does not offer such a scientific ideal, what perspective might offer a more accurate account? PA can be more fully understood by taking into account the rough-and-tumble organizational context in which these evaluations occur (Ferris & Judge, 1991; Folger et al., 1992). Organizations can be stormy places where people are driven by competing demands, goals, interests, and concerns. Accurate evaluations comprise only one such goal, and it may not even be a particularly important one (Longnecker, Sims, & Gioia, 1987). Next, we will discuss two aspects of real-world performance evaluation: (a) They are often sloppily done and (b) they are done in a political context.

The Sloppy Management of
Many PA Programs

It is difficult to describe organizational performance evaluations without taking note of the frequent poor management that characterizes such programs. Whereas senior managers profess to support PA (Patz, 1975), people in the lower ranks tend to disagree. Field research by Napier and Latham (1986, Study 1) indicated that supervisors perceived that subordinates' performance ratings did not actually affect pay raises or promotion opportunities. Supervisors also saw few consequences for conducting either decent or poor performance evaluations. There were no rewards for doing a good job rating someone's performance. Instead, Napier and Latham (1986, Study 2) found that raters actually believed that negative performance feedback would decrease employee morale and endanger the supervisor's own promotional opportunities. In general, Napier and Latham's (1986) respondents felt that accurate PA was not a very high managerial priority. Similar observations were also made by Longnecker and his colleagues (1987).

Perhaps the most unambiguous evidence for this discontent is illustrated in the dearth of rater training. Evidence shows that training can teach supervisors to conduct more effective PA interviews. (For quantitative evidence the reader is referred to French, Kay, & Meyer, 1966; Hillery & Wexley, 1974; Ivancevich, 1982; Nemeroff & Cosentino, 1979, and Taylor et al., 1995. For case studies, the reader is referred to Beer, Ruh, Dawson, McCaa, & Kavanagh, 1978; Gellerman & Hodgson, 1988.) Despite this evidence, many organizations do not supply sufficient training (Locher & Teel, 1977).

The net result of this inattention is a corrosive sloppiness. Often, PAs are not even conducted (Landy, Barnes, & Murphy, 1978). When they are held at all, PA interviews are often quite brief and may not even be scheduled in advance (Lawler, Mohrman, & Resnick, 1984). Further, managers tend to inflate performance ratings, often wildly so (Longnecker et al., 1987). For example, in one study by Pearce and Porter (1986), typical ratings were so high that workers thought of a "satisfactory" score as negative. At times, the ratings become so lenient that the resulting lack of variance renders them almost useless (Gellerman & Hodgson, 1988).

Interestingly, managers may not be aware of just how bad the problem can become. Several field studies have found that whereas supervisors see their appraisal interviews as participative, supportive, and planful, ratees see these same interviews as brief, vague, and generally less helpful (Fulk, Brief, & Barr, 1985; Ilgen, Peterson, Martin, & Boescher, 1981; Nemeroff & Wexley, 1979). Perhaps the best summary of the matter was provided by Lawler et al., (1984): "Performance appraisals seem to be events that focus on performance and content important to appraisers, take place in a relatively short period of time, and are not, according to subordinates, necessarily scheduled in advance" (p. 28).

Nowhere is this sloppiness more evident than in a phenomenon that Beer (1981) and Porter, Lawler, and Hackman (1975) termed the *vanishing performance appraisal*. Supervisors tend to indicate that they have conducted detailed and thorough appraisal interviews, whereas their supposedly "appraised" subordinates will report that they have not been evaluated for some time. The two parties cannot even agree as to whether or not an appraisal has taken place! Obviously, one cannot expect particularly profound consequences from something perceived as a nonevent.

As disinterested as senior management often appears, PA is extremely important to the people being appraised. When PA interviews are poorly conducted, ratees report heightened levels of anxiety, dissatisfaction, and injustice (Burke, Weitzel, & Weir, 1978; Burke & Wilcox, 1969; Fletcher & Williams, 1976; Greller, 1975; Greller, 1978; Kay, Meyer, & French, 1965;

Korsgaard & Roberson, 1995; Korsgaard et al., 1996; Taylor et al., 1995). This volatile mix of employee concern and managerial disregard places the rater in a precarious position. If the rater gives a negative evaluation, then he or she can expect nasty interpersonal consequences from a disgruntled coworker and limited support from his or her own boss. In this context, PA becomes a political dance, in which both the rater and the ratee bend, fold, tear, spindle, and mutilate the system in order to accomplish their personal objectives. In this fashion, performance evaluations become politically charged (Ferris & Judge, 1991; Ferris, Russ, & Fandt, 1989), and rating accuracy becomes less important (Ferris, Fedor, Chachere, & Pondy, 1989; Kennedy, 1980).

How and Why Politics Is in the PA Process

The trick in organizational politics is for one person to exert his or her agenda through pushing, pulling, or otherwise cajoling another person into going along. In the simplest and most common case, PA involves two people: a supervisor-rater and a subordinate-ratee. Each of these individuals has his or her own agenda. The supervisor wants high performance, and the subordinate wants high ratings. Neither individual is particularly concerned with rating accuracy, except to the extent that it furthers their individual goals.

Politics and the Supervisor. Giving negative feedback is an arduous and distasteful task (Baron, 1993; McGregor, 1957), for which managers may expect little organizational support and few rewards (Napier & Latham, 1986). In the short term, an accurate but negative rating may do a supervisor more harm than good. Small wonder that raters tend to bend the system (Patz, 1975).

Perhaps the most intriguing evidence for this comes from qualitative research carried out by Longnecker et al., (1987). These researchers conducted a series of interviews with 60 business executives. Longnecker and his colleagues concluded that "political considerations were *nearly always* part of the executive evaluation process" (p. 185, [italics added]). Supervisor-appraisers inflated or deflated their evaluations for a variety of reasons that had little or nothing to do with the person's actual performance. For example, ratings were inflated to avoid making a negative evaluation a permanent part of a subordinate's record. Similarly, if the merit ceiling was especially low, ratings could be inflated to ensure that a valued subordinate got at least a modest pay increase. At times, supervisors went so far as to actively hide the low performance of a worker. They feared that a poorly performing subordinate could reflect badly on the supervisor (recall the frequent lack of upper management support we mentioned earlier). Conversely, giving a poor performer a high evaluation could increase the possibility that an individual would be promoted out of the manager's work team. An inflated appraisal, therefore, was one way of passing off a low performer.

Ratings were also deflated for a variety of reasons. For example, if a subordinate was particularly lethargic and not performing up to potential, supervisors would sometimes administer a particularly pernicious evaluation in order to "shock" the individual out of inaction. Similarly, if a rater felt that a subordinate was being particularly rebellious, the supervisor might reassert authority by hitting the individual with a low appraisal.

Politics and the Subordinate. Traditionally, performance evaluations are conducted by the supervisor. A supervisor can bargain from a position of strength. After all, he or she makes the final decision. Nonetheless, the subordinate is hardly helpless. With interpersonal skill, verbal acumen, and a heavy dose of impression management, employees are able to impact their performance ratings without actually having to raise their performance (Liden & Mitchell, 1988; Ralston & Elsass, 1989; Villanova & Bernardin, 1989).

Several studies have demonstrated the powerful role played by impression management (e.g., Becker & Martin, 1995; Crant & Bateman, 1993; Sheppard & Arkin, 1991). For example, in one organizational simulation, Wayne and Ferris (1990, Study 1) found that subordinates who used a cluster of impression-management tactics, such as self-enhancement and complementing the rater, received higher performance ratings. In a field study, Wayne and Ferris (1990, Study 2) found that supervisor-focused influence tactics, such as taking an interest in the rater's personal life, were related to how well the supervisor liked the subordinate.

Wayne and Liden (1995) carried out a supportive longitudinal study. They found that when employees engaged in either supervisor-focused or self-focused impression-management behaviors, their managers reported liking them more and seeing them as similar to themselves. These perceptions of similarity, in turn, led managers to give high performance ratings.

Even more evidence was obtained in a follow-up experiment conducted by Wayne and Kacmar (1991). In this study, the participant played the role of a supervisor conducting a performance evaluation. Wayne and Kacmar had experimental accomplices play the role of a subordinate. Some of these simulated subordinates engaged in a great deal of impression management, doing such things as conforming to the supervisor's opinion and giving other-enhancing communications. Other subordinates did not engage in these behaviors. The result was intriguing. Impression-management behavior produced higher performance ratings. Impression management also caused the simulated supervisor to communicate in a more supportive, friendly, and open fashion. Consistent findings were also obtained by Ferris, Judge, Rowland, and Fitzgibbons (1994).

Another interesting study was conducted by Kipnis and Schmidt (1988). Among a sample of working individuals, certain influence tactics were positively associated with performance evaluations. The tactics in questions varied somewhat for men and women. For men, rational persuasion was the most effective means of raising one's appraisal, whereas for women, flattery or ingratiation was the most effective. Kipnis and Vanderveer (1971) also found that ingratiation was effective. Of course, this is not to say that flattery always works. For example, Ferris and Judge (1991) and Liden and Mitchell (1988, 1989) all review evidence indicating that if the flattery is too overt and obvious, it offends the supervisor and fails to "earn" higher performance ratings.

Conclusion: Is Their a Way Out of this Game?

As we can see, subordinates are not above manipulating the system to their own advantage. Nor, for that matter, are supervisors. Self-interested political machinations are facts of organizational life. However, it is important to note that this kind of nastiness does not always exist. It is not predestined. Instead, it seems that when the rater-ratee relationship is characterized by interpersonal trust, the PA process runs more smoothly and, perhaps, less politically. For example, Fulk et al. (1985) found that those individuals who had trusting relationships with their supervisor were more accepting of the PA process. Similar results were obtained by Nathan, Mohrman, and Milliman (1991). As was the case in the Fulk et al. (1985) sample, subordinates were more satisfied with the appraisal process to the extent they had a good relationship with their supervisor. Moreover, this effect was still present even after controlling for the favorability of the evaluation. Hence, when people trusted their supervisor, they were even accepting of negative evaluations. Clearly, these findings do not have the same flavor as those documenting self-interested political maneuvering.

Neither of the previous metaphors fully explicate these dynamics. The test metaphor does not tell us that politics exist at all. Conversely, the political metaphor tells us only about self-interested political behavior and does not emphasize the ameliorative role of interpersonal trust. People might have nasty relationships, to be sure, but this is not necessarily so. Thus, we need a broader, more inclusive model that maintains the strengths of both the test and political metaphors, while also taking these additional issues processes into account. In particular, we need a metaphor that emphasizes productive ways of building positive relationships between individuals and their employers. This is the key to avoiding both the academic idealism of the test metaphor and the grim self-interest of the political metaphor.

How PA Should Really Be Done: The
Due Process Metaphor as a Hopeful Suggestion

Before proceeding, let us reflect on the terrain we have already covered. PA is predicated on an intellectual base that emphasizes rational goals and scientifically sound standards. However, we have argued that sometimes there is no such standard and, even if one did exist, it would be rather difficult to operationalize with a great deal of psychometric precision.[1] When rating performance, supervisors have been asked to do an impossible task. As such, it is no surprise to find that corners get cut and a general sloppiness permeates the system. Within this context, both the rater and the ratee have little choice but to vie with each other for political influence. Life in some organizations can come to resemble a precivilized wasteland, where things are nasty, brutal, and short. But our Hobbesian metaphor also gives us a perspective for change. After all, human groups have always had to wrestle with the problems of diverse perspectives, debatable standards, and incomplete evidence. Understanding how these problems are dealt with in nonwork settings may offer some clues for work behavior.

We might find a better PA metaphor by examining the legal system. A "trial metaphor" might be a helpful way to supplement the test metaphor (Folger et al., 1992; Taylor et al., 1995). The Hobbesian brutality of early human groups is no longer with us (or, more accurately, is less ubiquitous) because of the rule of law. Laws were set up to regulate people's interactions with one another. Laws serve as abstract standards of behavior. When one violates a law, one stands trial. It is important to understand the purpose of a trial. It is, of course, true that trials attempt to ascertain the "truth" or, one might more properly say, *the facts of the case.* Hence, accurate judgments are important. Nevertheless, within our legal system, we also accept the fact that the truth can only be imperfectly known, and so we apply a *flexible standard of common law* (Folger et al., 1992). Essentially, we build in procedural safeguards that protect citizens from potentially capricious behavior by authority figures. These safeguards include such things as *innocent until proven guilty* and proof beyond a *reasonable doubt.* Carefully note that these safeguards can actually lower the "validity" of a particular trial. Although our statistical "best guess" might be guilt, this can only be established with a heavy preponderance of evidence. In psychometric jargon, our concern over a Type I error is so great that we may release potentially guilty suspects.

This underscores one fundamental goal of a trial. A trial is not a performance evaluation, in the sense that we generally use the term, because a trial is not exclusively seeking "test" accuracy. Our legal system is seeking something larger than simply accurate behavioral ratings. The purpose of a trial is to help maintain the greater social order. Our legal system seeks to maintain our society by guaranteeing the dignity and worth of the citizens that fall under its purview. A legal system that fails to preserve human dignity is automatically suspect.

We can understand this distinction by comparing a PA to a trial. It seems reasonable to most people to reward someone with a pay raise based on our best guess of past and future performance. It would seem less reasonable to use a best guess to send someone to prison. The best guess is the most accurate judgment possible, but using it for at least some purposes violates our standards of human dignity.

But why should dignity and worth be a consideration in some settings and not in others? Why is it acceptable to commit potentially injurious acts in a PA interview and not in a trial? The most common response would probably be the need for "profit." Our best guess, based on psychometrically sound criteria, should yield the most productive organization. This argument does have considerable merit. After all, it seems a bit legalistic and bureaucratic to establish poor performance beyond a strictly enforced "reasonable doubt." Clearly, one should not ignore important practical considerations, and a reasonable best guess is more realistic in organizational, as opposed to legal, settings. Nevertheless, if one pushes this profit argument too far, it runs into problems.

Even if accuracy were reasonably high, it is still not clear that this is the only, or even the best, criterion for a stable and effective social system (Ilgen, 1993). Probably the simplest way to illustrate this point is by considering an important observation made by Lind and Tyler (1988) and Shapiro (1993). As these authors noted, individuals typically do not have an isolated, one-shot interaction with important social institutions. Instead, people experience a series of justice episodes. The treatment they receive during any one of these events gives them two pieces of information. First, the experience allows them to know how much the system values and respects them. It gives individuals the opportunity to ascertain their worth. Second, one event has implications for what will occur in subsequent events.

This brings us to the crux of the trial metaphor. Fair procedures give one a sense of personal dignity and value (Lind & Tyler, 1988; Tyler, 1990; Tyler & Lind, 1992). Moreover, even if one particular judgment errs, over time, a procedurally fair system is still likely to avoid grossly unfair future outcomes (Shapiro, 1993). In essence, fair procedures give individuals a stake in the social structure. The system works to respect people's dignity, while trying to give them generally fair outcomes. If the system is working this well, then an individual would be foolhardy to damage it and sensible to maintain it. Certainly, one might tinker around the edges, but in the long run a procedurally fair system is more likely to give its participants what they want and, as such, will build the commitment and loyalty needed to maintain any social institution. In fact, several studies have shown this to be the case. After a trial, it has repeatedly been found that procedural justice is a stronger predictor of satisfaction than is the actual outcome (e.g., Lind & Tyler, 1988; Thibaut & Walker, 1975, 1978; Tyler, 1984, 1987).

Now let us return to the issue of performance evaluation. These ideas were tested in a quasi-experimental study carried out by Taylor et al. (1995). Taylor and her colleagues trained supervisors to conduct performance evaluations with due process considerations in mind. Untrained managers served as the control group. Performance ratings were actually lower in the treatment group. Despite this, both subordinates and their managers reported much more positive reactions to the due process procedures.

An appraisal may be accurate (if you are lucky), but this alone does not guarantee fairness. Further, in the absence of fairness, the social system of an organization can begin to come unglued. The stake that people have in the system is compromised. There is far less reason to maintain one's affiliation with the organization (Konovsky & Cropanzano, 1991) or perform helpful prosocial behaviors (Farh, Podsakoff, & Organ, 1990; Moorman, 1991). One might even be tempted to steal (Greenberg, 1990a) or engage in disruptive conflict (Cropanzano & Baron, 1991). To state the matter more starkly: Why should people respect a system that does not respect them? Organizations reap what they sow. If people are viewed as mere economic assets, then they will come to view their organization in the same way.

The upshot of all this is that the trial metaphor explicitly maintains that human dignity should be a central concern of PA. Of course, this is not to say that accuracy is unimportant. An inaccurate rating system is hardly a way to guarantee a person's worth! However, accuracy is only one thing that organizations should be pursuing. Organizations will also want to work for justice. This goal may seem vague and abstract (although, as we have seen, PA accuracy is no simple matter either). Fortunately, previous research has offered seven suggestions for doing fair performance evaluations: do appraisals on a regular basis, use appropriate criteria, have knowledgeable appraisers, use a fair rating format, consider multiple sources of ratings, conduct interpersonally fair performance interviews, and train subordinates to participate. These suggestions are displayed in Table 5.1. In the next few sections we will discuss each recommendation in more detail.

If You Promise to Do PA, Then Do It!

We already discussed the phenomenon of the vanishing PA. Organizations purport to do PA, and managers claim to have conducted the interview, but subordinates have no recollection of the matter (Beer, 1981; Porter et al.,

Table 5.1   How to Do a Fair Performance Appraisal

I.   If you promise to do a performance appraisal, then do it
II.   Appraise subordinates on the appropriate criteria
III.   Have knowledgeable appraisers
IV.   Use a fair rating format
V.   Consider the source of the ratings
VI.   Maintain interpersonal fairness in the performance appraisal interview
VII.   Train subordinates to participate

1975). This seems to be due to a lack of perceived rewards for good PAs (Dickinson, 1993; Napier & Latham, 1986) as well as a dearth of training (Locher & Teel, 1977). In any case, performance evaluation is not always done. It is not surprising that this can lower individuals' satisfaction with a PA program. One field study by Landy et al. (1978) found that subordinates were more satisfied with the evaluation process when it was done frequently.

Appraise Subordinates on the Appropriate Criteria

Performance reviews are seen as fairer to the extent that individuals are being appraised on fair criteria. For example, Landy et al. (1978) reported that workers were more satisfied with their performance ratings when they agreed with their supervisor as to their appropriate job duties. Additional supportive results were obtained in a cross-sectional study by Dipboye and de Pontbriand (1981) and a longitudinal study by Nathan et al. (1991). These standards must be more than simply appropriate. They must also be applied consistently to all ratees. The inconsistent application of performance standards is one important source of perceived injustice (Greenberg, 1986).

One way to help ensure that workers will perceive that fair performance criteria are being used is to allow some participation in the design of the PA program. This may be an effective means of producing fairness—even when a person's actual evaluation is low. One simple demonstration of this was a laboratory study by Cropanzano and Folger (1989). Cropanzano and Folger allowed laboratory participants either choice or no choice on the task for which they were being evaluated. Generally speaking, participants reported more anger and resentment when they failed on a task and also had no choice. When they were given a choice of tasks, however, they reported little ill will—even following a negative evaluation. Supportive results were also obtained in additional laboratory studies conducted by Earley and Lind (1987, Study 1) and Paese, Lind, and Kanfer (1988). Finally, in separate field studies reported by Silverman and Wexley (1984) and Earley and Lind (1987,

Study 2), it was again found that participation in the choice of task dimensions improved employee attitudes and led to greater perceived fairness.

Have Knowledgeable Appraisers

No PA instrument can be any better than the person completing it. If the rater lacks the appropriate expertise, then the PA is likely to be error ridden and inaccurate. As one might expect, employees report less justice when their evaluations are made by uninformed supervisors (Cederblom, 1982; Fulk et al., 1985; Greenberg, 1986; Landy et al., 1978), although this judgment may also depend on other aspects of the work environment (Stone, Gueutal, & McIntosh, 1984).

Some Rating Formats Are Fairer Than Others

Earlier, we noted that no particular rating format has been shown to be demonstrably more accurate than any other (e.g., Nathan & Alexander, 1985). However, some formats are perceived to be more or less fair. Generally speaking, a fair PA instrument has three characteristics: It provides for the setting of both performance and developmental goals, it is based on behaviors and not personal traits, and it is based on detailed information. Next, we will discuss evidence supporting the fairness of three formats that meet at least one of these criteria.

Formats Should Provide for Goal Setting: A Place for MBO. When an organization does PA, one hope is that employees will take the feedback to heart and improve the quality of their work. Thus, good PA interviews often involve some type of goal setting. In fact, a very consistent finding is that goal setting leads to more positive employee reactions (Burke et al., 1978; Burke & Wilcox, 1969; Dipboye & de Pontbriand, 1981; Fulk et al., 1985; Giles & Mossholder, 1990; Greller, 1975; Keaveny, Inderrieden, & Allen, 1987; Landy et al., 1978; Lawler et al., 1984; Nemeroff & Wexley, 1979). It seems safe to say that this finding is fairly well established. The positive effects of goal setting do not seem to be limited to simple performance goals. In one longitudinal study, Nathan et al. (1991) demonstrated that workers react more positively to PA systems that help them to develop their own career plans.

The positive effects of performance goals were also obtained in a laboratory experiment by Lind, Kanfer, and Earley (1990). This Lind et al. study is particularly important for theoretical reasons. Many of the experimental participants preferred to participate in goal setting, in part, because it impacted the goals they received. We can refer to this as an *instrumental* influence. However, participants also desired voice even after the goals had been set. That is, the process of allowing participation, even when it could not effect the actual goal, still improved perceptions of fairness. Apparently, simply having the opportunity to state one's opinion leads one to believe that he or she is more respected and valued (see Lind & Tyler, 1988). Thus, Lind and his colleagues provided us with important laboratory evidence of *noninstrumental* voice effects.

In all of the above studies, the goals were cited in a mutually participative fashion. Cross-sectional field studies by Keaveny et al. (1987) and Nemeroff and Wexley (1979) also found that individuals were especially likely to prefer goal setting when they were allowed to participate in the process. This suggests one important boundary condition. In an interesting field experiment, Ivancevich (1982) compared one group of people who were assigned goals to a "no goal" control group. Those subordinates who were assigned goals actually reported more anxiety than did those subordinates who were not assigned goals. Despite this finding, receiving assigned goals was seen as more equitable than not receiving goals. Thus, assigned goals caused tension, even though they did not seem to be particularly unfair.

All of these studies suggest that formal goal setting is a useful aspect of performance evaluation. It is likely, therefore, that formats that incorporate goal setting, such as Management by Objectives (MBO), will be more effective than those that do not. The data are generally consistent with this, although the need for more research must be acknowledged. In any case, MBO is a widely used technique (Campbell & Barron, 1982) that can produce substantial improvements in job performance (Rodgers & Hunter, 1991). Moreover, in a survey of organizations conducted by Lazer and Wikstrom (1977), 75% of the respondents rated MBO as an effective way to appraise the performance of managers. Other PA systems were not evaluated this favorably. Finally, Beer et al. (1978) implemented a performance-management system at Corning Glass. The system included MBO as well as other interventions. In general, the performance-management system was a success. Nevertheless, because so many aspects of PA were simultaneously manipulated, it is impossible to know for certain if formal goal setting, per se, was responsible for the program's success.

Formats Should Rate Behaviors: A Place for BARS. A variety of researchers have recommended that organizations adopt instruments for rating specific behaviors, as opposed to more general traits (e.g., DeVries et al., 1981). Although the evidence is still quite limited, the work that does exist tends to support this point of view. In a study of faculty evaluations, Dickinson and Zellinger (1980) compared a Behavioral Anchored Ratings Scale (or BARS) to a Mixed Standard Scale (MSS) and a more traditional Likert Scale. The students, who served as raters, preferred the BARS format to the other two procedures.

However, it should be noted that Dickinson and Zellinger (1980) did not have the ratees (faculty members) assess the fairness of these instruments.

Ivancevich (1980) conducted a more directly relevant study. Using a quasi-experimental design, Ivancevich introduced Behavioral Expectation Scales (BES) to 121 engineers. This treatment group was compared to a 128-person control group that was evaluated using the organization's regular trait-rating instrument. Twenty months after the BES was introduced, Ivancevich found that the treatment group responded far more favorably than the trait-rated control participants. In particular, engineers evaluated with the BES format had more positive attitudes and less work tension.

Formats Should Be Based on Good Record Keeping: A Place for Diaries. Earlier, we noted that appraisers should be knowledgeable souls who understand the worker's job. However, a rater must do more than memorize a job description. The rater also must have good information regarding the extent to which a given subordinate fulfills his or her responsibilities within that position. For example, Landy and his colleagues (1978) found that evaluations were seen more positively based on the extent to which ratees believed that their supervisors had a good idea of the subordinate's performance levels. It seems likely, therefore, that some formats may be seen as fair because they involve detailed record keeping and, presumably, high-quality information.

One particularly promising approach is use of performance diaries. Under this procedure, the rater-supervisor keeps a brief record of a person's day-to-day work activities. In one laboratory study, Greenberg (1987a) determined that ratings were perceived as particularly fair to the extent that they were based on diaries. Moreover, another laboratory study by DeNisi, Robbins, and Cafferty (1989) found that diaries could yield particularly accurate performance information, although this depends on the manner in which the diary is organized. DeNisi and his colleagues did not collect fairness ratings, however.

Who Rates?

In most PA systems, the supervisor rates his or her subordinates. In fact, except where explicitly noted, all of the previous comments were in regard to supervisory ratings. However, ratings can also be taken from other sources, most notably, peer and self-ratings. We will consider these next.

Peer Ratings. Psychometrically speaking, peer evaluations seem to be at least as reliable and valid as supervisory evaluations (Harris & Schaubroeck, 1988). However, this reasonably good validity does not necessarily translate into perceptions of social justice. The fairness data concerning peer ratings are mixed. In one study, Cederblom and Lounsbury (1980) found that workers did not like being rated by their peers. The respondents were particularly concerned with possible friendship bias, and there was also a perceived lack of feedback value.

However, these findings do not mean that peer ratings are always viewed negatively. Under the right conditions, peer evaluations can be viewed quite favorably. In particular, peer evaluations are considered fair when they are perceived to be lenient, when they are developmentally focused, and when they are free from friendship bias (McEvoy & Buller, 1987). McEvoy and Buller's findings are noteworthy for another reason as well. Although perceived leniency was positively correlated with ratee evaluations, actual leniency was not. In particular, the actual favorability of the ratee's evaluation was unrelated to his or her satisfaction with the peer appraisal. Hence, it might be that peers can give disadvantageous ratings, at least under certain conditions.

Another investigation of peer ratings was conducted by Barclay and Harland (1995). Like McEvoy and Buller (1987), Barclay and Harland (1995) found that peer ratings were desirable in some settings, but less so in others. In particular, individuals responded favorably to peer evaluations when they were correctable (in case of a disagreement) and when they were carried out by a competent rater.

Self-Ratings. Another source of appraisal data is self-ratings. Unlike peer ratings, the psychometric evidence for self-ratings is not particularly good. Self-ratings tend to be more lenient than peer and supervisory ratings (Harris & Schaubroeck, 1988). As such, they are not recommended for many purposes (Campbell & Lee, 1988).

On the other hand, including self-ratings seems to produce better employee attitudes than does an exclusive reliance on supervisory ratings. For example, in one longitudinal field study, Bassett and Meyer (1968) introduced self-appraisals into a PA system. (In this particular program, the manager still continued to make supervisory ratings, however.) The inclusion of self-ratings led to better ratee attitudes, more tolerance of managerial criticism, and higher work performance. Similarly, in a quasi-experimental field study, Folger and Lewis (1993) found that workers responded more favorably when they were allowed to perform self-appraisals. Not all of the research has been so positive, however. In a field experiment, Roberson et al. (1993) found that following self-ratings, individuals reported less influence over their supervisor, more disagreement, and less satisfaction. It is not entirely clear why these findings occurred. Roberson et al. (1993) suggested that managers may have attempted to retain their autocratic control under the self-appraisal system. To the extent that this occurred, employee voice was first promised (via the self-appraisals) and then de facto removed (via the manager's actions). This could have produced a deleterious frustration effect that lowered satisfaction with the self-evaluation procedures (Folger, 1977; Korsgaard et al., 1996). However, this is but one possible explanation. The findings of Roberson et al. (1993) suggested a need for more research.

This research suggests that self-ratings might have some use to organizations, despite their psychometric failings. For this reason, they put us in a quandary. Self-appraisals are perceived to be fair, which is good, but they are overly lenient, which is bad. Our sense is that justice should be pursued *in addition to* validity, not *in the face of* validity. For this reason, we would suggest a compromise. Although self-ratings may not be terribly valid, there are other voice mechanisms that could be incorporated into a PA system. The individual could, for example, provide an activities report or accomplishment log. This reporting function could be included in a performance review, without having each subordinate provide his or her own PA score. An additional option would be to allow subordinates to review and rebut their performance ratings. This guarantees input without automatically adding potentially inflated ratings.

Maintain Interpersonal Fairness in the PA Interview

After PA ratings have been made, based on a fair format and by a qualified rater, the results need to be communicated to the subordinate. Proper PA practice calls for the ratings to be communicated in a formal appraisal interview (e.g., DeVries et al., 1981). Unfortunately, as we have already seen, these sessions often depart from the ideal. Because appraisal interviews engender so much stress for the participants, while also being important for PA effectiveness, a great deal of research has examined ways to increase the usefulness of these sessions. This body of work allows us to make several suggestions for improving the interview process. These suggestions are illustrated in Table 5.2.

Be Supportive. Perhaps the most basic thing that a supervisor-rater can do is to be supportive. When conducting a PA interview, the evaluator should take a helpful attitude that shows concern for the subordinate. Several studies have shown that a supportive, helpful attitude on the part of the supervisor leads to higher ratee satisfaction with the appraisal interview (Burke et al., 1978; Cederblom, 1982; Dorfman, Stephen, & Loveland, 1986; Nemeroff & Wexley, 1979).

Be Participative. We have already seen the important role played by subordinate voice. Voice is central to procedural fairness. People want voice in selecting tasks (e.g., Cropanzano & Folger, 1989; Earley & Lind, 1987; Paese et al., 1988) and voice in setting performance goals (Keaveny et al., 1987; Lind

Table 5.2   How to Do a Fair Performance Appraisal Interview

I.   Be supportive
II.   Be participative
III. If desired, you can discuss both developmental information and the subordinate's evaluation
IV.   Use *only* constructive criticism

et al., 1990). However, voice has another purpose as well. Employees also like to participate in the actual evaluation. This sort of participation allows one to direct the rater to high-performance areas and also to explain why poor performance occurred. Consequently, it is a good general rule of thumb that the more participation people have, the happier they are with the process. This general finding was replicated in a variety of studies using a variety of different research designs, including a laboratory experiment (Kanfer, Sawyer, Earley, & Lind, 1987), two field experiments (French et al., 1966; Korsgaard et al., 1996), a longitudinal field study (Nathan et al., 1991), and a whole array of cross-sectional field studies (Burke & Wilcox, 1969; Burke et al., 1978; Ceder-blom, 1982; Dipboye & de Pontbriand, 1981; Giles & Mossholder, 1990; Greenberg, 1986; Greller, 1975, 1978; Keaveny et al., 1987; Korsgaard & Roberson, 1995; Landy et al., 1978; Nemeroff & Wexley, 1979; Wexley, Singh, & Yukl, 1973). Despite this collection of supportive data, at least one caveat may exist. Employees seem to want participation primarily when they perceive that they have some expertise. When individuals see themselves as lacking relevant job knowledge, participation becomes less important (Hillary & Wexley, 1974).

If Desired, You Can Discuss Both Developmental Information and Also the Subordinate's Evaluation. It has long been noted that a supervisor-rater has to play two distinct roles. On the one hand, he or she must take the role of a counselor and attempt to develop the subordinate. This requires trust and a good relationship. On the other hand, the supervisor-rater must also be evaluative and willing to give negative feedback. This role may cause fear and unease that can cast a pall over the manager-worker relationship. To solve this problem, several researchers have suggested holding two different PA inter-views: one for development and one for evaluation (Beer, 1981; Kindall & Gatza, 1963; McGregor, 1957; Meyer, Kay, & French, 1965).

There is some evidence attesting to the merits of this suggestion, but it is not conclusive. In one field study, Kay et al. (1965) found that when managers attempted to bring up areas for performance improvements, subordinates began to feel threatened and defensive. These negative reactions, in turn, led to a less constructive appraisal interview. Other research has shown that, not surprisingly, people are relatively dissatisfied with interviews in which they receive negative feedback (Pearce & Porter, 1986; Russell & Goode, 1988). However, it does not necessarily follow from these studies that developmental and evaluative sessions should be separated. They do tell us that employees prefer not to receive disadvantageous feedback (no big surprise here). However, sometimes such feedback has to be given. Thus, the proper comparison is not *negative feedback* versus *positive feedback,* as everyone prefers the latter. Instead, the relevant issue is whether or not negative feedback and developmental information can be presented in the same appraisal interview.

Leaving evaluative feedback out of the session seems to be something of an odd solution. Workers are well aware of the fact that organizations evaluate them. Omitting this information from the "developmental" interview only delays, and does not eliminate, the problems just mentioned. Research shows that a balanced and thorough review is better liked than none at all—even if it contains negative information. Individuals want to know where they stand, and they actively seek feedback to this effect. Denying or delaying this feedback can have ill effects. For example, Dorfman et al. (1986) found that workers were more satisfied when their PA interviews discussed salary and promotional opportunities. Finally, Prince and Lawler (1986) observed no ill effects from mixing developmental and evaluative information.

Based on these observations, we would argue that it serves little purpose to divide PA interviews into separate developmental and evaluative sessions. Besides, as we have already noted, many supervisors seem to have trouble doing one appraisal, much less two. However, this is only a partial answer to the problems raised by Meyer et al. (1965). These authors are quite correct in calling our attention to the unease and ill will generated by negative feedback. If having two interviews does not eliminate these problems, then what will? In the next section, we will suggest a way to address these concerns. We would argue that resentment and anger can be reduced by conducting the appraisal session in an interpersonally fair manner. Even the harsh blow of criticism can be eased by justice.

Evaluate, But Do So in a Respectful Fashion. Our previous comments may have left practitioners in something of a quandary. We noted that workers do not like negative feedback; however, often this kind of unpleasant feedback needs to be given. Unfortunately, we also argued that holding separate PA interviews does not seem to be the answer. What can be done?

It is important to note that negative feedback, properly given, can actually facilitate performance (Fedor, 1991). "Proper" performance feedback is given in a timely fashion, specifically designates the problem, and focuses on the errant behavior instead of the person (Ilgen, Fisher, & Taylor, 1979; Larsen,

1984). This is also consistent with a longitudinal field study by Landy, Barnes-Farrell, and Cleveland (1980). Landy and his colleagues found that workers' actual performance ratings were less closely related to their PA satisfaction than were their perceptions of the fairness and accuracy of these ratings. In other words, people could accept even negative ratings, so long as they were perceived to be fair. This suggests that the solution is not to stop giving negative feedback (which is not viable in any case), but instead, to supply this information in a way that is consistent with the principles of interpersonal justice. Negative feedback—one might say criticism—can be delivered effectively so long as it is offered in a constructive fashion. Baron (1993), for example, reviewed considerable evidence indicating that destructive criticism, and not criticism per se, is what produces the most odious consequences for work organizations. Constructive criticism, on the other hand, produces more favorable results.

As displayed in Table 5.3, Baron (1993) argued that helpful constructive criticism comprises six characteristics. It focuses on relevant behaviors. It does not presume that the person is the cause of the poor performance. (Of course, the manager may later determine that the individual is the culprit. However, this is not assumed a priori. Instead, the supervisor should investigate all possible causes before making such an attribution.) Constructive criticism does not contain threats. Moreover, it also attempts to maintain a considerate and respectful tone. For negative feedback to be constructive, it should be delivered in a timely fashion. Very often, managers hesitate to give criticism and save it until long after the event has taken place. Finally, constructive criticism is delivered in an appropriate setting, such as a PA interview.

Destructive criticism does not include these positive attributes. It is general in content. Often negative feedback becomes so vague and amorphous that it is even hard to recognize! When something bad has occurred, destructive criticism tends to blame the person or attributes of the person (i.e., "you are a shiftless bozo"). It contains nasty threats and is inconsiderate in tone. Moreover, when delivering destructive criticism, managers are often not very prompt or timely. Finally, managers often deliver their negative feedback in an inappropriate environment, such as a public meeting or social gathering. All of these things tend to lessen the effectiveness of the information.

A great deal of evidence is consistent with Baron's (1993) model. For example, a series of laboratory studies all found that criticism having destructive characteristics is less well received and more likely to cause interpersonal conflict (e.g., Baron, 1985, 1988b, 1990b; Bies & Moag, 1986; Cropanzano & Baron, 1991; Ohbuchi, Kameda, & Agarie, 1989). Destructive criticism might even lower task performance. For example, in one interesting study, Baron (1988a) trained simulated managers to give destructive or constructive negative feedback to laboratory participants. Baron (1988a) found that those

Table 5.3   Constructive and Destructive Criticism

I. Constructive Criticism
   A. Specifically focuses on the behavior or behaviors in question
   B. Does not attack the person as a cause of the poor performance
   C. Does not make threats
   D. Considerate in tone and content
   E. Delivered in a timely fashion
   F. Delivered in an appropriate setting
II. Destructive Criticism
   A. General in content
   B. Blames the person or attributes of the person as the cause of poor
      performance
   C. Makes threats
   D. Inconsiderate in tone and content
   E. Is delivered after too much time has passed since the negative
      behavior
   F. Delivered in an inappropriate setting

SOURCE: Based on Baron (1993, p. 158).

receiving the destructive criticism showed poorer attitudes toward the feedback and, relative to a group that received constructive criticism, actually showed poorer subsequent work performance.

Similar results were also obtained in field settings. For example, research by Burke et al. (1978) and Burke and Wilcox (1969) found that the amount of perceived threat was inversely related to PA satisfaction. Similarly, in a study of 287 bank employees, Greller (1978) found that criticism from the boss was detrimental to PA interviews. Taken together, these results would seem to indicate that destructive criticism damages the PA process. Unfortunately, these field studies also indicate that it does occur. The good news is that even after it does take place, all is not lost. In the next chapter we will discuss some ways of rectifying the harm done by pernicious interpersonal communication.

Train Subordinates to Participate

As we maintained, the test metaphor has long cautioned against the use of self-appraisals due to their dubious psychometric characteristics. It does not seem unlikely that managers have heeded this advice. For example, Roberson et al. (1993) suggested that even within the context of a voice-based system, managers may struggle to retain their traditional control. This poses a problem in implementing fair PAs. On the one hand, practitioners should continue to exhort and train managers to treat their workers fairly (e.g., Taylor et al.,

1995), for when judiciously implemented, fairness can benefit all. On the other hand, it would also be helpful if subordinates were given the skills they need to obtain justice for themselves. In this way, they would not remain passive but hopeful recipients of managerial actions.

This employee-focused perspective was taken in a field experiment conducted by Korsgaard and her colleagues (1996). In the context of a workplace performance evaluation, Korsgaard et al. assigned subordinates to three training conditions. The focal group received assertiveness training. This included such things as stating one's position in a confident manner, practicing non-verbal behavior, listening to the other point of view, checking for understanding, and so forth. Basically, trainees were taught to be both receptive to others but also honest with their own position. A second group received placebo training. In this condition, people were taught the PA system, but were not instructed in the use of assertive behavior. Finally, there was a no-training control group.

Following their instruction, employees later received their scheduled performance evaluations. Korsgaard and her colleagues (1996) then assessed their responses to the process. Although not all of their findings were perfectly supportive, the results of Korsgaard et al. strongly suggest that assertiveness training can promote PA fairness.

Conclusions

The test metaphor is one useful way of looking at PA. It stresses the importance of accuracy and offers us valuable suggestions for making ratings as valid as possible. However, this metaphor is ultimately limited because it does not emphasize that the objects being evaluated are actually human beings. The worth and value of a person cannot be as easily understood as the merits of a new automobile. With people, there is plenty of room for reasoned debate and different perspectives. Moreover, automobiles do not bite back. They do not form unions or sue when you forget to change their oil. (Otherwise both of the authors would have incurred significant legal expenses.) People are not so benign.

The political metaphor also has a great deal of truth. We reviewed considerable research attesting to the prevalence of self-interested game playing. People will work for their own self-interest, but not entirely so. We also experience loyalty and concern for others. Justice is a way of building the close interpersonal bonds of effective working relationships, because just treatment affirms the dignity and worth of an individual. This affirmation helps to build the kind of positive working relationships that produce successful organizations.

Note

1. None of this should be taken to indicate that precision should not be pursued. Our point here is that accuracy is only one goal for performance ratings. Even an accurate rating might still be seen as unfair under certain conditions (e.g., if ratings are made on "inappropriate" criteria). Performance evaluations must be considered in the larger organizational context; that is, in terms of how or if they influence organizational effectiveness. Accuracy, per se, may not be a suitable goal if the ratings also lower morale and work performance.

6 Organizational Justice and Conflict Management

SOCIAL ACCOUNTS, THIRD PARTIES, AND GRIEVANCE SYSTEMS

If the reader is ever motivated to conduct a quick-and-dirty justice study, it can be done easily enough. Just ask a few friends how they are getting along at work. You might get one or two who describe the office floor plan, benefits system, stock plan, or some such thing; but you probably won't. Instead, you are likely to hear about how this or that person made your friend miserable about such and such a thing. Someone said this or did that and then an argument (or at least a slow boil) ensued. And your friend will not understand how such a pathological person can function in the real world and will wonder if anyone else has to put up with this kind of office foolishness. In fact, we all put up with it. And, more than likely, someone has had occasion to "put up" with each of us. When human beings try to work together, their goals and interests will eventually clash, and, as a result, we often find ourselves on both the giving and receiving end of workplace conflict.

Conflict can be painful. In one study, Bolger, DeLongis, Kessler, and Schilling (1989) had a sample of adults complete a daily mood diary for 6 weeks. They found that interpersonal conflict was by far the most stressful daily event. Not only did it leave people in a bad mood, but unlike other events, individuals did not habituate to interpersonal conflict. It kept bothering people even the day after it occurred. One can see why conflict is taken so seriously. In fact, according to a survey by Thomas and Schmidt (1976), managers spend about 20% of their time managing workplace conflicts.

It is easy to visualize the negative effects of conflict—we all have firsthand experience with them. When conflict becomes too pernicious, workers experience severe interpersonal stress, and the environment becomes chaotic and characterized by mistrust, suspicion, and hostility. Cooperation and coordination become difficult or impossible. Instead, individuals may actually attempt to undermine or harm their coworkers through either passive or direct aggression.

Despite all of these potential problems, conflict, if it remains at moderate levels, is not totally bad. Imagine, for example, a workplace free of conflict. As noted by many observers (e.g., Baron, 1991; Boulding, 1963; Robbins, 1974, 1978; Thomas, 1993), when conflict drops to extremely low levels, workers may begin to feel a complacent contentment. Whereas this may promote inner peace, it may also lead to apathy and creative stagnation. The organization can become unimaginative and unable to adapt to environmental changes. There is a great deal of evidence to support this view (see Robbins, 1974, for a good review). However, perhaps the least ambiguous evidence comes from research on creativity. In a series of laboratory studies, for example, James and his colleagues (James, in press; James, Chen, & Goldberg, 1992) showed that moderately high levels of social conflict can actually promote innovative thinking.

Thus, organizational conflict is neither intrinsically bad nor intrinsically good. The challenge for organizations is to keep it high enough to promote adaptability and low enough to avoid disruption. Managers often find themselves walking a tightrope, trying to resolve conflicts between subordinates but not necessarily wanting to eliminate them altogether. In order to do this job more effectively, one needs to understand the causes of conflict. We believe that organizational justice (or injustice) is one important cause.

Does Injustice Cause Conflict?

From what we have seen, organizational conflict is a major worry for managers, workers, and organizations. This is as it should be. The right level of conflict can spur innovation and creativity; the wrong level can kill an organization or work team. For these reasons, it is important to consider justice in the conflict process. If justice is involved, then one might potentially maintain the appropriate level of conflict by raising or lowering the level of organizational fairness. In fact, from our earlier theoretical discussion (see Chapters 1 and 2), justice should be both a determinant of conflict and also a means of resolving it. Which is to say that injustice creates conflict, whereas restoring justice lowers it.

Evidence That Injustice Causes Conflict

Let us first consider the matter in theoretical terms. Conflict is posited to result when an individual believes that his or her goals were thwarted or could be thwarted sometime in the future. Individuals seek to recoup their losses, and conflict is one potentially viable strategy for doing so. However, this is usually not enough. Individuals choose conflict over other alternatives when they become angry over a perceived unfairness. This works in two steps. As we noted in our earlier discussion concerning Referent Cognitions Theory (see Chapter 3, and Cropanzano & Folger, 1989; Folger, 1986b, 1986c), these two steps are best captured in the words *would* and *should*. First, some disadvantageous outcome must occur. That is, things *would* have been better under some other circumstances. This is the *blocked objective* we already mentioned, and it is necessary but not sufficient for conflict to occur. After an unfavorable outcome, the individual looks around for someone to blame. If he or she finds someone, the injured party then asks, *should* the outcome have occurred? That is, the obtained outcome is evaluated against some normative criterion. The negative outcome that, ethically speaking, should not have occurred is the ultimate basis of resentment and moral outrage. And this outrage can lead to conflict (Mark & Folger, 1984).

So here's the kicker: It is not enough for something bad to happen. Rather, something bad must happen that is also morally indefensible. If the negative action can be justified, then the individual is less likely to experience anger. Thus, the basis for a perception of injustice is the understanding of why a person gave you something negative (see Bies, 1987b; Bies & Moag, 1986). Attributions, therefore, influence when someone will get angry and, by extension, when conflict will occur (Bies & Tripp, 1995a; Tripp & Bies, in press). Substantial evidence shows that if a negative outcome occurs, individuals will not get angry so long as they do not attribute fault to the harmdoer (Baron, 1985, 1988a, 1988b, 1990a, 1990b; Johnson & Rule, 1986).

This reasoning probably seems somewhat commonsensical, but it has been common for researchers to simply note that injustice causes conflict without citing sufficient empirical evidence in support of this proposition (e.g., Bies,

1987b; Cropanzano & Folger, 1989; Crosby, 1976; Mark & Folger, 1984). This assumption, made with insufficient research evidence, has lead some to question the injustice-conflict link altogether. Injustice may cause anger; however, it could be that neither this anger nor the unfairness is the central determinant of conflict.

Based on research regarding various social movements, McCarthy and Zald (1977) suggested that groups take social action when they have sufficient power and resources for success. Unfairness seemed to be a secondary concern. Unlike the justice literature reviewed previously, conflict is not seen as resulting from resentment or moral outrage. Rather, the decision to fight is based on a more or less rational calculation of its benefits for achieving a desired goal.

Martin, Brickman, and Murray (1984) supported this position in a role-playing field study. Working female managers were presented with vignettes describing large, moderate, or small inequities. Participants were then given the option of selecting various illegitimate responses such as work slowdowns or sabotage. Regardless of the size of the inequity, the amount of illegitimate actions was the same in all three groups. Martin and her colleagues interpreted this finding to mean that inequity, per se, is less important than the availability of power and resources.

Cropanzano and Baron (1991), however, noted that this study had no true control group. Individuals in all three conditions vicariously experienced at least some unfair treatment. Thus, there was no adequate way of distinguishing between behavior taken to restore equity and behavior taken to maximize benefits. To address this issue, Cropanzano and Baron (1991) conducted an experimental test of the injustice-conflict relation. In their study, undergraduate participants worked on an advertising campaign. Another "participant," actually an experimental accomplice, evaluated their work. Based on this evaluation, the accomplice divided a set of valued raffle tickets between himself or herself and the participant. Some participants were given an unfairly low performance evaluation that resulted in their losing most of the desired raffle tickets. Others were treated fairly, and the raffle tickets were split evenly between the participant and the accomplice.

Some participants were next allowed to act as appraisers. These participants divided a new set of raffle tickets based on the quality of a written advertising campaign. One third of the participants evaluated the accomplice, one third evaluated a neutral third person, and one third were not allowed to evaluate anyone at all. When given the opportunity to evaluate the accomplice, participants who had been treated unfairly allocated a larger number of tickets to themselves. Basically, they reciprocated the shoddy treatment they had received earlier. However, even when unfairly treated, participants gave the neutral person a fair distribution—participants ignored the opportunity to take extra raffle tickets. Moreover, when evaluating the accomplice, fairly treated participants actually gave the accomplice extra tickets! Clearly, these participants were not trying to maximize their (economic) outcomes.

After these two appraisal sessions, the participant and accomplice then negotiated the division of some hypothetical funds. Based on the quality of their negotiations, participants could earn extra raffle tickets at the expense of the accomplice. What happened? As one might expect, fairly treated individuals always tended to be more cooperative and more likely to accept an even division of the funds. The real action was in the unfairly treated conditions. Unfairly treated participants became more obstinate and stubborn negotiators, but only if they had had no earlier opportunity to appraise the accomplice. Unfairly treated individuals who had already restored outcome fairness by taking extra raffle tickets ceased trying to outdo the accomplice and agreed to divide the hypothetical funds evenly. Even after unfair treatment, participants did not seek to maximize their economic outcomes. Rather, they sought to maintain justice. With fairness restored, the unfair ticket allocations ceased.

Other research has produced similar findings. For example, Baron (1988b) exposed laboratory participants to either fair, constructive criticism or unfair, destructive criticism. Baron found that those participants who received the destructive criticism were in a poorer mood, had lower self-efficacy, and were more contentious negotiators. These findings were replicated and extended in additional experiments reported by Baron (1988a, 1990b). This research was reviewed by Baron (1990a, 1991, 1993).

It is not only Americans who meet injustice with conflict. In one role-playing study Leung, Chiu, and Au (1993) found similar effects in a Hong Kong sample. Leung et al. were attempting to understand when observers would support acrimonious industrial actions, such as grievances, sit-ins, and strikes. The authors found that participants were more sympathetic to, and more supportive of, these activities when workers were treated with interactional unfairness (e.g., management was insincere and treated "staff as profit-making machines," p. 784).

For now, the take-home point is only that under some conditions, injustice can produce organizational conflict, whereas restoring justice can reduce it. As a result, changing the level of justice can change the level of conflict. Nevertheless, the work of Martin and her colleagues (1984) is still important. Injustice does seem to be one cause of conflict, but it does not seem to be the only cause.

Retributive Justice as a Motivation for Revenge

Throughout this book, we have discussed how individuals seek outcomes and processes that are fair. Injustice takes something away from a person. A wronged person might lose something tangible, like a deserved pay raise, or intangible, such as their status or dignity within a group. In either case, the unfair treatment creates a deficit that did not exist before. Under conditions of injustice, it would seem normal for people to fill this open chasm by replacing what they have lost. In other words, it is common to seek retribution. From this perspective, retaliation becomes a means of *restoring* fairness (Tripp & Bies, in press). Building fairness through vengeance has been referred to as "retributive justice" (Hogan & Emler, 1981). It seems to be a powerful motivator of human behavior (Bies & Tripp, 1995b).

The process by which injustice and other perceived wrongs trigger retribution was theoretically articulated and empirically investigated in a series of studies by Robert Bies and Thomas Tripp. Bies, Tripp, and Kramer (1997) based their investigation on an analogy to thermodynamics. According to Bies and his colleagues, the retribution process typically moves through three steps. These are displayed in Figure 6.1. A *sparking event* creates a *heating up* of tensions. This heating is characterized by cognitive and motivational changes in the disputing individual. Usually the heat is released during a *cooling down* stage. This release may come in the form of conflict or it may be expressed through less contentious avenues, such as forgiveness. Next, we will review these stages in a little more detail. However, space permits only a cursory overview of these findings. We recommend the original source material to the interested reader.

Sparking Events. In an interesting qualitative study, Bies and Tripp (1995a) asked a series of open-ended questions to 90 MBA students. The respondents were asked to describe an episode in which they were motivated to take retaliatory action against a coworker. Although Bies and Tripp identified a variety of potential sparking events, these could be safely classified into two broad categories: damaged civic order and damaged personal identities.

As we discussed in the preface of this book, no group or organization can function unless the participants meet at least minimal obligations and social standards (Hosmer, 1995). If such expectations are not met, then interpersonal cooperation cannot be maintained. The institution will dissolve into anarchy. We can view these basic obligations and expectations as an organization's *civic order*. This order is part of the metaphorical "glue" that holds everyone together. An action that threatens this order concomitantly threatens the social group and, by extension, anyone who profits from the group. Thus, it should come as no great surprise to learn that damage to the civic order is frequently met with a quest for revenge.

Research by Bies and Tripp (1995a) identified at least three classes of events that could threaten the civic order. The first of these are gross *rule violations*. A rule violation is an act that undermines an agreement between two or more

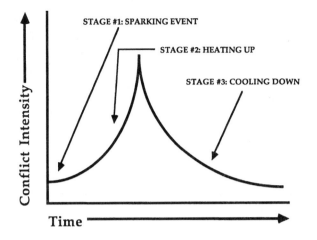

Figure 6.1. A model of Retributive Justice suggested by Bies, Tripp, and Kramer (1997).

individuals. For example, employees become extremely angry at breaches of contract or ex post facto rule changes. *Honor violations* comprise the second set of threats. These are acts that are inconsistent with "prevailing codes of ethics" (Bies & Tripp, 1995a, p. 249). Honor violations treat people dishonestly. As examples of honor violations, Bies and Tripp cited such things as broken promises and lies. Finally, an *abusive authority*, such as a disrespectful supervisor, is a third thing that may damage the civic order. Retributive justice can serve as one means of checking these types of abuses (Bies & Tripp, 1995b).

Civic order is not the only reason that people work. Individuals also work for personal reasons. These reasons include a need to develop and maintain their own identities. Given this, behaviors that damage a person's sense of self are apt to spur vengeance. Bies and Tripp (1995a) found that an identity damaged by such things as harsh criticism or insults triggers a need for retributive justice.

Heating Up. It is a well-known fact that, if left unchecked, conflicts often escalate (Glasl, 1982). Bies and his colleagues (1997) described this escalation as a process of heating up. Heating up is characterized by both emotional and cognitive changes. One's emotions become hot, perhaps even "white-hot" (Bies et al., 1997, p. 6). Individuals may become extremely angry. Such emotions are apt to color one's thinking about the conflict (Weiss & Cropanzano, 1996). For example, Bies and Tripp (1995a) found that, following a sparking event, individuals begin to see the other person's behavior in the most negative light possible. The other person's actions were apt to be attributed to selfishness or malevolence.

There is another cognitive change that bears mention here. Disputants also tend to exhibit what Bies et al. (1997, p. 7) referred to as a "biased punctuation of conflict." When seeking retribution, it is common to construe one's behavior as reactive. That is, individuals see themselves as responding to the bad behavior of others. Their opponent's malevolence justifies revenge. It is as if two wrongs make a right. Once the punctuation of conflict becomes biased, individuals are less likely to seek out and recognize their own culpability in the dispute. This problem looms especially large if both disputants are similarly biased. Each perceives himself or herself as reacting to the other person, not as the instigator of the conflict. Thus, each act of "retribution" by one individual sets up the need for additional "vengeance" by another. This can create a spiraling (and rather childish) game of "tit for tat."

Cooling Down. As shown in Figure 6.1, the rising heat from an escalating conflict demands a release. It comes in the final or so-called cooling down stage. Tripp and Bies (in press) and Bies and Tripp (1995a, in press) discussed several ways in which the conflict can wind down. For our purposes here, however, we will only consider a few.

Perhaps the purest example of conflict can be found in what Bies and Tripp (in press) termed an "explosion." Essentially, the dispute may culminate in a grand fireball that leads to legal action, formal grievances, public complaints, or even physical violence. A less extreme version of this can be found in "venting." Working people also report the gradual release of their anger. This might take the form of a "bitch session" with friends or perhaps vindictive fantasies. One thing should be noted, however. In one study, Tripp and Bies (in press) found that venting in these ways did not always reduce conflict. Instead, some respondents indicated that it increased their anger and made future battles more likely. More research is needed to determine when venting is constructive and when it is not. Tripp and Bies also found that conflicts could simply fade with time. Sometimes individuals experienced fatigue and decided to carry it no further. On other occasions, disputants simply forgave the other person and let the potential crisis pass. These findings suggest that although individuals often retaliate, they often do not.

Stimulating Conflict With Injustice

As we have seen, conflict can have both positive and negative consequences. The trick for managers is to crank up conflict so that organizations reap the benefits, but not to let it spiral out of control so that organizations and innocent people pay the costs. Thus, at least a modicum of conflict is necessary to promote effectiveness. At issue here is how this optimal level of conflict can be achieved. Because injustice is one cause of conflict, it may follow that injustice can be a good thing (at least from the point of view of the organization). That is, an apathetic organization can be stimulated by unfair treatment. In fact, this seems to have been the recommendation of some scholars. For example, Robbins (1987) suggested that one way to stimulate conflict is by presenting workers with "ambiguous or threatening messages" (p. 351). As another technique, Robbins went on to note that some units could be forced to "compete with each other for resources" (p. 352). These particular approaches to stimulating conflict could create the potential for perceived injustice.

Deliberately treating people unfairly strikes us as unethical.[1] Moreover, as we have argued throughout this book, justice is as much a business necessity as it is an ethical one. Treating people unfairly tends to create negative consequences for everyone involved, including the organization. Stimulating conflict in an unfair manner is likely to produce pernicious results. For example, we already noted that conflict can spur creativity (James, in press; James et al., 1992). However, this creativity need not be directed toward positive organizational innovations. Rather, these same creative urges can also be directed toward finding new and innovative ways to harm the organization. James, Clark, and Cropanzano (in press) referred to this as "negative creativity." This is when workers use their innovativeness to devise new strategies to hurt the organization.

When, then, will stimulating conflict lead to positive creativity and when will it lead to negative creativity? We would agree with Robbins (1974, 1978), Baron (1991), Thomas (1993), and others who suggest that conflict stimulation can lead to useful work outcomes (but see Wall & Callister, 1995, for a different perspective). However, we would add an important caveat. In our view, whether stimulated conflict results in positive or negative creativity is largely dependent on the justice of the stimulation techniques. If conflict is stimulated in a manner perceived to be fair, such as by increasing group diversity, then positive creativity is the more likely outcome. However, if conflict is stimulated in a manner perceived to be unfair, such as by giving threatening information, negative creativity is likely to result.

One good example of this comes from the management style of Henry Ford, Sr. According to Halberstam (1986), Ford took somewhat of a "Social Darwinism" perspective when dealing with his senior managers. He often played one against the other and forced them to compete for recognition and resources. At times, these political games could become virulent and nasty, but Ford believed that they allowed the strongest managers to prosper, while the weak were weeded out. Ultimately, things did not work out the way Ford hoped. The final result, according to Halberstam, was an organization rife with distrust, torn by labor strife, and marketing an obsolete product. In fact, Halberstam went so far as to suggest that only World War II military contracts saved the company from bankruptcy. It would seem, from this example, that Ford's efforts to stimulate conflict were unfair and therefore, misguided.

Although it seems reasonable to suggest that unfair stimulation produces adverse results, there is little hard research evidence to support these ideas. Fortunately, some suggestions can be found in the creativity literature. In a sample of researchers from the superconductor industry, Abbey and Dickson (1983) found that individuals who perceived that their work environment was fair were rated as more innovative. Similarly, Eisenberger, Fasolo, and Davis-LaMastro (1990) reported that the most innovative workers were those who saw their organization as more supportive. The converse of this may also be true. Work by Meglino (1977) and Talbot, Cooper, and Barrow (1992) indicated that individuals are less creative when placed under stressful working conditions. This research would suggest, but certainly not prove, that stimulating conflict in a fair way would lead to more positive creativity than would unfair stimulation. Unfortunately, none of these findings speak to the possibility of negative creativity in an unfair environment. More research is needed to clarify this point.

Given these observations, at least one thing does seem clear. At times, managers and organizations will want to reduce the level of conflict. It is also apparent that one way to do so is to restore fairness. Next, we will discuss conflict resolution from the perspective of workplace justice. This presentation is not meant to be comprehensive. Rather, our intention is to focus on only a few conflict-resolution techniques that seem to have particularly important implications for justice research and practice. For more comprehensive reviews, we refer the reader to Blake and Mouton (1984), Folger, Poole, and Stutman (1993), Rubin, Pruitt, and Kim (1994), Wall and Callister (1995), and Weeks (1992).

To accomplish this end, we will examine conflict resolution in three settings. First, we consider an interpersonal conflict between two individuals. Based on the justice literature, we will make some suggestions for defusing such a clash. Second, we will consider informal third-party interventions. We will focus on situations where the manager attempts to settle a dispute. Finally, we will examine formal third-party interventions. In particular, we will review research on the effectiveness of employee grievance systems.

Resolving Conflict, Part I:
One-on-One Conflict Resolution

We have said that justice can cause conflict when two things are present. The target person must believe that things would have been better under different circumstances and that they should have been better as well. Before engaging in conflict, therefore, a person will usually make both of these judgments. If this is the case, then a justice analysis suggests an easy way that we can defuse minor interpersonal crises—provide a *social account*. Social accounts, also called explanations, proffer new information regarding the nature of an injustice. There is now a large body of literature examining social accounts and attesting to their effectiveness (for a sampling of this literature, the reader is referred to Bies, 1987b, 1989; Bies & Sitkin, 1992; Folger & Bies, 1989; Greenberg, 1993; Greenberg, Bies, & Eskew, 1991; Sitkin & Bies, 1993b; Sitkin, Sutcliffe, & Reed, 1993; Tyler & Bies, 1990).

In general, social accounts allow us to manage someone's impression of us. Successful explanations make a wronged party think that we are not as bad as we might otherwise appear (Greenberg, 1991). As Greenberg (1988a, 1990b) argued, it is not always enough to be fair. We must also make sure that we appear fair. One way to accomplish this is to provide a social account or explanation when something negative occurs. Otherwise, interpersonal conflict is likely to result. As we saw in Chapter 4, these explanations can blunt the effects of ill treatment.

Let us consider a common example. Suppose you ask your boss for some additional resources. It goes without saying that every request cannot be granted. However, if your petition is denied, you'll likely feel a great deal better if your boss also supplies a good reason. If he or she does not, then you might experience a sense of injustice (Bies & Shapiro, 1986). Accounts work that way. They undo the damage that occurs when something goes wrong.

A great deal of research supports the efficacy of causal accounts. Soon we will review some it. However, despite this work, it is important to realize that theoretical needs still exist. There is as yet no complete theory of when and why some explanations produce beneficial effects. For organizational purposes, we have put together a tentative and cursory model (see Figure 6.2). Our framework is based on previous research and will serve as a guide to the discussion that follows. We should emphasize that this model has not been fully tested, although certainly some parts have received empirical support. Let us begin with a general overview.

Social accounts follow a negative event. The person responsible, or some related party, desires to deflect blame from himself or herself. For that reason, the individual provides an explanation or account. From Figure 6.1, we can see that at least four different types of accounts have received research attention: causal, ideological, referential, and penitential (Bies, 1987b). These different accounts impact how someone reacts to unfavorable treatment. If the explanation "works," then the seemingly wronged party will not experience feelings of injustice, nor will they engage in conflict. But what makes some accounts work whereas others fail?

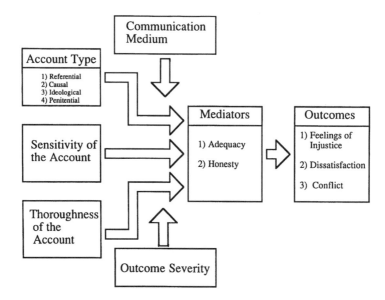

Figure 6.2. A model of social accounts.

An effective account is likely to meet two criteria: It should be seen as adequate and honest. For this reason, adequacy and honesty are said to mediate between the explanation and the outcomes (Bies et al., 1988; Shapiro, 1991). Other things besides the particular type of account also influence adequacy. Accounts can be more or less effective depending on their thoroughness (Shapiro et al., 1994, Studies 1-3) and on whether or not they are delivered in an interpersonally sensitive manner (Greenberg, 1994; Shapiro et al., 1994, Studies 1-3).

Finally, we should not neglect to mention two important moderators. The same social account may be more or less adequate, depending on whether it is presented in oral versus written form (Shapiro et al., 1994, Study 2) and on the severity of the original problem. Unfortunately, the precise nature of the severity interaction is not yet clear.

We will now examine each of these components in more detail. To accomplish this, we will begin with the main effects and then move to the moderators. As will be shown, the process by which social accounts exert their beneficial influences is a complicated one. Much more research is needed before we can be certain of these ideas. One other point bears mention: In the interest of brevity, we will emphasize research conducted in the last two decades. For a discussion of earlier work, see Bies (1987b), Sitkin and Bies (1993b), and Tyler and Bies (1990).

Types of Social Accounts

One can envision a wide variety of social accounts, each varying over an almost equally wide number of dimensions. This has led to many attempts at taxonomic classification. Over the years, several typologies have been offered (e.g., Goffman, 1967; Schlenker, 1980; Schönbach, 1990; Scott & Lyman, 1968), all of which have merit. However, in the organizational sciences, the most widely used taxonomy has been the one devised by Bies (1987b).

According to Bies (1987b), social accounts work because they manage a person's perceptions of a negative event. Sitkin and Bies (1993b, p. 353) maintained that they can do so in three ways. First, an explanation can articulate mitigating circumstances, which allow a decision maker to deny personal responsibility. These have been termed causal or mitigating accounts. Second, an explanation can justify the action with an appeal to higher values or shared goals. In this case, the decision maker accepts responsibility for the harm (Bobocel, Agar, Meyer, & Irving, 1996) but legitimizes the action based on higher motives. This has been named an ideological account, an exonerating account, or a justification. Third, the decision maker might attempt to minimize the perceived unfavorability of the event by encouraging the harmed party to engage in downward comparison. For instance, a manager might point out to an employee that others are worse off. This third type of explanation has been called a referential or reframing account. Finally, although not discussed by Sitkin and Bies (1993b), Bies (1987b) added a fourth account—penitential. A decision maker might simply admit that he made a mistake and apologize.

Causal Accounts. In order to restore justice, one can deflect blame away from himself or herself by making an excuse. One denies culpability. Bies (1987b) referred to these efforts as "causal accounts," because they do not deny that the outcome was unfair. Rather, the user of such an account simply states that he or she was not causally responsible. This involves attributing the alleged wrong to something external and beyond the control of the decision maker. Using slightly different terminology, Sitkin and Bies (1993b) referred to this as a "mitigating account," because powerful events make an individual less blameworthy.

Generally speaking, research evidence supports the efficacy of causal or mitigating accounts. For example, in one laboratory study, Bies and Shapiro (1987, Studies 1-2) found that after making a disadvantageous resource allocation decision, managers were perceived as fairer if they provided a causal account that appealed to mitigating circumstances. These findings were replicated in at least six other field studies (Bies & Moag, 1986; Bies & Shapiro, 1986; 1987, Study 3; 1988, Study 2; Bies et al., 1988; Greenberg, 1990a) and five more laboratory experiments (Baron, 1990b; Bies & Shapiro, 1988; Folger & Martin, 1986; Folger, Rosenfield, & Robinson, 1983; Shapiro, 1991). However, it should be noted that in an experiment by Bobocel and Farrell (1996, Study 1), a causal account failed to allay ill will. Similarly, Baron (1985, 1988a) found that a claim of mitigating circumstances was useless if it was not believed.

Although causal accounts can indeed be effective, they must be used with caution. In one role-playing experiment, Bobocel et al. (1996) examined the effect of mitigating circumstances in third-party conflict resolution. Bobocel and her colleagues (1996) had participants play the role of an individual who was responding to an unfavorable decision by his or her supervisor. The researchers found that participants perceived more fairness following a causal account, thereby replicating the results of earlier work. However, in providing this account, the manager claimed that he or she could not control the allocation decision. Although this impotent decision maker was seen as fairer, he or she was seen as a poor leader with circumscribed authority.

Ideological Accounts. A second means of diffusing anger is by offering an ideological account or justification. According to Bies (1987b), when making an ideological account one appeals to some higher value that legitimizes the wrongful action. For example, Bies suggested that one might recast a negative outcome as "necessary for company survival" or as "character building" (pp. 300-301). A bad outcome suddenly becomes a good one, based on its underlying motives. For this reason, Sitkin and Bies (1993b) termed these "exonerating accounts." An event might have caused some pain; however it was a good thing overall.

There is considerable research on justifications in work settings. For example, in one field study, Bies and Shapiro (1986) found that following a disadvantageous resource allocation decision, managers who offered ideological accounts were seen as more legitimate than were managers who offered no such account. Likewise, Konovsky and Cropanzano (1991) found that individuals were more approving of workplace drug testing when an adequate justification was provided. Explanations also help workers tolerate disadvantageous pay freezes (Schaubroeck, May, & Brown, 1994) and affirmative action hiring (Bobocel & Farrell, 1996). More evidence was obtained in a laboratory study by Shapiro (1991; although she termed these kinds of accounts "internal-altruistic") and Bies and Shapiro (1988). Justifications can also mitigate negative reactions to layoffs that would otherwise be manifested by both victims (Brockner et al., 1994, Study 1; Konovsky & Folger, 1991) and survivors (Brockner, DeWitt, Grover, & Reed, 1990). From this we can see that there is strong evidence attesting to the efficacy of ideological accounts. Indeed,

Bobocel et al. (1996) found these justifications to be more effective than causal accounts in mitigating ill will.

Referential Accounts. A referential account attempts to change a wronged party's frame of reference. For example, one might maintain that "You are better off than others" (Bies, 1987b, p. 304). When providing such an account, one is basically seeking to lower the other person's standards. Another approach is to direct the angered party toward the future and maintain that things might get better. Sitkin and Bies (1993b) also referred to this type of explanation as a "reframing account." These authors went on to note that there are two kinds of referential or reframing explanations: social and temporal. In a social-referential account, the person posing the explanation attempts to change another individual's referent standard. He or she attempts to steer the employee into a comparison with someone who is worse off. In a referential account that is temporal, the person proffering the explanation argues that things will get better sometime in the future. Let us now review the evidence for each.

Considerable laboratory research attests to the effectiveness of lowering someone's referent standard (Cropanzano & Folger, 1989; Folger, Rosenfield, Rheaume, et al., 1983). All other things being equal, people with lower comparison points are apt to be more easily satisfied than are those with higher standards. Consequently, it seems likely that if a decision maker or authority figure can guide someone into using a lower referent, then negative reactions should be mitigated. Although interesting, the work of Folger and his colleagues is limited for our purposes here. Although these experiments found that lower standards made ill will less likely, they did not test a decision maker's ability to directly reduce the participant's referent standards. Instead, Folger and his collaborators built the low standard into the research design—it was not an after-the-fact social account. Fortunately, more direct evidence does exist. Greenberg (1988c) found that production workers who received low performance evaluations exhibited better reactions when they were told to compare themselves to even lower performing coworkers. Similar findings were obtained by Bies (1982). In this light, it is interesting to consider a qualitative study of labor mediators conducted by Kolb (1985). Kolb observed that mediators often provided disputants with referents that either lowered their expectations or made their current state of affairs seem less onerous by comparison. Wall (1981) reviewed additional evidence attesting to the use of this tactic. It seems that shrewd mediators are well aware of referential accounts.

The other type of referential account is temporal. When offering a temporal-referential account, one is instructing an individual to look to the future, to his or her long-term outcomes, which should presumably be more advantageous. To examine this phenomenon, Folger, Rosenfield, Rheaume, et al. (1983) ran a laboratory experiment in which all of the participants failed to win a desired reward. Half of the participants were told by the experimenter that they had a good chance of earning the bonus in the future. The other half were given no such feedback. Consistent with predictions, Folger et al. found that individuals with a high likelihood of future success reported low levels of unfairness and resentment. Similar findings were obtained in a role-playing experiment conducted by Bernstein and Crosby (1980) and a field study by Bies (1982).

Nevertheless, the evidence is more equivocal than it would seem from these three studies. Mark (1985) had participants participate in a simulated work setting. Individuals again failed to earn a desired outcome. A second experimenter assured some of them, however, that they had a good chance of earning the reward some time in the future. Contrary to other research, Mark found that perceived unfairness and negative emotions were not reduced by the likelihood of future amelioration. Individuals remained upset even when they felt the reward would soon be forthcoming.

Mark's (1985) findings contradict the work of Folger, Rosenfield, Rheaume, et al. (1983), Bernstein and Crosby (1980), and Bies (1982). Why? One reason for these disparate findings was suggested by Cropanzano and Folger (1989). These authors argued that an individual experiences a sense of injustice when someone does something harmful and with provocation. That is, not only must an aversive state come about, but another person must be deliberately responsible for producing that aversive state. This is perhaps one reason why Mark's (1985) participants did not report lower levels of injustice: Although equity was restored, it was not restored by the person who had deliberately mistreated them. Although the individuals were likely thankful for the outcome, they were still displeased by the first experimenter's behavior.

In an experimental study, Cropanzano and Folger (1989) tested these ideas. Research participants failed to get a desired outcome (a bonus unit of experimental credit). The outcome was either not rectified (the control group), was rectified by a neutral third party (as in Mark, 1985), or was rectified by the original harmdoer (as in Bernstein & Crosby, 1980, and Folger, Rosenfield, Rheaume, et al., 1983). As expected, the sense of injustice was only reduced when the person who did the harm rectified the problem. There were no differences between participants in the other conditions. These data suggest that long-term improvement, in and of itself, may not be sufficient to reduce ill will. Rather, the person who created the problem needs to make amends.

Penitential Accounts. A final social account is "penitential." Here one admits that something bad happens and even accepts culpability. However, remorse is further expressed with an apology. Penitential accounts are quite effective. This may be surprising to some, for from an economic perspective, they shouldn't work. That is, the wronged party has still been wronged; the negative outcome has not been corrected. Nonetheless, asking for forgiveness seems to be quite effective. For example, in one laboratory experiment, Baron (1990b, Study 1) found that apologies were very effective in reducing ill will. Supportive results were also obtained in a field study (Baron, 1990b, Study 2). This finding does not seem to be limited to the United States. In one study with a Japanese sample, Ohbuchi et al. (1989) also found that penitential accounts reduce hostility and ill will. Saying you are sorry can go a long way.

Sensitivity of the Account

We have seen that four different types of accounts have had at least a modicum of research attention. However, we all know that the same words do not always convey the same meaning. A company explaining a pay cut, for example, might do so in a way that shows genuine concern for the well-being of the worker. Alternatively, the same pay cut could be justified in a manner that is callous and insensitive. As you might imagine, it is not enough to provide an explanation. Rather, one must also show some compassion for the one hurt.

In a field study, Greenberg (1990b) investigated the pay cut situation just mentioned. Workers at different manufacturing plants were forced to assent to a 15% reduction in salary. A control group had no pay cut. When the reduction was not explained in a sensitive and thorough manner, theft levels rose. On the other hand, when the 15% reduction was sensitively and thoroughly explained, theft did not show an increase. Unfortunately, the Greenberg (1990b) study confounds the dimensions of sensitivity (concern and compassion) and thoroughness (the detail and logic of the account). These were disentangled in a laboratory study by Greenberg (1993b). As expected, there was less theft when a pay cut was explained sensitively. Similar findings were later obtained in a field experiment by Greenberg (1994). In this study, smokers were found to be more accepting of a smoking ban if the prohibition was sensitively explained.

Slightly more complicated results were found by Shapiro et al. (1994). In one field survey, Shapiro et al. (1994, Study 1) did not find an effect for social sensitivity. However, this seemed to be due to the fact that sensitivity was highly correlated with information thoroughness. In another survey (Shapiro et al., 1994, Study 2) and one experiment (Shapiro et al., 1994, Study 3), social sensitivity did lower feelings of injustice. It is also noteworthy that in their Study 3, sensitivity and thoroughness interacted such that a sensitive presentation was maximally effective when it was also detailed. To our knowledge, this interaction has not been obtained elsewhere, so it should be interpreted cautiously pending replication. Finally, it should also be emphasized that Shapiro et al. offered the first three studies to directly compare sensitivity to thoroughness. In each case, account adequacy was better predicted by information thoroughness than by social sensitivity, although the interaction obtained in the third study could suggest that both are important.

Thoroughness of the Account

We already alluded to the fact that social accounts should be detailed, thorough, and logical if we hope to mitigate negative feelings. Greenberg (1990a) found that a thorough and sensitive explanation impeded workplace theft. However, as we already noted, this study confounded thoroughness with sensitivity. Fortunately, other evidence has addressed this concern. As indicated earlier, in three studies, Shapiro et al. (1994) found that detail improved account adequacy more than did sensitivity. Similar effects were found in other settings. Likewise, Daly and Geyer (1994) found that workers reacted less negatively to a facilities relocation if the move was fully explained. In a later study, Daly and Geyer (1995) also found that in firms experiencing a decline, full explanations mitigated ill will. Greenberg (1994) found that a thorough explanation made smokers more accepting of a workplace smoking ban.

Another approach to this problem is to assess how individuals respond to an incomplete account. In an experimental study, Ambrose and Rosse (1993) had participants complete a personality inventory for selection purposes. As we saw in Chapter 4, these types of devices are often seen as unfair. When justice issues were acknowledged, but not fully explained, participants became even more negative toward the personality test than when these concerns were not acknowledged at all. Incomplete accounts may be dangerous.

It seems to be the case that a detailed and complete account is better than one that is cursory and incomplete. However, a few caveats are in order. In a study of layoff survivors' reactions, Brockner and his colleagues (1990) found that explanations were most necessary when individuals were uncertain about the situation. It seems to be the case that thoroughness fills an information deficit. If this deficit does not exist, then the explanation can be less detailed.

Medium by Which the Account Is Communicated

As displayed in Figure 6.1, account type, social sensitivity, and account thoroughness also exert direct main effects on perceived adequacy. Adequacy, in turn, is what blunts the negative reactions to an unfavorable event. However, Figure 6.1 shows something else as well. There are also some things that moderate these relations.

The easiest moderator to discuss (given the current state of the research) is the medium of communication. In almost all of the research we have reviewed thus far, the account in question is provided via oral, face-to-face communication. This is a serious limitation. These days organizations use a wide variety of communication mediums—from letters to electronic messages to fax machines. It is unclear how strongly these effects will generalize to other forms of contact.

To our knowledge, only a single study has addressed this issue. Shapiro and associates (1994, Study 2) queried MBA students about a recent job rejection. The respondents were asked various questions about the explanation that they received. Shapiro and her colleagues discovered that the effectiveness of the account was greatest when the explanation was presented orally. The effects were weaker when the account was only presented in written form. It remains for future research to replicate these findings and to extend them to other mediums.

Outcome Negativity: Low- and High-Severity Effects

Outcome negativity presents us with an especially interesting situation for a couple of reasons. First, severity has both main and interactive effects (see Figure 6.1). Second, the nature of the interaction, when it has been found to exist, is not entirely consistent. Under certain conditions, it seems to reverse itself. Let us consider each of these in turn.

All other things being equal, when something terrible happens, explanations are apt to be seen as less adequate than when an event is not especially bad. In other words, it seems easier to explain away small problems than large ones. When people are very upset, this intense emotion can impact their reasoning, thereby making accounts less adequate than they would be if this emotion were not present (Shapiro, 1991). This main effect has been demonstrated in two field studies (Shapiro et al., 1994, Studies 1-2) and in one experiment (Shapiro, 1991). In each case, an explanation was rated as less adequate when a negative outcome was severe. It should be noted, however, that Shapiro and her colleagues (1994, Study 3) were unable to replicate these findings in a fourth study. Nevertheless, the balance of current evidence suggests that reactions are more negative when an individual is seriously harmed. This would not seem to be an especially controversial statement.

More intriguing is the obtained interaction between a social account and the severity of the outcome. Let us consider what is occurring. An individual experiences a negative event. An account is then proffered to mitigate the resulting ill effects. It seems to be the case that the event and the account interact together to determine employee responses. In and of itself, this would seem to make intuitive sense—an explanation may matter more or less, depending on what it is justifying. The problem is that, although this interaction has been obtained fairly consistently (Shapiro et al., 1994, Study 2 is one exception), the form of the interaction seems to vary from study to study. It is as if researchers have not found one interaction but two, although both involve the same variables.

Historically speaking, the first version of the interaction argued that accounts are less effective when an individual has experienced a particularly negative outcome and more effective when the event is less pernicious. Let us call this the *low-severity effect,* as explanations seem to function best when a deleterious event has minor negative consequences. There is good evidence for this. For example, Maier and Lavrakas (1976) had research participants play the role of someone whose coworker's lie cost them a great deal of money versus someone whose coworker's lie had cost them less. The participants were more likely to accept an apology when the consequences of the lie were less dire than when they were more harmful. Ten years later, Johnson and Rule (1986) compared the responses of individuals who had been badly insulted and were very upset to those whose insults were more mild. The upset participants were less likely to accept a causal account, whereas the mildly provoked were more accommodating. Maier and Lavrakas (1976) and Johnson and Rule (1986) found that accounts are more closely related to individual responses when the outcomes are less negative. If we expand our review to field studies, we find additional evidence. Shapiro et al. (1994, Study 1) found that accounts were most effective when the outcomes were less damaging and less effective when the outcomes were more damaging. Likewise, Shapiro et al. (1994, Study 3) also obtained the low-severity effect, although the actual form was a three-way interaction. In this laboratory study, an account was maximally effective if it was sincere, detailed, and delivered following an outcome that was low in severity.

There is a problem here. Social accounts are generally conceptualized as an aspect of procedure (Cropanzano & Greenberg, 1997; Folger & Bies, 1989; Tyler & Bies, 1990). As we discussed in Chapter 3, procedures and outcomes interact (Brockner & Wiesenfeld, 1996; Cropanzano & Folger, 1991; Cropanzano & Greenberg, 1997). This interaction takes a very specific form: Procedures are more closely related to sundry criteria (e.g., perceived fairness, organizational commitment, etc.) when the outcomes are unfavorable. When outcomes are acceptable, procedures predict less. This process × outcome interaction is not consistent with the low-severity effect. According to the data reviewed previously, accounts (a process) are *more* highly related to fairness when the outcome is favorable, or at least not especially negative. However, the process × outcome interaction described by Brockner and Weisenfeld (1996) suggests that procedures are *less* related to fairness when the outcomes are favorable.

This could suggest that the formal aspects of process (e.g., advance notice, voice, etc.) produce one interaction, whereas the social aspects of process (e.g., social accounts) produce another. This would be a meritorious conclusion only if we stopped our review here. In fact, there is also evidence for a *high-severity effect*—accounts sometimes work best when the outcome is unfavorable and work less well when the outcome is favorable. This high-severity effect, of course, parallels the process × outcome interaction discussed by Brockner and Wiesenfeld (1996), although it seems to contradict the low-severity effect reviewed previously.

Nevertheless, it does show up in the data. For example, an experiment by Shapiro (1991) garnered the high-severity effect. Even more evidence comes from field research. In a study mentioned earlier, Greenberg (1994) helped implement a workplace smoking ban. Thorough and sensitive social accounts improved the responses of smokers but had little effect on nonsmokers. Of course, a smoking ban would seem to be a more severe event for a person who consumes cigarettes than for one who does not. Likewise, Cropanzano and Konovsky (1995) found that justifications were better predictors when the consequences of an employee drug-testing program were punitive than when they were lenient. Similarly, Brockner and his collaborators (1990) found that layoff survivors responded more positively to an account when the outcome of the termination decision was important. The account showed smaller effects when the outcome of the decision was less important. Daly and Geyer (1995) found that explanations mattered more in periods of firm decline (when things were going poorly) than in periods of growth (when things were going well).

Seldom are two effects in such stark disagreement. On the one side is the low-severity effect, which maintains that pernicious events overwhelm social accounts. On the other is the high-severity effect, which suggests that accounts only matter when there is some initial harm done to the individual. Both interactions have empirical support. Unfortunately, there has been little speculation and no research addressing this seeming contradiction.

It seems likely that severity exerts a curvilinear effect on account effectiveness. When the outcome is not severe, or when it is positive, there is at most only a weak "trigger" for injustice perceptions. Most everyone will remain content, regardless of the accounts. In essence, no explanation is required to explain good or neutral events. And any account would be superfluous to one's reactions. As the outcomes worsen, however, people are moved into a negative emotional state. When something goes wrong, individuals are apt to become disenchanted and discontented. At this time, an account can be useful because it mitigates these negative reactions. However, suppose the unfavorable event is even worse still. Indeed, suppose it is extremely pernicious. It could be that in very harsh circumstances simple explanations are simply inadequate. An account can diffuse ill effects only if the effects are of moderate magnitude. However, when things are especially negative, the account is apt to fall short and produce no effect on reactions.

If our analysis is correct, social accounts only work when the event is moderately harmful. If the event is harmless or positive, the explanation is moot. If the event is disastrous, the explanation is feeble and impotent. This theory could produce both the low- and high-severity effects, depending on which levels of severity are sampled. If a moderately poor outcome is compared to an extremely miserable one, the researcher will see a low-severity effect. The account will succeed in the former case but fail in the latter. If a harmless or positive outcome is compared to a moderately negative one, the researcher will see the high-severity effect. The account will fail in the former case but succeed in the latter. Whereas this explanation seems reasonable to us, we caution the reader that it has never been tested. To do so would require a study that sampled at least three levels of outcome severity: none, moderate, and high. Until this research is conducted, our explanation can only be seen as speculative.

Account Adequacy

Let us refer back to Figure 6.1. We started on the distal side of the causal sequence by noting that accounts should be thorough and sensitive. We also suggested that the effectiveness of accounts is moderated by the medium through which it is delivered and by the severity of the event that it is attempting to explain (severity also exerts main effects). For all that, however, even sensitive and thorough accounts are not going to be 100% effective.

Explanations do not act directly on workers' reactions. Instead, they must be seen as adequate. As noted by Sitkin and Bies (1993b, p. 358) an effective account must offer reasons that are sufficient and credible to the listener. The reasons must fully justify or explain the event, and they must be plausible. When the reasons are incomplete or unreasonable, the account is seen as inadequate and will be of limited utility.

There is a lot of evidence to support this proposition. In one field study, Bies and Shapiro (1986) had employees recall a time when their manager could not meet their demands for resources. As noted earlier, when managers offered the worker either a causal or an ideological account, the employee reported more procedural justice and greater endorsement of their boss. However, these effects were mediated by account adequacy. In short, the effects of the accounts were more profound when they were perceived as adequate. The effect for the ideological account was fully mediated, whereas the effect for the causal account was only partially mediated. In either case, adequacy was important. Three later field studies by Bies and Shapiro (1987, Study 3), Bies et al. (1988), and Greenberg (1990a) also found that adequacy mediated the effects of a causal account. In order to allow for stronger causal inferences, Bies and Shapiro (1987, Study 2) and Shapiro (1991) replicated the adequacy effect in laboratory studies. Additionally, these findings are fully consistent with earlier experimental research conducted by Folger, Rosenfield, Rheaume, et al. (1983) and Folger and Martin (1986).

The current evidence for the adequacy effect would seem to be overwhelming. For this reason, recent research has taken a step back in the causal sequence and begun to examine the things that determine judgments of adequacy. We already reviewed these findings, but for completeness we can restate them now. In keeping with Figure 6.1, accounts are seen as more adequate to the extent that they are detailed (e.g., Shapiro et al., 1994), based on sound reasoning (e.g., Bies et al., 1988), sensitive (e.g., Greenberg, 1994), and delivered orally (Shapiro et al., 1994, Study 2). Outcome severity also matters, but here the effect is less clear. Finally, Bobocel and Farrell (1996) presented evidence that ideological accounts are more adequate than causal accounts. Although promising, this finding is in need of further replication.

Account Honesty and Sincerity

In a series of experiments, Baron (1985, 1988a, 1990b) identified another mediator. Let us consider one straightforward example of Baron's work. Baron (1990b) had simulated managers deliver nasty, destructive criticism. A causal account claiming mitigating circumstances was among the most effective means for reducing anger. However, it only seemed to work when the account was seen as sincere (see also Baron, 1985, 1988a). Obviously, an explanation that is not believed will not make anyone feel better. Two field studies by Bies (1987a) and Bies et al. (1988) also found that sincerity was important. Accounts that were not sincere did little to reduce ill will.

The role of sincerity has been the subject of some confusion. Shapiro (1991) proposed a model in which honesty, along with account type and outcome severity, were causes of adequacy. However, when the effect of adequacy was controlled, sincerity was still an important predictor of participant reactions. This suggests that adequacy is at most a partial mediator of the honesty effect. Moreover, when the effect of honesty was controlled, the relations of account type and outcome severity to participant reactions were not significant. This suggests that sincerity acts as a mediator in its own right (see Bies, 1989, Bies et al., 1988, and Sitkin & Bies, 1993b, for a similar perspective). This status is reflected in Figure 6.1. However, our model is qualified in a very important way. At the present time, very little is known about the causes of perceived honesty. We simply do not have a complete idea as to why some accounts are seen as sincere, whereas others are not. We speculate that perceptions of honesty spring from many of the same sources as perceptions of adequacy. However, only future research will inform these ideas.

Conclusions

Social accounts are generally used when one person is angry at another. If they are perceived to be adequate and sincere, then they will likely be effective. But as the research reviewed demonstrates, an account will not always work. Conflict may continue to spiral upward. This being the case, work may be disrupted and people hurt. The manager may have to intervene. It is to these managerial interventions that we now turn.

Resolving Conflict, Part II:
Informal, Third-Party Conflict Resolution

If a social account is effective, a conflict can be blunted before it even develops. Unfortunately, this does not always happen. Conflicts do break out, and they often continue to grow. Eventually, they may come to the attention of a manager or supervisor. Once the manager becomes involved, we can say that he or she has taken on the role of a third-party decision maker (Sheppard, 1984). In this section, our purpose is to explain how managers operate within this third-party role. We will first discuss a series of common conflict-resolution tactics that are frequently utilized by supervisors. We will then examine them in light of organizational justice, emphasizing the nature of the solution first and participant reactions next.

How Managers Resolve Conflicts

Despite the effort and importance placed on conflict resolution, surprisingly little systematic research has been devoted to the issue of managerial conflict-resolution tactics. Thus, although we know much about managers' resolution goals (e.g., Rahim, 1983), we have only a very preliminary understanding of their behavioral tactics and the fairness associated with them.

According to Sheppard (1984), a principal reason for this lack of research involves measurement. Fortunately, recent work has moved to address this deficiency. Extending earlier research by Thibaut and Walker (1975), Sheppard (1984) and Sheppard, Saunders, and Minton (1988) argued that a conflict episode moves through four discreet stages: definition, discussion, alternative selection, and reconciliation. In the definition stage, the nature of the dispute is defined, some resolution procedure is chosen, and the relevant evidence is assessed. In the discussion stage, arguments are presented for each side and the relevant information is clarified. Following this, in the alternative selection stage, individuals assess the validity of the arguments and select a resolution alternative. Finally, in the reconciliation stage, appeals are heard and the decision is enforced. When resolving a conflict, managers can exert control at any or all of these four stages. Based on stages at which control is exerted, Sheppard (1983) identified three common managerial intervention strategies: inquisitorial, providing impetus, and adversarial.

The most common intervention used an *inquisitorial* strategy. In this approach, the manager exerts considerable control over the discussion, alternative selection, and outcome stages. Both Sheppard (1983) and Shapiro and Rosen (1994) likened this intervention to that of a parent. The second most common technique was *providing impetus.* Here, managers tended to ignore the first three stages. Most of their control was exerted in the final, or reconciliation, phase of the process. In particular, managers provided motivational incentives to the individuals so that they might work out their own conflict. Often these incentives were negative, such as a real or implied threat. Shapiro and Rosen referred to this tactic as *offering incentives.* They compared it to a "kick in the pants." The third most common intervention was the *adversarial* tactic. When using an adversarial approach, managers did not "actively seek or restrict the content of particular evidence and arguments from the disputing parties" (Sheppard, 1983, p. 205). Rather, managers tended to step aside and let each employee present his or her own case free from harassment. After this presentation of evidence, however, managers selected the resolution alternative and enforced the decision. This adversarial strategy has also been called *arbitration* (e.g., Shapiro & Rosen, 1994; Kolb & Glidden, 1986) or *adjudication* (Karambayya & Brett, 1989).

More recently, Shapiro and Rosen (1994) included a fourth procedure. Shapiro and Rosen presented evidence that a commonly used *intervention* tactic is simply to ignore the problem. Kolb and Glidden (1986) referred to this as *avoidance* and, consistent with Shapiro and Rosen (1994), also maintained that this is commonly used.

Later research by Lewicki and Sheppard (1985) added a fifth tactic called *mediation.* Under this procedure, the decision maker controls the presentation of information but does not select the resolution alternative. Lewicki and Sheppard noticed an important problem with defining this procedure: The term *mediation* has been used in a variety of ways. For example, in the Lewicki and Sheppard study, managers used the term *mediation* to refer to a fairly rigid style of gathering information with a high degree of process control. Lewicki and Sheppard observed that managers in their study thought of mediation as being fairly close to an inquisitorial style. However, the authors conceptualized mediation somewhat differently than the respondents. Lewicki and Sheppard defined mediation as "a facilitative, problem-solving style similar to process consultation" (p. 62). Using this tactic, the manager serves as a catalyst to bring the disputants together and to help them work out their problems. Kolb (1986) termed this type of facilitative style *advising*. When using this strategy, managers are posited to share process control, but to forgo decision control. In particular, the manager only exerts process control to the extent that it is necessary to facilitate discussion and debate among the two disputants. Thus, subordinates have a great deal of discretion in determining the topic(s) of discussion. As the third party, therefore, the supervisor is a relatively passive moderator. The real work of resolving the conflict is left to the subordinates.

In sum, we have six different conflict-resolution strategies: inquisitorial, providing impetus (or incentives), adversarial (or arbitration), overlooking (or avoidance), mediational, and advising (a form of mediation where the third party shares process control). Further, research by Sheppard (1983), Lewicki and Sheppard (1985), and Shapiro and Rosen (1994) demonstrated that, with the possible exception of advising, all of these tactics are commonly used by managers.

The research cited previously is still incomplete and in need of further elaboration. There are relatively few studies and none of them would claim to be representative of American managers—much less of the rest of the world. Nevertheless, the available work does suggest important progress. These papers, although small in number, afford us at least a tentative picture of what managers do. With this in mind, we now need to turn our attention to how these various tactics work.

Consequences of Using the Intervention Tactics: The Nature of the Solution

When a conflict episode occurs, a variety of solutions are possible. Karambayya and Brett (1989), for example, argued that the conflict could conclude with (at least) an impasse, a compromise, or one of the disputants winning. In a simulated organizational conflict, these authors found that compromise was most likely when mediation was used and was least likely when the third party provided incentives. The inquisitorial strategy was intermediate with respect to the other two. Although informative, Karambayya and Brett's findings need to be extended for two reasons.

The first limitation in Karambayya and Brett's (1989) study is that it does not include the possibility of an integrative solution. That is, many conflicts can be resolved by a "win-win" alternative that is mutually advantageous to both disputants (Thomas, 1993). Unfortunately, this limitation is shared by other research as well. The problem is not fatal, however, as it does not invalidate Karambayya and Brett's (1989) findings. It only reminds us of the need for further research.

The second concern is more problematic. Karambayya and Brett (1989) used factor-analytic techniques to derive measures of various conflict-resolution tactics, such as mediation and inquisition. Their measures tended to be unifactorial. However, the conceptual definitions of the tactics seem to include multiple factors, as a third party can exert control during different conflict stages (Sheppard, 1984). Consequently, the measures and theory may not match.

Perhaps an example will add clarity. According to Thibaut and Walker (1975), Sheppard (1983, 1984), Kolb (1986), and others, many of the major conflict-intervention strategies involve both the extent to which the third party controls information and also the extent to which he or she controls the final decision. However, in some cases, Karambayya and Brett's (1989) measures of conflict-intervention strategies involved either information or decision control. For example, their items measuring an inquisitorial or autocratic strategy included "imposed own ideas," "made final decision," and "let disputants work it out" (negatively loaded; p. 696). These seem to refer primarily to decision control. We cannot be certain if the disputants controlled the process—as in Sheppard's (1983) adversarial tactic—or if the third party retained process control—as in Sheppard's (1983) inquisitorial tactic. Conversely, the items for mediation included "shuttled back and forth," "questioned parties," and "listened to disputants' views." These items seem to emphasize the process component. Consequently, we do not know if Karambayya and Brett's (1989) mediation tactic proffers decision control to the disputants—as in Kolb's (1986) *advising*—or retains it for the manager—as in Sheppard's (1983) adversarial tactic.

It is not clear that Karambayya and Brett's (1989) measurement scales adequately capture the multidimensional nature of conflict intervention. If forced to guess, we would argue that the Karambayya and Brett's autocratic tactic corresponds to the inquisitorial tactic of Sheppard (1983) and others. Based on items such as the reverse-scored "let disputants work it out," it seems likely that the third party was believed to retain both process and decision control. Conversely, because the mediation factor was independent of the inquisitorial factor, it would not be unreasonable to assume that the third party released both process and decision control to the disputants. If our speculation is correct, then Karambayya and Brett's (1989) mediational tactic is actually close to Kolb's (1986) advising. Although we cannot be certain of this, it could be that advising yields more compromises and fewer impasses than do other tactics. Obviously, we would like to have more research on this issue. Unfortunately, besides Karambayya and Brett's (1989) work, there is little other systemic research that could allow us to predict which conflict-management tactic is associated with which outcome. Nevertheless, there has been enough conceptual development to allow us to make some tentative suggestions.

Heuer and Penrod (1986) suggested that winner-take-all solutions are most likely to occur when the third party retains decision control. Thus, clean wins and losses are most likely under inquisitorial and adversarial proceedings. A clean win would probably seem fair to the winning party (Karambayya & Brett, 1989), but would be a bitter pill for the loser. These types of all-or-none judgments should, therefore, be avoided, as the latent hostility could express itself in the form of future conflict. Resolving one conflict by creating another would not be sound managerial policy.

Of course, *more likely* is not the same as *always.* Compromises can occur even when the third party possesses decision control. For example, in formal labor arbitration (similar to what we termed *adversarial* proceedings), the arbitrator will often "split the difference" and implement a compromise (Notz & Starke, 1987). Thus, compromises are common solutions that can result from a variety of conflict-resolution strategies. In terms of distributive justice, these compromise solutions are at least sometimes perceived as fair (Karambayya & Brett, 1989), even though each party gets an incomplete portion of what he or she feels entitled to.

Another important outcome is the presence of an integrative solution. These win-win integrative settlements seem most apt to occur when everyone has an opportunity to present their views and, in addition, when the cost of failure is high for both disputants. This makes sense. Integrative solutions are usually not obvious. As a result, they typically require more information and more effort. All other things being equal, one maximizes information quantity by giving everyone a chance to speak. Likewise, the high cost of failure motivates participants to do their best. Although direct empirical evidence is unavailable, these conditions are most likely to be met when the third party uses Kolb's (1986) advising strategy, or provides motivational incentives, or both. Under these conditions, the disputants are pressured to work out a deal, but only a mutually satisfactory arrangement is allowed.

Impasses are the most unfortunate of all outcomes, because neither of the disputants gets anything. Impasses are likely to occur when the third party has no decision control, for in the case of inquisitorial and adversarial tactics, the manager could always resolve an impasse by imposing a settlement. Thus, we would expect impasses to exist primarily when the third party uses mediation and advising. This creates something of a dilemma for managers. A strategy that is likely to produce a maximally fair integrative solution (i.e., advising) is also likely to yield an impasse. The same is true for mediation, which can produce a partially fair compromise. The way out of this dilemma is for managers to use the different strategies sequentially. They could begin with a low-control tactic (e.g., advising). If that yields an impasse, the manager could step up control, perhaps through arbitration. Unfortunately, little empirical work has examined the sequential use of different conflict-resolution tactics. This would be an interesting line of inquiry for future investigations.

Consequences of Using the Intervention Tactics: Disputant Preference and Procedural Fairness

In the fluid work environment, disputants usually want to retain some process and decision control (as we shall see, this is not true in all situations; see Folger, Cropanzano, Timmerman, Howes, & Mitchell, 1996; Rubin, 1980; Sheppard, 1985; Thibaut & Walker, 1975). Thus, employees generally favor mediation and what Kolb (1986) termed *advising* to arbitration (for a review, see Karambayya & Brett, 1994). With these two strategies, of course, the worker retains considerable influence over the final decision.

As this evidence seems fairly extensive, we need only consider a few representative examples here. In one interesting study, Rasinski (1992, Study 1) examined school teachers. He found that teachers preferred to resolve student conflict using participative methods. Similarly, managers in the Lewicki and Sheppard (1985) survey reported preferring mediation to other conflict intervention styles that took decision control away from the actual disputants (whether or not supervisors actually *use* mediation is another issue entirely). Heuer and Penrod (1986, Study 1) reported similar findings. The positive reaction to participative procedures is not exclusive to U.S. samples. Kozan and Ilter (1994) found that Turkish supervisors tended to resolve conflicts between subordinates by using either arbitration (Kozan & Ilter termed it *mediation*) or advising (these researchers used the term *facilitation*). Likewise, in a role-playing experiment, Cropanzano, Aguinis, Schminke, and Denham (in press) noted that respondents in the United States, Argentina, Mexico, and the Dominican Republic all preferred participative tactics. One important laboratory study was conducted by Schoorman and Champagne (1994). Schoorman and Champagne provided supervisors with negative information about a simulated subordinate. At times, the supervisor and subordinate discussed the information openly and at other times, they did not. The researcher discovered that the negative information hurt the relationship between the two people. However, if the supervisor and subordinate discussed the issue, their relationship improved.

This evidence seems fairly compelling. Both managers and subordinates usually rate participative tactics (e.g., mediation and advising) as procedurally fair. These findings contain something of a paradox. Disputants are desirous of voice. This implies that they prefer to have some control over the process (Thibaut & Walker, 1975). If this is the case, then it poses an important question: Why would disputants willingly turn over control to a third party? Indeed, one might go so far as to argue that an overlooking or avoidance strategy should offer the best route to justice. Unfortunately, this advice flies in the face of the data we reviewed earlier. Cropanzano et al. (in press), for example, found that individuals did not like overlooking. Additionally, in the classic work of Thibaut and Walker (1975), disputants were repeatedly found to grant a neutral third party decision control (as opposed to process control).

People seem to be somewhere in the middle. Too much third-party control breeds discontent. Too little control also creates trouble. Although this proposition is intuitively reasonable, it begs the question of how these control decisions are made. A few researchers have examined this issue. One suggestion comes from Rubin (1980). Based on a detailed review of the empirical literature, Rubin argued that individuals prefer to defer to a third party only when the conflict is relatively intense. When the conflict is less severe, people are satisfied with working things through themselves. Heuer and Penrod (1986, Study 2) examined another possibility. In one experimental study, they found that individuals preferred to maintain both process and decision control when the problem lent itself to a complex or integrative solution. On the other hand, when the only resolution seemed to be all-or-none, the disputants were more willing to defer to a third party. Although suggestive, this type of research is indeed tentative. More work is necessary to determine when it is best for managers to get involved.

So Why Don't Managers Participate More?

By now, the careful reader will have noticed something unusual. Participative tactics likely lend themselves to integrative solutions and procedural fairness perceptions. For this reason they should be commended. On the other hand, considerable evidence suggests that when (American) supervisors intervene, they often prefer more autocratic methods (Dworkin, 1994). The literature suggests a gap between prescription (what researchers recommend to managers) and description (what managers actually do). If participation is so effective, then why don't more supervisors use it?

To answer this question, Sheppard, Blumenfeld-Jones, Minton, and Hyder (1994) interviewed a number of supervisors. They had each participant describe a conflict between subordinates that he or she had recently settled. The results of Sheppard and associates replicated the usual tendency for managers to favor autocratic resolution tactics. This was to be expected. The unique contribution of that study, however, was that Sheppard and his colleagues identified two reasons for this inquisitorial tilt. First, whereas participation may yield higher quality solutions, it often takes longer. When speed was a concern, individuals tended to be autocratic. When speed was less important and quality mattered, then supervisors became more likely to sanction participative tactics. Second, practicing supervisors see their job as involving decision making. As a result, they tend to frame conflicts as decision-making tasks. Inquisitorial tactics allow the supervisor to make a choice.

Another reason why managers use autocratic tactics was identified in a role-playing experiment conducted by Karambayya, Brett, and Lytle (1992). Karambayya and her colleagues compared inexperienced MBA students to a group of actual managers who had experience resolving conflicts. When the two groups lacked formal power, students and managers behaved similarly— they were participative. The differences occurred when power was granted. Once in possession of power, the students became autocratic. However, the managers remained the same. They were participative regardless of their ascribed authority. Karambayya et al. suggested that sometimes people are autocratic because they simply do not know any better. Presumably, with experience or training they can become more participative.

Other Situational Factors That Determine the Success of Third-Party Intervention

As we can see, the manager's tactics seem to be important determinants of resolution success. If an intervention is appropriate, then fairness is preserved. Otherwise, justice is compromised, thereby leading to undesirable outcomes. Despite the importance of these interventions, however, more is going on. Other factors influence fairness. In this section we will discuss three of these factors: the timing of the intervention, third-party partisanship, and interactional fairness.

Timing of the Intervention. As we already saw, there are many occasions when workers would rather work through their differences personally, away from the authoritarian gaze of their supervisor (for a recent review, see Bergmann & Volkema, 1994; for a review of earlier work, see Rubin, 1980). When managers get involved too quickly, subordinates are likely to be ill at ease. It is sometimes better to wait. For example, Conlon and Fasolo (1990) discovered that when third parties intervened too hastily, the disputants responded less favorably to the process.

Third-Party Partisanship. When an individual goes before a court, or some other institution formally charged with resolving conflict, neutrality is presumed. To the extent that the decision maker is not dispassionate, justice is compromised (Lind, 1995; Tyler, 1990; Tyler & Lind, 1992). However, when a manager informally intervenes, this can become a problem. Managers often have a vested interest in how a conflict is decided. As such, it is difficult for them to meet the neutrality criteria. In fact, when a third party stands to gain from a conflict, fairness is apt to be doubted (Welton & Pruitt, 1987; Wittmer, Carnevale, & Walker, 1991).

Other than scrupulously avoiding the appearance of impropriety, the problem of partisanship affords few solutions. One possibility was suggested by Lind and Lissak (1985). In their experiment, participants saw a decision maker chatting with a bogus disputant (both were experimental confederates). To the participant, this chummy discourse appeared to suggest bias. The gregarious decision maker than resolved a dispute. When his or her resolution favored the "friendly" confederate, the participant reacted quite negatively. However, when the seemingly biased decision maker favored the participant, the participant was especially pleased with the fairness of the outcome. Lind and Lissak interpreted this to mean that the apparent friendship between the decision maker and the participant's opponent lowered expectations of success. When these negative expectations were not met, the individual reacted quite favorably. Thus, in the Lind and Lissak experiment, a bit of partisanship actually boosted fairness, but only so long as the final decision was in the participant's favor. In two more experiments, Conlon and Ross (1993) extended these ideas. Conlon and Ross found that initial partisanship lowered expectations for success. For this reason, an unfavored person was more willing to reach a settlement. Consequently, conflicts were more easily resolved.

Maintaining Interactional Justice. Earlier, we discussed evidence suggesting that interactional injustice can cause antagonism (e.g., Baron, 1991). However, the converse also seems to be true. When a third party maintains interactional fairness, this can help reduce workplace strife. Unfortunately, with the exception of research on apologies (e.g., Baron, 1990b; Ohbuchi et al., 1989), the evidence is limited.

In one experiment, Preskitt and Olson-Buchanan (1996) had undergraduate students play the role of an organizational member who was involved in a conflict. The conflict was either of high intensity (racist harassment) or low intensity (a coworker caused the participant to miss a meeting). In each case, the "worker" discussed the case with his or her manager, and in each case the manager handled the problem in the same fashion—by sending out a company-wide memo. Thus, the outcomes and formal process were invariant across conditions. What varied was the interpersonal treatment that the individual received from the supervisor. Half of the participants experienced a supervisor who was respectful, truthful, and provided explanations (i.e., high interactional fairness). The other half read about a supervisor who was disrespectful and asked inappropriate questions (i.e., low interactional fairness). Preskitt and Olson-Buchanan measured participants' responses on three dimensions: fairness, satisfaction with the resolution, and intent to pursue the conflict further. All three of these variables were impacted by the interactional justice manipulation. This suggests that managers should maintain interpersonal decorum when resolving conflicts.

Resolving Conflict, Part III:
Formal Grievance Procedures

It is perhaps easiest to understand grievance systems in reference to their historical context. In North America, as in other parts of the world, the process of industrialization did not come easily. During the Second Industrial Revolution, from about 1870 until the beginning of World War I, one of the most salient distinctions in U.S. society was that between labor and capital. The term *labor* is easily grasped. It referred to those who worked in the factories, mines, and mills. *Capital,* as the term was then understood, is a bit trickier for some modern readers. In contemporary parlance the term *capital* suggests wealth. In particular, it suggests the wealth used in commerce. This type of business capital is partially money, but also includes the physical plant, equipment, and so forth. But the term *capital* has another meaning: *Capital* is also a collective term for those who own the business wealth. Nowadays, this would include stockholders and banks, but when Marx and others used the term during the 1800s, *capital* had more substantive connotations. In this sense, *capital* referred to those who both owned and managed large industrial and mining firms.

In the North American economy of the late 20th century, owners and operators are generally separate individuals. Officially, large corporations are usually the property of shareholders. Often managers possess only a modest portion of a firm's business capital. Sizable, family-owned organizations— such as Campbell's soup—still exist, but in the United States, these tend to be the exception to the rule. In large firms, the owners and the managers tend to be different people. This separation was not always the case. In the late 1800s, owners and managers tended to overlap a great deal more (Moore & Sinclair, 1995). As Fukuyama (1995) discussed, many large businesses were both owned and operated by the entrepreneurs who founded them. This list includes such luminaries as Andrew Carnegie (steel), Henry Ford I (automobiles), Andrew Mellon (banking), John D. Rockefeller (oil), and Cornelius

Vanderbilt II (railroads). It was only later that ownership turned to stockholders and "managership" turned to professional supervisors (Fukuyama, 1995).

From this, we can see that the term *capital* once had a more profound meaning. Used in this way, *capital* simply refers to those who own and run things. *Labor* designates those who took orders and did the work. Put differently, the only things of value that labor "owned" were their skills and motivation. These were "sold" to the capitalist for profit (Moore & Sinclair, 1995). Capital, as understood here, underscores differences in social class and highlights the potential, if not the reality, of exploitation and conflict (Fantasia, 1988).

Although lacking in wealth, labor was not entirely powerless. To a greater or lesser extent, they were represented by their unions. They also had the sporadic support of various intellectuals, activists, and clergy. Workers were more than capable of putting up a fight (see Bettmann, 1974, and Painter, 1987, for histories of this period). Bettmann (1974, p. 82) reported that in the 19 years from 1881 to 1900, there were a full 2,378 strikes idling over six million workers. Not that these strikes were especially successful. Capital responded with private armies of goons and, failing this, had the strong support of the local police and even the Federal army. In such a situation, it is difficult to find someone who clearly benefits. Clearly, there were appreciable costs to both sides. With World War I acting as an impetus, the federal government encouraged greater cooperation between labor and capital (Painter, 1987). Self-interest (and prompting from the government in regard to national interest) led to the present system of collective bargaining enforced by grievance proceedings.

The current pattern of industrial relations grew from the conflicts of these earlier years. We can apprehend the present state of affairs by realizing a simple point: Labor works when it has a contract. Lacking a contract, the cooperation between labor and management breaks down. The central goal of industrial relations is to establish and maintain a viable contract. For this reason, conflicts often break out when a contract has expired and another is in need of negotiation. For instance, unions may use this time to request a raise, or management might ask for a pay rollback. It is during contract negotiations that the grievance system is usually devised.

Grievance procedures do not set up a labor-management contract. Rather, they are a mechanism for making certain that an existing contract functions smoothly. Even the best specified compact will contain some ambiguities and grounds for disagreement. There will invariably be misunderstandings or new situations that were not specifically anticipated. For example, workers may receive assignments that seem to contradict their negotiated job duties. If these differences are not somehow resolved, the contract will break down, perhaps precipitating a strike. In order to maintain the agreement, some system must be in place to address these inevitable disagreements. This is the purpose of grievance systems.

Grievance systems grew out of disputes between labor and capital. Although nonunion grievance systems exist (Feuille & Chachere, 1995; Lewin, 1990), the origins of the institution are firmly grounded in organized struggles for worker rights. This history helps shape the character of present-day grievance procedures. By their historical nature, grievances involve an exchange between parties who may be deeply suspicious of one another (Brett, 1980). This poses an interesting question: Why do low-trust parties maintain procedures that demand their interaction? The answer would seem to be self-interest. Workers and managers did not organize grievance systems because they suddenly decided to become friends. Rather, the two sides came together because they needed each other. Labor and capital have an association that is simultaneously symbiotic and adversarial (Brett, 1980). Collective bargaining and grievance systems are institutional tools that allow the two parties to navigate this contradictory relationship. In other words, grievance procedures allow both workers and managers to put aside their enmity long enough to accomplish mutually beneficial objectives.

Conduct of Workplace Grievances

Grievance policies involve quasi-legal proceedings (Gordon & Miller, 1984). Like the laws of nations and communities, the systems are not necessarily the same, but they often share many commonalties. In most systems, a worker's grievance moves through a series of stages. For example, he or she might open with a written grievance to a supervisor, later appeal to the business unit, and conclude with a similar appeal to the CEO (Brett & Goldberg, 1983; Lewin, 1987).

This stage-based quality is important. Appeals typically move forward one step at a time. This is intended to encourage the resolution of grievances at the lower stages (Lewin & Peterson, 1988; Ury, Brett, & Goldberg, 1989). This stage-based procession has another advantage. In a properly designed system, the lowest-cost steps appear first and the higher-cost steps only come into play when those fail (Brett, Goldberg, & Ury, 1990). This functions to keep costs down—no mean consideration for a large firm (e.g., Ichniowski, 1986). For these reasons, it is generally useful to resolve disputes in the earliest possible stages, although this depends somewhat on the nature of the grievance and settlement (Gordon & Bowlby, 1988).

A typical system will have four or five steps. Lewin (1987, p. 471) presented some specific examples. Let us take the fairly typical, four-step case of an aerospace firm. The plaintiff-worker (a) first addresses a written appeal to his or her supervisor; (b) files another appeal with the personnel officer, thereby triggering a hearing; (c) writes an appeal to the vice president for employee relations, thereby triggering a board of inquiry; and (d) addresses a final appeal to an adjustment board that includes an outside arbitrator. Remember: Proceedings vary from firm to firm. For example, many companies conclude their policies in-house. They might have the CEO render a final decision rather than using an outside arbitrator. It is also very common for firms to require plaintiffs to speak informally with their supervisor before filing the initial, written appeal. Even where this is not a requirement, it is often encouraged.

What Happens When Grievance Systems Cease to Function Effectively?

Many grievance systems are fairly elaborate and seemingly thorough. A well-working system has the support of both management and workers and thereby maintains the smooth functioning of the contract. On the other hand, these systems often fail to accomplish their objectives. Workers and managers can lose faith in appeals policies (e.g., Ury et al., 1989). When this occurs, the symbiotic relationship between labor and capital begins to fracture, tipping away from mutual dependence and ever more closely toward contentiousness. Gradually, the organization begins to fall apart. A flagging grievance system is associated with declining industrial productivity (Ichniowski, 1986; Katz, Kochan, & Gobeille, 1983; Katz, Kochan, & Weber, 1985; Norsworthy & Zabala, 1985).

When the system is functioning badly, some supervisors seem inclined to retaliate against grievants by biasing performance ratings downward (Carnevale, Olson, & O'Connor, 1992; Klaas & DeNisi, 1989; Lewin, 1987) and curtailing the offending workers' promotion opportunities (Lewin, 1987). Angered workers may actually lower their job performance (Bretz & Thomas, 1992; Olson-Buchanan, 1996b), miss work (Klaas, Heneman, & Olson, 1991), leave the firm (Bretz & Thomas, 1992; Lewin, 1987; Olson-Buchanan, 1996b), and crowd the grievance system with so many appeals that it is unable to function effectively (Ury et al., 1989). Of course, it must be strongly emphasized that none of these pernicious responses are necessary. In fact, although beyond the scope of the present review, the research cited here shows that there are many moderators of these contentious reactions (see Klaas, 1989, for a review and theoretical model). Nevertheless, grievance systems can malfunction from time to time, and when they do, people get hurt.

It is for this reason that organizational justice researchers have begun to examine grievance systems. Clearly, fairness is not the only consideration necessary to design a smoothly working procedure (for others, see Brett et al.,

1990). Nevertheless, to the extent that appeals policies promote a sense of procedural justice, they do seem to function more effectively (Gordon & Fryxell, 1993). For example, in one large-scale study, Fryxell and Gordon (1989) examined five samples of unionized workers. They found that the presence of a procedurally fair grievance system led to higher satisfaction with the union among all five groups. Similarly, distributive justice boosted union satisfaction in four of the five samples. In a later study, Fryxell (1992) found that fair grievance procedures predicted workers' beliefs that there was a moral order at work. For this reason, we can see workplace fairness as one important issue in policy administration.

Grievance Systems and Social Justice: Voice as Process Control

In this section, we will consider how grievance systems can be made fairer. The quasi-legal nature of grievance appeals allows us to gain some insights from research on courtroom proceedings. This work is substantial. A classic series of studies was conducted by Thibaut and Walker (1975, 1978). According to Thibaut and Walker (1975, 1978), formal third-party dispute resolution involves three individuals: two disputants and a decision maker. In the courtroom, the decision maker is usually a judge. In work settings he or she is likely to be a mediator or arbitrator. These researchers maintained that these three people move together through two stages. First, there was a process stage in which evidence was presented, debated, and evaluated. This was followed by a decision stage in which a verdict was reached. Different people can exert control at different stages. Examining dispute resolution from the perspective of the third party yields five possible dispute resolution processes: (a) The decision maker controls both stages (autocratic), (b) the decision maker controls the outcome stage but not the process stage (arbitration), (c) the decision maker controls the process stage but not the outcome stage (mediation), (d) the decision maker controls neither stage (moot), or (e) a decision maker is not even involved (bargaining).

As this chapter already considered the case of dispute resolution without a third party, we will ignore here the bargaining procedure. In large measure, Thibaut and Walker (1975) were concerned with comparing the legal systems of various nations. In particular, they equated the Anglo-American adversarial system with their arbitration procedure. Conversely, the European inquisitorial system was equated with the autocratic process. Thibaut and Walker (1975, 1978) maintained that the inquisitorial procedure affords the disputants less process control than does its adversarial counterpart. From this line of inquiry, Thibaut and Walker (1975, 1978) determined that disputants in legal settings preferred to retain voice in the process stage. In this way, disputants ensured that their case was adequately presented. However, people were also willing to forgo voice in the decision stage (assuming the outcome was all-or-none; see Heuer & Penrod, 1986). From this, Thibaut and Walker (1975, 1978) concluded that disputants generally found adversarial proceedings to be the fairest. That is, participants were satisfied by process, as opposed to decision, control.

It is interesting to revisit Thibaut and Walker's (1975, 1978) findings in light of more recent research. Part of it has withstood the test of time, but another part has not. Let us begin with the revisions to their earlier model. Sheppard (1985) observed that Thibaut and Walker (1975, 1978) tended to somewhat malign the European inquisitorial system. He pointed out that, in fact, European inquisitors typically allow disputants some free time to present their own cases. Thus, some process control is given to the people engaged in the conflict. In a series of role-playing studies, Sheppard (1985) found that a more accurately represented inquisitorial procedure was seen to be just as fair as the adversarial process. This revision not withstanding, Thibaut and Walker's (1975, 1978) most important conclusion still holds. Recent work has confirmed that disputants are desirous of voice during the process stage (Folger et al., 1996). Unfortunately, none of this work directly examines grievance systems. One would suspect that the determinants of fairness are similar for both courtrooms and workplace appeals, but for this evidence we must turn elsewhere.

In one field study, Shapiro and Brett (1993) examined a large group of coal miners who had filed grievances. Coal miners reported more procedural fairness when they had some control over the process. Thus, Shapiro and Brett's findings are fully consistent with Thibaut and Walker's (1978) work in legal settings. Shapiro and Brett (1993) reported a few other things as well. They also examined a variable termed *third-party enactment* or *third-party fairness.* Third-party enactment referred to the behavior of the mediator or arbitrator. It included such things as whether or not the third party understood the grievance, considered the disputants' viewpoints, and acted impartially. Third-party enactment turned out to be an especially important predictor. In fact, it acted on procedural justice in two different ways. For one, enactment exerted a statistically significant main effect. For another, it interacted with process control, such that process control was more closely related to procedural justice perceptions when third-party enactment was high (i.e., the mediator or arbitrator behaved impartially, considered the disputant's opinion, etc.). Finally, people cared about the process and its enactment even when the grievance was not resolved in their favor.

In another field study, Conlon (1993) examined the reactions of university employees and students who appealed a parking violation. Consistent with Shapiro and Brett (1993) and Thibaut and Walker (1975), Conlon (1993) found that individuals reported more procedural fairness when they believed that they were provided voice. However, unlike Shapiro and Brett (1993), in Conlon's (1993) sample, the favorability of the outcome overrode the amount of process control. That is, the primary influence on justice perceptions was whether or not the claimants won their case. When they did, they reported more fairness; when they did not, they reported less.

In a third study, Giacobbe-Miller (1995) moved away from workplace grievances and focused on contract negotiations. Giacobbe-Miller determined that when impasse resolution procedures allowed for disputant voice, both union members and managers reported more procedural fairness. Consistent with Shapiro and Brett (1993) but not with Conlon (1993), process control was a more important predictor than was outcome control or pay level.

Taken together, this research suggests that process control or voice is an important predictor of fairness. However, these data are not completely consistent. In particular, Conlon (1993) did not find strong process-control effects. This makes it reasonable to ask whether any additional variables could be moderating the process control-procedural justice relation. As implied by Shapiro and Brett's (1993) findings, at least one such moderator does seem to exist. Unfortunately, it has received surprisingly little attention in workplace settings. In one early field study, Tyler (1984) assessed defendants' reactions to courtroom verdicts. Tyler found that even when the results of the case went against them, defendants derogated neither the courts nor the judge so long as they exercised some process control (this is consistent with the research discussed earlier) *and* the judge seriously considered their viewpoint. In short, voice produced more positive reactions only when that voice was given due consideration. In later work, Tyler and his colleagues replicated this consideration effect and extended it to police officers (Tyler, 1987; Tyler et al., 1985). Clearly, Shapiro and Brett's (1993) findings with respect to third-party enactment are consistent with this research, although it should be noted that third-party enactment contains elements other than just simple consideration.

Given these findings, Shapiro (1993) set out to more clearly articulate what is meant by *consideration*. According to Shapiro, individuals believe their views have been considered when two conditions are met. First, the disputants must perceive that they have the potential to influence the process. Whereas this potential need not be realized, individuals must at least feel that the procedure was not a sham, that they at least had a chance to achieve a desirable resolution. Second, disputants must also feel that the decision maker is interpersonally responsive. That is, he or she should be receptive and attentive to their ideas. Shapiro offered several suggestions for promoting both the potential to influence, as well as interpersonal responsiveness. Besides clarifying the nature of consideration, Shapiro's theoretical work raises an important conceptual question. What is the difference between interpersonal responsiveness and the social aspects of procedural justice? Responsiveness would seem to be similar to interpersonal sensitivity. If this is so, then Shapiro (1993) is implicitly suggesting that one form of procedural justice (interpersonal sensitivity) is moderating another (the structural elements of process). Unfortunately, this intriguing possibility has not yet been investigated.

Clearly, processes that supply voice are more apt to be viewed as fair. However, throughout this book we have also seen that other attributes matter as well. Voice is only one determinant (Cropanzano & Greenberg, 1997; Leventhal, 1976). Thus, much of the work we have discussed is limited by its heavy emphasis on voice. Research in legal settings suggests that other elements of process may also be important (e.g., Krzystofiak, Lillis, & Newman, 1995; Lind, Kulik, Ambrose, & de Vera-Park, 1993). Future work on grievance systems should expand its focus to include such things as procedural consistency, accuracy, and opportunity for further appeals.

Conclusion

This chapter was about conflict in work organizations. But implicit in any discussion of conflict is the idea of a social fabric—a pliable collection of people that from time to time will be torn apart and patched back together. From this metaphor we can see the centrality of justice to social life. Injustice destroys the social fabric and sends its constituents spiraling into conflict. But justice repairs the fabric and rebuilds the whole. In large measure, work organizations can be held together through fairness. In this way, justice represents the greatest of lost opportunities and also the greatest of future challenges.

Note

1. It should be noted that we have only selected these two particular stimulation techniques because they raise potential justice issues. As such, they are especially relevant to the present book. We strongly emphasize that the vast majority of Robbins's (1987) suggestions raise no such concerns. In fact, some of his recommendations, such as increased participation and increased group heterogeneity, strike us as promoting the goal of workplace fairness.

7 Toward a General Theory of Fairness

This chapter presents an integrative framework for earlier models of organizational justice. The framework—Fairness Theory—focuses on accountability for events with negative impact on material or psychological well-being. The theory could also be extended to positive events, at least in principle, but we have chosen to focus on negative events in order to keep the presentation more concise.

An event's negative impact can affect responses to those held accountable. Fairness Theory addresses separate determinants of (a) an event's negative impact and (b) accountability for the event. Nonetheless, responding to others also combines negativity and accountability. We use these themes to integrate the justice literature, noting where previous approaches have emphasized some determinants to the neglect of others.

Accountability as Grounds for Integration

Work on organizational justice has introduced numerous concepts relating to various topics. Considerable fragmentation has resulted. Although an

173

integrative theory might not necessarily incorporate all preceding findings into a tidy package, it might at least give greater coherence of direction in the future. Also, showing how the various concepts fit together can provide a "forest" overview otherwise lost by a "trees" focus. In this chapter, we show how Fairness Theory ties together relational approaches (e.g., Lind & Tyler, 1988; Tyler & Lind, 1992), Referent Cognitions Theory (RCT) (e.g., Folger, 1987b, 1993), and other conceptual developments in the justice literature.

Justice approaches share a common focus: how people who experience unfairness respond to those held accountable for the unfairness. Adams (1965), for example, asked whether a disadvantageous inequity would result in more than mere feelings of dissatisfaction. He pointed out that anger toward the perpetrator of an injustice could lead to equity restoration attempts involving actions directed against the perpetrator (e.g., reducing Other's outcomes or increasing Other's inputs). Similarly, RCT (Folger, 1987b, 1993) discussed the conditions that would maximize resentment toward such a violator of justice norms. Bies (1986) introduced the concept of interactional justice in part to note the important role of explanations that the violator might give to avoid retaliation from the person feeling unfairly treated. This conception explicitly took into account the prospects for hostile responses directed toward an agent of injustice. Finally, Lind and Tyler's (1988) group value model was later elaborated as a relational model of authority (Tyler & Lind, 1992). The latter version of their model explicitly focused on the implications of unfair treatment exhibited by authorities for individuals' acceptance of the same authority figures and their willingness to comply with rules or evaluations advanced by these figures. Holding someone else accountable for injustice, and directing responses toward the accountable party, emerges as an overall integrative theme across various models of justice. Thus, we propose that certain basic processes involving accountability are central for understanding the way individuals react to injustice, whether their reactions are directed toward another person or a social institution, such as a workplace organization.

Elements for a Theory of Fairness
Counterfactuals: The Nature of Moral Reasoning

The moral codes of a given society serve to constrain social conduct that can have repercussions for the material and psychological well-being of others in the society. Similarly, norms of fairness call for exercising discretion with others' well-being in mind. Reasoning about social justice, therefore, involves applying moral principles that hold people accountable for the implications of their discretionary behavior.

Fairness Theory characterizes moral accountability as involving (a) *conduct*—the commission or omission of actions capable of having effects on others (i.e., social conduct); (b) *principles*—tenets about constrained discretionary conduct, where a lack of restraint might jeopardize others' well-being (guidelines regulating conduct); and (c) *states* of well-being of affected parties—when human actions have implications for others' welfare (the impact of social conduct and its repercussions). People's perceptions concerning these aspects of moral accountability—discretionary conduct, applicable principles, and implications for states of well-being—are characteristically influenced by the implicit use of contrastive reasoning. An event, such as a layoff, and its implications, such as financial hardship, for example, can be contrasted with the implications for well-being associated with some alternative event that comes to mind even though it did not actually occur (a laid-off employee's thoughts about the financial security associated with having a job). Observed social conduct, such as the manner in which top executives determined what proportion of employees to lay off, can be contrasted with other types of actions that come to mind (some other manner of deliberation). Where other people's actions are concerned, alternative actions can be brought to mind both in reflecting on what alternative actions were possible and in reflecting on what alternative actions might be considered morally superior.

The psychological literature on this type of implicit contrastive reasoning has seen an explosion of work associated with the term *counterfactual thinking* (for a review, see Roese, 1997), and we find it helpful to use counterfactual language in describing our model. Actual occurrences—events and their implications for states of well-being, in conjuction with the actions of others—are the objects of comparison with counterfactual alternatives that come to mind. *Counterfactual*, as Roese (1997) noted, literally means "contrary to the facts" (p. 133). He used the following illustrations:

> Some focal factual outcome typically forms the point of departure for the counterfactual supposition (e.g., Madame Bovary's or Cyrano's angst). Then, one may alter (or *mutate*) some factual antecedent (e.g., her decision to marry dull Henry and his inability to court Roxanne directly) and assess the consequences of that alteration. (p. 133)

Whereas those examples refer to alternative states of well-being for Bovary or Cyrano based on mutations of their own actions, we focus on the moral accountability of others' conduct because the theory aims at explaining perceptions of social fairness. Because discretionary conduct refers to choices among feasible alternatives, first note the relevance of a contrast between what another person actually did and one type of counterfactual, namely what he or she *could* have done. Second, judging another's discretionary conduct by moral principles implies the contrast between what was done and and what *should* have been done. Finally, the experienced state of well-being of an affected party is implicitly compared with what it *would* have been otherwise (e.g., had some other event occurred instead of the one associated with the other party's discretionary conduct).

Take the example of a high-level manager, Sarah, who downsizes part of an organization by laying off employees. Consider this downsizing as an event with implications for the well-being state of Joe, one of those laid-off employees. Our discussion of Fairness Theory addresses some of the following points relevant to such situations:

1. What impacts Joe adversely? Prior theories have emphasized issues of distributive, procedural, and interactional justice; in other words, Joe's well-being might seem adversely affected to the extent that his actual state is deemed unfair in any of these three ways. For example, he might evaluate his amount of severance pay according to distributive principles such as equity. He might evaluate the procedural justice underlying various aspects of the layoff decision—such as those concerning whom to dismiss or how much severance pay to award—by considering whether the decision making took into account the interests of affected parties such as Joe (e.g., whether employee representatives were put on a task force to determine criteria for layoff selection and severance benefits). Also, Joe might react to the degree of interpersonal sensitivity Sarah shows when laying off employees (e.g., the extent and quality of explanations given, as well as the timing of dismissals and the manner in which they are implemented).

Despite the noted distinctions among outcomes distributed, procedures used, and interpersonal manner displayed, Fairness Theory also emphasizes one way in which the perceived impact of experience cuts across such distinctions: Each can vary with respect to perceived negativity. Any experience is subject to differing perceptions as a function of contextual factors that influence how negative the impact seems. For example, consider two people who each fail to win a door prize after having purchased a $5 ticket. Even though the objective financial loss is the same, the subjective experience differs according to the counterfactual that the given situation evokes, such as a drawing for a $50 prize versus for a $5,000 prize. A loss of $5 compared to the counterfactual of winning $5,000 seems worse than a loss of $5 compared to the counterfactual of winning $50. Counterfactuals play exactly the same role in reactions to procedures and reactions to interpersonal treatment: A given negative experience (based on negative features of the procedure used or treatment received) will seem only mildly negative if its evoked counterfactual (an alternative procedure or form of treatment that comes to mind) does not seem much better, whereas the same experience will seem much worse if its evoked counterfactual is much better.

We call these *Would* counterfactuals, which refers to a mental comparison indicating how something else *would* feel instead of the state of well-being actually experienced. In the interactional justice realm concerning perceived interpersonal sensitivity of treatment, for example, a difference in Would counterfactuals might make the same comment about performance seem like a mild admonition to one person but like a scathing insult to another. Please note, however, that Would counterfactuals refer only to the emotional implications of thinking about what an alternative experience would feel like, disregarding the analysis of why the actual experience occurred rather than its counterfactual alternative. If Joe spends a lot of time thinking about how nice it would be to have his old job back, such thoughts are likely to sustain feelings of misery about being out of work, regardless of the reason for being out of work. The loss of a $150,000 job presumably might feel worse than the loss of a $15,000 job, for example. Such a difference is conceptually independent of the reason for job loss (e.g., Joe victimized by unscrupulous office politics vs. a "just cause" dismissal for Joe's egregious contractual violations).

2. Does the negative impact constitute unfair treatment? Partly that depends on whether the unfairness is personal (i.e., single party) or social (i.e., two or more parties). If Joe's own conduct did not warrant the extent of negative impact, this personal unfairness sets up the potential for perceptions of social unfairness. If Joe attributes the unwarranted adversity (e.g., job loss despite top-notch performance) to factors beyond anyone's control, he will hold no one else accountable and will not perceive social unfairness (unwarranted adversity attributable to another social agent).

3. What determines whether another party is held accountable for an experience that is perceived as both adverse and unwarranted, based on one's own conduct? We see that question as having a two-part answer. In part, such matters depend on perceptions of whether aspects of events were subject to changes at the discretion of the other party. For example, Sarah and Joe might differ in their perceptions of her discretionary authority—which courses of action were or were not among her feasible alternatives. Our discussion of *Could* counterfactuals addresses that topic, integrating it with a recent interpretation of the relational model with parallels between trust—a relational element—and intentionality.

4. Holding someone accountable also depends on perceptions about which moral principles were in force, and how they apply with respect to the party in question. What *should* Sarah have done?

Much of our discussion focuses on so-called two-party cases such as the example of Sarah and Joe. These occur when discretionary conduct by Person A (e.g., a supervisor) has implications associated with the well-being state of Person B (e.g., a laid-off employee). Moral principles such as fairness norms permit individuals to connect their state of well-being with the conduct of others. The nature of that connection influences perceptions of A as an offending party and B as a grievant, based on what A did (his or her conduct) and what B experienced (his or her state). In the layoff example used earlier, Could and Should factors refer to Sarah's conduct in terms of (a) her capacity for managerial discretion and (b) an evaluation based on applicable moral imperatives. Conversely, Would factors refer to Joe's state as compared to other possible outcomes. As we have emphasized, the negativity of that state might be determined by many factors, including a focus on lost pay, a missed opportunity to participate in decision making, diminished pride or self-esteem stemming from the manner in which the layoff was announced, and so forth. Because we want to emphasize how different situations operate in the same fashion despite key differences between them, our examples often depict two extremes—a purely material or financial matter, such as money, and a psychologically, symbolically significant matter, such as receiving an insult or otherwise being subjected to demeaning interpersonal treatment. Because only the latter situations are inevitably social, involving more than one party, we first turn to clarifying the nature of effects in terms of social parties before addressing the theory proper.

Before classifying effects based on the number of parties, however, we must stress that Would factors have a conceptually separate function from that of Could and Should. Could and Should factors function to determine account-ability (e.g., whether to hold the immediate supervisor responsible for the amount of pay received or the manner in which criticism was delivered). Conversely, Would factors determine only the degree of negativity of the outcome. Separate discussions of Would, Could, and Should will precede our discussion of their interrelation. But be forewarned: We propose that some factors said to involve procedural or interactional justice nonetheless function as determinants of negative event impact, whereas some previous discussions (e.g., Folger, 1987b) tended to focus almost exclusively on outcomes as deter-minants of negative impact.

Effects to Be Explained

Fairness Theory addresses one-party, two-party, and three-party cases of perceived unfairness. This abstract classification system is the background context for our treatment of Fairness Theory in this chapter, which focuses primarily on the two-party case.

Single-Party (Personal) Unfairness

"How unfair that it's raining and I can't get a tan." If someone uses fairness language in that manner, they seem to mean something like the following: (a) My experience is negative, although (b) I have not done anything negative (to cause the negative experience or deserve it). Not being personally accountable for misfortune makes it seem unfair; the more misfortune, the more perceived unfairness. But when impersonal forces—rather than another party's actions—cause misfortune, greater magnitudes of misfortune increase the perception of only personal, not social, unfairness.

Unfairness in the Two-Party Case

Two-party situations include those in which the focal party holds another party accountable and those in which the focal party does not hold anyone else accountable. The latter reduce conceptually to an equivalent of one-party cases in which impersonal forces (e.g., meteorological factors) cause misfortune (e.g., rain). Again, an event's negative impact on someone's experienced well-being has no influence on responses directed toward another person, unless the former holds the latter accountable for key implications of that event.

Suppose, for example, an employee loses her job during a layoff. If she does not consider anyone at the firm responsible for the layoff, then she tends not to direct any retribution against the former employer or managers at the organization. Now consider a group of employees who do not consider anyone at the firm responsible for the layoff—perhaps because they all believe that layoffs are inevitable under certain types of market conditions (cf. impersonal forces such as meteorological conditions causing rain). The negative implications of being laid off might seem severe to some and only mild to others. Nonetheless, the variations in experienced negativity would tend not to be correlated with negative responses that target management, such as calling management unfair or increasing the level of retribution to correspond with the level of negativity experienced.

In the other type of two-party case, the focal party feels aggrieved because he or she *does* hold another party responsible for an event's negative implications. Here, negative responses toward the other party *do* vary directly with the magnitude of the event's negative implications for the aggrieved (e.g., the severity of the aggrieved's sense of loss). Among employees who do hold a firm's management accountable for jobs lost through layoff, for example, differences in the perceived magnitude of impact from the implications of being laid off (i.e., variations in experienced sense of loss across employees) will tend to be associated with differences in the propensity to direct certain types of responses—typically those exhibiting hostility—toward the organization and its leaders as targets.

This description of contrasting effects among two-party cases also fits the classic Process × Outcome pattern confirmed across numerous lab and field studies testing predictions about fairness from theories such as RCT (for a review, see Brockner & Wiesenfeld, 1996). As we will show, however, Fairness Theory recasts this interaction in ways that go beyond the distinction between process and outcome, yet retain what is useful about it. In particular, we argue that accountability and impact are related to process and outcome but also differ from them in ways that potentially overcome some of their limitations. Moreover, as we will discuss subsequently, the experienced negativity of the impact from an event can be determined by either the factors traditionally associated with "outcomes" and distributive justice, or the "process" factors traditionally associated with procedural or interactional justice.

Unfairness From the Perspective of a Third-Party Observer

Most explanations about sources of felt injustice try to give reasons that such a person does or does not feel unfairly treated, and what that person might do when feeling unfairly treated. These are the two-party cases of victim and perpetrator, analyzed from the standpoint of the victim's desire for righting wrongs and requiring others to answer for injustices they commit. But society also has an interest in righting wrongs and holding people accountable. Thus, accounts of perceived injustice that involve explanatory mechanisms, such as the loss of one's material comfort or self-esteem, then seem ill-suited to explaining why third-party observers can react with a strong sense of moral outrage and righteous indignation, even though their material comfort and self-esteem have not suffered. We try to take this potential anomaly into account even as we shape an explanation for the two-party cases.

Elements of a Theory of Fairness: Would, Could, and Should Counterfactuals

The next three subsections provide more details about the Would, Could, and Should counterfactuals as separate elements of Fairness Theory. We also draw parallels between these concepts in Fairness Theory and related concepts in other approaches. Note, however, that we postpone discussing their combined effects in the two-party case until a later section on how Fairness Theory integrates previous approaches. The following three sections concentrate on comparison, therefore, whereas a subsequent major section concentrates on integration.

Our integrative model—Fairness Theory—emphasizes a distinction between an event's negative impact (e.g., the impact of a less-than-expected raise vs. a large pay cut, or scathing insult vs. mild admonition) and whether someone is held accountable for the event (e.g., whether to hold the immediate supervisor solely responsible for the amount of pay received or the manner in which criticism was delivered). Fairness Theory proposes conceptually separable psychological processes governing perceptions of impact magnitude and perceptions of accountability, much like a distinction between the amount of damage (or its severity) versus how and why it occurred. As we noted, the Would aspect of the theory concentrates on magnitude impact, whereas Could and Should concentrate on accountability.

The impact-accountability distinction is also not unlike the difference between determining guilt (accountability) and deciding how much punishment to administer based on the magnitude of negative impact. In the U.S. justice system, for example, civil juries sometimes award punitive damages according to their perceptions of the amount of harm done or suffering experienced. As a response directed toward some social party, however, negative sanctions (e.g., punishment) reflect not only the negative impact of harm or suffering but also the assignment of accountability for that harm or suffering. The decision to apply a negative sanction requires accountability judgments to determine the direction of the response (toward the party designated for sanctions) as well as impact-negativity judgments to determine the intensity or magnitude of the response.

Fairness theory argues that judgments about the Would, Could, and Should factors do not occur in any particular order. Unlike guilt determination followed by punishment assignment, therefore, the accountability-impact judgments need not occur in any particular order. Sometimes accountability is determined prior to knowledge of impact, such as when an employee knows that management has mandated job rotation but does not yet know details about a new assignment that will result. Alternatively, damage to company property might be evident before the perpetrator is discovered, for example, or the perpetrator might never be discovered. Regulations about sabotage of a firm's property by its employees might stipulate the magnitude of specific penalties in advance, but a case of sabotage handled by a civil jury (or, for that matter, by an internal disciplinary hearing) might take into account mitigating or exacerbating aspects of accountability in determining the amount of punishment. Thus, although we begin with Would counterfactuals, we want to stress that the order of presentation is arbitrary and does not imply a necessary order of occurrence.

Would Counterfactuals: Variations in the Negativity of an Event's Impact on Experience

Would determinants affect perceived negative impact. As noted earlier, RCT explanations of resentment (e.g., Folger, 1987b) sometimes implied that experienced negative impact was determined by referent (i.e., counterfactual) outcomes. Fairness Theory revises RCT, however, by pointing out how experienced negative impact can also stem from variations in factors previously associated with procedural justice (e.g., voice as conceived by Thibaut & Walker, 1975) or interactional justice (e.g., demeaning interpersonal conduct in the role noted by Bies, 1987a). To put it another way, this subsection on Would counterfactuals reconceptualizes outcome, procedure, and interactional conduct in terms of the feature they share when influencing experienced negative impact.

The Would criterion refers to matters of degree regarding the importance (significance) of an offense. If an employee feels insulted or deprived as an implication of unfair treatment, how serious is the offense? The language of seriousness, severity, importance, and significance connotes variations in magnitude. We suggest that this magnitude judgment can be conceptualized as the size of a discrepancy between a person's experienced implications and what the person assumes it would feel like to experience something else instead. For example, this discrepancy can involve the classic counterfactual experience about "what would have been" otherwise ("if only . . . "). Sometimes such counterfactuals come to mind because of a tendency for people to mutate or mentally "undo" unusual, abnormal aspects of experience; the discrepant image is replaced with a more normal, typical image (its default value). Fairness can act as a default value. Treated unfairly, therefore, an employee might readily consider what it would feel like to have been treated fairly instead. As we shall see, the logic of counterfactual reasoning also applies to Could and Should judgments, a parallel that gives the model theoretical cohesion.

Consider an affected party (e.g., laid-off employee) who feels aggrieved by an offending party (e.g., the management of the company that conducted the layoff). The description of what the aggrieved's state *is* at present (e.g., unemployed) has different implications depending on the use of various alternatives as descriptions of what that state might be instead; put another way, what an experience is like can depend on thoughts about what it *would* have been like under other circumstances (e.g., the employee would have been eligible for retirement in 2 months, if not for having been laid off yesterday).

In referring to Would-counterfactual factors, we mean aspects of an event's context that shape its meaning and significance. Part of an event's context involves the social relationships in which the event is imbedded. However, we postpone discussing those types of social factors until a later section on the integration of Fairness Theory and relational approaches. That section will cover variations in negative impact based on differences in the importance of belonging to a social group. The nature of role relationships can obviously lead to variations in magnitude of impact. For the sake of simplification, however, we temporarily discuss Would counterfactuals as a residual category reflecting aspects of context other than the nature of associated relationships.

In particular, various studies of cognitive, perceptual, and psychophysical phenomena, for example, have all illustrated contextual effects of nonsocial stimuli. For example, consider Helson's (1954) work on the establishment of a subjective adaptation level, which showed that the same object could appear comparatively light or heavy, depending on its location in a series of other weights (the physical, nonsocial context of related stimuli). Similar work on numerous cognitive heuristics (e.g., availability, anchoring-and-adjustment; see Kahneman, Slovik, & Tversky, 1982) provides additional illustrations of how contextual stimuli affect the processing of a target stimulus.

Indeed, RCT grew out of related work, especially the seminal piece by Kahneman and Tversky (1982) on the simulation heuristic. Specifically, RCT referred to mentally simulated alternatives as implicit or explicit comparisons that contribute to the affect associated with an outcome. Subsequent work on automaticity (for a summary, see Bargh, 1996) indicates that such comparisons can occur outside conscious awareness and thus need not literally involve an active process of generating mental alternatives to actually experienced events. Instead, the ease with which a preferred alternative comes to mind can influence the intensity of negative affect associated with a nonpreferred outcome (another way of conceptualizing impact magnitude). Thus, automatically activated counterfactual outcomes might have an even greater negative impact than those produced by the conscious simulation of imagined scenarios. That result would be expected if the conscious mental process took more effort and had to be deliberately initiated in order to *bring* the preferred alternative to mind, whereas the automatic process made the preferred alternative *come* to mind (even when the person tried to avoid thinking about it). Our point is that when people respond to the subjective magnitude of impact they experience in a situation, variations in that magnitude of impact can be conceptualized as the size of the discrepancies between a factual event and different counterfactual alternatives—whether those alternatives are automatic and implicit or elaborated explicitly in conscious awareness. In this way, Fairness Theory differs from the characteristic treatment of such alternatives by RCT, which tended to imply the creation of alternative scenarios by a *conscious* process of mental simulation.

Whether brought to mind spontaneously or only after deliberate reflection, counterfactual alternatives to an event in question will represent "what would have been." We invoke that expression to show a parallel with the "Would-Should" analysis of RCT (e.g., Cropanzano & Folger, 1989). The Would-Should analysis described circumstances maximizing resentment as those in which a preferred alternative would have occurred, if only someone had done what should have been done. Referring to counterfactual thoughts about what a situation would have been like, if only the target event had not occurred, thus provides a way in which Fairness Theory can integrate RCT within a broader framework.

The negative impact factor—Would—illustrates how Fairness Theory puts the strengths of RCT in context and also helps transcend its weaknesses. In RCT, the Would concept involves the salience of referent outcomes: The easier it is to bring unrealized consequences to mind (making someone think more often what it would have been like to have experienced such consequences instead of those actually encountered), the greater the importance of that perceived discrepancy is likely to seem. For example, losing a job during downsizing is painful enough by itself, but suppose the laid-off employee learns that the CEO who ordered massive layoffs also earned an enormous bonus during the same year. One of the RCT strengths lies in identifying a variety of ways that such gaps can become salient and thereby magnify the importance of the sense of deprivation.

On the other hand, the expanded conception of Would as negativity also points to limitations of the RCT approach. RCT treats the sense of outcome discrepancy or deprivation in a generic sense, whereas the accountability model's expanded analysis of Would acknowledges that the negativity of an event's impact can vary in several different ways and for several different reasons, a point we discuss later in reviewing group-membership importance as a factor identified by the relational model.

It is also important to note two key differences between RCT and Fairness Theory, thereby further highlighting what now appear to us as some deficiencies in the RCT analysis. First, RCT associated the term *Would* with the discrepancy between an actual and a referent outcome. We now see this emphasis on outcomes as being too narrow or too limited in terms of the scope of events to which people respond. Based on the findings from research on the relational approach, Fairness Theory uses the term *Event* to include both the traditional focus of exchanged outcomes (the staple of studies about distributive justice), as well as an emphasis on procedural and interactional considerations. Thus, the Event to which people respond might not be a physical deprivation or a subjective representation of material loss; rather, such events might also be cases of another person's rudeness and inconsiderate conduct (e.g., a supervisor's condescending tone in talking with employees). Process events might just as easily be the source of reflections about "what it would be like if this had not occurred."

As a second deficiency, RCT tended to imply that thoughts about what Would have happened were inevitably linked to thoughts about what should have been done. Conversely, Fairness Theory proposes that each of these comparisons can occur separately, along with a third aspect concerning feasibility (the *Could* aspect). We stress that comparisons stimulated by the violation of moral guidelines (e.g., concerning what a supervisor should do) are not the sole source of thoughts about what would have occurred; other contextual factors can instigate implicit or explicit alternatives to the Event in question (see Bargh, 1996). Recall that in the first chapter of this book, we used examples from *Liar's Poker* to illustrate just such a point: Michael Lewis had a number of different points of reference flash through his mind when he first heard about the size of his bonus.

Research stimulated by Norm Theory (Kahneman & Miller, 1986) and related developments in the counterfactual literature (e.g., Olson & Roese, 1995) can be mined as a rich source of ideas about context factors influencing impressions of events. Theoretical progress on understanding the dynamics of counterfactual thinking, therefore, will help provide insights into Would factors as contextual determinants of event perceptions. The same rich veins can also be mined when exploring accountability determinants from a counterfactual perspective—the Could and Should counterfactuals that we address next.

Accountability I: Could Counterfactuals, Feasible Options, and Discretionary Conduct

The Could component refers to a feasibility aspect of accountability, namely, discretionary conduct—having the capacity to make a difference in what happened. In the case of a layoff, people tend not to direct hostile responses toward a supervisor who found it impossible to implement downsizing other than the way it occurred—such as when emergency surgery prevented the supervisor from being present when certain key decisions were made. Perhaps even if a supervisor's actions seem unfair, employees might tend to hold hostile responses in check when they perceive that the supervisor had no choice (although hostility might be directed at others who put the supervisor in that position, such as upper management). Before responding negatively toward someone as a source of unfairness, people in essence ask whether that person had other feasible options—alternatives over which personal control could be exercised. The relevant comparison question is this: If the person had intended otherwise and had tried hard enough to implement that intention, could that person have acted in ways with implications other than those considered unfair? Such questions address a necessary but not sufficient condition for holding someone morally accountable for unfair conduct: It was possible to have acted otherwise.

Discussions of ethical philosophy often make the following point about a prerequisite of accountability (Velasquez, 1982): It makes no sense to hold someone morally responsible for the implications of events over which he or she could not have any influence (i.e., could not control or anticipate). If a man is deaf, it is unreasonable to demand that he respond to sounds he cannot detect. Similarly, codes of moral conduct must entail actions that people can bring under their personal control. Holding people accountable for what they should have done, therefore, requires attending to what they could have done. Could counterfactuals thus refer to aspects of someone's conduct that involve feasible options and discretionary control over them (e.g., willful, intentional effort; volitional acts).

Focusing on feasible options as a prerequisite for moral accountability highlights one reason that the attribution of intent can become crucial. If people fail to do something, it makes sense to ask whether they tried (and how hard they tried). Effort intensity provides a way to gauge intention. For example, employees asked "To what extent did your supervisor try to be fair?" would vary their responses according to their perceptions of the supervisor's fairness intentions.

Feasibility, Intention, and Relational Approaches to Justice. We emphasize how feasibility relates to such indicators of intentions (e.g., the tried-to-be-fair item) because they are central to the measurement of what is called *trust* in writings on the relational approach to justice (Tyler & Degoey, 1996). *Relational* is our summary term for the group-value (Lind & Tyler, 1988) and relational-model (Tyler & Lind, 1992) approaches. Also, Brockner and Siegel (1996) reinterpreted trust as playing an influential role in fairness judgments because it assesses intent. We agree, and indeed, think the point made by Brockner and Siegel extends also to the relational concepts of status recognition and neutrality.

According to the relational approach, people feel threatened by loss of self-esteem when marginalized by leaders who fail to treat them as full-fledged group members worthy of respect. Suppose the leader is perceived to embody the values of a group from which the reacting person gains self-identity through group membership. Such a leader's failure to display the relational components of trust, neutrality, and status recognition threatens to undermine an important basis for the person's sense of identity. In the case of all three types of actions—the failure to be trustworthy (not acting with benevolent intent), the failure to recognize status (not acting with intent to respect), and the failure to act in a neutral and impartial manner (not acting with intent to hold personal interest in check)—it is the intentional failure on the part of the leader or other group members, rather than accidental failure, that would be threatening to self-esteem.

In sum, within this section, (a) we identified feasibility as one set of perceptions that contributes to the overall assessment of accountability; (b) we indicated how feasibility perceptions relate to intention; and (c) we noted how other authors have linked intention to one of the relational themes (trust), and we extended the same logic to the other two (status recognition and neutrality). This discussion, therefore, shows how Fairness Theory integrates the relational approaches to justice within the context of an overarching framework.

Subtleties Requiring Further Investigation and Attention. Feasibility is a catch-all term standing for judgment processes that require much more detailed study. Understanding its role will improve with further advances in the study of causal attribution, which is a close conceptual relative. As discussions of accountability (e.g., Schlenker, 1997) have emphasized, however, judgments of what people could have done are more complex when related to moral accountability than in the case of only physical causality. In particular, sometimes people are held accountable not simply for their own actions (based on intent) but also for the actions of those under their charge, as when an executive officer of a corporation has responsibility for an unethical and illegal behavior on the part of his employees. Future research might well focus on when a person is held accountable simply as a function of being in a position of authority, versus when judgments about matters such as intent are more crucial.

We believe that people often think in terms of questions about whether a person could have prevented some untoward consequences (e.g., whether management could have avoided having to conduct large-scale layoffs). Was it feasible to act differently? By framing the issue this way, Fairness Theory is able to benefit from prior work on counterfactual cognitions (e.g., Olson & Roese, 1995). However, feasibility also applies both to intent and to responsibility assigned along with authority. "Was it feasible to prevent *X*?" could be answered by making a judgment about what a person could do by exerting effort with intent, or by making a judgment that a duty to prevent certain consequences "goes with the job." In the latter case, it is less important to know whether a person could actually have prevented negative consequences than to believe that feasibility is a fait accompli concomitant with the role. For example, one employee might hold management responsible for the negative impact of layoffs because of actual evidence about how the layoff might have been prevented, whereas another employee might hold management responsible simply because of the belief that the duties and obligations of organizational leadership entail management accountability for whatever employment consequences occur.

Feasibility judgments, therefore, serve to connect a person with an event in ways considered necessary if the person is to be held accountable for the event. This type of connection is usually based on the person's actions as well as the person's role, either of which may provide that person the opportunity to make a difference. If someone could not have made a difference with respect to events being considered (e.g., a supervisor in no feasible way could have created a job opening), then such a person has no feasible connection with the events and cannot be held accountable for them.

Feasibility considerations may also determine whether someone whose connection with events has already been established on the basis of physical, cause-and-effect evidence is to be held accountable. For example, suppose a supervisor opens a door that hits an employee approaching from the other side. The supervisor might not be held accountable for the employee's black eye if the supervisor could not have foreseen the danger. If the supervisor did not intend harm and could not have anticipated the employee's approach, the employee is less likely to hold the supervisor accountable, even though the causal description of events does connect this supervisor with this door. In that respect, feasibility is notable for what it excludes from consideration: Each aspect of the process of judgment (e.g., was this supervisor present, did she open the door, did she know to expect employees approaching from the other side?) functions either to connect a possible harmdoer with some harm done or to disconnect the person from the harm in ways making the person not accountable for it.

Accountability II: Should Counterfactuals as Moral Guidelines

Should counterfactuals, which refer to a morality aspect of accountability, provide a key basis for linking people's discretionary conduct with the consequences of that conduct. People tend not to direct hostile responses toward others who did what they were supposed to do. If a supervisor's actions seem unfair, for example, employees tend to hold hostile responses in check when they perceive that the supervisor acted in full accord with relevant moral precepts (ethical standards for treating other people fairly—acting as one should). Again, the relevant reasoning is counterfactual in nature: Among the feasible set of alternative actions that the other person could have taken, were there other discretionary options that he or she should have exercised instead (i.e., options morally superior to those actually taken)?

Morally superior alternatives in the feasible set will tend to indict someone of misconduct to the extent that two subconditions are met: (a) The modes of conduct "required" are relevant to the circumstances (i.e., they apply clearly to the given situation being considered); and (b) the precept also applies directly to the person whose conduct is under consideration, due to aspects of that person's official position and other reasonable expectations about what the person ought to do (Schlenker, 1997).

For example, expecting supervisors to treat people equally or with consistency might not apply unequivocally under some circumstances that seem to involve special exceptions reasonable to consider. The moral precept of equality or consistency might not apply, that is, in the case of a given employee. As another example, positions of authority in the upper levels of a management hierarchy might be expected to exercise greater discretion, whereas lower levels might be held more accountable for "going by the book."

Summary of Guilt Criteria Involving Feasibility (Could) and Morality (Should)

The Could and Should criteria affect the extent to which someone is held accountable for violating a moral norm of fairness only if both sets of requirements for guilt meet a sufficiency test (as options sufficiently feasible and morally compelling enough to "trump" other priorities and obligations). Analogies include glue-like substances that must have enough of two ingredients for a tight bond, or legal-like criteria of guilt (e.g., motive, opportunity) that must be met jointly to make an indictment "stick." If either component fails to reach a bonding threshold, the bond is broken, and the initially accused party cannot be held accountable after all.

Feasibility connects a person to an event by focusing on what the person did or did not do and on what the person could or could not have done. In contrast, permissibility focuses on what people did or did not do in relation to what they should or should not have done (and what should or should not have happened). As we noted, feasibility is prerequisite: It is unreasonable to claim someone should have done something that was impossible. Feasibility is only necessary, however, and not sufficient for holding someone accountable. A judgment of feasibility helps distinguish between (a) those whose presence and conduct have some relevant bearing on an event and (b) those who have no feasible or plausible connection with an event whatsoever. But those feasibility-based grounds for making a connection between events and potentially accountable parties represent only a background condition establishing that such parties do, indeed, belong in a set of those eligible for being held accountable. Actually holding such parties morally accountable assumes not only their membership in this eligibility set but also a set of moral guidelines applicable to both (a) the party in question, given his or her role and (b) the focal events in a given situation. Those guidelines bring to mind Should counterfactuals for comparison with discretionary conduct as it was actually exercised.

Integrating Equity, RCT, Interactional Justice, and Relational Approaches

Recall that Would counterfactuals can affect perceived negative impact regarding material deprivation or purely symbolic suffering, such as a negative experience from interpreting a remark as an insult. We now illustrate the integrative potential of Fairness Theory first by relating it in further ways to RCT and, thereby, also to equity theory. We refer to material deprivation in our RCT and equity theory examples, although we mean deprivation as perceived not in material or objective terms, but in subjective terms as relative deprivation. Then we turn to the notion of insult and use it to illustrate how Fairness Theory accommodates the type of unfairness that interactional justice (Bies, 1987b) and relational approaches (Tyler & Lind, 1992) high-lighted. Note that we have chosen to apply Fairness Theory to all these cases as a way of showing the basic similarity they share in common, despite some grounds for differentiation.

Fairness Theory, RCT, and Equity

Because the early descriptions statement of RCT (e.g., Cropanzano & Folger, 1989; Folger, 1987b; Folger, Rosenfield, & Robinson, 1983) corre-sponds more directly to equity theory, we discuss equity and that version of RCT jointly here. A subsequent version of RCT (Folger, 1993) comes closer to Fairness Theory, so we postpone our discussion of Fairness Theory as an RCT successor until after our presentation of the interactional and relational approaches.

The first three chapters of this book included a discussion of equity theory's failure to adequately specify the determinants of responses to unfair depriva-tion. This deficiency created ambiguities in the theory's explanation for why people sometimes try to resolve an inequity by decreased outcomes as op-posed to increased inputs. We also suggested that early versions of RCT modified equity theory by indicating how resolution modes tend to follow the attribution of blame: If the disadvantages I experience from an inequity are those I can blame on others, then the mode of responding tends to be consistent with retributive actions directed toward the other person as a source of the inequity (or discrepancy from the referent outcome, in RCT terms). If the disadvantages flow from my mistakes or I am more at fault than anyone else, on the other hand, cognitive distortion becomes more likely. Fairness Theory, therefore, incorporates the equity and the early RCT approaches because it outlines the considerations that determine whether accountability resides with the other person or not.

Fairness Theory, Interactional Justice, and the Relational Approach to Procedural Justice

In this discussion, we combine Bies's (1987b) concept of interactional justice with the relational approaches of Tyler and Lind (1992), primarily as a matter of rhetorical convenience. Separating those approaches from equity and RCT is somewhat like the aggression literature's distinction between mere insult versus frustration as the blocking of goal-directed action, which is the reason we refer to insult versus deprivation. However, we suggest that frustration-deprivation and insult have more in common than first meets the eye. Our discussion of interactional justice and the relational approach, therefore, begins by noting their unique aspects but continues by noting which factors insult (their distinctive feature) has in common with deprivation (the salient feature of inequity and RCT as originally conceived).

Both the concept of interactional justice as formulated by Bies (1986), as well as relational approaches that include the group value model (Lind & Tyler, 1988) and relational model of authority (Tyler & Lind, 1992), tend to involve what Tyler and Lind referred to as "dignitary concerns"—that is, concerns about face saving or threat to face and social status, such as when people feel demeaned by rude or insulting conduct. When a supervisor does not bother to provide any explanation for some decision that affects employees or provides an explanation regarded as inadequate and insincere, the employees are more likely to take this as a sign of contempt for them on the supervisor's part. They can feel insulted by such conduct. This is the same type of result that Tyler and Lind described as making a person feel marginalized—like ostracism or exclusion from a group important to one's identity—when encountering conduct by an authority that violates aspects of trust (not trying to be fair, failing to consider a person's needs sufficiently), or of recognition and status (denying status as a group member, not granting rights and privileges of membership), or of neutrality (acting from bias, such as a choice based on favoritism rather than accurate information).

Although insults from demeaning conduct do seem different from deprivation—the frustration that results from having the path to a goal blocked—
the accountability determinants of responses to such conduct are the same as
those that influence the response to unfair deprivation. Could some other
form of conduct have occurred instead? That is, was it possible for the other
person (e.g., manager or other authority) to act in a manner not so demeaning? If not, then the bond of culpability is broken and hostile response
tendencies thereby mitigated. For example, employees who think that they,
too, would have found it very difficult to stay calm when facing what their
supervisor faced (e.g., a mother dying of cancer; inexorable pressure from
higher-ups in the company) might decide that a less demeaning manner was
not an especially feasible option available to the supervisor. Even if treating
the employees in this case more politely and with a greater degree of dignity
is perceived as a highly feasible alternative for the supervisor, the question
remains as to whether such treatment ought to be considered a moral imperative. Is it clearly what the supervisor should have done—how he or she was
obligated to behave—under the circumstances? If so, then these inferences
(especially taking intent into account) tend to convict the supervisor as being
guilty of unfair treatment; if not, then the conclusion amounts to innocence
or at least a lack of sufficiently compelling blame.

Finally, suppose the insulting conduct seems to stem from unfair intentions
for which the other person, such as a supervisor, can be held morally accountable (could and should have acted otherwise). What, then, is the magnitude
of the implications? What makes such conduct so insulting—or is it really
significant, after all? Such questions about what the implications would have
been otherwise (the would or magnitude factor for adjusting levels of punishment that apply when guilt has been determined) apply the third criterion
of Fairness Theory.

Further Topics on Which Fairness Theory
Might Shed Light: A Theme for Investigation

As one way to illustrate further some of our reasons for proposing an
integrative model, we turn to topics on which that model might shed some
light. We think further exploration of these topics is one of the potential
growth areas for future investigations.

Reformulating the Outcome × Process Interaction

Recently, Brockner and Siegel (1996) suggested that intentions play a piv-
otal role in providing a way for relational approaches to account for the

Outcome × Process interaction. Consistent with similar reasoning expressed by Tyler and Degoey (1995), Brockner and Siegel (1996) argued that the authority-trustworthiness aspect of the relational approach signals whether an authority intended to be fair. If an authority violates this trustworthiness obligation, then adverse and possibly unfair outcomes reflect something like a malevolent intention (or at least a failure to be other-regarding to an adequate extent). This interpretation sounds very much like the way Fairness Theory extends RCT, which suggests that we are right in assuming that a high degree of integrative potential has been tapped. To capitalize even more on a potential thus far dormant in work on organizational justice, however, requires some additional analysis as well. Next, we outline some further implications as sets of related topics for future research and theory.

Main Effects as Embedded Interactions

As much research has found (Lind & Tyler, 1988), sometimes interpersonal sensitivity (e.g., insult as a form of interactional injustice) or a violation of procedural fairness (e.g., procedures that fail to provide voice or do not allow for adequate consideration of those affected by decisions) produces a main effect rather than interacting with an outcome factor. Fairness Theory implies that it might make sense to examine whether such main effects result from a hidden or embedded interaction.

The concept of an embedded interaction calls for distinguishing between (a) the focal outcomes allocated or exchanged, which typically involve material resources or the wherewithal for obtaining such resources (e.g., wages exchanged for labor); and (b) the symbolic outcomes that stem directly from another person's conduct and that typically involve something like the notion of insult that we explored earlier. Previously, the typical test for an Outcome × Process interaction involved treating only the former as an outcome, such as when the manner of conducting a layoff was treated as a process factor and the severity of the consequences from being laid off constituted the outcome (cf. *outcome severity*, Brockner et al., 1995). Sometimes measures will fail to show an interaction of process with such an outcome but will instead reveal a main effect for the process factor alone. Note that one variation on this theme is the oft-reported finding that more "global" measures (e.g., organizational commitment, support for supervisor) are more strongly associated with the process factor than with the outcome factor.

We argue that such main effects conceal an "embedded" Outcome × Process interaction that is actually an impact-accountability interaction in terms of Fairness Theory. Recall that Fairness Theory involves a different view of process (in terms of accountability) and a different view of outcome (in terms of the negativity of an event's impact). First consider the insulting form of interactional process as a symbolic outcome in its own right. Process (the insulting conduct) and outcome (the experience of being insulted) occur so simultaneously and are bound so inextricably together that they do not fit the usual pattern of a cause-effect sequence; rather, the symbolic outcome implications (threat to self-esteem) are an inherent part of what it means to conduct a process in a demeaning behavioral manner (a manner that yields the inference of an intention to insult).

The reconceptualized view of process, however, suggests an embedded or concealed causal factor that does exist prior to the insulting conduct and operates instrumentally in bringing it about: the other person's intentions. To reveal this embedded interaction requires distinguishing between intended and unintended procedures and manifestations of interpersonal conduct (the interactional-justice view of process). When intended, the magnitude of insult would affect a given measure (e.g., organizational commitment) in the manner previous research has suggested. Conversely, if someone perceives that the demeaning procedure or interpersonal conduct was unintentional, then his or her reaction to such treatment will tend to remain largely unaffected by variations in the perceived unfairness of the procedure or interpersonal process.

A second way of commenting on the reconceptualized interaction has even broader implications. We want to make explicit what was only implicit in discussing the "embedded interaction": The Could-Should determinants of guilt in Fairness Theory act as its Process factor (moral accountability added to the more purely instrumental aspect of causal responsibility), whereas the factor of Would—as a punishment determinant—acts in the role of Outcome. Put another way, under Fairness Theory, the issue of process translates into questions about holding people accountable by virtue of their actions and intentions, and the issue of outcome translates into questions about the magnitude of the implications for which someone is held accountable. That magnitude is irrelevant for determining responses oriented toward some person unless the person meets the criteria of accountability, which yields exactly the form of interaction typically found (see Brockner & Wiesenfeld, 1996).

As an illustration of this reconceptualization in the broadest possible terms, consider how it reshapes thinking about RCT and the relational approaches. Previously, RCT referred only to exchanged outcomes—largely those with material rather than symbolic implications—as the second of the two factors used to predict the Outcome × Process interaction (a feature true even in the most recent version; Folger, 1993). Fairness Theory, however, suggests that any kind of event can vary in the magnitude of its importance (e.g., as regards reasons for sanctioning negatively, such as the importance of setting an example or of expressing repudiation because "of the principle of the thing"). Rather than conceptualizing referent outcomes (as the Would factor) solely in terms of exchanged material resources, therefore, expanding beyond that limitation of RCT would entail an analysis about the symbolic importance of implications such as those associated with another person's conduct.

The focus of that analysis could profit from the insight of the relational approach. Recent evidence designed to test relational predictions (e.g., Tyler & Degoey, 1995; Van den Bos, Vermunt, & Wilke, 1996), for instance, invoked the concept of importance quite independently of its role in Fairness Theory (which in turn borrows from Schlenker, Britt, Pennington, Murphy, & Doherty, 1994). Because the relational approach points to group membership as a source of implications about identity and self-esteem, the tested predictions revolved around questions about the importance of group membership. Specifically, the research hypothesized that factors such as trust, neutrality, and standing would have a greater impact when the group was an important source of self-identity, whereas access to material resources as outcomes would have greater impact when the group was not so important.

Summary of Implications From Fairness Theory for Reformulating the Outcome × Process Interaction

For convenience, we can summarize several of the points from this Outcome × Process reformulation by referring chiefly to ways that it modifies both RCT and the relational approach while also integrating them. First, the reformulated Would (magnitude) factor replaces the role of referent outcomes in RCT, while still retaining the original emphasis on counterfactual reasoning. Second, a broader spectrum of events is seen as affecting this magnitude. Following the relational analysis, for example, symbolic implications of procedures and conduct tend to vary in magnitude as a function of the relationship between the (a) allocator, exchange partner, decision maker, dispute resolver, or authority; and (b) the person affected by that person's actions.

Consider, for example, how a supervisor's actions could affect the importance of money versus recognition. Money tends to act as a universalistic resource (cf. Foa & Foa, 1976); that is, the specific nature of the relationship with a particular supervisor has little if any implication with regard to the purchasing power of the employee's salary per se (i.e., the same salary enables the same ability to purchase groceries, regardless of which supervisor or member of management determines the size of the employee's raise). Recognition, on the other hand, might more likely be of varying importance to the employee, depending on that employee's opinions about the supervisor and the nature of the relationship.

Third, this reformulated approach also helps overcome a potential limitation in the relational approach. As articulated in published material (e.g., Lind & Tyler, 1988; Tyler & Lind, 1992), the relational approach tends to focus on implications for self-esteem and self-identity—based on the importance of group identity—as the source of motivations that affect responses toward injustice. According to Fairness Theory, however, the importance of a moral precept need not be grounded in specific relationships. Indeed, some analyses of morality (e.g., Kohlberg, 1984) argued that higher levels of morality appeal to principles that tend to be shared more universally. Presumably, this relative independence from the context of specific group membership helps explain reactions of moral outrage to such incidents as those involving Susan Smith's murder of her children and subsequent lies about their death, or reactions to genocide and other atrocities committed around the globe.

8 Future Directions

This chapter contains topics that we think represent promising future directions. Some relate to points made in the preceding chapter, but here we place less emphasis on the relation of the topic or theme to the integrative framework we presented in that chapter.

We start with recent research indicating that the Outcome × Process interaction occurs in three distinct patterns, discussing what is likely to contribute to each. Next, we address sources of ambiguity and a distributional-procedural-interactional continuum that runs from the most ambiguity about intent (outcome distributions) to the least (interactional conduct).

We then introduce the possibility of a negative-positive asymmetry—and the implications of that possibility—as a general topic. If such an asymmetry exists, that would suggest the inadvisability of treating positive and negative events (or evaluative reactions to events) as opposite poles of the same continuum. For that reason, we examine positive and negative topics separately. An example of a positive topic is trust. Our discussion of trust will tie that topic back to our comments about intention (a theme discussed in this chapter as well as the previous one). We also explore the further connection with fairness of a possible "snap judgment" involving "swift trust."

Turning to negative topics, we next deal with reactions to unfairness and potential implications for "the dark side" of human behavior (e.g., retaliatory responses to perceived injustice). We then raise a question related to dark-side behavior: If unfair actions often cause such negative reactions, and if more considerate treatment that conveys intended fairness is familiar and easy to implement, why do sources of perceived unfairness occur so frequently under some common conditions? This question shifts the discussion from reactions against unfair behavior, where a supervisor's conduct can cause vengeful repercussions, to questions about the source of that supervisor's unfair behavior. In other words, we explore designs using a dependent variable (supervisor's behavior as an effect) that has usually been an independent variable (supervisor's behavior as cause).

Our final set of topics is a loosely collected set of thoughts conveying prejudices we have developed over the years. As frequent reviewers of manuscripts on organizational justice, we have developed likes and dislikes that color our comments. This last section of the chapter gives us a chance to express those in writing. At the very least, those who plan to submit manuscripts and anticipate that one or the other of us might become reviewers will have had a chance to see our prejudices revealed in advance! We, of course, hope that they are more than mere prejudices—hence, we will present them in the spirit of advice. We tried to think about the kind of advice we would give to new graduate students who might be thinking about the study of organizational justice as a topic. Our comments, therefore, have the flavor of "do this, and don't do that," even though we admit that neither of us has ever been accused of giving infallible advice. Our version of the classic Latin warning to the reader, *caveat lector,* is the following: Our advice is free—and remember that you get what you pay for.

More Than One Form of Interaction

Research by Van den Bos, Vermunt, and Wilke (1997) suggested that outcome and process can interact in three different ways, shown in Table 8.1. Pattern 1 takes a form consistent with RCT predictions (e.g., Folger, 1993), as confirmed in numerous lab and field studies (for a review, see Brockner & Wiesenfeld, 1996). Specifically, it matches the shape depicted in figures displaying actual results (Folger, 1993) or summarized in an idealized fashion as depicting "typical" results (Brockner & Wiesenfeld, 1996, Figure 1).

We made up the i-iv entries of Pattern 1, however, by matching them to specific results from Van den Bos, Vermunt, et al. (1997, Experiment 1, distributive justice measure).[1] For example, we simply duplicated two Van den Bos, Vermunt, et al. means from Pattern 2, v and vi, as the idealized entries for Cells i and ii of Pattern 1. Cells v and vi share a common subscript (viz., *a*) and hence do not differ significantly. We used those Van den Bos, Vermunt, et al. means in Pattern 1 because that lack of significant difference mirrors a

Table 8.1   Three Interaction Patterns of Outcome × Process

Pattern	Outcome Level	
	Unfavorable Outcome	*Favorable Outcome*
Pattern 1: standard pattern[1]		
Procedural level:		
High process fairness	i, 5.6	ii, 5.7
Low process fairness	iii, 1.75	iv, 5.5
Pattern 2: Van den Bos, Vermunt, et al.[2] procedure-first conditions		
Procedural accuracy:		
Accurate procedure	v, 5.6$_a$	vi, 5.7$_a$
Inaccurate procedure	vii, 1.9$_c$	**viii, 3.4**$_b$
Pattern 3: Van den Bos, Vermunt, et al.[2] outcome-first conditions		
Procedural accuracy:		
Accurate procedure	**ix, 3.6**$_b$	x, 5.6$_a$
Inaccurate procedure	xi, 1.6$_c$	xii, 5.5$_a$

SOURCE: Adapted from Van den Bos, Vermunt, et al. (1997).
NOTE: Entries are distributive justice means from Van den Bos, Vermunt, et al. (1997), also used artificially to illustrate Pattern 1 (i.e., i = v, ii = vi, and iii = average of vii and xi). Van den Bos, Vermunt, et al. means with different subscripts differed at $p < .05$ by a Fisher LSD test.
1. See, for example, Brockner & Wiesenfeld, 1996; Folger, 1993.
2. 1997, Experiment 1.

typical, Pattern 1 finding. Cells ii and iv also typically do not differ significantly. We duplicated the mean of Cell xii as the Cell iv entry, therefore, consistent with the lack of significant difference between x and xii. As we will discuss, this procedure for artificially constructing Pattern 1 from results actually obtained by Van den Bos, Vermunt, et al. also highlights two of their means that differed from standard findings: Cells viii and ix (both of which are underlined and bolded in Table 8.1).

Table 8.1 indicates, therefore, what needs explaining in order to interpret the reason for differences among the three patterns. Pattern 2 differs from Pattern 1 only in the case of Cell viii, just as Pattern 3 differs from Pattern 1 only in the case of Cell ix. Explanations should thus focus on (a) why the *procedural* main effect is strengthened in Pattern 2 relative to Pattern 1 and (b) why the *outcome* main effect is strengthened in Pattern 3. The general nature of such explanations, even if not their exact details, starts to become clear when describing the patterns in those terms. It is not altogether surprising, in other words, to note greater differences due to procedures in *Procedure-first* conditions and greater differences due to outcomes in *Outcome-first* conditions. We first describe the methodology of the Van den Bos, Vermunt, et al. (1997) Experiment 1 as it pertains to this difference in the order of information (procedure or outcome first) and then discuss Pattern 2 and Pattern 3 separately.

Using either a role-playing or a laboratory methodology, Van den Bos, Vermunt, et al. (1997) consistently found both Pattern 2 and Pattern 3; we describe only the former, role-playing version (Experiment 1) for convenience. Respondents read a vignette about applying for a desired job that required nine selection tests. One form of interaction (Pattern 3) came from Outcome-first conditions, in which respondents learned whether they were hired (favorable outcome) or not (unfavorable outcome) 1 week after applying. A month later they were sent further information on how many parts of the selection process had been graded (1/9 vs. 9/9 tests, in the inaccurate vs. accurate procedure conditions). The Procedure-first conditions reversed the order of information and produced a second form of interaction (Pattern 2). Notification about the number of tests graded (1/9 vs. 9/9) purportedly came first, 1 week after testing. Then respondents learned that additional information, delivered a month after that notification, subsequently stated whether they got the job or not.

A Strengthened Main Effect When Procedural Violations Are Salient

Compare Patterns 1 and 2: In Pattern 1, only Cells i and iii (both involving unfavorable outcomes) differ on the basis of variations in procedural fairness. By contrast, Pattern 2 shows significant procedure effects at each level of outcomes (favorable, unfavorable)—producing an overall main effect of procedure that is quite robust, rather than being qualified by outcome level. This strengthened main effect is consistent with Fairness Theory's suggestion (see the preceding chapter) that the heightened negative impact of an event can result directly from a procedure's violation of normative precepts—in this case, a failure to use all information (i.e., Inaccurate Procedure = only one out of nine tests graded).

Van den Bos, Vermunt, et al. (1997) suggested that procedural violations become salient when information about such violations occurs first, followed by information about outcomes. Such means of highlighting procedural impropriety might cause perceivers to encode it so negatively that subsequent information about favorable outcomes only compensates somewhat, rather than fully offsetting it. The difference between Cell iv in Pattern 1 and Cell viii in Pattern 2 shows this lack of compensatory impact from favorable outcomes as a lower distributive justice rating when information about the procedure came first rather than after outcome favorability (i.e., viii = 3.4 < iv = 5.5; or ii = iv, whereas viii < vi).

Not much is yet known about the more general determinants of such results. Presumably differences other than order might also affect salience. We think developments in the study of counterfactual thinking (also mentioned by Van den Bos, Vermunt, et al., 1997) could provide some insights on this matter. When an employee has time to reflect on procedural irregularities (e.g., because information about outcomes is not yet forthcoming), such rumination might amplify the adverse implications about arbitrary, capricious, unilateral power (e.g., "Even my worst nightmare might come true"). Knowing immediately that outcomes are favorable, on the other hand, might short-circuit such "what if" speculations. One message from the Van den Bos, Vermunt, et al. (1997) results is that reassuring outcomes sometimes come too late: "I'm OK now" fails to adequately placate someone who had already been thinking "You have the chance to do anything with me that you want."

A Strengthened Main Effect When Unfavorable Outcomes Are Salient

Now compare Patterns 1 and 3: In Pattern 1, only Cells iii and iv (both involving low process fairness) differ on the basis of variations in outcome favorability. By contrast, Pattern 3 shows significant effects of outcome at each level of procedure (accurate as well as inaccurate). Pattern 3 suggests that when the negative impact from an unfavorable outcome is made highly salient (e.g., when outcomes come first, prior to information about procedures), fair procedures do not always offer security and protection from reproach for those who administer them. A procedure might be fair and "by the books," therefore, yet the salience (or extremity) of an associated negative outcome could bias an otherwise more dispassionate assessment of blame. Highly salient negative outcomes, or outcomes with extremely negative implications, might encourage a tendency to externalize blame away from oneself by reducing the perceived fairness of procedures (because unfavorable outcomes from a fair procedure imply self-blame). This same point about fair procedures can also apply to excuses and justifications: They can mitigate negative reactions, but a severely negative outcome might at times reduce or eliminate that mitigating effect.

A complete account of such biases awaits further study. We suspect, as did Van den Bos, Vermunt, et al. (1997), that enhanced outcome main effects are rarer than enhanced process effects. They noted that procedural information is often available prior to information about resulting outcomes. Receiving outcome information first might change perceptions in unusual ways.

Summary of Interaction Patterns in Relation to Fairness Theory

The RCT explanation of Outcome × Process interactions emphasized two conditions: adverse events and reasons to hold the other accountable for those events. If each component is essential, the predicted interaction is Pattern 1. That theory, therefore, ignored other influences (heightened impact of outcome or procedure) that could alter responses in the mixed cases of favorable outcome and unfair process, or unfavorable outcome and fair process.

In contrast with RCT, Fairness Theory emphasizes that because the strength of the two subcomponents—impact and accountability—can vary independently, each might contribute to a main effect as well as to an interaction. Distinguishing these subcomponents conceptually and noting their potential independence, however, does not preclude their both being affected by the same cause under some circumstances. The same reason for considering some consequences to be horrendous might also increase the likelihood of assigning external accountability for it, such as blaming an unfair procedure. Although Fairness Theory considers holding another accountable for harm as tantamount to perceptions that an injustice is socially unfair (by definition, meaning caused by another), the conditions that contribute to perceptions of accountability (e.g., an unfair procedure) can also affect perceptions of harmful impact (e.g., outcome unfavorability), and vice versa. Fairness Theory thus provides a means by which specific variables' effects (e.g., primacy, salience, extremity) can contribute to the development of an integrative framework.

Related Issues: The Nature of Dependent Measures and the Role of Accountability

Two points warrant further comment. First, investigators should examine the nature of dependent measures carefully. As we noted in the preceding chapter (see discussion of differences between nonsocial unfairness vs. social unfairness), people do not always give expressions of unfairness a specific target by pinning blame on someone else. Fate, a word for nonsocial forces, might be the cause of undeserved outcomes. When Van den Bos measured perceptions of distributive and procedural unfairness (which, interestingly, showed identical patterns), it is unclear how the potential mix of social and nonsocial unfairness might have influenced the ratings expressed by respondents. People asked "Is this fair?" might answer (a) in terms of personal deservingness (my outcome is negative, and I am not at fault) or (b) in terms of another's unfairness toward them (my outcome is negative and the other is at fault). The latter tends to imply the former, but not vice versa.

The second point is related to the first: Issues of accountability should be addressed in interpreting results. When Van den Bos et al. designed their experiments, for example, they relied on a principle called the "fairness heuristic" (cf. Lind et al., 1993). This principle suggests that perceptions of fairness crystallize quickly, and that early fairness judgments thereby "serve as a heuristic for interpreting subsequent events" (Van den Bos et al., 1997, p. 96). Although that idea makes sense, it does not tell the whole story. Judgments about accountability for unfairness also determine the nature of a response to perceived unfairness. Perhaps, for example, an early judgment about procedural unfairness might establish blame more firmly than would be likely from an early judgment about outcome unfairness (which might or might not have been determined on the basis of an unfair procedure).

Fairness Ambiguity: Effects of Knowing or Not Knowing Others' Opinions Versus Their Treatment

Responses to injustice can depend on how sure a person feels that he or she has been mistreated. There are three sources of ambiguity that have not been differentiated, much less treated in detail. Two involve different roles of social comparison (others' opinions vs. others' outcomes), which we discuss under two corresponding subheadings in this section. We address the third in a separate section on accountability, outcome, and process.

Ambiguity and the Opinions of Others

Why might others' opinions about fairness matter? Theoretical discussions (Degoey, in press; Greenberg & Folger, 1983) and empirical evidence on effects of social influence (Folger et al., 1979) suggest that the answer can involve others' opinions as evidence or as approval. Consider others as a source of information—providing evidence otherwise unavailable. Suppose, for example, a new employee cannot tell how good his or her performance is. This uncertainty would diminish if seasoned veterans gave independently concurring opinions about the quality of his or her work.

Second, consider others as a source of approval. Social fairness involves a certain degree of willingness to exercise constraint when trying to obtain favorable resources—that is, a constraint conditioned by some regard for the interests of others who desire the same resources. The threat of social disapproval accompanies efforts to exploit others with no regard for their welfare, or to show hostility when none is warranted (e.g., an employee punished or humiliated by a supervisor even though the employee has done nothing wrong). Calling something unfair invites retribution by the moral community. When a supervisor dispenses rewards, and an employee complains about not getting a fair share, the complaints imply rebuke or reproach: Calling the rewards unfair is only one step removed from calling the supervisor unfair. If criticizing outcomes as unfair tends to reflect poorly on decision makers and looks like an attack on them (e.g., impugning character), then the implied hostility of the criticism or complaint might elicit something equivalent to counteraggression in return. Indeed, whistle-blowers often run the risk of losing their jobs or seeing their subsequent career progression jeopardized. For that reason, it pays to have some reassurance of social support. Strength in numbers is an asset, and the person who has approval for bringing charges (e.g., an employee assured of a union's active role in pursuing the employee's grounds for discontent) will be more likely to issue a protest.

Ambiguity About the Treatment
Received by Others

Van den Bos, Lind, et al. (1997) looked at social comparison from a second angle—the presence versus absence of information about others' actual outcomes. Knowing others' outcomes can help when interpreting one's own, and the absence of information about others' outcomes could make distributive justice ambiguous. In contrast, the fairness of a procedure might seem more readily interpretable. If so, then people would tend to rely on perceptions of procedural fairness in order to make distributive fairness assessments when information about others' outcomes was absent, whereas those distributive fairness assessments would tend not to be influenced by the fairness of the procedure when outcome information was present. In an experiment and in a role-playing scenario designed to test this hypothesis, Van den Bos, Lind, et al. found evidence consistent with their reasoning: Unambiguously unfair outcomes (confirmed by social comparison about others' outcomes) caused the ordinarily positive impact of fair procedures—the fair-process effect—to disappear.

The argument from the Van den Bos, Lind, et al. (1997) studies can be extended. Van den Bos, Lind, et al. referred only to ambiguity about outcomes based on the absence of social comparison information about others' outcomes. But what about more informationally rich situations? In some cases, conflicting cues might suggest alternative distribution norms. One employee might think that need would be a relevant consideration for certain types of health benefits, arguing that people with families deserved more than single men or women. Some members of a team might think that a group bonus should be distributed equally, whereas others might want to reward individual contributions to overall productivity. Even when people agree on a criterion such as equity, differences can exist about how to calculate and weight relevant determinants (cf. debates about comparable worth). It would be premature, therefore, to assume that social comparison information about outcomes always reduces ambiguity about distributive justice or that no other sources of ambiguity exist.

In addition, a similar analysis could be applied to norms about fair procedures. Perhaps it is often true that certain relatively universal principles seem applicable to judging the fairness of procedures and conduct—such as, for example, treating people with dignity and allowing parties some say in matters that affect them. Nonetheless, situations can arise in which equally valid principles have competing implications. Methods of random assignment such as lotteries can ensure equality of opportunity and a form of nonbiased evenhandedness, but not every person wants every matter decided by chance. More needs to be known regarding when a given principle of conduct or procedure receives widespread acceptance and when it becomes controversial instead. After all, procedural empowerment through enhanced opportunities for decision-making input is, itself, not always welcomed with open arms—as when people dread the burden of responsibility that goes with authority or autonomy, or when the increased responsibilities for having input to decision making are not accompanied by any increased sources of financial or other forms of compensation.

Ambiguity About Intent and Issues of Accountability: Outcome and Process Differences

Despite the possibility for ambiguity and disagreement about *norms* regarding procedural norms or the propriety of conduct, we think that conduct and procedures often allow more direct inferences of *intent* than do distributions. To our knowledge, no research has investigated this idea. If true, however, it would indicate an additional reason why procedures and conduct often outweigh equity or other distributive criteria in determining the nature of responses to perceived unfairness—namely, because inferences of intent might follow more directly from procedures or conduct than from distributions, and perceived intent can influence responses to unfairness. Fairness Theory notes that if an action seems intended, that inference links the action with its unfair implications and thereby connects the intentional actor with the unfairness—making the actor a target for resentment and hostility.

What might make it more difficult to infer intent from outcomes than from conduct or procedures? Consider what happens when outcomes are based on aspects of those receiving the outcomes. Because aspects of an employee's labor result in compensation, for example, the employee is a partial cause of the outcome. A supervisor who evaluates the worth of an employee's contribution, of course, is also a partial cause of the size of the outcome award made. Distribution thus often partakes of joint responsibility, and the relative influence of the two parties in actually "determining" what happened can be unclear.

Procedures, on the other hand, can have fewer sources of ambiguity regarding intent. Someone in charge often selects methods, writes policies, or chooses to use one procedure rather than another. Various features of available options presumably lead to one being used rather than another. What will result from applying the chosen option—the outcomes it will cause—is less well known in advance. Because people can choose among means by referring to characteristics of those means, such choices appear to provide evidence about intent. On the other hand, a process once set in motion can yield unintended results. We speculate, therefore, that people might in general be held more accountable for the means they choose than for the ends that result, especially if the methods for determining outcomes are seen as interacting with the raw material of decisions (information for deciding) in complex ways.

Similar reasoning suggests that certain forms of conduct allow inferences of intent even more readily than procedures. If it is unclear who decided to use a procedure, for example, judging intent and accountability becomes ambiguous. In contrast, suppose a supervisor treats an employee in an egregiously rude, inconsiderate, demeaning, or insulting manner that causes unwarranted discomfort. Everyday reasoning, as also embodied in some legal doctrines, often notes that even a person deserving punishment should not be treated in certain ways (e.g., injunctions against "cruel and unusual punishment"). Although what the person did is seen as warranting negative sanctions, people frequently agree about limits on the manner in which those sanctions are applied (e.g., allowing neither torture nor testimony against oneself or one's spouse, no matter what the suspected offense). Common discourse abounds with expressions such as *there's no excuse for being so rude* that illustrate this point. A person who violates moral guidelines regarding such conduct, therefore, runs the risk of having others readily infer ill will—or at least not benign intent. Moreover, deciding whether someone has intentionally treated you impolitely or in a demeaning manner is often easier than deciding whether a punishment fits an alleged offense.

We speculate, therefore, that a crude rank ordering exists among distributive, procedural, and interactional justice. The violation of distributive justice should occasion the greatest uncertainty; it will often be unclear who is to blame, even when it is clear that an outcome is unfair. Procedures tend to occupy a middle position on this imaginary continuum of accountability or the inferential readiness to assume intent. On the one hand, choices about procedures frequently occur on a direct basis (e.g., making a decision to implement a new pay-for-performance policy), whereas outcomes follow subsequently as an indirect by-product of procedures operating jointly with other determining factors (e.g., an employee's performance). Finally, interactional conduct—such as the degree of interpersonal sensitivity shown by supervisors toward employees—perhaps provides the most direct basis for inferring intent. If such speculations are correct, then those differences might help explain why the reactions to outcomes are often conditioned by perceptions of procedures and conduct.

An Asymmetry Between
Negative and Positive Outcomes?

Growing evidence suggests that human brains, and perhaps those of most other species as well, operate with two distinct systems (e.g., Gray, 1990; LeDoux, 1996). One functions in an appetitive, consummatory, or approach-like fashion; that is, the organism seeks pleasure and the enjoyment of rewarding experiences. Brain mechanisms in the second mode tend to function more like an alarm system that warns the person about negative events. This second system activates tendencies to escape or avoid adverse conditions. Evidence consistent with the existence of two such systems also appears in reviews of their possible manifestations (e.g., Taylor, 1991). Two of the so-called Big 5 personality traits are sometimes referred to as positive and negative affectivity, for example, and evidence indicates that they are largely uncorrelated with one another (e.g., Watson, Pennebaker, & Folger, 1986). More generally, Taylor (1991) reviewed wide-ranging evidence that negative events evoke stronger and more rapid physiological, cognitive, emotional, and social responses than do positive events or neutral events.

In a related development, a recent conceptualization of attitudes (Cacioppo, Gardner, & Berntson, 1997) extended the consideration of asymmetry and drew conclusions about the need to alter measurement practices (e.g., calling for separate measurement of the negative and positive aspects of attitudes as evaluative reactions to events). The implications of this model include a call for investigating the unique antecedents and consequences of positive and negative evaluative processes as separable constructs. In the Cacioppo et al. model, "the activation of positivity and of negativity is conceived as representing the outcome of distinguishable motivational (and brain) processes with only partially overlapping antecedents and somewhat different transfer functions" (p. 6). We think this line of evidence and argument can be extended informally into the justice arena.

Consider, for example, the affect associated with relationships. In two recent studies, positive affect was associated with other relationship measures whereas negative affect was not (i.e., failed to show an inverse association). Cacioppo et al., (1997) examined the attitudes that female undergraduates had toward their dormitory roommates. Those authors used the PANAS (Watson, Clark, & Tellegen, 1988), a measurement instrument that contains separate scales for positive and negative affect, in asking the women how they

felt about their roommates. Positive affect correlated directly with two measures of relationship: (a) reports of the extent to which roommates were
considered friends and (b) reported amounts of time spent with roommates.
In contrast, the respective correlation coefficients involving negative affect
were nonsignificant. Similar results in the political arena were obtained by
Abelson, Kinder, Peters, and Fiske (1982). In organizations, this asymmetry
might have a bearing on labor-management relationships; however, we do not
know of research that has separated positive and negative affect from one
another in that context.

There may be related reasons to think about fairness in terms of a negative-
positive asymmetry. Although discredited methodologically, Herzberg's
(1968) motivator-hygiene distinction might contain a kernel of truth (cf.
Watson et al., 1986; Weiss & Cropanzano, 1996). In some respects, that is,
reactions to another person's actions and their implications might range from
extreme perceptions of unfairness (very negative) to fairness perceptions that
are only neutral in affect (the absence of unfairness).

Implications of this asymmetry bear noting. For example, scale measures
might function improperly if anchored with bipolar endpoints (e.g., fair vs.
unfair). Perhaps separate scales (e.g., not at all unfair to very unfair; not at all
fair to very fair) might be more effective. Similarly, fair behaviors might not
always induce exceptionally positive reactions, such as the spontaneous innovation and helpfulness of organizational citizenship behavior. Rather, a fair
person might be viewed more neutrally as simply acting in an expected,
acceptable manner—much like a person who drives on the right-hand side of
the highway (in the United States) and who does not benefit from strong
accolades as a result.

The idea of a positive-negative asymmetry has at least an intuitive appeal
as captured in such commonplace examples, regardless of its scientific status
or implications for research and theory. Consider, for example, colloquial
references to "a fish in water" as a way to illustrate the difficulty of attending
to an unvarying stimulus (related to phenomena discussed more technically
in the literature on habituation). Humans assume that fish are not very
consciously aware of water. Analogously, experiencing positive events more
often than negative—and therefore tending to expect a positive event to be
more likely than a negative one—fits the human experience of habituation to
the positive (cf. our earlier example of driving on the right-hand side of the
road in the United States and other countries). On the other hand, imagine
the experience of "a fish out of water." The intensity of this negative experience is intense for two separate reasons. For one thing, it cannot be ignored.
As the fish gasps frantically, the absence of oxygenated water acts like what
Kahneman and Tversky (1982) called a *close counterfactual*: This particular
alternative to reality (being in water, in contrast to having been removed from

it) "comes to mind" in an especially powerful and almost inescapable way. Switching examples to a human whose head is being held under water, we can avoid being anthropomorphic by saying that such a person could not help but think about what it would feel like to be able to breathe again.

The fish out of water, or the human with his or her head being held under water, also represents an intensely negative experience for a second reason. We said that a fish ordinarily is not aware of water's presence (and its usefulness in providing oxygen), just as humans do not ordinarily spend much time thinking about the presence of oxygen in the air. For both, the positive experience of being able to breathe habituates and hence fades into the background of awareness. Lack of awareness about a positive experience, however, does not necessarily make it less positive in principle—as the sudden absence of that positive experience makes clear in the case of a fish out of water or a human drowning in water. We are suggesting that intensely negative experiences are especially likely to differ qualitatively from positive experiences when the sudden onset of the negative occurs after habituation to the positive. Such a situation magnifies the psychologically experienced discrepancy between the hedonic quality of the positive experience and the hedonic quality of the negative experience. In summary, then, these intensely negative experiences gain their asymmetrically different quality because of two factors operating simultaneously: The negative experience (not breathing) contrasts with a positive experience (breathing) that is (a) hedonically far away (i.e., far better), yet at the same time (b) counterfactually close (i.e., inescapably brought to mind).

What does that have to do with fairness? We suspect that in some environments, certain behavior by others can operate for a time like an unvarying stimulus—as part of an expected routine, it becomes comfortably expected and taken for granted. Often, fair behavior is like that. When treated with civility, decency, and common courtesy, people might not even think to remark that they have experienced a "fair outcome" or "fair procedure" as a result. The positive quality of fair treatment might differ qualitatively from the experience of unfairly negative treatment, therefore, in the same asymmetric fashion as being in or out of water produces qualitatively different experiences for fish or humans. The unfair experience would tend to have a more profound impact, so it would seem, just as starting to drown produces intense motivation in humans, and being removed from water produces intense motivation in fish. (Note that this analogical reasoning also suggests the importance of interactional justice, consistent with our earlier discussion of a possible distributive-procedural-interactional continuum.)

Considering the possibility of qualitative differences in experience as suggested by the positive-negative asymmetry, we segmented most of our remaining discussion into positive and negative topics. We next discuss trust as a positive topic, then turn to retaliation and other forms of negative behavior as "dark side" topics. Parenthetically, we note that different streams of research in organizational justice seem to have pursued either a positive or negative orientation. The group-value and relational-model approaches have tended to focus, for example, on positive topics such as the acceptance of decisions and the endorsement of leaders or the social institutions they represent. RCT, on the other hand, focused on resentment and retaliation. Could an underlying asymmetry have been at work in causing the former to emphasize main effects and the latter an Outcome × Process interaction?

Nonselfish Fairness and Swift Trust

In the preceding chapter we suggested that most, perhaps all, existing theories of fairness view norms of justice as drawing support by virtue of the implications for long-term self-interest: Although I might gain a larger immediate return from behaving exploitatively rather than fairly, various side effects of unfair actions can "catch up to me" in the long run. Mutual advantage and the benefits of cooperation can be gained from fairness. Relatedly, managers or firms that take actions based on fairness considerations tend to gain at least some long-term benefits from establishing a reputation for being a trustworthy exchange partner. Even an economic actor acting on a rational and calculative basis to maximize long-run reward maximization, therefore, might not be oblivious to potential gains from fairness and might willingly constrain some short-term exploitation tendencies in order to sustain better future prospects.

We also argued, however, that this type of account tells only part of the story. Many human actions seem less understandable when described as exhibiting nothing more than ordinary self-aggrandizement. Instead, using concepts such as altruism, communal feelings, other-regarding sympathy, and commitments to collective well-being seems to shed greater light on certain behaviors that do not fit the model of economic self-interest maximizers. Whether it is a Mother Theresa, a soldier diving on top of a live hand grenade to save comrades-in-arms, or merely someone who leaves a tip in an out-of-town restaurant unlikely to be revisited, behavior that takes others' interests into account seems both too common and too self-sacrificial (high cost, with minimal prospects for any direct, immediate return) to match standard economic accounts of human motivation.

The previous chapter contained a related theme as well—namely, that conceptions of trust might have something to do with fairness. We embellished slightly a theme first developed by Brockner & Siegel (1996). They reexamined the concept of trust as a component of the relational approach (as distinct from the other relational elements of a status-regarding orientation and a stance of impartiality or neutrality). They suggested that the most crucial aspect of attributing trustworthiness to a leader was the inference of a particular type of intention or motive: an attitude of benevolent intent regarding the well-being of the perceiver. We think such grounds for examining possible interrelation of trust and fairness bear further scrutiny, especially as regards the nonselfish version of fairness motives. Occasionally, similar themes are expressed in discussions about trust. Kramer, Brewer, & Hanna (1996), for example, spoke of "moralistic trust" in the following way: "We view moralistic trust as noncontingent. It is presumed to be explicitly predicated not on calculations of risks and benefits but rather on general ethical convictions and intrinsic values" (p. 376).

What parallels exist and what suggestions for future research might emerge from a search for those parallels? We can envision a research agenda somewhat analogous to the thrust of a program begun by Shapiro (1993). She noted Tyler's (1994) finding that voice without consideration is ineffective; that is, employees given voice ordinarily react more positively but might not if they think the decision maker's solicitation of opinions was a sham. Someone who asks what you think, then yawns and seems not to consider what you say seriously, has not really provided a meaningful version of voice. Shapiro, therefore, investigated what consideration might mean. Using a critical-incident approach, she generated a list of behavioral cues signifying that the other person has seriously considered your opinion.

It seems to us that a related program of research might examine nonselfish fairness motives in the "swift trust" context mentioned by Meyerson, Weick, & Kramer (1996). They observed that teams and task forces often group and regroup within short time frames and operate more effectively the more quickly they coordinate, cooperate, and learn to trust one another. For that reason, the ordinary conception of trust as something that builds up over time, allowing for evidence of consistency and reliable delivery of favorable outcomes, has drawbacks on grounds of inadequate timeliness. What might instead contribute to more instantaneous judgments that the other person is trustworthy? Perhaps a methodology like that used by Shapiro would be helpful. Respondents could be asked to recall incidents in which they intuitively, instinctively concluded that they could trust another person "right away." If recall also generated a list of behavioral cues signaling the basis for such judgments, their presence versus absence could then be manipulated in a new team context. Just as Konovsky and Pugh (1994) looked at trust as a mediator between fairness perceptions and citizenship behavior, this type of investigation would reverse the sequence. Grounds for trust would be established first, then perceptions of fairness could be measured as an effect.

Lacking evidence from such studies, we speculate meanwhile on how nonselfish versions of fairness could relate to the capacity for swift trust judgments. This approach reverts back to the fairness-causes-trust sequence but tries to conceptualize what behavioral cues might signal that another person adheres to fairness norms not for the sake of long-term personal benefit through cooperation, but even more fundamentally because being fair is simply "the right thing to do." What indicators suggest that someone would "try hard to be fair" (one of the most common items measuring *trust* as a relational element) because of commitment to moral principle?

Some hints appear occasionally in extant literature, and other themes for exploration suggest themselves as extensions from the logic of various existing frameworks. For example, the economist Robert Frank (1988) tried to account for the survival of cooperators in mixed-motive interdependent relationships with others who are sometimes competitors. He argued that certain behavioral characteristics might act as signals of trustworthiness and thereby act as the basis for establishing a reputational advantage (i.e., someone with whom more people would like to have dealings). He mentioned such characteristics as blushing because they are not subject to personal control. Why would evolution have contributed to the continued existence of a trait such as the tendency to blush when ashamed? Perhaps those who blush (as a response not readily subject to volitional control) can capitalize on the advantage of identifying themselves as people who have a harder time acting deceptively than nonblushers. Even more generally, nonfeignable behaviors might become grounds for perceptions that a person intends fairness and can be trusted. A fake smile does not involve the zygomatic muscle whereas a genuine smile does (DePaulo, 1992; Ekman, 1993), for example. Such issues raise a host of questions well worth exploring.

Those who act fairly for its own sake—as the right means to use regardless of other ends found desirable—also might provide signaling cues whose effects run counter to ordinary, more coldly calculative motives. What might be called "ordinary trust," for example, looks for stable and predictable consistency in rewards. By that token, simply recognizing grounds for similarity and common interest might help provide a basis for relatively instantaneous trust ("Oh, so you like fly-fishing, too?"). In contrast, the grounds for swift trust could instead stem from what might be called "extraordinary trust," which has closer ties to nonselfish fairness as a principled value held dear. If a way could be found to pit opposing predictions against each other, the research paradigm might include some of the features that we explore subsequently.

First, ordinary or calculative trust seems to have certain natural boundary conditions that could be specified on an a priori basis and perhaps be made the basis for manipulations. For example, we already alluded to time as one boundary condition: Predicting consistency and reliability tends to reflect a cumulative judgment that gains in confidence as the experiential database grows through repeated encounters (e.g., from a long-term encounter). If anything roughly equivalent to that effect were achievable even in a short-term context, it might be similarity and commonality. Seeing evidence for shared interests immediately might allow someone to extrapolate, even without direct evidence, that long-term prospects for favorable returns look promising.

In contrast, cues that signal principled allegiance to fairness as a moral obligation need not be grounded in similarity. Overlapping, similar interests actually signal the unfair grounds for favoritism—a willingness to help those of "our own kind, because they're like us." Alternatively, a leader might inspire trust not because he or she shares our own in-group interests and similarities, but because of a moral commitment to treating everyone fairly, impartially, evenhandedly, and without favoritism. In some sense, the latter perception might even be more reassuring than the former. After all, counting on the other person to recognize similarity and commonality of interest might not always pan out, whereas moral fiber might more readily stand up against the sirens of interest calling from several different directions. What if, for example, a decision maker not only shares some grounds of similarity and commonality of interest with you and your group, but also shares some other ground with another set of people whose interests do not coincide with your group?

Dark Times and Revenge: Unfairness Prevalence and "Going Over to the Dark Side"

What aspects of motivation will trigger greater productivity in today's workplace? Increasingly, it seems as if current organizational climates encompass more rampant cynicism and distrust than appeared to be the case in earlier times. It might even be true that "the buttons to push" for motivation today are different than yesterday. In the aftermath of ubiquitous downsizing and talk of a "survivor syndrome" that involves decreased loyalty and commitment by employees, it seems small wonder that issues of fairness now loom more prominently as motivational hot buttons.

A related phenomenon has been the rise of interest in what we call "dark-side" responses. Workplace behaviors might be crudely classified as either positive or negative from the perspective of management—those that management believes will help the organization's well-being and those believed to be harmful instead. Referring to dark-side behaviors reflects that managerial orientation. Antiorganization, antimanagement activity might be seen as traitorous and rebellious, or even as evil and malevolent. Such images recall the Star Wars language of the universe's underlying "force" in its malevolent manifestation, "the dark side of the force." Sabotage, arson, industrial espionage by insiders to "aid and abet the enemy," embezzlement, and workplace violence come to mind as illustrations of such imagery.

The academic literature on organizations has seen a steadily growing interest in such themes. Correspondingly, authors have used a plethora of terms to capture the flavor of the relevant behaviors. Recent terminology has included *anticitizenship* (Youngblood, Trevino, & Favia, 1992) and *deviant workplace behaviors* (Robinson & Bennett, 1995). As Lind (1995) noted, however, such treatments tend to share a hidden source of potential bias. Often, the negative connotations of such terms imply that only negative consequences will result. Just as conflict can be constructive in fostering flexibility or innovation, so, too, can seemingly antagonistic responses, if managed properly; they should not be treated automatically as evil or bound to bring about nothing but harmful consequences. We use dark-side terminology and imagery very loosely and somewhat reluctantly, therefore, merely to signal an orientation whose connotations tend to clash with the tone of more "positive" concepts such as Organizational Citizenship Behavior or Prosocial Behavior. In the following three sections, we simply touch on three recent themes whose emergence tends to reflect the dark-side zeitgeist.

Psychological Contract Violation

Here we focus on only one article (Morrison & Robinson, 1997), and one specific topic that it addresses, as a sampler from amongst a flurry of recent writings on the psychological contract (e.g., Guzzo, Noonan, & Elron, 1994; Lucero & Allen, 1994; McLean-Parks & smith, in press; Robinson, Kraatz, & Rousseau, 1994; Rousseau & McLean-Parks, 1993). Morrison and Robinson (1997) referred to psychological contracts as constituted by employee beliefs concerning reciprocal obligations that exist between themselves and their organizations. A distinguishing feature of such covenants is that they consist of promises regarding mutual obligations—that is, each party to the contract promises to live up to certain obligations so long as the other does likewise. The quid-pro-quo nature of a psychological contract is clearest in discussions about breach of contract, which Morrison and Robinson defined in terms of employee perceptions:

> For a breach of contract to be perceived, an employee must determine not only that a promise has not been met, but also that he or she has made contributions in exchange for that promise that have not been adequately reciprocated. (p. 239)

This aspect of mutuality or reciprocity led Morrison and Robinson to describe perceived breach of contract as involving a comparison between two ratios, one representing provided:promised benefits by the organization and the other provided:promised contributions by the employee. A breach is perceived when the organization's side of the equation comes up short (i.e., it delivers less than promised, in comparison with the more abundant rate at which the employee provides promised contributions to the organization). Although conceptually similar to the pair of outcome-input ratios described by Adams (1965) in his equation for equity, the ratios for the psychological contract differ in that they involve promises: "An employee's perception of past promises plays a prominent role in the determination of contract breach. In contrast, evaluations of equity include all job-relevant inputs and outcomes, regardless of promises" (Morrison & Robinson, 1997, p. 242).

We will focus on promises even though Morrison and Robinson also noted the following as a second possible divergence from equity theory: "In most discussions of equity theory, the referent other is not in a direct exchange relationship with the focal employee. Rather, the referent is someone in a similar exchange relationship with a similar third party" (p. 242). That difference is more apparent than real. Although equity is often misconstrued as pertaining to the exchange relationship between one party and a similar Other, Adams (1965) explicitly referred to that as simply a way of indexing the fairness of the relationship between an employee and the employer.

We think exciting new directions for research have been opened by this attention to perceived contracts, obligations, and promises. At the same time, we think the differentiation from equity is both somewhat misleading and ultimately a possible detriment to integration. On the one hand, it makes sense to note the special quality of promises. People who break promises, whose words cannot be trusted because of a hypocritical disconnection with subsequent deeds, certainly incite a special form of condemnation. On the other hand, there are surely additional ways in which equally strong grounds can emerge for feeling that people should meet their moral obligations, whether such obligations were incurred on the basis of promises or not. The violation of moral obligations seems important even though "according to most researchers, if a perceived obligation is not accompanied by the belief that promise has been conveyed . . . , then it falls outside the psychological contract" (Morrison & Robinson, 1997, p. 228). Put another way, does a promise add to the intensity of an obligation, or does it change the underlying psychological dynamics in a way that makes unfilled promises qualitatively different from unfulfilled obligations? Only future research can answer that question. If promises create a qualitatively different dynamic from violated obligations, however, we think that would make the ultimate integration of these seemingly related concepts (e.g., promises as a special subcategory of obligations) more difficult than rigorous advocates of Occam's razor would hope.

Organizational Retaliatory Behaviors and Workplace Aggression

Again, we touch only lightly on a rapidly expanding literature. The topic of retaliation at work is hardly new, being traceable at least to the earliest writings on the frustration-aggression hypothesis (Dollard et al., 1939). Subsequently, Spector undertook a program of research that specifically related organizational frustration to aggression in the workplace (e.g., Chen & Spector, 1992; Leatherwood & Spector, 1991; Spector, 1975, 1997; Storms & Spector, 1987). Other authors have also published related work (e.g., Day & Hamblin, 1969; Lehman & Simpson, 1992; Mangione & Quinn, 1977; Moretti, 1986; Tucker, 1993).

Although the frustration-aggression model has been applied often in the context of workplace antagonism, we think a justice perspective can enrich this work considerably. Passages from Roger Brown's (Brown & Herrnstein, 1975) discussion of the relation between these concepts (also quoted in Folger & Baron, 1996) provide an overview:

> Frustration correctly conceived may not be fundamentally different from injustice, inequity, and relative deprivation. All may conceivably be considered variations on a single kind of instigator. . . . The basic notion is that all these instigating circumstances may be placed under the rubric of "the disappointment by illegitimate means of legitimate expectations". . . . Legitimacy implies operating according to norms, prescriptions for the way people in groups ought to think or act, which when violated lead to reproach, anger, even violence. (pp. 271, 274, 285)

We find the use of justice rather than frustration-aggression preferable for two reasons. First, a significant modification to the frustration-aggression hypothesis was suggested by Pastore (1950), who argued that frustrations do not provoke aggressiveness unless the frustration seems arbitrary, capricious, or otherwise illegitimate and unjustified. This modification is consistent with the role played by procedural and interactional justice in moderating reactions to unfair outcomes. Second, the role of interactional justice seems especially relevant to findings that insults often provoke greater aggressiveness than do frustrations (Baron & Richardson, 1994).

Other terminology also relates to retaliation as a dark-side alternative to its more frequently studied, positive counterpart, organizational citizenship behaviors (Organ, 1988). Indeed, Youngblood et al. (1992) referred to anticitizenship behaviors. Similarly, Robinson and Bennett (1995) referred to deviant workplace behaviors. Although these phrases are all variants on a common theme, and terminology is always somewhat arbitrary, we use *organizational retaliatory behaviors* as our preferred label (see Skarlicki & Folger, 1997).

Anticitizenship, for example, seems to connote the willingness not to live up to civic duty. In contrast, we think much retaliation for perceived unfairness in the workplace is seen (at least by the participant in that activity) as a justifiable response to the lack of civic responsibility on the employer's part.

Relatedly, we think the potentially pejorative connotations of deviant workplace behavior are also unfortunate, because it seems to presume "unnormal" and hence contranormative behavior by employees. Although many antagonistic actions in response to perceived unfairness can, indeed, be aggressive enough to deviate from the bounds of ordinary, socially acceptable behavior, it would seem problematic to impugn motives by implication or connotation. The danger that an employee's motives might be mistakenly impugned looms larger when labeling responses to perceived injustice as deviant. It is not outside the realm of possibility for some employees at some corporations to be treated unfairly—at times, shamefully so. Negative and even hostile reactions to such treatment might too easily be dismissed as abnormal and hence, sick, in some sense, if described only as deviant behaviors.

Despite the extent of the citations listed for dark-side behaviors and the growing popularity of the topic as reflected in numerous different terms for related concepts, the empirical investigation of actual dark-side behaviors is almost nonexistent. That is, the evidence amassed thus far pertains almost exclusively to self-reports of antagonism on survey questionnaires. Recently, that trend has changed, even if only ever so slightly. Work by Catalano, Novaco, & McConnell (1997), for example, examined the impact of layoffs in which people lose their jobs undeservedly, through no fault of their own. Up to a point, increased layoff rates increased the incidents of civil commitment for violence. Beyond that point, violence decreased, however, suggesting that the fear of layoffs inhibited violence by those who still had jobs. It is also possible that extremely high layoff rates serve to legitimize or justify the layoffs more than might otherwise be the case, thereby also contributing to a decrease in violence based on a reduced sense of injustice.

Perhaps the most direct test of a relation between unfairness perceptions and retaliatory behaviors used coworkers as observers of those behaviors, having also obtained ratings of perceived organizational injustice—distributive, procedural, and interactional—from the employees whose retaliation behaviors were observed (Skarlicki & Folger, 1997). In using peers to record actual aggressive behavior, this method goes beyond self-report and thereby avoids the problem of common method variance. The retaliation data revealed a three-way interaction among the types of injustice, with the most incidents of retaliation occurring when all three were at unfair levels. Consistent with Fairness Theory, variations in distributive justice had no impact on retaliation except when both procedural and interactional justice were low in fairness; when both were low, retaliation tendencies grew stronger with increasingly unfair outcomes. Moreover, the results showed the classic (RCT) pattern for a two-way interaction of distributive and procedural justice only when interactional justice was low, and showed a similar pattern for combined distributive-interactional impact only when procedural justice was low.

These results imply possible substitution effects involving tradeoffs between procedural and interactional justice. When a supervisor's interpersonal conduct drops below fair levels, employees are anxious to see procedural safeguards in place, to substitute for the trust in their supervisor that they do not have. Similarly, when procedural safeguards are not in place, employees are anxious to find indications of fair interpersonal conduct as evidence that they can trust the supervisor. Either source of fairness can provide a reassurance of well-intentioned efforts to do the right thing. Thus, either source of fairness can make an unfair outcome more tolerable, especially by suggesting that a particular outcome (despite whatever level of unfairness it exhibits) does not indicate the organization's lack of willingness to meet moral obligations owed employees. Such inferences make retaliation unlikely regardless of distributive injustice levels otherwise associated with a given outcome (e.g., perceptions of pay not at adequate levels of fairness). Simply stated, either fair procedures or fair interpersonal conduct can cancel the impact that disadvantageous outcomes would otherwise have on retaliation (i.e., the more distributively unfair the outcomes, the greater the retaliatory tendencies). Other authors have also provided similar accounts about employee desires for revenge against unfair bosses (e.g., Bies & Tripp, 1995a; Folger & Baron, 1996; Folger & Skarlicki, in press-a; Greenberg & Alge, in press; Lucero & Allen, 1994; Spector, 1997; Tripp & Bies, 1997).

The Churchill Effect: In Dark Times, Why Will Good People Sometimes Do Bad Things?

Consider a reversal of the independent variable-dependent variable sequence normally encountered in justice research. Usually, organizational justice researchers have studied manipulations of (or measured variations in) managerial fairness behaviors as causes and then examined employee reactions as effects. For example, ample evidence indicates how employees react when encountering what they consider unfair treatment by management. Both victims and survivors of layoffs, for example, respond far less antagonistically when management implements the negative decision with proper attention to procedural propriety and civil, courteous, respectful conduct (e.g., Brockner et al., 1994). Now reverse the sequence and go back in the causal chain: Take what was the independent variable (e.g., procedural or interactional justice by management) and treat it instead as a dependent variable (the frequency of occurrence of such behaviors, or presence vs. absence of their display, as an effect rather than a cause). Switching fairness behaviors into dependent variable status means treating them as effects and going back in the causal chain to identify their antecedent determinants. This introduces a new research question: What causes fair or unfair behaviors? Research addressing this question would try to determine the conditions under which otherwise good people—such as those who ordinarily would follow sound management practices—act in a manner that employees consider unfair.

Often procedural fairness (e.g., voice as letting people have their say) and interactional fairness (e.g., interpersonal sensitivity as politeness and showing respect for people's dignity) seem so much like Golden Rule versions of "what I learned in kindergarten" that no significant variation in their occurrence would seem likely. As discussed in connection with the possibility of a positive-negative asymmetry, normal decency goes underappreciated because people habituate to its occurrence. If there were a ceiling effect for such behavior as a socially desirable response, there would be little point in launching research studies to look for interesting causal antecedents. The way downsizing has actually played out, however, suggests otherwise. At the very time when employees might respond most favorably to some display of sympathy, some representatives of management have at times seemed to have turned so coldhearted, aloof, and distancing (or even downright brutally abusive) as to have inspired countless Dilbert cartoon caricatures (Folger & Skarlicki, in press-b).

Some related theorizing and research has begun, albeit only on a small scale, as work on what is called the *Churchill effect* (Folger & Pugh, 1997; Folger & Skarlicki, in press-b). Essentially, the effect refers to creating psychological distance from victims on whom harm is imposed, and its presumed cause is the desire to avoid psychological or other "costs" anticipated from failing to maintain such distance. The term comes from an expression used by England's wartime Prime Minister and found in his memoirs (Churchill, 1950). In writing about the events of World War II, Churchill related having sent a telegram to the Japanese ambassador when Great Britain declared war on Japan. The note adopted a very proper British writing style and closed with "I have the honor, sir, to be your humble servant, Winston S. Churchill." The Prime Minister, therefore, was following conventions of politeness as regards his interpersonal conduct toward the Japanese ambassador.

The public, however, was inclined to treat the enemy otherwise. Consistent with the animosity often generated toward those whom we are about to harm (perhaps in conjunction with a dissonance-reducing principle of generating dislike for our victims and justifying their treatment by assuming they deserve it), the British people could not understand why Churchill would take the trouble to display good manners when dealing with the enemy. Churchill's answer, as he recorded it later for posterity, was wry: "But after all, when you have to kill a man it costs nothing to be polite."

The significance of that statement is twofold. First, note that it served as a reminder of how people ought to act. No person about to be harmed, implied Churchill, deserves additional insult; let the punishment fit the action (according to reciprocity principles of fairness), but do not implement the chosen punishment in a demeaning, humiliating manner. Instead, act with politeness and thereby administer harmful consequences in an interpersonally sensitive, considerate manner—continuing to treat people with the respect and dignity they deserve as human beings, despite their having drawn negative sanctions on themselves. Simple acts of politeness and other indications of interpersonal sensitivity embody the ethic of Kant's categorical imperative, which requires never treating people merely as means to private ends but always also as ends themselves (i.e., as being worthy of respect). When we refer to the Churchill effect, therefore, we refer to situations in which people *violate* this ethic of interactional fairness. When good people do bad things (mistreat others by adding insult to injury), it is as if they need reminding that it would "cost nothing" to do the right thing instead.

The second significant feature of Churchill's remark is that reference to cost. The Churchill effect, which violates another's dignity when imposing harm, involves a perception of cost that Churchill's reminder was meant to reprove and correct. He tried to make his point by hyperbole, stating that politeness (and by extension, the interpersonal sensitivity of interactional justice) would impose no cost. If people "forget" this principle and seem inclined to act insensitively—even brutally and abusively—when imposing harm, however, then perhaps they do so when they instead perceive greater cost from acting considerately than when not. Perhaps Churchill exaggerated about the lack of cost in order to counteract the opposite tendency for people to exaggerate the costliness of showing kindness, consideration, and sensitivity to the victims of harm. Such costs do not have to be financial or material, of course. In fact, they are far more likely to be symbolic and psychological—such as the discomfort and awkwardness experienced when interacting with someone who has a fatal disease, a disfigurement, or some other stigmatizing feature (e.g., Roth, Sitkin & House, 1994).

These issues have been discussed thoroughly elsewhere (e.g., Folger & Pugh, 1997; Folger & Skarlicki, in press-a, in press-b), and we will not go into further detail here. Our point is simply that we think there is another reminder needed: When studying the dark side, investigators should not focus only on employee reactions considered to be antagonistic toward the organization or labeled dysfunctional, deviant, antisocial, and the like. Rather, a balanced scorecard also calls for studying managerial conduct and the causes of actions by managers perceived by employees to be unfair. Sometimes such perceptions might have a kernel of truth to them. Sometimes even good people do bad things. Instead of attributing unfair actions to character defects and thereby running the risk of the fundamental attribution error (viz., neglecting situational determinants of conduct), we think it worthwhile to examine different types of conditions that can evoke less than honorable behavior even from otherwise well-intentioned people. We think it worthwhile to investigate when people need Churchill's reminder.

Preliminary investigations (Folger & Skarlicki, in press-b) obtained evidence consistent with a few hypotheses, and other research (e.g., Gilliland & Schepers, 1997) promises to uncover additional contributing factors. We refer to the Folger and Skarlicki research illustratively. In it, the tendency to reduce levels of interactional fairness as interpersonal sensitivity was measured in terms of a single, simple indicator: the amount of time that a manager designated to spend with the victim of a layoff (as part of a role-playing exercise using an in-basket technique). To date, research with this paradigm has used only a limited number of manipulations as independent variables. Each conceptualizes increased psychological cost associated with harming a victim as a function of increasingly negative reactions anticipated from the victim.

Employees should react with greater animosity when they suspect that mismanagement has caused the need to reduce labor costs by laying off workers, for example, in comparison with the situation in which employees perceive that ineluctable market forces caused declining profits and the need to cut costs. One Churchill-effect study by Folger and Skarlicki (in press-b), therefore, introduced one or the other of those descriptions as the background to a layoff scenario in which role-playing managers had to decide how much time they would allocate for telling their laid-off employees about the terminations. When it was plausible to assume hostility by employees because of perceived mismanagement, the communicators dedicated less time to such messages than when they felt that inexorable market forces would instead be blamed. Other data (Folger, 1997) showed a similar tendency toward moral disengagement by harmdoers (cf. Bandura, 1990) and the creation of increased psychological distance from victims (less time devoted to communicating with them and providing explanations; see Milgram, 1974, for a related discussion of distancing). Managers who thought that layoffs had come at a time of large financial bonuses to the CEO, for example, designated less time to spend on layoff conversations with victims than did managers told that the CEO's compensation increased only to a very modest degree during the layoff period.

The theoretical importance of this research lies in the framework it provides for distinguishing conditions under which managers may be inclined to distance their victims—that is, when "tough times make tough bosses." Research also suggests that the costs of being a tough boss (e.g., distancing, interpersonal insensitivity) are significant both to the victim and the organization. Moreover, research has shown that a manager can minimize costs of the delivery of bad news by demonstrating interpersonal sensitivity. Hence, it is necessary to better understand conditions under which a manager is likely to approach or avoid victims of management decision making.

From a practical perspective, it appears that in difficult economic times, managers often focus on costs to the organization that are measurable (e.g., salaries, severance packages) and tend to overlook the costs of their own actions. This research provides a first step in understanding what managers can do to mitigate the costs of management decision making in hard times— namely, demonstrate interpersonally sensitive behaviors. Future investigations might involve talking to managers to get their implicit theories regarding their tendency to approach or avoid victims of managerial decision making in tough times.

"Do This," "Don't Do That": Recommendations for Theory and Research

We discussed the Churchill effect as a prelude to this section for the following reason: That effect involves turning what had been an independent variable (managerially insensitive—hence, interactionally unfair—behavior, as a factor influencing employee reactions) into a dependent variable (managerially insensitive distancing as itself a reaction, possibly caused by perceived costs such as anticipated hostility from employees who feel unfairly victimized by layoffs). This idea extends research in a new direction, rather than applying a well-established finding (e.g., the fair-process effect demonstrating that fair procedures produce enhanced acceptance even of otherwise unfair outcomes) to an increasingly larger set of topic domains (e.g., perceptions of drug testing, selection tests, performance appraisal ratings).

Much of this book has catalogued applications of known effects to new domains in human resource management. Although this progress has been remarkable, it threatens to look faddish and to become stale unless theorists and researchers exert continued creativity. Otherwise, finding related effects across content domains might eventually lead to such reactions as "this is just old wine in new wineskins." To flourish, the field of organizational justice should stretch its boundaries not only by generalizing across domains for increasing external validity, but also by solving new intellectual puzzles that demand insight about causal mechanisms and the corresponding attention to internal-validity problems as the ruling-out of alternative explanations. Much has been learned by conducing field surveys that obtain correlational data useful for generalization and external validity, for example, but far too few field experiments have occurred to allow confident interpretation about some of the correlational findings now commonly cited. True, some of the field studies have replicated effects previously obtained on the basis of experimental manipulations in the laboratory. Nonetheless, we think the rigor of experimental methodology—whether in lab or field—must continue to play a vital role in the further refinement of understanding about organizational justice.

In what follows, we extend our editorializing about how we think theory and research on organizational justice might best progress. Originally, we conceived this section as an initial set of "don't do that" principles, to be followed by a set of "do this" principles. We found it difficult, however, to hold onto the distinction in pure form: A discussion of what not to do invariably starts to include comments about what to do, and vice versa. The result is a potpourri of loosely collected thoughts and immodest pontificating in the form of advice. Our advance caution to the reader, therefore, is to bear in mind our own inevitable fallibility.

"Unfair Comparisons"

The first topic addressed we will call "unfair comparisons," in honor of an eponymous article by Cooper and Richardson (1986). The unfairness to which they referred has nothing to do with justice in the sense of this book (e.g., employee perceptions of fairness in treatment by supervisors). Rather, they referred to methods of scientific investigation that pit two or more competing theories against one another in a biased manner. Unfair comparisons lack a level playing field on which opposing viewpoints might vie as equals; instead, one position has an advantage or disadvantage not based on relative merit. In addition to the case of contests among two or more theories, unfairness of this type can also occur when investigators compare "the predictive or relational strength of two or more factors or variables" (Cooper & Richardson, 1986, p. 179). An example would be comparing the strength of distributive and procedural factors in their respective ability to predict variance in some criterion. Such a comparison can be unfair unless both predictors are measured with equivalent fidelity, neither has problems of restricted range or variance, and so on.

The potentially problematic aspects of tests to compare the relative strength or importance of two or more factors (e.g., as predictors accounting for variance in a criterion) have been amply described elsewhere (e.g., Budescu, 1993; Cooper & Richardson, 1986). We recapitulate those arguments in a reduced form. Briefly, there are two major categories of problems:

1. When dealing with more than two factors or theoretical models being compared, conclusions about the relevant importance or strength (henceforth, impact) of a given factor or model must be drawn with great care. Budescu (1993), for example, reviewed several statistical approaches to this issue, discussed weaknesses associated with each, and proposed a general solution—"dominance analysis," which is equivalent to the Darlington usefulness analysis in the two-variable case but differs from it with more than two predictors.

2. Independently of the type of statistical analysis performed (e.g., usefulness vs. dominance), substantive issues can arise when two factors or models are not represented with equal care. These issues constitute the concerns about unfair comparisons to which we referred earlier.

We concentrate primarily on the nature of unfair comparisons rather than on problematic aspects of statistical analyses because the latter seem to us less troublesome in the major part of the organizational literature. As we noted, the statistical problems arise when more than two factors or models are compared for relative impact. Many tests within the organizational justice literature, however, pit one factor or model against another—the two-variable case, which is statistically uncontroversial. Drawing conclusions about the relative impact of procedural versus distributive justice is unproblematic in a statistical sense, so long as any of several valid techniques are used (Budescu, 1993). Caution should be exercised, however, when more than two such factors or models are compared. The investigator faced with such a situation would do well to consider Budescu's discussion carefully; we do not know of ways to justify an approach other than dominance analysis when comparing more than two predictors for relative impact.

Even in the two-predictor case analyzed with the appropriate statistical tests, however, important substantive concerns must be addressed— issues of potentially unfair comparisons. Notably, the Cooper and Richardson (1986) discussion used the language of distributional and procedural properties when addressing questions about the equivalence of two factors or models. Although those two categories of equivalence (or nonequivalence) do not involve unfairness in the sense of outcome distributions or procedures for making decisions, the reasoning is analogous to the categories of distributive and procedural justice. The procedural fairness of comparative tests refers to measurement procedures and calls for an equivalence of measurement. The distributive fairness of comparative tests refers to the moments of a variable's distribution—in particular, involving restrictions to range or variance, as they create unequal dispersion across two variables. Jointly, these two criteria of comparative test fairness dictate caution in interpreting results. As Cooper and Richardson stated, "if one theory, factor, or variable is found to be stronger than others, the researchers are obliged to show that procedural slippages and distributional compressions are not one-sided, favoring the results that are found" (p. 184).

These requirements, it seems to us, may be especially hard to meet in the case of correlational survey data. When variables are measured rather than manipulated, distributional equivalence requires that researchers "first select samples that are expected to contain sufficient variance on each of the competing variables (as well as on the dependent variable(s))" (Cooper & Richardson, 1986, p. 183). Cooper and Richardson also offered the related advice of using measures for which norms are available, then correcting for differential range (or variance) restriction where necessary. Establishing procedural equivalence is even more demanding. Overall, this requirement dictates "no differential slippage" (p. 182) in the process of translating constructs into operational measures: "Look at everything you plan to do, think of all the ways you could deliberately favor one theory, factor, or variable, and then search your procedures to see if you approximated any one of them" (p. 183). Similarly, tests of competing theories require demonstrating "equivalent respect for each of their boundary conditions . . . by first saying what the boundary conditions are and then describing exactly how the procedures meet the conditions" (p. 183). We think that organizational justice research has rarely exercised such care in tests of competing models or tests of the relative strength of more than one variable or factor.

An example concerns testing for main effects versus interactions. Some models explicitly predict ordinal or fan-shaped interactions (e.g., RCT), whereas others (e.g., the group-value or relational model) have always focused on main effects. Two opposite types of problems exist. On the one hand, an Outcome × Process interaction can be produced artifactually when the outcome distribution contains a ceiling effect (as might be indicated by skewness). Lind and Tyler (1988) discussed that possibility in arguing why an interaction might be obtained despite the theoretical correctness of predicting a procedural main effect (or a main effect both for outcomes and for procedures) instead. On the other hand, McClelland and Judd (1993) noted that "the theoretical constraint of ordinal interactions . . makes such effects more difficult to detect in field studies" (p. 377). Indeed, numerous commentators have noted that interactions—moderator effects in multiple regression—are difficult to obtain from correlational data (e.g., Aiken & West, 1991; Morris, Sherman, & Mansfield, 1986; Zedeck, 1971).

Inadvertently Reducing Fairness to Selfishness

Next, we return to the theme with which we concluded the preceding chapter: making organizational justice research and theory more congruent with general ethical principles. Oddly enough, empirical work on fairness seems to have lost touch with its ultimate grounding in the literature on ethics and morality. At best, the morality of psychological egoism prevails—an ostensibly ethical set of precepts hardly distinguishable from simple self-interest and greed.

The influence of egoism (Folger, in press) occurs in two ways. First, some research has emphasized that when people make judgments of fairness, they express a self-interested bias. That is, fairness preferences are aligned with self-interest all too conveniently, such as when people endorse a given procedure as fair only because it is also the one most likely to give them the outcomes they want. We do not deny that self-interest often biases fairness perceptions, preferences, choices, and reactions. Nonetheless, if the language of fairness is to have a meaningful link with its ethical roots, theory and research ought also to address the circumstances under which people sacrifice self-regard for the sake of genuine fairness (e.g., taking into account the rights, interests, and well-being of others).

The scientific study of fairness has tended to be egoistical in a second respect as well. Fundamentally, each existing psychological theory of justice tries to understand and explain why a person might react in certain ways to perceived fairness or unfairness. The fair or unfair treatment being considered, however, always pertains to the perceiver as someone affected quite directly by the actions of others. The theory of inequity (Adams, 1965), for example, asks when a person will perceive that he or she has been treated unfairly. Similarly, the origins of work on procedural justice (Thibaut & Walker, 1975) asked what procedures might enhance the acceptability of decisions even when the outcome otherwise seemed unfair (or was unfavorable) to the perceiver as the person receiving an outcome from that procedure (viz., an allocation decision-making or dispute-resolution procedure). The vantage point of the spectator whose perceptions matter, therefore, is always one of self-interest. That is, the perceiver is one whose interests are at stake because they stand to be affected by procedures, decisions, outcomes, consequences, and interpersonal treatment from some other person. Missing is the vantage point of the neutral, "disinterested" spectator—the third party observer whose own material well-being and self-regard are not directly jeopardized, but who nonetheless cares about what happens (i.e., how other people are affected) as a member of the moral community.

How would adopting such a perspective alter theory and research? First, it would imply the need for a type of research different from what the extant literature contains most commonly. Rather than obtaining reactions only from those most directly involved (i.e., those who stand to gain or lose directly), research would investigate the views of neutral, third-party observers (or those able to adopt that role). Some past research has adopted that viewpoint, of course, in asking people hypothetically what type of procedure seems fairest. When people read a description of a courtroom trial conducted either by an adversarial or inquisitorial procedure, for example, their preferences represent third-party views in the sense that the respondents are not the actual participants in the trial portrayed. A similar paradigm uses respondents who are not trial participants but portrays merely the abstract, structural features of the decision-making procedure (e.g., abstract descriptions of adversarial, inquisitorial, or hybrid models; Folger et al., 1996; Sheppard, 1984). There, too, the respondents have nothing at stake directly, even if asked to indicate their preference for the procedure that would be used if they were brought to trial at some point in the future.

This type of research harks back to a distinction made by Greenberg (e.g., 1984), who noted the difference between *reactive* and *proactive* research on justice. Reactive research examines reactions (e.g., perceived fairness, absenteeism, turnover) to conditions that presumably vary with regard to their fairness. The conditions are those that have already been brought about (e.g., by someone else's actions, such as by distributing outcomes in a particular way or by selecting a particular procedure to use for resolving a dispute). The reactions involve those who have experienced those conditions (e.g., someone who feels underpaid). Proactive research, on the other hand, would investigate people's preferences and selections as regards how to distribute outcomes, which procedure to use, or what manner of interpersonal conduct to display.

When introducing the distributive-procedural distinction to the field of organizational behavior by incorporating it into a typology, Greenberg (1984) also included the proactive-reactive distinction. At that time, he could point to a small set of existing studies that had explored the proactive-distributive combination (e.g., Leventhal et al., 1980). None then existed at the proactive-procedural interface, with the possible exception of some early work by Thibaut and his colleagues (e.g., LaTour, Houlden, Walker, & Thibaut, 1976) and by Sheppard (1984). Virtually none have been conducted since that time (one exception being Folger et al., 1996). Moreover, we are not aware that anyone has ever studied interactional justice from a proactive perspective.

In addition to suggesting a different type of research to explore, there is also a second implication to derive from considering the observer perspective—a change in theoretical orientation. We suspect that current theoretical explanations of justice effects would be hard-pressed to account for certain types of effects possible to obtain from observers' reactions. That is, current explanations are built from assumptions about the thoughts and feelings of people who experience an injustice affecting them personally (e.g., being paid less than a similarly qualified coworker). A different type of psychological mechanism would have to be used to explain the reactions of neutral, third-party observers—that is, if such observers showed outrage over an injustice that has no effect on them personally.

Illustratively, suppose a theorist's favorite explanation for justice effects involves a particular assumption involving how it feels to be unfairly treated and why it feels that way. We can take threats to self-esteem, for example, as a general psychological mechanism underlying many such explanations. A threat to the self can explain why a person becomes antagonistic when treated unfairly, but how can the same type of antagonism be explained by the same type of psychological mechanism (threat to self, such as sense of personal identity or status) when the unfairness happens to another person instead? Third-party reactions of outrage to another person's unfair treatment would seem to require some other type of explanation. But then, however, Occam's razor suggests that the number of explanatory mechanisms has been unnecessarily expanded. Why not seek a single mechanism that can account for both types of reactions? Such a mechanism might imply, for example, that all members of the moral community have a stake in upholding standards of decent, fair treatment. We urge the development of such theorizing.

Changing Moderators Into Mediators

Our advice about unfair comparisons and reducing fairness to selfishness can combine into an overall plea for theory and research aimed at explanation in terms of underlying mechanisms. If interactions are hard to find in non-experimental field research, that means the detection of moderator effects is problematic. But predictions of moderator effects do not always rise above mere description to begin with. Saying that males will react more strongly than females to some form of information does not explain why sex differences would produce such an effect, for example, just as saying that differences in outcomes affect reactions more strongly given unfair procedures than given fair procedures does not explain why procedures would produce such an effect. A possible solution to the dilemma of predicting moderator effects, yet having problems obtaining them, therefore, might be to concentrate on mediators instead. That approach, in turn, jibes with our call for more thought about the nature of the psychological mechanisms that mediate reactions to unfairness.

Work by Van den Bos, Lind, et al. (1997) is suggestive in this regard, although not definitive because only the theoretical reasoning dealt with mediation—the results themselves still involved only a moderator analysis (i.e., a test for an interaction by an ANOVA involving experimentally manipulated factors). Van den Bos, Lind, et al. manipulated an outcome factor and a process factor, the latter in terms of differences in voice. The outcome manipulation pertained to the number of lottery tickets obtained by the participant and, ostensibly, by another person with equivalent performance in the same experiment. A given participant always received three lottery tickets, but information varied about the lottery tickets received by the other person. In an Unknown (ambiguous information) condition, the participant did not know how may tickets the other person received. In the remaining conditions (the other person's outcome Better than, Worse than, or Equal to the participant's), information created known conditions of clearly disadvantageous inequity, advantageous inequity, or equity, respectively. Contrary to the usual finding of a fair-process effect, the procedure containing voice failed to improve perceptions of satisfaction or fairness relative to the procedure that contained no voice. That absence of an effect for procedures was obtained, however, only in the Better, Worse, and Equal conditions—that is, in the conditions where distributive justice had clearly been violated or clearly been preserved. In contrast, a positive effect of voice on perceived outcome fairness was obtained in the Unknown condition.

As Van den Bos and colleagues noted, such findings cast some doubt on one way of interpreting an Outcome × Process interaction—one not only cited by Brockner and Wiesenfeld (1996) in their review of such interactions, but also invoked by Van den Bos himself in a prior study (Van den Bos, Vermunt, et al., 1997). The nature of that discredited explanation is as follows: "A negative outcome may serve as a negative event, an unexpected event, or both, and hence is more likely to initiate sense-making or information-seeking activity than a positive outcome" (Van den Bos, Lind, et al., 1997, p. 1043). Comparing the impact of procedures on reactions in the Better and the Unknown conditions shows how such an explanation is disconfirmed. Specifically, the clearly negative event (Better conditions) did not lead to information seeking about intent as revealed by the procedure or sense making in light of the procedure; rather, the impact of procedural differences on outcome perceptions occurred only when the relative negativity of the outcome was uncertain (Unknown conditions). As the authors themselves put it, "the present results cast doubt on the . . . procedure-by-outcome explanation rooted in conceptions about informational search" (p. 1043).

When procedural impact thus varies as a function of differences among the conditions of another, cross-cutting factor, the results indicate an interaction. The interaction obtained by manipulating outcome ambiguity showed that procedural differences had no impact when equity or inequity was clear-cut, but had an impact when an uncertain chance of inequity was possible. This interaction, therefore, showed the impact of procedures moderated by outcome information. Although suggestive in the sense of its inconsistency with the information-search explanation, that result does not reveal a specific mediator of procedure's impact (cf. the mediator-moderator distinction drawn by Baron & Kenny, 1986). We think that future theory and research will advance to the extent that specification of mediators and tests of mediation occur.

According to Fairness Theory, for example, the mediation of reactions to unfairness resides in inferences about the causal and moral context. When an outcome at first seems unfair, but evidence eventually implicates the victim, hostility by that person will tend to abate. Attributing blame to oneself as the cause and assigning oneself the moral responsibility for a negative outcome, that is, are incongruent with antagonism toward others about any unfairness. With the absence of personal responsibility by the victim, however, two other possibilities arise: Either purely external factors in the natural, physical world were at work (e.g., a rainstorm as the cause of a canceled trip), or the blame rests with another person held morally accountable for the negative event. This reasoning is consistent with data indicating that reactions to inequity differ according the potential assignment of blame based on which person, victim or other, made crucial choices with consequences for outcomes obtained (e.g., Cropanzano & Folger, 1989; Folger, Rosenfield, & Hays, 1978).

In the future, measures of moral accountability might be developed, thereby allowing for tests of this factor as a mediator. Although tests of mediation will depend on obtaining reliable and valid measurement, we can speculate in the meantime about how such a measure might help to explain different patterns of results. The results of unknown versus known equity or inequity serve as a case in point. Apparently, a clear-cut inequity can simplify the assignment of blame and moral accountability—anyone who would impose exceedingly disparate outcomes despite equivalent inputs (e.g., three lottery tickets vs. five lottery tickets, despite identical performance) is ordinarily presumed to have acted unfairly with willful intent. How about the case where the other person's outcomes are unknown, but the presence versus absence of voice characterizes a difference in procedural treatment? Here the procedure acts both as a substitute outcome and as a source of information on which to base an inference of intent. As a substitute outcome, the absence of voice can demean and belittle the person subjected to this unfair procedural treatment (imposing a loss of dignity, especially if seen as a manner of treatment more befitting a child than an adult). As the basis for inferring intent, the use of procedures without voice implies a decision maker who deliberately avoids obtaining information potentially relevant to the interests and well-being of those affected by the results of implementing the procedure.

Moral Accountability as a Mediator: An Explanation of How Procedural Justice Moderates the Impact of Outcomes. Building on the analysis that Van den Bos,

Lind, et al. (1997) proposed, we see possible advances in understanding the nature of differences among distributive, procedural, and interactional justice. In particular, we believe that procedural and interactional justice often act to moderate the impact of outcome distributions because of the role played by the two former justice concepts in relation to inferences about moral accountability. Said more directly, evidence about procedures and interactional conduct often conveys underlying motives and intentions in ways not often so readily apparent from differences in outcomes.

We start with the assumption of Van den Bos, Lind, et al. (1997) that "concerns related to procedural fairness may be easier to interpret than those related to distributive fairness" (pp. 1042-1043). They meant that the unfairness of outcomes is often more difficult to establish than the unfairness of procedures. In particular, they suggested that direct, unequivocal information about others' outcomes is often unavailable—hence the reason for their Unknown condition.

We think this line of reasoning can be extended in ways consistent with pointing to causal and moral attributions (e.g., of intent) as a crucial mediator of reactions. Outcome unfairness need not represent a difficult judgment only when information about others' outcomes is missing. Even when known, those outcomes and their disparity from one's own can constitute ambiguous information for a variety of reasons, especially with regard to the prospects for inferring a decision maker's motives merely from the pattern of a distribution. In some cases, the distribution pattern will clearly imply the decision maker's intent. In many cases, however, inferring the intent behind the pattern will be fraught with uncertainty—because it is unclear how much of a determinative role the decision maker played, because more than one fairness norm might reasonably be applied, and so on.

Often, the conditions for assigning moral accountability will be more clear cut in the case of procedural-fairness differences than in the case of distributive-outcome differences. For one thing, a given society or culture might have a higher degree of social consensus about normatively appropriate procedures than about norms for distributional fairness. The absence of an appropriate procedural feature, therefore, would more clearly be identified as a definite loss. Moreover, the choice of which procedural variation to use might seem to be in the purview of an authority. If procedural details are at the decision maker's discretion, then the omission of a normatively required element can be seen not only as the loss of a desired procedural feature (e.g., absence of voice) but also as a loss attributable to the motives and intentions of the decision maker. Procedural unfairness is thus doubly unfair in the sense of incorporating both aspects of injustice specified by Fairness Theory: It harms or insults someone by imposing an undeserved deprivation (e.g., of procedural rights as "outcomes"), and it constitutes improper conduct by another person—a social actor held morally accountable under the circumstances.

Interactional Justice in Light of Moral Accountability as a Mediator. Interactional justice, we suggest, might prove even more important than either distributive or procedural justice in its impact on the crucial, mediating processes that govern reactions to unfairness. We want to clarify our sense of the difference between procedural and interactional justice first, before arguing for the claim just made. Assuming the mediating role of attributions and accountability actually provides a guide to making this distinction.

Consider, for example, the legal concept of premeditation as it refers to action performed by design, in accordance with a predetermined plan (cf. "with malice aforethought"). We think of procedural features as similarly premeditated. By procedural features, we mean characteristic design elements that structure the process governing how certain mechanisms operate to determine a distribution of outcomes. Administrative policy might be a good synonym for such features, which represent the predetermined structure of governance mechanisms. Such policies describe applicable rules and regulations in advance. Some of those regulatory statutes stipulate certain aspects of the roles to be played by various parties, as exemplified by the manner in which Thibaut and Walker (1975, 1978) distinguished between adversarial and inquisitorial procedures according to the roles of disputants and a third party with respect to both process and decision control. Other regulations might establish procedural safeguards against some of the problems identified by Leventhal's (1980) analysis. Some rules might call for certain types of consistent application across persons and times, for example, just as others might provide forms of protection against some standard sources of inaccuracy, bias, and even innocent mistakes (e.g., an appeal mechanism whose procedural details are prespecified).

In contrast, interactional justice does not constitute fair treatment by obeying rules about structural features dictated by a predesigned, administrative plan. Formal institutions publish rules in constitutions, for example, whereas the fairness of interactional conduct comes from conformity with the informal dictates of culture and custom (a society's unwritten rules of conduct regarding fairness in human interaction). The various ways that interactional justice has been defined, and the various examples usually given to illustrate it, can be understood in light of this basis for distinguishing it from procedural justice.

One such illustrative differentiation described interactional justice as the "enacted" fairness of a procedure, as contrasted with its structural features as dictated on an a priori basis. In terms of inferences about moral accountability, that difference suggests the role of two different social actors—or at least points to actions (decisions) occurring at two different stages or points in time. First, some decision maker or group (e.g., legislative body, governing council, top echelon of executives or administrators) establishes formal policy regarding decision-making structures, often in distributing published copies of rules and regulations. Then, as those governing mechanisms operate to regulate the process for making a particular decision on a particular occasion, someone then in charge of making that decision presumably follows those predetermined guidelines as applicable. The enactment might differ from, or go beyond, some characteristics of the a priori, structural features. The person in charge might misinterpret how a procedural rule should apply or be interpreted. Deliberate disobedience of a rule can occur. Also, rules for all possible aspects of a situation cannot be specified in advance; personal discretion reigns "in between the cracks" of rules as another entry point for variations in interactional fairness.

A way to think about the distinction in general, therefore, is to differentiate (a) an initial set of intentions, often inferred from documents and other sources of official pronouncements about policy and procedure, from (b) a "realized" set of intentions, as enacted by someone in charge at the time final decisions are actually made. The former, as one possible description of procedural justice, is analogous to codified law as it pertains to regulations that govern decision-making processes. The latter, as one possible description of interactional justice, is analogous to actions that can raise questions regarding whether they conform with the spirit or the letter of the law.

Why suggest a distinction along those lines? We have introduced it now, at the end of the book rather than at its beginning, because it does not represent a neutral use of terminology. Rather, it is theory laden in being driven by assumptions characteristic of Fairness Theory. Because Fairness Theory reserves a central role for assigning moral accountability among prospective social actors (e.g., victim's own fault vs. unfairly exploited by another), its conceptual foundations call for distinguishing among justice terms according to differences in the basis for inferring accountability. When procedural fairness is violated, it matters whether the procedure was flawed by design or was improperly implemented—whether the governing body is at fault (for establishing unfair procedural policy) or one of its minions (for failing to follow fair guidelines). When interactional fairness is violated, on the other hand, the predesignated criteria are those established by the moral community itself. The inference of an a priori failure to abide by fair principles would not make sense, because it would be self-contradictory. A case of interactional injustice exists when social conduct violates a moral community's precepts considered legitimate by the perceiver, so a previous-stage violation of fairness (a flaw in predetermined criteria) is ruled out by definition. By the same token, less confusion exists regarding whom to blame—the "system" or the person in charge (i.e., the system in question is the one already deemed fair by the perceiver, hence, it cannot be at fault). This relative reduction in ambiguity, in comparison with the case of procedural justice, suggests one reason why interactional justice might be a more powerful moderator of outcome impact.

Other reasons also exist. Consider two types of outcomes resulting from an unfair procedure: (a) the tangible outcome whose distribution the procedure was designed to influence (i.e., outcomes distributed as ends, and procedures used instrumentally as the means for trying to ensure the greater likelihood of certain ends considered desirable); and (b) the deprivation of procedural rights by virtue of the procedural system and structure imposed. Potential ambiguity exists regarding the moral accountability for each.

A procedure for making decisions, for example, starts by acquiring information and ends by reaching conclusions presumably based on that information. If the information pertains to the behavior and qualifications of someone to whom benefits will be distributed (or from whom some might be withheld), then sources of ambiguity can involve several factors. Does the decision accurately reflect the person's behavior or qualifications, or was it a product of poor-quality information (with noise potentially entering the system in a variety of ways)? Or could the decision maker have been prejudiced? Similarly, it is not always clear whom to hold accountable for the deprivation of procedural rights. Was a policy mandated by someone at the corporate offices? Was a procedural feature implemented for no particular reason and as a mere function of habit, or chosen deliberately to deny certain parties their chance for potential influence?

By contrast, instances involving violated codes of interpersonal conduct often come bound unmistakably with clear-cut implications about their source and presumed reasons for their occurrence. Suppose a supervisor notes an employee's production error, marches onto the shop floor, confronts the employee, and makes a public announcement about the error in ways obviously calculated to humiliate the employee. Or suppose an applicant can tell that an interviewer has lied about promising to get back in touch, and the interviewer rudely fails to return calls of inquiry thereafter. Such interpersonal slights and indignities leave little doubt whom to blame. Moreover, they ordinarily seem deliberately intended rather than accidental or coerced.

In sum, the role of moral accountability as a mediator shows promise as a way to clarify the nature of nuanced differences among distributive, procedural, and interactional justice. We have also implied that interactional justice might have some of the strongest impact in moderating reactions to suspected injustices. With that possibility having been suggested, we have come full circle: Despite having warned against the "unfair comparisons" that pit one factor against another, we have also indicated some reasons to suspect that interactional justice will play an especially powerful role. This reminder about the difficulty of comparing the relative impact from various factors, therefore, also suggests why it will be helpful to construct explanations in terms of underlying psychological mechanisms as mediators. Only with such analyses will the most complete characterization of relevant constructs be forthcoming, and only on the basis of those richer and more thorough descriptions will it be possible to conduct comparisons among constructs in a fair manner. We think that in a book on fairness, it is fitting to end by reminding investigators about their obligation to be fair when conducting research.

Note

1. For convenience, we present only the means for one measure, distributive justice, obtained from Experiment 1 (a role-playing study). A procedural justice measure in Experiment 1, as well as distributive and procedural justice measures in Experiment 2 (a laboratory study), yielded essentially identical results.

References

Abbey, A., & Dickson, J. W. (1983). Organizational structure and innovation. *Journal of Business, 40,* 497-510.

Abdenour, T. E., Miner, M. J., & Weir, N. (1987). Attitudes of intercollegiate football players toward drug testing. *Athletic Training, 22,* 199-201.

Abelson, R. P., Kinder, D. P., Peters, M. D., & Fiske, S. T. (1982). Affective and semantic components in political person perception. *Journal of Personality and Social Psychology, 42,* 619-630.

Adams, J. S. (1965). Inequity in social exchange. In L. Berkowitz (Ed.), *Advances in experimental social psychology* (Vol. 2, pp. 267-299). New York: Academic Press.

Aiken, L. S., & West, S. G. (1991). *Multiple regression: Testing and interpreting interactions.* Newbury Park, CA: Sage.

Alder, G. S., & Ambrose, M. L. (1996). *Designing, implementing, and utilizing computerized performance monitors for procedural and distributive justice.* Unpublished manuscript.

Alderfer, C. P. (1969). An empirical test of a new theory of human needs. *Organizational Behavior and Human Performance, 4,* 142-175.

Alderfer, C. P. (1972). *Existence, relatedness, and growth: Human needs in organizational settings.* New York: Free Press.

Alexander, S., & Ruderman, M. (1987). The role of procedural and distributive justice in organizational behavior. *Social Justice Research, 1,* 177-198.

Ambrose, M. L., & Rosse, J. G. (1993). *Relational justice and personality testing: Sometimes nice guys do finish last.* Unpublished manuscript, University of Colorado, Boulder.

Aronson, E. (1969). The theory of cognitive dissonance: A current perspective. In L. Berkowitz (Ed.), *Advances in experimental social psychology* (Vol. 4, pp. 1-34). New York: Academic Press.

Arvey, R. D. (1991, June). *Frontier issues in personnel psychology.* Paper presented at the annual meeting of the International Personnel Management Assessment Association, Chicago.

Arvey, R. D. (1992). Fairness and ethical considerations in employee selection. In D. M. Saunders (Ed.), *New approaches in employee selection* (Vol. 1, pp. 1-19). Greenwich, CT: JAI.

Arvey, R. D., & Campion, J. E. (1982). The employment interview: A summary and review of recent research. *Personnel Psychology, 35,* 281-322.

Arvey, R. D., Gordon, M. E., Massengill, D. P., & Mussio, S. J. (1975). Differential dropout rates of minority and majority job candidates due to "time-lags" between selection procedures. *Personnel Psychology, 28,* 175-180.

Arvey, R. D., & Sackett, P. R. (1993). Fairness in selection: Current developments and perspectives. In N. Schmitt & W. Borman (Eds.), *Personnel selection* (pp. 171-202). San Francisco: Jossey-Bass.

Austin, J. L. (1961). A plea for excuses. In J. O. Urmson & G. J. Warnock (Eds.), *Philosophical papers of J. L. Austin* (pp. 123-152). Oxford, UK: Oxford University Press.

Austin, J. T., & Villanova, P. (1992). The criterion problem: 1917-1992. *Journal of Applied Psychology, 77,* 836-874.

Bandura, A. (1990). Selective activation and disengagement in moral control. *Journal of Social Issues, 46,*(1), 27-46.

Banks, C. G., & Roberson, L. (1985). Performance appraisers as test developers. *Academy of Management Review, 10,* 128-142.

Barclay, J. H., & Harland, L. (1995). Peer performance appraisals: The impact of rater competence, rater bias, and correctability. *Group and Organizational Studies, 20,* 39-60.

Bargh, J. A. (1996). Automaticity in social psychology. In E. T. Higgins & A. W. Kruglanski (Eds.), *Social psychology: Handbook of basic principles* (pp. 169-183). New York: Guilford.

Baron, R. A. (1985). Reducing organizational conflict: The role of attributions. *Journal of Applied Psychology, 70,* 434-441.

Baron, R. A. (1988a). Attributions and organizational conflict: The mediating role of apparent sincerity. *Organizational Behavior and Human Decision Processes, 41,* 111-127.

Baron, R. A. (1988b). Negative effects of destructive criticism: Impact on conflict, self-efficacy, and task performance. *Journal of Applied Psychology, 73,* 199-207.

Baron, R. A. (1990a). Attributions and organizational conflict. In S. Graham & V. Folkes (Eds.), *Attribution theory: Applications to achievement, mental health, and interpersonal conflict* (pp. 185-204). Hillsdale, NJ: Lawrence Erlbaum.

Baron, R. A. (1990b). Countering the effects of destructive criticism: The relative efficacy of four potential interventions. *Journal of Applied Psychology, 75,* 235-245.

Baron, R. A. (1991). Conflict in organizations. In K. R. Murphy & F. E. Saal (Eds.), *Psychology in organizations: Integrating science and practice* (pp. 197-216). Hillsdale, NJ: Lawrence Erlbaum.

Baron, R. A. (1993). Criticism (informal negative feedback) as a source of perceived unfairness in organizations: Effects, mechanisms, and countermeasures. In R. Cropanzano (Ed.), *Justice in the workplace: Approaching fairness in human resource management (pp. 155-170). Hillsdale, NJ: Lawrence Erlbaum.*

Baron, R. A., & Richardson, D. R. (1994). *Human aggression* (2nd ed.). New York: Plenum.

Baron, R. M., & Kenny, D. A. (1986). The moderator-mediator variable distinction in social psychological research: Conceptual, strategic, and statistical considerations. *Journal of Personality and Social Psychology, 51*(6), 1173-1182.

Barrett, G. V., & Depinet, R. L. (1991). A reconsideration of testing for competence rather than for intelligence. *American Psychologist, 46,* 1012-1024.

Barrett-Howard, E., & Tyler, T. R. (1986). Procedural justice as a criterion in allocation decisions. *Journal of Personality and Social Psychology, 50,* 296-304.

Barrick, M. R., & Mount, M. K. (1991). The big five personality dimensions and job performance: A meta-analysis. *Personnel Psychology, 44,* 1026.

Bassett, G. A., & Meyer, H. H. (1968). Performance appraisal based on self-review. *Personnel Psychology, 21,* 421-430.

Becker, T. E., & Martin, S. L. (1995). Trying to look bad at work: Methods and motives for managing poor impressions in organizations. *Academy of Management Journal, 38,* 174-199.

Beehr, T. A., & Taber, T. D. (1993). Perceived intra-organizational mobility: Reliable versus exceptional performance as means to get ahead. *Journal of Organizational Behavior, 14,* 579-594.

Beehr, T. A., Taber, T. D., & Walsh, J. T. (1980). Perceived mobility channels: Criteria for intraorganizational job mobility. *Organizational Behavioral and Human Performance, 26,* 250-264.

Beer, M. (1981). Performance appraisal: Dilemmas and possibilities. *Organizational Dynamics, Winter,* 24-36.

Beer, M., Ruh, R., Dawson, J. A., McCaa, B. B., & Kavanagh, M. J. (1978). A performance management system: Research, design, introduction, and evaluation. *Personnel Psychology, 31,* 505-535.

Bergmann, T. J., & Volkema, R. J. (1994). Issues, behavioral responses and consequences in interpersonal conflicts. *Journal of Organizational Behavior, 15,* 467-471.

Bernstein, M., & Crosby, F. (1980). An empirical examination of relative deprivation theory. *Journal of Experimental Social Psychology, 16,* 442-456.

Bettmann, O. L. (1974). *The good old days—They were terrible!* New York: Random House.

Bies, R. J. (1982, August). *The delivery of bad news in organizations: A social information perspective.* Paper presented at the annual meetings of the Academy of Management, New York.

Bies, R. J. (1986, August). *Identifying principles of interactional justice: The case of corporate recruiting.* In the "Moving beyond equity theory: New directions in research on justice in organizations" symposium conducted at the annual meeting of the Academy of Management, Chicago.

Bies, R. J. (1987a). Beyond "voice": The influence of decision-maker justification and sincerity of procedural fairness judgments. *Representative Research in Social Psychology, 17,* 3-17.

Bies, R. J. (1987b). The predicament of injustice: The management of moral outrage. In L. L. Cummings & B. M. Staw (Eds.), *Research in organizational behavior* (Vol. 9, pp. 289-319). Greenwich, CT: JAI.

Bies, R. J. (1989). Managing conflict before it happens: The role of accounts. In M. A. Rahim (Ed.), *Managing conflict: An interdisciplinary approach* (pp. 83-91). New York: Praeger.

Bies, R. J., & Moag, J. S. (1986). Interactional justice: Communication criteria for fairness. In B. Sheppard (Ed.), *Research on negotiation in organizations* (Vol. 1, pp. 43-55). Greenwich, CT: JAI.

Bies, R. J., & Shapiro, D. L. (1986, August). *It's not my fault, but it's for the greater good: The influence of social accounts on perceptions of managerial legitimacy.* Paper presented at the annual meeting of the Academy of Management, Chicago.

Bies, R. J., & Shapiro, D. L. (1987). Interactional fairness judgments: The influence of causal accounts. *Social Justice Research, 1,* 199-218.

Bies, R. J., & Shapiro, D. L. (1988). Voice and justification: Their influence on procedural fairness judgments. *Academy of Management Journal, 31,* 676-685.

Bies, R. J., Shapiro, D. L., & Cummings, L. L. (1988). Causal accounts and managing organizational conflicts: Is it enough to say its not my fault? *Communications Research, 15,* 381-399.

Bies, R. J., & Sitkin, S. B. (1992). Explanation as legitimation: Excuse-making in organizations. In M. L. McLaughlin, M. J. Cody, & S. J. Read (Eds.), *Explaining one's self to others: Reason-giving in a social context* (pp. 183-198). Hillsdale, NJ: Lawrence Erlbaum.

Bies, R. J., & Tripp, T. M. (1995a). Beyond distrust: "Getting even" and the need for revenge. In R. M. Kramer & T. Tyler (Eds.), *Trust in organizations* (pp. 246-260). Newbury Park, CA: Sage.

Bies, R. J., & Tripp, T. M. (1995b). The use and abuse of power: Justice as social control. In R. Cropanzano & K. M. Kacmar (Eds.), *Organizational politics, justice, and support: Managing the social climate of work organizations* (pp. 131-145). New York: Quorum Books.

Bies, R. J., & Tripp, T. M. (in press). A passion for justice: The rationality and morality of revenge. In R. Cropanzano (Ed.), *Justice in the workplace (Volume II): From theory to practice*. Mahwah, NJ: Lawrence Erlbaum.

Bies, R. J., Tripp, T., & Kramer, R. M. (1997). At the breaking point: Cognitive and social dynamics of revenge in organizations. In J. Greenberg & R. Giacalone (Eds.), *Anti-social behavior in organizations* (pp. 18-36). Thousand Oaks, CA: Sage.

Bies, R. J., & Tyler, T. R. (1993). The "litigation mentality" in organizations: A test of alternative psychological explanations. *Organizational Science, 4,* 352-366.

Bigelow, R. (1972). The evolution of cooperation, aggression, and self-control. In J. K. Cole & D. D. Jensen (Eds.), *The Nebraska symposium on motivation* (Vol. 20, pp. 1-57). Lincoln: University of Nebraska Press.

Blake, R. A., & Mouton, J. S. (1984). *Solving costly organizational conflicts.* San Francisco: Jossey-Bass.

Bobocel, D. R., Agar, S. E., Meyer, J. P., & Irving, P. G. (1996, April). *Managerial accounts and fairness perceptions in third-party conflict resolution: Differentiating the effects of shifting responsibility and providing a justification.* Paper presented at the annual meeting of the Society for Industrial and Organizational Psychology. San Diego, CA.

Bobocel, D. R., & Farrell, A. C. (1996). Sex-based promotion decisions and interactional fairness: Investigating the influence of managerial accounts. *Journal of Applied Psychology, 81,* 22-35.

Bok, S. (1978). *Lying: Moral choice in public and private life* (1st ed.). New York: Pantheon.

Bolger, N., DeLongis, A., Kessler, R. C., & Schilling, E. A. (1989). Effects of daily stress on negative mood. *Journal of Personality and Social Psychology, 57,* 808-818.

Borman, W. C. (1978). Exploring the upper limits of reliability and validity in job performance ratings. *Journal of Applied Psychology, 60,* 561-565.

Boudreau, J. W., & Rynes, S. L. (1985). The role of recruitment in staffing utility analysis. *Journal of Applied Psychology, 70,* 354-366.

Boulding, K. E. (1963). *Conflict and defense: A general theory.* New York: Harper.

Bourgeois, R. P., Leim, M. A., Slivinski, L. W., & Grant, K. W. (1975). Evaluation of an assessment center in terms of acceptability. *Canadian Personnel and Industrial Relations Journal, 22*(3), 17-20.

Brett, J. M. (1980). Behavioral research on unions and management systems. In B. M. Staw & L. L. Cummings (Eds.), *Research in organizational behavior* (Vol. 2, pp. 177-213). Greenwich, CT: JAI.

Brett, J. M., & Goldberg, S. B. (1983). Grievance mediation in the coal industry: A field experiment. Industrial and labor relations of a layoff and survivors' reactions to the layoff. *Journal of Experimental Social Psychology, 26,* 389-407.

Brett, J. M., Goldberg, S. B., & Ury, W. L. (1990). Designing systems for resolving disputes in organizations. *American Psychologist, 45,* 162-170.

Bretz, R. D., Jr., & Thomas, S. L. (1992). Perceived equity, motivation, and final-offer arbitration in major league baseball. *Journal of Applied Psychology, 77,* 280-287.

Brockner, J., DeWitt, R. L., Grover, S., & Reed, T. (1990). When it is especially important to explain why: Factors affecting the relationship between managers' explanations of a layoff and survivors' reactions to the layoff. *Journal of Experimental Social Psychology, 26,* 389-407.

Brockner, J., Konovsky, M., Cooper-Schneider, R., Folger, R., Martin, C., & Bies, R. (1994). Interactive effects of procedural justice and outcome negativity on victims and survivors of job loss. *Academy of Management Journal, 37,* 397-409.

Brockner, J., & Siegel, P. (1996). Understanding the interaction between procedural and distributive justice: The role of trust. In R. M. Kramer & T. R. Tyler (Eds.), *Trust in organizations: Frontiers of theory and research* (pp. 390-413).Thousand Oaks, CA: Sage.

Brockner, J., & Wiesenfeld, B. M. (1996). An integrative framework for explaining reactions to decisions: The interactive effects of outcomes and procedures. *Psychological Bulletin, 120,* 189-208.

Brockner, J., Wiesenfeld, B. M., & Martin, C. L. (1995). Decision frame, procedural justice, and survivors' reactions to job layoffs. *Organizational Behavior and Human Decision Processes, 63,* 59-68.

Brown, R. (1965). *Social psychology.* New York: Free Press

Brown, R., & Herrnstein, R. J. (1975). *Introductory psychology.* Boston: Little, Brown.

Budescu, D. (1993). Dominance alliance: A new approach to the problem of relative importance of predictors in multiple regression. *Psychological Bulletin, 114,*(3) 542-551.

Burke, R. J., Weitzel, W., & Weir, T. (1978). Characteristics of effective employee performance review and development interviews: Replication and extension. *Personnel Psychology, 31,* 903-919.

Burke, R. J., & Wilcox, D. S. (1969). Characteristics of effective employee performance review and development interviews. *Personnel Psychology, 22,* 291-305.

Burnstein, E., & Worchel, P. (1962). Arbitrariness of frustration and its consequences for aggression in a social situation. *Journal of Personality, 30,* 528-540.

Cacioppo, J. T., Gardner, W. L., & Berntson, G. G. (1997). Beyond bipolar conceptualizations and measures: The case of attitudes and evaluative space. *Personality and Social Psychology, 1,* 3-25.

Campbell, B. C., & Barron, C. L. (1982). How extensively are HRM practices being utilized by the practitioners? *The Personnel Administrator, 27*(5), 67-71.

Campbell, D. J., & Lee, C. (1988). Self-appraisal in performance evaluation: Development versus evaluation. *Academy of Management Review, 13,* 302-314.

Campbell, J. P., & Pritchard, R. D. (1976). Motivation theory in industrial and organizational psychology. In M. D. Dunnette (Ed.), *Handbook of industrial and organizational psychology* (Vol. 1, pp. 63-130). Chicago: Rand McNally.

Carnevale, P. J., Olson, J. B., & O'Connor, K. M. (1992). *Formality and informality in a laboratory grievance system.* Paper presented at the annual meeting of the International Association for Conflict Management, Minneapolis.

Cascio, W. F., & Phillips, N. (1979). Performance testing: A rose among thorns? *Personnel Psychology, 32,* 751-766.

Catalano, R., Novaco, R., & McConnell, W. (1997). A model of the net effect of job loss on violence. *Journal of Personality and Social Psychology, 72,* 1440-1447.

Cederblom, D. (1982). The performance appraisal interview: A review, implications, and suggestions. *Academy of Management Review, 7,* 219-227.

Cederblom, D., & Lounsbury, J. W. (1980). An investigation of user acceptance of peer evaluations. *Personnel Psychology, 33,* 567-579.

Chen, P. Y., & Spector, P. E. (1992). Relationships of work stressors with aggression, withdrawal, theft, and substance abuse: An exploratory study. *Journal of Occupational and Organizational Behavior, 65,* 177-184.

Churchill, W. S. (1950). *The grand alliance.* Boston: Houghton Mifflin.

Conlon, D. E. (1993). Some tests of the self-interest and group-value models of procedural justice: Evidence from an organizational appeal procedure. *Academy of Management Journal, 36,* 1109-1124.

Conlon, D. E., & Fasolo, P. M. (1990). Influence of speed of third-party intervention and outcome on negotiator and constituent fairness judgments. *Academy of Management Journal, 33,* 833-846.

Conlon, D. E., & Ross, W. H. (1993). The effects of partisan third parties on negotiator behavior and outcome perceptions. *Journal of Applied Psychology, 78,* 280-290.

Cooper, W. H., & Richardson, A. T. (1986). Unfair comparisons. *Journal of Applied Psychology, 71,* 179-184.

Cosmides, L. (1989). The logic of social exchange: Has natural selection shaped how humans reason? Studies with the Watson selection task. *Cognition, 31,* 187-276.

Cowherd, D. M., & Levine, D. I. (1992). Product quality and pay equity between lower-level employees and top management: An investigation of distributive justice theory. *Administrative Science Quarterly, 37,* 302-320.

Crant, J. M., & Bateman, T. S. (1989). A model of employee responses to drug-testing. *Employee Responsibilities and Rights Journal, 2,* 173-190.

Crant, J. M., & Bateman, T. S. (1990). An experimental test of the impact of drug-testing programs on potential job applicants' attitudes and intentions. *Journal of Applied Psychology, 75,* 127-131.

Crant, J. M., & Bateman, T. S. (1993). Potential job applicant reactions to employee drug testing: The effect of program characteristics and individual differences. *Journal of Business and Psychology, 7,* 279-290.

Cropanzano, R. (1994). The justice dilemma in employee selection: Some reflections on the trade-offs between fairness and validity. *The Industrial—Organizational Psychologist, 31*(3), 90-93.

Cropanzano, R., Aguinis, H., Schminke, M., & Denham, D. L. (in press). Disputant reactions to managerial intervention strategies. *Group & Organization Management.*

Cropanzano, R., & Baron, R. A. (1991). Injustice and organizational conflict: The moderating role of power restoration. *International Journal of Conflict Management, 2,* 5-26.

Cropanzano, R., & Folger, R. (1989). Referent cognitions and task decision autonomy: Beyond equity theory. *Journal of Applied Psychology, 74,* 293-299.

Cropanzano, R., & Folger, R. (1991). Procedural justice and worker motivation. In R. M. Steers & L. W. Porter (Eds.), *Motivation and work behavior* (5th ed., pp. 131-143). New York: McGraw-Hill.

Cropanzano, R., & Greenberg, J. (1997). Progress in organizational justice: Tunneling through the maze. In C. L. Cooper & I. T. Robertson (Eds.), *International review of industrial and organizational psychology* (pp. 317-372). New York: John Wiley.

Cropanzano, R., James, K., & Citera, M. A. (1993). A goal hierarchy model of personality, motivation, and leadership. In L. L. Cummings & B. M. Staw (Eds.), *Research in organizational behavior* (Vol. 15, pp. 267-322). Greenwich, CT: JAI.

Cropanzano, R., & Konovsky, M. A. (1992). *Drug testing practices as determinants of employee fairness perceptions.* Paper presented at the Annual Meeting of the Academy of Management, Las Vegas, NV.

Cropanzano, R., & Konovsky, M. A. (1993). Drug use and its implications for employee drug testing. In G. R. Ferris & K. M. Rowland (Eds.), *Research in personnel and human resource management* (Vol. 11, pp. 207-257). Greenwich, CT: JAI.

Cropanzano, R., & Konovsky, M. A. (1995). Resolving the justice dilemma by improving the outcomes: The case of employee drug screening. *Journal of Business and Psychology, 10,* 221-243.

Cropanzano, R., & Randall, M. L. (1995). Advance notice as a means of reducing relative deprivation. *Social Justice Research, 8,* 217-238.

Cropanzano, R., & Schminke, M. (in press). Using social justice to build effective work groups. In M. Turner (Ed.), *Groups at work: Advances in theory and research.* Hillsdale, NJ: Lawrence Erlbaum.

Cropanzano, R., & Wright, T. (1996). *A tale of two paradigms: Psychometrics meets social justice in the conduct of psychological assessment.* Unpublished manuscript, Colorado State University.

Crosby, F. (1976). A model of egoistical relative deprivation. *Psychological Review, 83,* 85-113.

Crowne, D. F., & Rosse, J. G. (1988). A critical review of the assumptions underlying drug testing. *Journal of Business and Psychology, 3,* 22-41.

Daly, J. P., & Geyer, P. D. (1994). The role of fairness in implementing large-scale change: Employee evaluations of process and outcome in seven facility relocations. *Journal of Organizational Behavior, 15,* 623-638.

Daly, J. P., & Geyer, P. D. (1995). Procedural fairness and organizational commitment under conditions of growth and decline. *Social Justice Research, 8,* 137-151.

Davis, R. (1993). When applicants rate the examinations: Feedback from 2,000 people. In B. Nevo & R. S. Jäger (Eds.), *Educational and psychological testing: The test taker's outlook* (pp. 221-237). Toronto: Hogrefe & Huber.

Dawes, R. (1986). *Group identification and collective action.* Paper delivered at the Nag's Head Conference on Social Dilemmas, Nag's Head, NC.

Day, R. C. & Hamblin, R. L. (1969). Some effects of close and punitive styles of supervision. *American Journal of Sociology, 69,* 499-510.

Deci, E. L. (1975). *Intrinsic motivation.* New York: Plenum.

Degoey, P. (in press). Justice and influence. In B. M. Staw & L. L. Cummings (Eds.), *Research in organizational behavior.* Greenwich, CT: JAI.

Deming, R. H. (1968). *Characteristics of an effective management control system in an industrial organization.* Boston: Harvard University, Division of Research, Graduate School of Business Administration.

DeNisi, A. S., Cafferty, T. P., & Meglino, B. M. (1984). A cognitive view of the performance appraisal process: A model and research propositions. *Organizational Behavior and Human Performance, 33,* 360-396.

DeNisi, A. S., Robbins, T., & Cafferty, T. P. (1989). Organization of information used for performance appraisals: Role of diary-keeping. *Journal of Applied Psychology, 74,* 124-129.

DeNisi, A. S., & Williams, K. J. (1988). Cognitive research in performance appraisal. In K. Rowland & G. S. Ferris (Eds.), *Research in personnel and human resources management* (Vol. 6, pp. 109-156). Greenwich, CT: JAI.

DePaulo, B. M. (1992). Nonverbal behavior and self-presentation. *Psychological Bulletin, 111*(2), 203-249.

DeVries, D. L., Morrison, A. M., Shullman, S. L., & Gerlach, M. L. (1981). *Performance appraisal on the line.* New York: Wiley.

de Waal, F. (1996). *Good natured: The origins of right and wrong in humans and other animals.* Cambridge, MA: Harvard University Press.

de Wolff, C. J. (1993). The prediction paradigm. In H. Schuler, J. L. Farr, & M. Smith (Eds.), *Personnel selection and assessment: Individual and organizational perspectives* (pp. 125-139). Hillsdale, NJ: Lawrence Erlbaum.

Diamond, J. (1992). *The third chimpanzee: The evolution and future of the human animal.* New York: HarperCollins.

Dickinson, T. L. (1993). Attitudes about performance appraisal. In H. Schuler, J. L. Farr, & M. Smith (Eds.), *Personnel selection and assessment: Individual and organizational perspectives* (pp. 141-162). Hillsdale, NJ: Lawrence Erlbaum.

Dickinson, T. L., & Zellinger, P. M. (1980). A comparison of the behaviorally anchored rating and mixed standard scale formats. *Journal of Applied Psychology, 65,* 147-154.

Dipboye, R. L. (1995). How politics can destructure human resources management in the interest of empowerment, support, and justice. In R. Cropanzano & M. K. Kacmar (Eds.), *Organiza-*

tional politics, justice, and support: Managing the social climate of work organizations (pp. 55-80). Westport, CT: Quorum Books.

Dipboye, R. L., & de Pontbriand, R. (1981). Correlates of employee reactions to performance appraisals and appraisal systems. *Journal of Applied Psychology, 66,* 248-251.

Dodd, W. E. (1977). Attitudes toward assessment center programs. In J. L. Moses & W. C. Byham (Eds.), *Applying the assessment center method.* New York: Pergamon.

Dollard, J., Doob, L. W., Miller, N. E., Mowrer, O. H., & Sears, R. R. (1939). *Frustration and aggression.* New Haven, CT: Yale University Press.

Donaldson, T., & Dunfee, T. W. (1994). Toward a unified conception of business ethics: Integrative social contracts theory. *Academy of Management Review, 19,* 252-284.

Dorfman, P. W., Stephen, W. G., & Loveland, J. (1986). Performance appraisal behaviors: Supervisor perceptions and subordinate reactions. *Personnel Psychology, 39,* 579-597.

Dworkin, J. B. (1994). Managerial third party dispute resolution: An overview and introduction to the special issue. *Employee Responsibilities and Rights Journal, 7,* 1-8.

Earley, P. C., & Lind, E. A. (1987). Procedural justice and participation in task selection: The role of control in mediating justice judgments. *Journal of Personality and Social Psychology, 52,* 1148-1160.

Eisenberger, R., Fasolo, P., & Davis-LaMastro, V. (1990). Perceived organizational support and employee diligence, commitment, and innovation. *Journal of Applied Psychology, 75,* 51-59.

Ekman, P. (1993). Facial expression and emotion. *American Psychologist, 48*(4), 384-392.

England, G. W. (1961). *Development and use of weighted application blanks.* Dubuque, IA: William C. Brown.

Fantasia, R. (1988). *Cultures of solidarity: Consciousness, action, and contemporary American workers.* Berkeley: University of California Press.

Farabee, K., & Lehman, W. E. K. (1991). *Peripheral impacts of co-workers substance abuse.* Fort Worth: Institute of Behavioral Research, Texas Christian University.

Farh, J., Podsakoff, P. M., & Organ, D. W. (1990). Accounting for organizational citizenship behavior: Leader fairness and task scope versus satisfaction. *Journal of Management, 16,* 705-722.

Fedor, D. B. (1991). Recipient responses to performance feedback: A proposed model and its implications. In G. R. Ferris & K. M. Rowland (Eds.), *Research in personnel and human resources management* (Vol. 9, pp. 73-120). Greenwich, CT: JAI.

Feldman, J. M. (1981). Beyond attribution theory: Cognitive approaches to performance appraisal. *Journal of Applied Psychology, 60,* 736-741.

Ferris, G. R., Fedor, D. B., Chachere, J. G., & Pondy, L. R. (1989). Myths and politics in organizational contexts. *Group and Organization Studies, 14,* 83-103.

Ferris, G. R., & Judge, T. A. (1991). Personnel/human resources management: A political influence perspective. *Journal of Management, 17,* 447-488.

Ferris, G. R., Judge, T. A., Rowland, K. M., & Fitzgibbons, D. E. (1994). Subordinate influence and the performance appraisal process: Test of a model. *Organizational behavior and human decision processes, 58,* 101-135.

Ferris, G. R., Russ, G. S., & Fandt, P. M. (1989). Politics in organizations. In R. A. Giacalone & P. Rosenfeld (Eds.), *Impression management in the organization* (pp. 143-170). Hillsdale, NJ: Lawrence Erlbaum.

Feuille, P., & Chachere, D. R. (1995). Looking fair or being fair: Remedial voice procedures in nonunion workplaces. *Journal of Management, 21,* 27-42.

Fiske, S. T., & Talyor, S. E. (1984). *Social cognition.* New York: Random House.

Fletcher, C., & Williams, R. (1976). The influence of performance feedback in appraisal interviews. *Journal of Occupational Psychology, 49,* 75-83.

Foa, E.B., & Foa, U.G. (1976). Resource theory of social exchange. In J. S. Thibaut, J. Spence, & R. Carson (Eds.), *Contemporary topics in social psychology* (pp. 99-111). Morristown, NJ: General Learning Press.

Folger, J. P., Poole, M. S., & Stutman, R. K. (1993). *Working through conflict: Strategies for relationships, groups, and organizations* (2nd ed.). New York: Harper-Collins.

Folger, R. (1977). Distributive and procedural justice: Combined impact of "voice" and improvement on experienced inequity. *Journal of Personality and Social Psychology, 35,* 108-119.

Folger, R. (1984). Perceived injustice, referent cognitions, and the concept of comparison level. *Representative Research in Social Psychology, 14,* 88-108.

Folger, R. (1986a). Mediation, arbitration, and the psychology of procedural justice. In R. J. Lewicki, B. H. Sheppard, & M. H. Bazerman, (Eds.), *Research on negotiation in organizations* (Vol. 1, pp. 57-79). Greenwich, CT: JAI

Folger, R. (1986b). A referent cognitions theory of relative deprivation. In J. M. Olson, C. P. Herman, & M. P. Zanna (Eds.), *Social comparison and relative deprivation: The Ontario symposium* (Vol. 4, pp. 33-55). Hillsdale, NJ: Lawrence Erlbaum.

Folger, R. (1986c). Rethinking equity theory: A referent cognitions model. In H. W. Bierhoff, R. L. Cohen, & J. Greenberg (Eds.), *Justice in social relations* (pp. 145-162). New York: Plenum.

Folger, R. (1987a). Distributive and procedural justice in the workplace. *Social Justice Research, 1,* 143-159.

Folger, R. (1987b). Reformulating the preconditions of resentment: A referent cognitions model. In J. C. Masters & W. P. Smith (Eds.), *Social comparison, justice, and relative deprivation: Theoretical, empirical, and policy perspectives* (pp.183-215). Hillsdale, NJ: Lawrence Erlbaum.

Folger, R. (1987c). Theory and method in social science. *Contemporary Social Psychology, 12,* 51-54.

Folger, R. (1988, August). *Justice as dignity.* Discussion presented at the Symposium on Theoretical Developments in Procedural Justice at the American Psychological Association, Atlanta, GA.

Folger, R. (1993). Reactions to mistreatment at work. In K. Murnighan (Ed.), *Social psychology in organizations: Advances in theory and research* (pp. 161-183). Englewood Cliffs, NJ: Prentice Hall.

Folger, R. (1997). [Not letting them down gently: Data on why some layoffs are conducted abusively]. Unpublished data.

Folger, R. (in press). Fairness as moral virtue. In M. Schminke (Ed.), *Managerial ethics: Morally managing people and processes.* Mahwah, NJ: Lawrence Erlbaum.

Folger, R., & Baron, R. A. (1996). Violence and hostility at work: A model of reactions to perceived injustice. In G. R. VandenBos & E. Q. Bulatao (Eds.), *Violence on the job: Identifying risks and developing solutions* (pp. 51-85). Washington, DC: American Psychological Association.

Folger, R., & Bies, R. J. (1989). Managerial responsibilities and procedural justice. *Employee Responsibilities and Rights Journal, 2,* 79-90.

Folger, R., Cropanzano, R., Timmerman, T. A., Howes, J. C., & Mitchell, D. (1996). Elaborating procedural fairness: Justice becomes both simpler and more complex. *Personality and Social Psychology Bulletin, 22,* 435-441.

Folger, R., & Greenberg, J. (1985). Procedural justice: An interpretative analysis of personnel system. In G. R. Ferris & K. M. Rowland (Eds.), *Research in personnel and human resource management* (Vol. 3, pp. 141-183). Greenwich, CT: JAI.

Folger, R., & Konovsky, M. A. (1989). Effects of procedural justice, distributive justice, and reactions to pay raise decisions. *Academy of Management Journal, 32,* 115-130.

Folger, R., Konovsky, M. A., & Cropanzano, R. (1992). A due process metaphor for performance appraisal. In B. M. Staw & L. L. Cummings (Eds.), *Research in organizational behavior* (Vol. 14, pp. 129-177). Greenwich, CT: JAI.

Folger, R., & Lewis, D. (1993). Self-appraisal and fairness in evaluations. In R. Cropanzano (Ed.), *Justice in the workplace: Approaching fairness in human resource management* (pp. 107-131). Hillsdale, NJ: Lawrence Erlbaum.

Folger, R., & Martin, C. (1986). Relative deprivation and referent cognitions: Distributive and procedural justice effects. *Journal of Experimental Social Psychology, 22,* 532-546.

Folger, R., & Pugh, D. (1997). *The Churchill effect in managing hard times: Kicking employees when they're down and out.* Unpublished manuscript.

Folger, R., Rosenfield, D., Grove, J., & Corkran, L. (1979). Effects of "voice" and peer opinions on responses to inequity. *Journal of Personality and Social Psychology, 37,* 2243-2261.

Folger, R., Rosenfield, D., & Hays, R. P. (1978). Equity and intrinsic motivation: The role of choice. *Journal of Personality and Social Psychology, 36,* 556-564.

Folger, R., Rosenfield, D., Hays, R. P., & Grove, R. (1978). Justice versus justification effects on productivity: Reconciling equity and dissonance findings. *Organizational Behavior and Human Performance, 22,* 465-478.

Folger, R., Rosenfield, D., Rheaume, K., & Martin, C. (1983). Relative deprivation and referent cognitions. *Journal of Experimental Social Psychology, 19,* 172-184.

Folger, R., Rosenfield, D., & Robinson, T. (1983). Relative deprivation and procedural justifications. *Journal of Personality and Social Psychology, 45,* 172-184.

Folger, R., & Skarlicki, D. P. (in press-a). A popcorn metaphor for workplace violence. In R. W. Griffin, A. O'Leary-Kelly, & J. Collins (Eds.), *Dysfunctional behavior in organizations, Vol. 1: Violent behaviors in organizations.* Greenwich, CT: JAI.

Folger, R., & Skarlicki, D. P. (in press-b). When tough times make tough bosses: Managerial distancing as a function of layoff blame. *Academy of Management Journal.*

Frank, R. H. (1988). *Passions within reason: The strategic role of emotions.* New York: Norton.

French, J. R. P., Jr., Kay, E., & Meyer, H. H. (1966). Participation and the appraisal system. *Human Relations, 19,* 3-20.

Fryxell, G. E. (1992). Perceptions of justice afforded by formal grievance systems as predictors of a belief in a just workplace. *Journal of Business Ethics, 11,* 635-647.

Fryxell, G. E., & Gordon, M. E. (1989). Workplace justice and job satisfaction as predictors of satisfacton with unions and management. *Academy of Management Journal, 32,* 851-866.

Fukuyama, F. (1995). *Trust: The social virtues and the creation of prosperity.* New York: Free Press.

Fulk, J., Brief, A. P., & Barr, S. H. (1985). Trust-in-supervisor and perceived fairness and accuracy of performance evaluations. *Journal of Business Research, 13,* 301-313.

Garland, H., Giacobbe, J., & French, J. L. (1989). Attitudes toward employee and employer rights in the workplace. *Employee Responsibilities and Rights Journal, 2,* 49-59.

Gaugler, B. B., Rosenthal, D. B., Thornton, G. C., III, & Bentson, C. (1987). Meta-analysis of assessment center validity. *Journal of Applied Psychology, 72,* 493-511.

Gellerman, S. W., & Hodgson, W. G. (1988, May-June). Cyanamid's new take on performance appraisal. *Harvard Business Review,* pp. 36-37, 40-41.

Giacobbe-Miller, J. (1995). A test of the group-values and control models of procedural justice from competing perspectives of labor and management. *Personnel Psychology, 48,* 115-142.

Giles, W. F., & Mossholder, K. W. (1990). Employee reactions to contextual and session components of performance appraisal. *Journal of Applied Psychology, 75,* 371-377.

Gilliland, S. W. (1993). The perceived fairness of selection systems: An organizational justice perspective. *Academy of Management Review, 18,* 694-734.

Gilliland, S. W. (1994). Effects of procedural and distributive justice on reactions to a selection system. *Journal of Applied Psychology, 79,* 691-701.

Gilliland, S. W. (1995). Fairness from the applicant's perspective: Reactions to employee selection procedures. *International Journal of Selection and Assessment, 3,* 11-19.

Gilliland, S. W., & Honig, H. (1994a, April). *Development of the selection fairness survey.* Paper presented at the annual meeting of the Society for Industrial and Organizational Psychology, Nashville, TN.

Gilliland, S. W., & Honig, H. (1994b, April). *The perceived fairness of employee selections systems as a predictor of attitudes and self-concept.* In the "Selection from the applicant's perspective: Justice and employee selection procedures" symposium conducted at the meeting of the Society for Industrial and Organizational Psychology, Nashville, TN.

Gilliland, S. W.,& Schepers, D. H. (1997, August). *Civility in organizational downsizing: Antecedents and consequences of fairness in layoff practices.* Paper presented at the meeting of the Academy of Management, Boston.

Glasl, F. (1982). The process of conflict escalation and roles of third parties. In G. B. J. Bomers & R. B. Peterson (Eds.), *Conflict management and industrial relations* (pp. 119-140). Boston: Kluwer-Nijhoff.

Goffman, E. (1967). *Interaction ritual: Essays on face-to-face behavior.* Chicago: Aldine.

Gomez-Mejia, L. R., & Balkin, D. B. (1987). Dimensions and characteristics of personnel manager perceptions of effective drug-testing programs. *Personnel Psychology, 40,* 745-763.

Gordon, M. E., & Bowlby, R. L. (1988). Propositions about grievance settlements: Finally consultation with grievants. *Personnel Psychology, 41,* 107-123.

Gordon, M. E., & Fryxell, G. E. (1993). The role of interpersonal justice in organizational grievance systems. In R. Cropanzano (Ed.), *Justice in the workplace: Approaching fairness in human resources management* (pp. 231-255). Hillsdale, NJ: Lawrence Erlbaum.

Gordon, M. E., & Miller, S. J. (1984). Grievances: A review of research and practice. *Personnel Psychology, 37,* 117-146.

Gould, S. J. (1981). *The mismeasure of man.* New York: Norton.

Gouldner, A. W. (1960). The norm of reciprocity: A preliminary statement. *American Sociological Review, 25,* 161-179.

Gray, J. A. (1990). Brain systems that mediate both emotion and cognition. Special Issue: Development of relationships between emotion and cognition. *Cognition and Emotion, 4,* 269-288.

Greenberg, J. (1982). Approaching equity and avoiding inequity in groups and organizations. In J. Greenberg & R. L. Cohen (Eds.), *Equity and justice in social behavior* (pp. 389-435). New York: Academic Press.

Greenberg, J. (1984). On the apocryphal nature of inequity distress. In R. Folger (Ed.), *The sense of injustice: Social psychological perspectives.* New York: Plenum.

Greenberg, J. (1986). Determinants of perceived fairness of performance evaluations. *Journal of Applied Psychology, 71,* 340-342.

Greenberg, J. (1987a). Reactions to procedural injustice in payment distributions: Do the ends justify the means? *Journal of Applied Psychology, 72,* 55-61.

Greenberg, J. (1987b). Using diaries to promote procedural justice in performance evaluations. *Social Justice Research, 1,* 219-234.

Greenberg, J. (1988a). Cultivating an image of justice: Looking fair on the job. *Academy of Management Executive, 1,* 155-158.

Greenberg, J. (1988b). Equity and workplace status: A field experiment. *Journal of Applied Psychology, 73,* 606-613.

Greenberg, J. (1988c, August). *Using social accounts to manage impressions of performance appraisal fairness.* Paper presented at the annual meeting of the Academy of Management, Anaheim, CA.

Greenberg, J. (1989). Cognitive re-evaluation of outcomes in response to underpayment inequity. *Academy of Management Journal, 32,* 174-184.

Greenberg, J. (1990a). Employee theft as a reaction to underpayment inequity: The hidden cost of pay cuts. *Journal of Applied Psychology, 75,* 561-568.

Greenberg, J. (1990b). Looking fair vs. being fair: Managing impressions of organizational justice. In B. M. Staw & L. L. Cummings (Eds.), *Research in organizational behavior* (Vol. 12, pp. 111-157). Greenwich, CT: JAI.

Greenberg, J. (1990c). Organizational justice: Yesterday, today, and tomorrow. *Journal of Management, 16,* 399-432.

Greenberg, J. (1991). Using explanations to manage impressions of performance appraisal fairness. *Employee Responsibilities and Rights Journal, 4,* 51-60.

Greenberg, J. (1993a). The social side of fairness: Interpersonal and informational classes of organizational justice. In R. Cropanzano (Ed.), *Justice in the workplace: Approaching fairness in human resource management* (pp. 79-103). Hillsdale, NJ: Lawrence Erlbaum.

Greenberg, J. (1993b). Stealing in the name of justice. *Organizational Behavior and Human Decision Processes, 54,* 81-103.

Greenberg, J. (1994). Using socially fair treatment to promote acceptance of a work site smoking ban. *Journal of Applied Psychology, 79,* 288-297.

Greenberg, J. (1997). The STEAL motive: Managing the social determinants of employee theft. In R. A. Giacalone & J. Greenberg (Eds.), *Antisocial behavior in organizations* (pp. 85-108). Thousand Oaks, CA: Sage.

Greenberg, J., & Alge, B. (in press). Aggressive reactions to workplace injustice. In R. Griffin, A. O'Leary-Kelly, & J. Collins (Eds.), *Dysfunctional work behavior in organizations, vol. 1: Violent behaviors in organizations.* Greenwich, CT: JAI Press.

Greenberg, J., Bies, R. J., & Eskew, D. E. (1991). Establishing fairness in the eye of the beholder: Managing impressions of organizational justice. In R. Giacalone & P. Rosenfeld (Eds.), *Applied impression management: How image making affects managerial decisions* (pp. 111-132). Newbury Park, CA: Sage.

Greenberg, J., & Folger, R. (1983). Procedural justice, participation and the fair process effect in groups and organizations. In P. B. Paulus (Ed.), *Basic group processes* (pp. 235-256). New York: Springer-Verlag.

Greenfield, P. A., Karren, R. J., & Giacobbe, J. K. (1989). Drug testing in the workplace: An overview of legal and philosophical issues. *Employee Responsibilities and Rights Journal, 2,* 1-10.

Greller, M. M. (1975). Subordinate participation and reactions to the appraisal interview. *Journal of Applied Psychology, 60,* 544-549.

Greller, M. M. (1978). The nature of subordinate participation in the appraisal interview. *Academy of Management Journal, 21,* 646-658.

Guastello, S. J., & Rieke, M. L. (1991). A review and critique of honesty test research. *Behavioral Sciences and the Law, 9,* 501-523.

Guzzo, R. A., Noonan, K. A., & Elron, E. (1994). Expatriate managers and the psychological contract. *Journal of Applied Psychology, 79,* 617-626.

Hackman, J. R., & Oldham, G. R. (1980). *Work redesign.* Reading, MA: Addison-Wesley.

Halberstam, D. (1986). *The reckoning.* New York: Morrow.

Hanson, A. (1990, July). What employees say about drug testing. *Personnel,* 32-36.

Harland, L. K., & Biasotto, M. M. (1993, August). *An evaluation of the procedural fairness of personality tests.* In "Procedural Justice" symposium conducted at the annual meeting of the Academy of Management, Atlanta, GA.

Harn, T. J., & Thornton, G. C., III. (1985). Recruiter counselling behaviours and applicant impressions. *Journal of Occupational Psychology, 58,* 57-65.

Harris, M. M., Dworkin, J. B., Park, J. (1990). Preemployment screening procedures: How human resource managers perceive them. *Journal of Business and Psychology, 4,* 279-292.

Harris, M. M., & Schaubroeck, J. (1988). A meta-analysis of self-supervisor, self-peer, and peer-supervisor ratings. *Personnel Psychology, 41,* 43-62.

Hartigan, J. A., & Wigdor, A. K. (1989). *Fairness in employment testing: Validity generalization, minority issues, and the General Aptitude Test Battery.* Washington, DC: National Academy Press.

Hattrup, K., Schmitt, N., & Landis, R. S. (1992). Equivalence of constructs measured by job-specific and commercially available aptitude tests. *Journal of Applied Psychology, 77,* 298-308.

Hayes, T. L., Citera, M., Brady, L. M., & Jenkins, N. M. (1995). Staffing for persons with disabilities: What is "fair" and "job related"? *Public Personnel Management, 24,* 413-428.

Hegtvedt, K. A. (1993). Approaching distributive and procedural justice: Are separate routes necessary? In E. J. Lawler, B. Markovsky, K. Heimer, & J. O'Brien (Eds.), *Advances in group processes* (Vol. 10, pp. 195-221). Greenwich, CT: JAI.

Helson, H. (1954). *Adaptation-level theory.* New York: Harper & Row.

Herriot, P. (1989). Selection as a social process. In M. Smith & I. T. Robertson (Eds.), *Advances in selection and assessment* (pp. 171-187). New York: Wiley.

Herzberg, F. (1968). One more time: How do you motivate employees. *Harvard Business Review, 46,* 53-62.

Heuer, L. B., & Penrod, S. (1986). Procedural preference as a function of conflict intensity. *Journal of Personality and Social Psychology, 51,* 700-710.

Hillary, J. M., & Wexley, K. N. (1974). Participation effects in appraisal interviews conducted in a training session. *Journal of Applied Psychology, 59,* 168-171.

Hirschman, A. O. (1970). *Exit, voice and loyalty: Responses to decline in firms, organizations, and states.* Cambridge, MA: Harvard University Press.

Hoffman, A., & Silvers, J. (1987). *Steal this urine test: Fighting drug hysteria in America.* New York: Penguin.

Hogan, R., & Emler, N. P. (1981). Retributive justice. In M. J. Lerner & S. C. Lerner (Eds.), *The justice motive in social behavior* (pp. 125-143). New York: Plenum.

Homans, G. C. (1961). *Social behavior: Its elementary forms.* New York: Harcourt, Brace & World.

Hosmer, L. T. (1995). Trust: The connecting link between organizational theory and philosophical ethics. *Academy of Management Review, 20,* 379-403.

Huffcutt, A. I. (1990). Intelligence is not a panacea in personnel selection. *The Industrial-Organizational Psychologist, 27*(3), 66-67.

Huffcutt, A. I., & Arthur, W., Jr. (1994). Hunter and Hunter (1984) revisited: Interviewer validity for entry-level jobs. *Journal of Applied Psychology, 79,* 184-190.

Huffcutt, A. I., & Woehr, D. J. (1992, May). *A meta-analytic examination of the relationship between employment interview validity and degree of structure.* Paper presented at the Annual Meeting of the Society for Industrial and Organizational Psychology, Montreal, Quebec.

Hunter, J. E., & Hunter, R. F. (1984). Validity and utility of alternative predictors of job performance. *Psychological Bulletin, 96,* 72-98.

Ichniowski, C. (1986). The effects of grievance activity on productivity. *Industrial and Labor Relations Review, 40,* 75-89.

Iles, P. A., & Robertson, I. T. (1989). The impact of personnel selection procedures on candidates. In P. Herriot (Ed.), *Assessment and selection in organizations* (pp. 257-271). Chichester, UK: Wiley.

Ilgen, D. R. (1993). Performance-appraisal accuracy: An illusive or sometimes misguided goal? In H. Schuler, J. L. Farr, & M. Smith (Eds.), *Personnel selection and assessment: Individual and organizational perspectives* (pp. 235-252). Hillsdale, NJ: Lawrence Erlbaum.

Ilgen, D. R., & Feldman, J. M. (1983). Performance appraisal: A process focus. In B. M. Staw & L. L. Cummings (Eds.), *Research in organizational behavior* (Vol. 5, pp. 141-197). Greenwich, CT: JAI.

Ilgen, D. R., Fisher, C. D., & Taylor, M. S. (1979). Consequences of individual feedback on behavior in organizations. *Journal of Applied Psychology, 64,* 349-371.

Ilgen, D. R., Peterson, R. B., Martin, B. A., & Boescher, D. A. (1981). Supervisor and subordinate reactions to performance appraisal sessions. *Organizational Behavior and Human Performance, 28*, 311-330.

Ivancevich, J. M. (1980). A longitudinal study of behavioral expectation scales: Attitudes and performance. *Journal of Applied Psychology, 65*, 139-146.

Ivancevich, J. M. (1982). Subordinates' reactions to performance appraisal interviews: A test of feedback and goal-setting techniques. *Journal of Applied Psychology, 67*, 581-587.

Jaikumar, R. (1986). Post-industrial manufacturing. *Harvard Business Review*, November-December, 69-79.

James, K. (in press). Goal conflict and individual creativity. *Creativity Research Journal.*

James, K., Chen, J., & Goldberg, C. (1992). Organizational conflict and individual creativity. *Journal of Applied Social Psychology, 22*, 545-566.

James, K., Clark, K., & Cropanzano, R. (in press). Positive and negative creativity in groups, institutions, and organizations: A model and theoretical extension. *Creativity Research Journal.*

Johnson, T. E., & Rule, B. G. (1986). Mitigating circumstance information, censure, and aggression. *Journal of Personality and Social Psychology, 30*, 537-542.

Jones, J. W. (1991). Assessing privacy invasiveness of psychological test items: Job reference versus clinical measures of integrity. *Journal of Business and Psychology, 5*, 531-535.

Jones, T. M. (1991). Ethical decision making by individuals in organizations: An issue-contingent model. *Academy of Management Review, 16*, 366-395.

Kahneman, D., & Miller, D. T. (1986). Norm theory: Comparing reality to its alternatives. *Psychological Review, 93*, 136-153.

Kahneman, D., Slovik, P., & Tversky, A. (Eds.). (1982). *Judgement under uncertainty: Heuristics and biases.* Cambridge, UK: Cambridge University Press.

Kahneman, D., & Tversky, A. (1982). The simulation heuristic. In D. Kahneman, P. Slovic, & A. Tversky, (Eds.), *Judgment under uncertainty: Heuristics and biases* (pp. 201-208). New York: Cambridge University Press.

Kane, J., & Lawler, E. (1979). Performance appraisal effectiveness: Its assessment and determinants. In B. M. Staw (Ed.), *Research in organizational behavior* (Vol. 1, pp. 425-478). Greenwich, CT: JAI.

Kanfer, R., Sawyer, J., Earley, P. C., & Lind, E. A. (1987). Fairness and participation in evaluation procedures: Effects on task attitudes and performance. *Social Justice Research, 1*, 235-249.

Karambayya, R., & Brett, J. M. (1989). Managers handling disputes: Third-party roles and perceptions of fairness. *Academy of Management Journal, 32*, 687-704.

Karambayya, R., & Brett, J. M. (1994). Managerial third parties: Intervention strategies, process, and consequences. In J. Folger & T. Jones (Eds.), *New directions in mediation: Communication research and perspectives* (pp. 175-192). Thousand Oaks, CA: Sage.

Karambayya, R., Brett, J. M., & Lytle, A. (1992). Effects of formal authority and experience on third-party roles, outcomes, and perceptions of fairness. *Academy of Management Journal, 35*, 426-438.

Karren, R. J. (1989). An analysis of the drug testing decision. *Employee Responsibilities and Rights Journal, 2*, 27-37.

Katz, H. C., Kochan, T. A., & Gobeille, K. R. (1983). Industrial relations performance, exonomic performance, and QWL programs: An interplant analysis. *Industrial and Labor Relations Review, 37*, 3-17.

Katz, H. C., Kochan, T. A., & Weber, M. R. (1985). Assessing the effects of industrial relations systems and efforts to improve the quality of working life on organizational effectiveness. *Academy of Management Journal, 28*, 509-526.

Katzell, R. A., & Austin, J. T. (1992). From then to now: The development of industrial-organizational psychology in the United States. *Journal of Applied Psychology, 77*, 803-835.

Kay, E., Meyer, H. H., & French, J. R. P., Jr. (1965). Effects of threat in a performance appraisal interview. *Journal of Applied Psychology, 49,* 311-317.

Keaveny, T. J., Inderrieden, E. J., & Allen, R. J. (1987). An integrated perspective of performance appraisal interviews. *Psychological Reports, 61,* 639-646.

Keeley, M. (1983). Values in organizational theory and management education. *Academy of Management Review, 8,* 376-386.

Kennedy, M. M. (1980). *Office politics: Seizing power wielding clout.* New York: Warner Books.

Kindall, A. F., & Gatza, J. (1963). Positive programs for performance appraisal. *Harvard Business Review, 41,* 153-166.

Kipnis, D., & Schmidt, S. W. (1988). Upward influence styles: Relationship with performance evaluations, salary, and stress. *Administrative Science Quarterly, 33,* 528-542.

Kipnis, D., & Vanderveer, R. (1971). Ingratiation and the use of power. *Journal of Personality and Social Psychology, 17,* 266-280.

Klaas, B. S. (1989). Determinants of grievance activity and the grievance system's impact on employee behavior: An integrative perspective. *Academy of Management Review, 14,* 445-458.

Klaas, B. S., & DeNisi, A. S. (1989). Managerial reactions to employee dissent: The impact of grievance activity on performance evaluations. *Academy of Management Journal, 32,* 705-717.

Klaas, B. S., Heneman, H. G., III, & Olson, C. A. (1991). Effects of grievance activity on absenteeism. *Journal of Applied Psychology, 76,* 818-824.

Kluger, A. N., & Rothstein, H. R. (1993). The influence of selection test type on applicant reactions to employment testing. *Journal of Business and Psychology, 8,* 3-25.

Kohlberg, L. (1984). *The psychology of moral development.* San Francisco: Harper & Row.

Kolb, D. M. (1985). To be a mediator: Expressive tactics in mediation. *Journal of Social Issues, 41,* 1-25.

Kolb, D. M. (1986). Who are organizational third parties and what do they do? In R. J. Lewicki, B. H. Sheppard, & M. H. Bazerman (Eds.), *Research on negotiations in organizations* (Vol. 1, pp. 207-278). Greenwich, CT: JAI.

Kolb, D. M., & Glidden, P. (1986). Getting to know your conflict options. *Personnel Administration, 31*(6), 77-90.

Konovsky, M. A., & Cropanzano, R. (1991). The perceived fairness of employee drug testing as a predictor of employee attitudes and job performance. *Journal of Applied Psychology, 76,* 698-707.

Konovsky, M. A., & Cropanzano, R. (1993). Justice considerations in employee drug testing. In R. Cropanzano (Ed.), *Justice in the workplace: Approaching fairness in human resource management* (pp. 171-192). Hillsdale, NJ: Lawrence Erlbaum.

Konovsky, M. A., & Folger, R. (1991). The effects of procedures, social accounts, and benefits level on victims' layoff reactions. *Journal of Applied Social Psychology, 21,* 630-650.

Konovsky, M. A., & Pugh, S. D. (1994). Citizenship behavior and social exchange. *Academy of Management Journal, 37,* 656-669.

Korsgaard, M. A., & Roberson, L. (1995). Procedural justice in performance evaluation. *Journal of Management, 21,* 657-699.

Korsgaard, M. A., Roberson, L., & Rymph, D. (1996, April). *Promoting fairness through subordinate training: The impact of communication style on manager's effectiveness.* Paper presented at the annual meeting of the Society for Industrial and Organizational Psychology, San Diego, CA.

Kozan, M. K., & Ilter, S. S. (1994). Third party roles played by Turkish managers in subordinates' conflicts. *Journal of Organizational Behavior, 15,* 453-466.

Kramer, R. M., Brewer, M. B., & Hanna, B. A. (1996). Collective trust and collective action: The decision to trust as a social decision. In R. M. Kramer & T. R. Tyler (Eds.), *Trust in organizations* (pp. 357-389). Thousand Oaks, CA: Sage.

Kravitz, D. A., & Brock, P. (1997). Evaluations of drug testing programs. *Employee Responsibilities and Rights Journal, 10,* 65-86.

Kravitz, D. A., Stinson, V., & Chavez, T. L. (1996). Evaluations of tests used for making selection and promotion decisions. *International Journal of Selection and Assessment, 4,* 24-34.

Krzystofiak, F. J., Lillis, M., & Newman, J. M. (1995, August). *Justice along the scarcity continuum.* Paper presented at the annual meeting of the Academy of Management, Vancouver, British Columbia.

Kulik, C. T., & Ambrose, M. L. (1992). Personal and situational determinants of referent choice. *Academy of Management Review, 17,* 212-237.

Kulik, J. A., & Brown, R. (1979). Frustration, attribution of blame, and aggression. *Journal of Experimental Social Psychology, 15,* 183-194.

Labig, C. E., Jr. (1992). Supervisory and nonsupervisory employee attitudes about drug testing. *Employee Responsibilities and Rights Journal, 5,* 131-141.

Landy, F. J., Barnes, J. L., & Murphy, K. R. (1978). Correlates of perceived fairness and accuracy of performance evaluation. *Journal of Applied Psychology, 63,* 751-754.

Landy, F. J., Barnes-Farrell, J., & Cleveland, J. N. (1980). Perceived fairness and accuracy of performance evaluation: A follow-up. *Journal of Applied Psychology, 65,* 355-256.

Landy, F. J., & Farr, J. L. (1980). Performance rating. *Psychological Bulletin, 82,* 72-107.

Lane, R. E. (1988). Procedural goods in a democracy: How one is treated versus what one gets. *Social Justice Research, 2,* 177-192.

Larsen, J. R., Jr. (1984). The performance feedback process: A preliminary model. *Organizational Behavior and Human Performance, 33,* 42-76.

Latham, G. P. (1986). Job performance and appraisal. In C. L. Cooper & I. Robertson (Eds.), *Review of industrial and organizational psychology* (pp. 117-155). Chichester, UK: Wiley.

Latham, G. P., & Finnegan, B. J. (1993). Perceived practicality of unstructured, patterned, and situational interviews. In H. Schuler, J. L. Farr, & M. Smith (Eds.), *Personnel selection and assessment: Individual and organizational perspectives* (pp. 41-56). Hillsdale, NJ: Lawrence Erlbaum.

LaTour, S., Houlden, P., Walker, L., & Thibaut, J. (1976). Procedure: Transnational perspectives and preferences. *Yale Law Review, 86,* 258-290.

Lawler, E. E., III, Mohrman, A. M., Jr., & Resnick, S. M. (1984, Summer). Performance appraisal revisited. *Organizational Dynamics,* pp. 20-35.

Lazer, R. I., & Wikstrom, W. S. (1977). *Appraising managerial performance: Current practices and future directions* (Conference Board Rep. No. 732). New York: Conference Board.

Leatherwood, M. L., & Spector, L. C. (1991). Enforcements, inducements, expected utility and employee misconduct. *Journal of Management, 17,* 553-569.

LeDoux, J. E. (1996). *The emotional brain: The mysterious underpinnings of emotional life.* New York: Simon & Schuster.

Lee, C. (1985). Increasing performance appraisal effectiveness: Matching task types, appraisal process, and rater training. *Academy of Management Review, 10,* 322-331.

Lehman, W. E. K., & Simpson, D. D. (1992). Employee substance abuse and on-the-job behaviors. *Journal of Applied Psychology, 77,* 309-321.

Lerner, B. (1981). Representative democracy, "men of zeal," and testing legislation. *American Psychologist, 36,* 270-275.

Leung, K., Chiu, W.-H., & Au, Y.-F. (1993). Sympathy and support for industrial actions: A justice analysis. *Journal of Applied Psychology, 78,* 781-787.

Leventhal, G. S. (1976). Fairness in social relationships. In J. W. Thibaut, J. T. Spence, & R. C. Carson (Eds.), *Contemporary topics in social psychology* (pp. 211-240). Morristown, NJ: General Learning Press.

Leventhal, G. S. (1980). What should be done with equity theory? In K. J. Gergen, M. S. Greenberg, & R. H. Willis (Eds.), *Social exchanges: Advances in theory and research* (pp. 27-55). New York: Plenum.

Leventhal, G. S., Karuza, J., & Fry, W. R. (1980). Beyond fairness: A theory of allocation preferences. In G. Mikula (Ed.), *Justice and social interaction* (pp. 167-218). New York: Springer-Verlag.

Lewicki, R. J., & Sheppard, B. H. (1985). Choosing how to intervene: Factors affecting the use of process and outcome control in third party dispute resolution. *Journal of Occupational Behavior, 6,* 49-64.

Lewin, D. (1987). Dispute resolution in the nonunion firm: A theoretical and empirical analysis. *Journal of Conflict Resolution, 31,* 465-502.

Lewin, D. (1990). Grievance procedures in nonunion workplaces: An empirical analysis of usage, dynamics, and outcomes. *Chicago-Kent Law Review, 66,* 823-844.

Lewin, D., & Peterson, R. B. (1988). *The modern grievance procedure in the United States.* New York: Quorum Books.

Lewin, R. (1988). *In the age of mankind.* Washington, DC: Smithsonian Books.

Lewis, M. (1989). *Liar's poker.* New York: Norton.

Liden, R. C., & Mitchell, T. R. (1988). Ingratiatory behaviors in organizational settings. *Academy of Management Review, 13,* 572-587.

Liden, R. C., & Mitchell, T. R. (1989). Ingratiation in the development of leader-member exchanges. In R. A. Giacalone & P. Rosenfeld (Eds.), *Impression management in the organization* (pp. 343-361). Hillsdale, NJ: Lawrence Erlbaum.

Liden, R. C., & Parsons, C. K. (1986). A field study of job applicant interview perceptions, alternative opportunities, and demographic characteristics. *Personnel Psychology, 39,* 109-122.

Lilienfeld, S. O. (1993). Do "honesty" tests really measure honesty? *Skeptical Inquirer, 18,* 32-41.

Lind, E. A. (1995). Justice and authority relations in organizations. In R. Cropanzano & M. K. Kacmar (Eds.), *Organizational politics, justice, and support: Managing the social climate of the workplace* (pp. 83-96). Westport, CT: Quorum Books.

Lind, E. A., Kanfer, R., & Earley, P. C. (1990). Voice, control, and procedural justice: Instrumental and noninstrumental concerns in fairness judgements. *Journal of Personality and Social Psychology, 59,* 952-959.

Lind, E. A., Kulik, C. T., Ambrose, M., & de Vera-Park, M. W. (1993). Individual and corporate dispute resolution: Using procedural fairness as a decision heuristic. *Administrative Science Quarterly, 38,* 224-251.

Lind, E. A., & Lissak, R. I. (1985). Apparent impropriety and procedural fairness judgments. *Journal of Experimental Social Psychology, 21,* 19-29.

Lind, E. A., MacCoun, R. J., Ebener, P. E., Felstiner, W. L. F., Hensler, D. R., Resnik, J., & Tyler, T. R. (1989). *The perception of justice: Tort litigants' views of trials, court-annexed arbitration, and judical settlement conferences.* Santa Monica, CA: RAND.

Lind, E. A., & Tyler, T. R. (1988). *The social psychology of procedural justice.* New York: Plenum.

Locher, A. H., & Teel, K. S. (1977). Performance appraisal—a survey of current practices. *Personnel Journal, 56,* 245-247 & 254.

Longnecker, C. O., Sims, H. P., Jr., & Gioia, D. A. (1987). Behind the mask: The politics of employee appraisal. *Academy of Management Executive, 1,* 183-193.

Lord, R. G., & Foti, R. J. (1986). Schema theories, information processing, and organizational behavior. In H. P. Sims, Jr. & D. A. Gioia (Eds.), *The thinking organization* (pp. 20-48). San Francisco: Jossey-Bass.

Lounsbury, J. W., Bobrow, W., & Jensen, J. B. (1989). Attitudes toward employment testing: Scale development, correlates, and "known-group" validation. *Professional Psychology: Research and Practice, 20,* 340-349.

Lucero, M. A., & Allen, R. E. (1994). Employee benefits: A growing source of psychological contract violations. *Human Resource Management, 3,* 425- 446.

Macan, T. H., Avedon, M. J., Paese, M., & Smith, D. E. (1994). The effects of applicants' reactions to cognitive ability tests and an assessment center. *Personnel Psychology, 47,* 715-738.

MacCoun, R. J., Lind, E. A., Hensler, D. R., Bryant, D. L., & Ebener, P. A. (1988). *Alternative adjudication: An evaluation of the New Jersey automobile arbitration program.* Santa Monica, CA: Institute for Civil Justice, RAND.

Maier, R. A., & Lavrakas, P. J. (1976). Lying behavior and eveluation of lies. *Perceptual and Motor Skills, 42,* 575-658.

Mangione, T. W., & Quinn, R. P. (1977). Job satisfaction, counterproductive behavior, and drug use at work. *Journal of Applied Psychology, 59,* 114-116.

Mark, M. M. (1985). Expectation, procedural justice, and alternative reactions to being deprived of a desired outcome. *Journal of Experimental Social Psychology, 21,* 114-137.

Mark, M. M., & Folger, R. (1984). Responses to relative deprivation: A conceptual framework. In P. Shaver (Ed.), *Review of personality and social psychology* (Vol. 5, pp. 192-218). Beverly Hills, CA: Sage.

Mars, G. (1973). Hotel pilferage: A case study in occupational theft. In P. Rock & M. McIntosh (Eds.), *Deviance and social control* (pp. 209-228). London: Tavistock.

Martin, J., Brickman, P., & Murray, A. (1984). Moral outrage and pragmatism: Explanations for collective action. *Journal of Experimental Social Psychology, 20,* 484-496.

Maslow, A. H. (1954). Motivation and personality. New York: Harper & Row.

McCarthy, J. D., & Zald, M. N. (1977). Resource mobilization and social movement: A partial theory. *American Journal of Sociology, 82,* 1212-1241.

McClelland, G. H., & Judd, C. M. (1993). Statistical difficulties of detecting interactions and moderating effects. *Psychological Bulletin, 114,* 376-390.

McEnrue, M. P. (1989). The perceived fairness of managerial promotion practices. *Human Relations, 42,* 815-827.

McEvoy, G. M., & Buller, P. F. (1987). User acceptance of peer appraisals in an industrial setting. *Personnel Psychology, 40,* 785-797.

McEvoy, G. M., & Cascio, W. F. (1985). Strategies for reducing employee turnover: A meta-analysis. *Journal of Applied Psychology, 70,* 342-353.

McFarlin, D. B., & Sweeney, P. D. (1992). Distributive and procedural justice as predictors of satisfaction with personal and organizational outcomes. *Academy of Management Journal, 35,* 626-637.

McGregor, D. (1957). An uneasy look at performance appraisal. *Harvard Business Review, 34,* 89-94.

McLean-Parks, J., & Smith, F. (in press). Organizational contracting: A "rational" exchange? In J. Halpern & R. Stern (Eds.), *Debating rationality: Non-rational elements of organizational decision making* (pp. 168-210). Ithaca, NY: ILR Press.

Meglino, B. M. (1977, Autumn). The stress-performance controversy. *Michigan State University Business Topics,* pp. 53-59.

Meyer, H. H., Kay, E., & French, J. R. P., Jr. (1965). Split roles in performance appraisal. *Harvard Business Review, 43,* 123-129.

Meyerson, D., Weick, K. E., & Kramer, R. M. (1996). Swift trust and temporary groups. In R. M. Kramer & T. R. Tyler (Eds.), *Trust in organizations* (pp. 166-195). Thousand Oaks, CA: Sage.

Milgram, S. (1974). *Obedience to authority.* New York: Harper & Row.

Milkovich, G. T., & Newman, J. M. (1987). *Compensation* (2nd ed.). Plano, TX: Business Publications.

Moore, R. W., & Stewart, R. M. (1989). Evaluating employee integrity: Moral and methodological problems. *Employee Responsibilities and Rights Journal, 2,* 203-215.

Moore, S., & Sinclair, S. P. (1995). *Sociology.* Lincolnwood, IL: NTC Publishing Group.

Moorman, R. H. (1991). Relationship between organizational justice and organizational citizenship behaviors: Do fairness perceptions influence employee citizenship? *Journal of Applied Psychology, 76,* 845-855.

Moretti, D. M. (1986). The prediction of employee counterproduction through attitude assessment. *Journal of Business and Psychology, 1,* 134-147.

Morris, J. H., Sherman, J. D., & Mansfield, E. P. (1986). Failures to detect moderated effects with ordinary least squares-moderated multiple regression: Some reasons and a remedy. *Psychological Bulletin, 99,* 282-288.

Morrison, E. W., & Robinson, S. L. (1997). When employees feel betrayed: A model of how psychological contract violation develops. *Academy of Management Review, 22,* 226-256.

Motowidlo, S. J., Carter, G. W., Dunnette, M. D., Tippins, N., Werner, S., Burnett, J. R., & Vaughan, M. J. (1992). Studies of the structured behavioral interview. *Journal of Applied Psychology, 77,* 571-587.

Mowday, R. T. (1996). Equity theory predictions of behavior in organizations. In R. M. Steers, L. W. Porter, & G. A. Bigley (Eds.), *Motivation and leadership at work* (pp. 53-71). New York: McGraw-Hill.

Muchinsky, P. M. (1979). The use of reference reports in personnel selection: A review and evaluation. *Journal of Occupational Psychology, 52,* 287-297.

Murnighan, J. K., & Pillutla, M. M. (1995). Fairness versus self interest: Asymmetric moral imperatives in ultimatum bargaining. In R. Kramer & D. Messick (Eds.), *Negotiation in its social context* (pp. 240-267). Thousand Oaks, CA: Sage.

Murphy, K. R. (1986). When your top choice turns you down: Effect of rejected offers on the utility of selection tests. *Psychological Bulletin, 99,* 133-138.

Murphy, K. R., Thornton, G. C., III., & Prue, K. (1991). Influence of job characteristics on the acceptability of employee drug testing. *Journal of Applied Psychology, 76,* 447-453.

Murphy, K. R., Thornton, G. C., III., & Reynolds, D. H. (1990). College students' attitudes toward employee drug testing procedures. *Personnel Psychology, 43,* 615-631.

Murray, H. A. (1938). *Explorations in personality.* New York: Oxford University Press.

Napier, N. K., & Latham, G. P. (1986). Outcome expectancies of people who conduct performance appraisals. *Personnel Psychology, 39,* 827-837.

Nathan, B. P., & Alexander, R. A. (1985). The role of inferential accuracy in performance ratings. *Academy of Management Review, 10,* 109-115.

Nathan, B. P., Mohrman, A. M., Jr., & Milliman, J. (1991). Interpersonal relations as a context for the effects of appraisal interviews on performance and satisfaction: A longitudinal study. *Academy of Management Journal, 34,* 352-369.

Nemeroff, W. F., & Cosentino, J. (1979). Utilizing feedback and goal setting to increase performance appraisal interviewer skills of managers. *Academy of Management Journal, 22,* 566-576.

Nemeroff, W. F., & Wexley, K. N. (1979). An exploration of the relationship between performance feedback interview characteristics and interview outcomes as perceived by managers and subordinates. *Journal of Occupational Psychology, 52,* 25-34.

Neter, E., & Ben-Shakhar, G. (1989). The predictive validity of graphological inferences. *Personality and Individual Differences, 10,* 737-745.

Nevo, B. (1993). Face validity revisited. In B. Nevo & R. S. Jäger (Eds.), *Educational and psychological testing: The test taker's outlook* (pp. 17-28). Toronto, Canada: Hogrefe & Huber.

Noe, R. A., & Steffy, D. B. (1987). The influence of individual characteristics and assessment center evaluation on career exploration behavior and job involvement. *Journal of Vocational Behavior, 30,* 187-202.

Normand, J., Salyards, S. D., & Mahoney, J. J. (1990). An evaluation of preemployment drug testing. *Journal of Applied Psychology, 75,* 629-639.

Norsworthy, J. R., & Zabala, C. A. (1985). Worker attitudes, worker behavior, and productivity in the U.S. automoble industry, 1959-1976. *Industrial and Labor Relations Review, 38,* 544-557.

Notz, W. W., & Starke, F. A. (1987). Arbitration and distributive justice: Equity or equality? *Journal of Applied Psychology, 72,* 359-365.

O'Bannon, R., Goldringer, L., & Appleby, G. (1989). *Honesty and integrity testing.* Atlanta, GA: Applied Information Services.

Ohbuchi, K., Kameda, M., & Agarie, N. (1989). Apology as aggression control: Its role in mediating appraisal of and response to harm. *Journal of Personality and Social Psychology, 56,* 219-227.

Olson, J. M., & Roese, N. J. (1995). The perceived funniness of humorous stimuli. *Personality and Social Psychology Bulletin, 21,* 908-931.

Olson-Buchanan, J. B. (1996a). *To grieve or not to grieve: Factors related to voicing discontent in an organizational simulation.* Unpublished manuscript.

Olson-Buchanan, J. B. (1996b). Voicing discontent: What happens to the grievance filer after the grievance? *Journal of Applied Psychology, 81,* 52-63.

Ones, D. S., Viswesvaran, C., & Schmidt, F. L. (1993). Comprehensive meta-analysis of integrity test validities: Findings and implications for personnel selection and theories of job performance. *Journal of Applied Psychology, 78,* 679-703.

Organ, D. W. (1988). *Organizational citizenship behavior.* Lexington, MA: Lexington Books.

Owens, W. A. (1976). Background data. In M. D. Dunnette (Ed.), *Handbook of industrial and organizational psychology* (1st ed., pp. 609-644). Chicago: Rand McNally.

Paese, P. W., Lind, E. A., & Kanfer, R. (1988). Procedural fairness and work group responses to performance evaluation systems. *Social Justice Research, 2,* 193-205.

Painter, N. I. (1987). *Standing at Armageddon: The United States, 1877-1919.* New York: Norton.

Parducci, A. (1965). Category judgment: A range-frequency model. *Psychological Review, 72,* 407-418.

Pastore, N. (1950). A neglected factor in the frustration-aggression hypothesis: A comment. *Journal of Psychology, 29,* 271-279.

Patz, A. L. (1975). Performance appraisal: Useful but still resisted. *Harvard Business Review, 53,* 74-80.

Pearce, J. L., & Porter, L. W. (1986). Employee responses to formal performance appraisal feedback. *Journal of Applied Psychology, 71,* 211-218.

Perelman, C. (1967). *Justice.* New York: Random House.

Peters, L. H., O'Connor, E. J., & Eulberg, J. R. (1985). Situational constraints: Sources, consequences, and future considerations. In K. M. Rowland & G. R. Ferris (Eds.), *Research in personnel and human resources management* (pp. 79-113). Greenwich, CT: JAI.

Pfeffer, J. (1981). *Power in organizations.* Cambridge, MA: Ballinger.

Pfeffer, J., & Davis-Blake, A. (1992). Salary dispersion, location in the salary distribution, and turnover among college administrators. *Industrial and Labor Relations Review, 45,* 753-763.

Pfeffer, J., & Langton, N. (1993). The effects of wage dispersion on satisfaction, productivity, and working collaboratively: Evidence from college and university faculty. *Administrative Science Quarterly, 38,* 382-407.

Porter, L. W., Lawler, E. E., III, & Hackman, J. R. (1975). *Behavior in organizations.* New York: McGraw-Hill.

Premack, S. L., & Wanous, J. P. (1985). A meta-analysis of realistic job preview experiments. *Journal of Applied Psychology, 70,* 709-719.

Preskitt, S. K., & Olson-Buchanan, J. B. (1996, April). *Impact of interactional justice on fairness in organizational conflict resolution.* Paper presented at the annual meeting of the Society of Industrial and Organizational Psychology, San Diego, CA.

Prince, J. B., & Lawler, E. E., III. (1986). Does salary discussion hurt the developmental performance appraisal? *Organizational Behavior and Human Decision Processes, 37,* 357-375.

Rahim, M. A. (1983). A measure of styles of handling interpersonal conflict. *Academy of Management Journal, 26,* 368-376.

Ralston, D. A., & Elsass, P. M. (1989). Ingratiation and impression management in the organization. In R. A. Giacalone & P. Rosenfeld (Eds.), *Impression management in the organization* (pp. 235-249). Hillsdale, NJ: Lawrence Erlbaum.

Randall, D. M., & Gibson, A. M. (1990). Methodology in business ethics research: A review and critical assessment. *Journal of Business Ethics, 9,* 457-471.

Rasinski, K. A. (1992). Preference for decision control in organizational decision making. *Social Justice Research, 5,* 343-357.

Rawls, J. (1971). *A theory of justice.* Cambridge, MA: Harvard University Press.

Reilly, R. R., & Chao, G. T. (1982). Validity and fairness of some alternative employee selection procedures. *Personnel Psychology, 35,* 1-61.

Robbins, S. P. (1974). *Managing organizational conflict: A nontraditional approach.* Englewood Cliffs, NJ: Prentice Hall.

Robbins, S. P. (1978, Winter). "Conflict management" and "conflict resolution" are not synonymous terms. *California Management Review,* pp. 67-75.

Robbins, S. P. (1987). *Organization theory: Structure, design, and applications* (2nd ed.). Englewood Cliffs, NJ: Prentice Hall.

Roberson, L., Torkel, S., Korsgaard, A., Klein, D., Diddams, M., & Cayer, M. (1993). Self-appraisal and perceptions of the appraisal discussion: A field experiment. *Journal of Organizational Behavior, 14,* 129-142.

Robertson, I. T., & Downs, S. (1989). Work-sample tests of trainability: A meta-analysis. *Journal of Applied Psychology, 74,* 402-410.

Robertson, I. T., Iles, P. A., Gratton, L., & Shapley, D. (1991). The impact of personnel selection and assessment methods on candidates. *Human Relations, 44,* 963-982.

Robertson, I. T., & Kandola, R. S. (1982). Work sample tests: Validity, adverse impact and applicant reactions. *Journal of Occupational Psychology, 55,* 171-183.

Robertson, I. T., & Makin, P. J. (1986). Management selection in Britain: A survey and critique. *Journal of Occupational Psychology, 59,* 45-57.

Robinson, S. L., & Bennett, R. J. (1995). A typology of deviant workplace behaviors: A multidimensional scaling study. *Academy of Management Journal, 38,* 555-572.

Robinson, S. L., Kraatz, M. S., & Rousseau, D. M. (1994). Changing obligations and the psychological contract: A longitudinal study. *Academy of Management Journal, 37,* 137-152.

Rodgers, R., & Hunter, J. E. (1991). Impact of management by objectives on organizational productivity. *Journal of Applied Psychology, 77,* 322-336.

Roese, N. J. (1997). Counterfactual thinking. *Psychological Bulletin, 121,* 133-148.

Roese, N. J., & Olson, J. M. (1995). *What might have been: The social psychology of counterfactual thinking.* Mahwah, NJ: Lawrence Erlbaum.

Rokeach, M. (1973). *The nature of human values.* New York: Free Press.

Rosse, J. G., Miller, J. L., & Ringer, R. C. (1996). The deterrent value of drug and integrity testing. *Journal of Business and Psychology, 5,* 431-445

Rosse, J. G., Miller, J. L., & Stecher, M. D. (1994). A field study of job applicants' reactions to personality and cognitive ability testing. *Journal of Applied Psychology, 79,* 987-992.

Rosse, J. G., Ringer, R. C., & Miller, J. L. (1996). Personality and drug testing: An exploration of perceived fairness of alternatives to urinalysis. *Journal of Business and Psychology, 5,* 459-475.

Roth, N. L., Sitkin, S. B., & House, A. (1994). Stigma as a determinant of legalization. In S. B. Sitkin & R. J. Bies (Eds.), *The legalistic organization* (pp. 137-168). Thousand Oaks, CA: Sage.

Rousseau, D. M., & McLean-Parks, J. M. (1993). The contract of individuals and organizations. In L. L. Cummings & B. M. Staw (Eds.), *Research in organizational behavior* (Vol. 15, pp. 1-43). Greenwich, CT: JAI.

Rubin, J. Z. (1980). Experimental research on third-party intervention in conflict: Toward some generalizations. *Psychological Bulletin, 87,* 379-391.

Rubin, J. Z., Pruitt, D. G., & Kim, S. H. (1994). *Social conflict: Escalation, stalemate, and settlement* (2nd ed.). New York: McGraw-Hill.

Russell, J. S., & Goode, D. L. (1988). An analysis of managers' reactions to their own performance appraisal feedback. *Journal of Applied Psychology, 73,* 63-67.

Ryan, A. M., & Sackett, P. R. (1987). Pre-employment honesty testing: Fakability, reactions of test takers, and company image. *Journal of Business and Psychology, 1,* 248-256.

Rynes, S. L. (1993). When recruitment fails to attract: Individual expectations meet organizational realities in recruitment. In H. Schuler, J. L. Farr, & M. Smith (Eds.), *Personnel selection and assessment: Individual and organizational perspectives* (pp. 27-40). Hillsdale, NJ: Lawrence Erlbaum.

Rynes, S. L., Bretz, R. D., Jr., & Gerhart, B. (1991). The importance of recruitment in job choice: A different way of looking. *Personnel Psychology, 44,* 487-521.

Rynes, S. L., & Connerley, M. L. (1993). Applicant reactions to alternative selection procedures. *Journal of Business and Psychology, 7,* 261-277.

Sackett, P., Burris, L., & Callahan, C. (1989). Integrity testing for personnel selection: An update. *Personnel Psychology, 42,* 491-529.

Schaubroeck, J., May, D. R, & Brown, F. W. (1994). Procedural justice explanations and employee reactions to economic hardship: A field experiment. *Journal of Applied Psychology, 79,* 455-460.

Schlenker, B. R. (1980). *Impression management: The self-concept, social identity, and interpersonal relations.* Monterey, CA: Brooks/Cole.

Schlenker, B. R. (1997). Personal responsibility: Applications of the triangle model. In L. L. Cummings & B. M. Staw (Eds.), *Research in organizational behavior* (pp. 241-301). Greenwich, CT: JAI.

Schlenker, B. R., Britt, T. W., Pennington, J. W., Murphy, R., & Doherty, K. J. (1994). The triangle model of responsibility. *Psychological Review, 101,* 632-652.

Schmidt, F. L. (1988). The problem of group differences in ability test scores in employment selection. *Journal of Vocational Behavior, 33,* 272-292.

Schmidt, F. L., Greenthal, A. L., Hunter, J. E., Berner, J. G., & Seaton, F. W. (1977). Job sample vs. paper-and-pencil trades and technical tests: Adverse impact and examinee attitudes. *Personnel Psychology, 30,* 187-197.

Schmitt, N. (1993). Group composition, gender, and race effects on assessment center ratings. In H. Schuler, J. L. Farr, & M. Smith (Eds.), *Personnel selection and assessment: Individual and organizational perspectives* (pp. 315-332). Hillsdale, NJ: Lawrence Erlbaum.

Schmitt, N., & Coyle, B. W. (1976). Applicant decisions in the employment interview. *Journal of Applied Psychology, 61,* 184-192.

Schmitt, N., & Gilliland, S. W. (1992). Beyond differential prediction: Fairness in selection. In D. M. Saunders (Ed.), *New approaches to employee management: Fairness in employee selection* (Vol. 1, pp. 21-46). Greenwich, CT: JAI.

Schmitt, N., Gilliland, S. W., Landis, R. S., & Devine, D. (1993). Computer-based testing applied to selection of secretarial applicants. *Personnel Psychology, 46,* 149-165.

Schmitt, N., Gooding, R. Z., Noe, R. A., & Kirsch, M. (1984). Metaanalysis of validity studies published between 1964 and 1982 and the investigation of study characteristics. *Personnel Psychology, 37,* 407-422.

Schönbach, P. (1990). *Account episodes: The management and escalation of conflict.* Cambridge, UK: Cambridge University Press.

Schoorman, F. D., & Champagne, M. V. (1994). Managers as informal third parties: The impact of supervisor-subordinate relationships on interventions. *Employee Responsibilities and Rights Journal, 7,* 73-84.

Schuler, H. (1993a). Is there a dilemma between validity and acceptance in the employment interview? In B. Nevo & R. S. Jäger (Eds.), *Educational and psychological testing: The test taker's outlook* (pp. 239-250). Toronto, Canada: Hogrefe & Huber.

Schuler, H. (1993b). Social validity of selection situations: A concept and some empirical results. In H. Schuler, J. L. Farr, & M. Smith (Eds.), *Personnel selection and assessment: Individual and organizational perspectives* (pp. 11-26). Hillsdale, NJ: Lawrence Erlbaum.

Schuler, H., Farr, J. L., & Smith, M. (1993). The individual and organizational sides of personnel selection and assessment. In H. Schuler, J. L. Farr, & M. Smith (Eds.), *Personnel selection and assessment: Individual and organizational perspectives* (pp. 1-5). Hillsdale, NJ: Lawrence Erlbaum.

Schuler, H., & Fruhner, R. (1993). Effects of assessment center participation on self-esteem and on evaluation of the selection situation. In H. Schuler, J. L. Farr, & M. Smith (Eds.), *Personnel selection and assessment: Individual and organizational perspectives* (pp. 109-124). Hillsdale, NJ: Lawrence Erlbaum.

Schwarzwald, J., Koslowsky, M., & Shalit, B. (1992). A field study of employees' attitudes and behaviors after promotion decisions. *Journal of Applied Psychology, 77,* 511-514.

Scott, M. B., & Lyman, S. M. (1968). Accounts. *American Sociological Review, 23,* 46-62.

Seymour, R. T. (1988). Why plaintiffs' counsel challenge tests, and how they can successfully challenge the theory of "validity generalization." *Journal of Vocational Behavior, 33,* 331-364.

Shapiro, D. L. (1991). The effects of explanations on negative reactions to deceit. *Administrative Science Quarterly, 36,* 614-630.

Shapiro, D. L. (1993). Reconciling theoretical differences among procedural justice researchers by re-evaluating what it means to have one's view "considered": Implications for third-party managers. In R. Cropanzano (Ed.), *Justice in the workplace: Approaching fairness in human resource management* (pp. 51-78). Hillsdale, NJ: Lawrence Erlbaum.

Shapiro, D. L., & Brett, J. M. (1993). Comparing three processes underlying judgments of procedural justice: A field study of mediation and arbitration. *Journal of Personality and Social Psychology, 65,* 1167-1177.

Shapiro, D. L., Buttner, E. H., & Barry, B. (1994). Explanations for rejection decisions: What factors enhance their perceived adequacy and moderate their enhancement of justice perceptions? *Organizational Behavior and Human Decision Processes, 58,* 346-368.

Shapiro, D. L., & Rosen, B. (1994). An investigation of managerial interventions in employee disputes. *Employee Responsibilities and Rights Journal, 7,* 37-51.

Sheppard, B. H. (1983). Managers as inquisitors: Some lessons from the law. In M. H. Bazerman & R. J. Lewicki (Eds.), *Negotiation in organizations* (pp. 193-213). Beverly Hills, CA: Sage.

Sheppard, B. H. (1984). Third party conflict intervention: A procedural framework. In B. M. Staw & L. L. Cummings (Eds.), *Research in organizational behavior* (Vol. 6, pp. 141-191). Greenwich, CT: JAI.

Sheppard, B. H. (1985). Justice is no simple matter: Case for elaborating our model of procedural fairness. *Journal of Personality and Social Psychology, 49,* 953-962.

Sheppard, B. H., Blumenfeld-Jones, K., Minton, W. J., & Hyder, E. (1994). Informal conflict intervention: Advice and dissent. *Employee Responsibilities and Rights Journal, 7,* 53-72.

Sheppard, B. H., Lewicki, R. J., & Minton, J. W. (1992). *Organizational justice: The search for fairness in the workplace.* New York: Macmillan.

Sheppard, B. H., Saunders, D. M., & Minton, J. W. (1988). Procedural justice from the third party perspective. *Journal of Personality and Social Psychology, 54,* 629-637.

Sheppard, J. A., & Arkin, R. M. (1991). Behavioral other-enhancement: Strategically obscuring the link between performance and evaluation. *Journal of Personality and Social Psychology, 60,* 79-88.

Silverman, S. B., & Wexley, K. N. (1984). Reactions of employees to performance appraisal interviews as a function of their participation in rating scale development. *Personnel Psychology, 37,* 703-710.

Simon, H. A. (1983). A mechanism for social selection and successful altruism. *Science, 250,* 1665-1668.

Singer, M. (1993). *Fairness in personnel selection.* Aldershot, New Zealand: Avebury.

Singer, P. (1981). The expanding circle: Ethics and sociobiology. New York: Farrar, Straus, & Giroux.

Sitkin, S. B., & Bies, R. J. (1993a). The legalistic organization: Definitions, dimensions, and dilemmas. *Organization Science, 4,* 345-351.

Sitkin, S. B., & Bies, R. J. (1993b). Social accounts in conflict situations: Using explanations to manage conflict. *Human Relations, 46,* 349-370.

Sitkin, S. B., Sutcliffe, K. M., & Reed, G. L. (1993). Prescriptions for justice: Using social accounts to legitimate the exercise of professional control. *Social Justice Research, 6,* 87-111.

Skarlicki, D., & Folger, R. (1997). Retaliation for perceived unfair treatment: Examining the roles of procedural and interactional justice. *Journal of Applied Psychology, 82,* 434-443.

Smither, J. W., Reilly, R. R., Millsap, R. E., Pearlman, K., & Stoffey, R. W. (1993). Applicant reactions to selection procedures. *Personnel Psychology, 46,* 49-76.

Spector, P. E. (1975). Relationships of organizational frustration with reported behavioral reactions of employees. *Journal of Applied Psychology, 60,* 635-637.

Spector, P. E. (1997). The role of frustration in antisocial behavior at work. In R. A. Giacalone & J. Greenberg (Eds.), *Antisocial behavior in organizations* (pp. 1-36). Thousand Oaks, CA: Sage.

Steel, M., Balinsky, B., & Lang, H. (1945). A study on the use of a work sample. *Journal of Applied Psychology, 29,* 14-21.

Steiner, D. D., & Gilliland, S. W. (1996). Fairness reactions to personnel selection techniques in France and the United States. *Journal of Applied Psychology, 81,* 134-141.

Stepina, L. P., & Perrewe, P. L. (1991). The stability of comparative referent choice and feelings of inequity: A longitudinal field study. *Journal of Organizational Behavior, 12,* 185-200.

Stoffey, R. W., Millsap, R. E., Smither, J. W., & Reilly, R. R. (1991, April). *The influence of selection procedures on attitudes about the organization and job pursuit intentions.* In the "Perceived validity of selection procedures: Implications for organizations" symposium conducted at the annual conference of the Society for Industrial and Organizational Psychology, Saint Louis, MO.

Stone, D. L., & Bommer, W. (1990, August). *Effects of drug testing selection method and justification provided for the test on reactions to drug testing.* Paper presented at the annual meeting of the Academy of Management, San Francisco, CA.

Stone, D. L., & Bowden, C. (1989). Effects of job applicant drug testing practices on reactions to drug testing. In F. Hoy (Ed.), *Academy of Management Best Paper Proceedings* (pp. 190-195).

Stone, D. L., Gueutal, H. G., & McIntosh, B. (1984). The effects of feedback sequence and expertise of the rater on perceived feedback accuracy. *Personnel Psychology, 37,* 487-506.

Stone, D. L., & Kotch, D. A. (1989). Individuals' attitudes toward organizational drug testing policies and practices. *Journal of Applied Psychology, 74,* 518-521.

Stone, E. F., O'Brien, T. E., & Bommer, W. (1989, June). *Individuals' reactions to job applicant drug testing practices.* Paper presented at the Annual Conference of the American Psychological Society, Washington, DC.

Stone, E. F., & Stone, D. L. (1990). Privacy in organizations: Theoretical issues, research findings, and protection mechanisms. In G. R. Ferris & K. M. Rowland (Eds.), *Research in personnel and human resource management* (Vol. 8, pp. 349-411). Greenwich, CT: JAI.

Stone, E. F., Stone, D. L., & Hyatt, D. (1989, April). *Personnel selection procedures and invasion of privacy*. Paper presented at the annual meeting of the Society for Industrial and Organizational Psychology, Boston.

Stone, E. F., Stone, D. L., & Pollack, M. (1990). *The effects of precipitation events and coerciveness of the procedures on individuals' reactions to drug testing*. Unpublished manuscript.

Storms, P. L. & Spector, P. E. (1987). Relationships of organizational frustration with reported behavioral reactions: The moderating effect of locus of control. *Journal of Occupational Psychology, 60,* 227-234.

Stouffer, S., Lumsdaine, M., Williams, R., Smith, M., Janis, I., Starr, S., & Cottrell, L. (1949). *The American soldier*. Princeton, NJ: Princeton University Press.

Sweeney, P. D., & McFarlin, D. B. (1993). Workers' evaluations of the "ends" and the "means": An examination of four models of distributive and procedural justice. *Organizational Behavior and Human Decision Processes, 55,* 23-40.

Sweeney, P. D., McFarlin, D. B, & Inderrieden, E. J. (1990). Using relative deprivation theory to explain satisfaction with income and pay level: A multistudy examination. *Academy of Management Journal, 33,* 423-436.

Talbot, R., Cooper, C., & Barrow, S. (1992). Creativity and stress. *Creativity and Innovation Management, 1,* 183-193.

Taylor, D. M., Moghaddam, F. M., Gamble, I., & Zellerer, E. (1987). Disadvantaged group responses to perceived inequality: From passive acceptance to collective action. *Journal of Social Psychology, 127,* 259-272.

Taylor, M. S., Tracy, K. B., Renard, M. K., Harrison, J. K., & Carroll, S. J. (1995). Due process in performance appraisal: A quasi-experiment in procedural justice. *Administrative Science Quarterly, 40,* 495-523.

Taylor, S. E. (1991). Asymmetrical effects of positive and negative events: The mobilization-minimization hypothesis. *Psychological Bulletin, 110,* 67-85.

Teel, K. S., & Dubois, H. (1983). Participants' reactions to assessment center. *Personnel Administrator, March,* 85-91.

Tepper, B. J., & Braun, C. K. (1995). Does the experience of organizational justice mitigate the invasion of privacy engendered by random drug testing? An empirical investigation. *Basic and Applied Social Psychology, 16,* 211-225.

Tett, R. P., Jackson, D. N., & Rothstein, M. (1991). Personality measures as predictors of job performance: A meta-analysis. *Personnel Psychology, 44,* 703-742.

Thibaut, J., & Kelley, H. H. (1959). *The social psychology of groups*. New York: Wiley.

Thibaut, J. W., & Walker, L. (1975). *Procedural justice: A psychological perspective*. Hillsdale, NJ: Lawrence Erlbaum.

Thibaut, J. W., & Walker, L. (1978). A theory of procedure. *California Law Review, 66,* 541-566.

Thomas, K. W. (1993). Conflict and negotiation process in organizations. In M. D. Dunnette & L. M. Hough (Eds.), *Handbook of industrial and organizational psychology* (2nd ed., Vol. 3, pp. 651-717). Palo Alto, CA: Consulting Psychologists Press.

Thomas, K. W., & Schmidt, W. H. (1976). A survey of managerial interests with respect to conflict. *Academy of Management Journal, 19,* 315-318.

Thorndike, R. L. (1949). *Personnel selection: Test and measurement techniques*. New York: John Wiley.

Thornton, G. C., III. (1992). *Assessment centers in human resource management*. Reading, MA: Addison-Wesley.

Thornton, G. C., III. (1993). The effect of selection practices on applicants' perceptions of organizational characteristics. In H. Schuler, J. L. Farr, & M. Smith (Eds.), *Personnel selection and assessment: Individual and organizational perspectives* (pp. 57-69). Hillsdale, NJ: Lawrence Erlbaum.

Thornton, G. C., III., & Byham, W. C. (1982). *Assessment centers and managerial performance.* New York: Academic Press.

Thornton, G. C., III, & Cleveland, J. C. (1990). Developing managerial talent through simulation. *American Psychologist, 45,* 190-199.

Tripp, T. M., & Bies, R. J. (1997). What's good about revenge? The avenger's perspective. In R. J. Lewicki, R. J. Bies, & B. H. Sheppard (Eds.), *Research on negotiation in organizations* (Vol. 6, pp. 145-160). Greenwich, CT: JAI.

Tripp, T. M., & Bies, R. J. (in press). *Seeking revenge in organizations: An exploration into the hearts and minds of avengers.* Unpublished manuscript.

Tucker, J. (1993). Everyday forms of employee resistance. *Sociological Forum, 8,* 25-45.

Tyler, T. R. (1984). The role of perceived injustice in defendants' evaluations of their courtroom experience. *Law and Society Review, 18,* 51-74.

Tyler, T. R. (1987). Conditions leading to value expressive effect in judgments of procedural justice: A test of four models. *Journal of Personality and Social Psychology, 52,* 333-344.

Tyler, T. R. (1988). What is procedural justice? Criteria used by citizens to assess the fairness of legal procedures. *Law and Society Review, 22,* 301-355.

Tyler, T. R. (1989). The quality of dispute resolution processes and outcomes: Measurement problems and possibilities. *Denver University Law Review, 66,* 419-436.

Tyler, T. R. (1990). *Why people obey the law: Procedural justice, legitimacy, and compliance.* New Haven, CT: Yale University Press.

Tyler, T. R. (1994). Psychological models of the justice motive: Antecedents of distributive and procedural justice. *Journal of Personality and Social Psychology, 67,* 850-863.

Tyler, T. R., & Bies, R. J. (1990). Beyond formal procedures: The interpersonal context of procedural justice. In J. S. Carroll (Ed.), *Applied social psychology and organizational settings* (pp. 77-98). Hillsdale, NJ: Lawrence Erlbaum.

Tyler, T. R., & Caine, A. (1981). The role of distributional and procedural fairness in the endorsement of formal leaders. *Journal of Personality and Social Psychology, 41,* 642-655.

Tyler, T. R., & Degoey, P. (1995). Collective restraint in social dilemmas: Procedural justice and social identification effects on support for authorities. *Journal of Personality and Social Psychology, 69,* 482-497.

Tyler, T. R., & Degoey, P. (1996). Trust in organizational authorities: The influence of motive attributions on willingness to accept decisions. In R. M. Kramer & T. R. Tyler (Eds.), *Trust in organizations: Frontiers of theory and research* (pp. 331-356). Thousand Oaks, CA: Sage.

Tyler, T. R., & Folger, R. (1980). Distributional and procedural aspects of satisfaction with citizen-police encounters. *Basic and Applied Social Psychology, 1,* 281-292.

Tyler, T. R., & Lind, E. A. (1992). A relational model of authority in groups. In M. P. Zanna (Ed.), *Advances in experimental social psychology* (Vol. 25, pp. 115-191). San Diego, CA: Academic Press.

Tyler, T. R., Rasinski, K., & Spodick, N. (1985). Influence of voice and satisfaction with leaders: Exploring the meaning of process control. *Journal of Personality and Social Psychology, 42,* 333-344.

Tyler, T. R., & Smith, H. J. (in press). Social justice and social movements. In D. Gilbert, S. T. Fiske, & G. Lindzey (Eds.), *Handbook of social psychology* (4th ed.). New York: McGraw-Hill.

Ury, W. L., Brett, J. M., & Goldberg, S. B. (1989). *Getting disputes resolved: Designing systems to cut the costs of conflict.* San Francisco: Jossey-Bass.

Van den Bos, K. (1996). *Procedural justice and conflict.* Unpublished doctoral dissertation, University of Leiden, Netherlands.

Van den Bos, K., Lind, E. A., Vermunt, R., & Wilke, H. A. M. (1997). How do I judge my outcome when I do not know the outcome of others? The psychology of the fair process effect. *Journal of Personality and Social Psychology, 72,* 1034-1046.

Van den Bos, K., Vermunt, R., & Wilke, H. A. M. (1996). The consistency rule and the voice effect: The influence of expectations in procedural fairness judgments and performance. *European Journal of Social Psychology, 26,* 411-428.

Van den Bos, K., Vermunt, R., & Wilke, H. A. M. (1997). Procedural and distributive justice: What is fair depends more on what comes first than on what comes next. *Journal of Personality and Social Psychology, 72,* 95-104.

Velasquez, M. J. (1982). *Business ethics: Concepts and cases.* Englewood Cliffs, NJ: Prentice Hall.

Villanova, P., & Bernardin, H. J. (1989). Impression management in the context of performance appraisal. In R. A. Giacalone & P. Rosenfeld (Eds.), *Impression management in the organization.* Hillsdale, NJ: Lawrence Erlbaum.

Vroom, V. H. (1969). Industrial social psychology. In G. Lindzey & E. Aronson (Eds.), *The handbook of social psychology* (Vol. 5, pp. 196-268). Reading, MA: Addison-Wesley.

Wall, J. A., Jr. (1981). Mediation: An analysis, review, and proposed research. *Journal of Conflict Resolution, 25,* 157-180.

Wall, J. A., & Callister, R. R. (1995). Conflict and its management. *Journal of Management, 21,* 515-558.

Walster, E., Walster, G. W., & Berscheid, E. (1978). *Equity: Theory and research.* Boston: Allyn & Bacon.

Wanous, J. P. (1993). Newcomer orientation programs that facilitate organizational entry. In H. Schuler, J. L. Farr, & M. Smith (Eds.), *Personnel selection and assessment: Individual and organizational perspectives* (pp. 125-139). Hillsdale, NJ: Lawrence Erlbaum.

Waterman, A. S. (1988). On the uses of psychological theory and research in the process of ethical inquiry. *Psychological Bulletin, 103,* 283-298.

Watson, D., Clark, L. A., & Tellegen, A. (1988). Development and validation of brief measures of positive and negative affect: The PANAS scales. *Journal of Personality and Social Psychology, 54,* 1063-1070.

Watson, D., Pennebaker, J., & Folger, R. (1986). Beyond negative affectivity: Measuring stress and satisfaction in the workplace. *Journal of Organizational Behavior Management, 8*(2), 141-157.

Wayne, S. J., & Ferris, G. R. (1990). Influence tactics, affect, and exchange quality in supervisor-subordinate interactions: A laboratory experiment and field study. *Journal of Applied Psychology, 75,* 487-499.

Wayne, S. J., & Kacmar, K. M. (1991). The effects of impression management on the performance appraisal task. *Organizational Behavior and Human Decision Processes, 48,* 70-88.

Wayne, S. J., & Liden, R. C. (1995). Effects of impression management on performance ratings: A longitudinal study. *Academy of Management Journal, 38,* 232-260.

Weeks, D. (1992). *The eight essential steps to conflict resolution: Preserving relationships at work, at home, and in the community.* New York: Putnam.

Weick, K. E. (1964). Reduction of cognitive dissonance through task enhancement and effort expenditure. *Journal of Abnormal and Social Psychology, 68,* 533-539.

Weiss, H. M., & Cropanzano, R. (1996). An affective events approach to job satisfaction. In B. M. Staw & L. L. Cummings (Eds.), *Research in organizational behavior* (Vol. 18, pp. 1-74). Greenwich, CT: JAI.

Welton, G. L., & Pruitt, D. G. (1987). The mediation process: The effect of mediator bias and disputant power. *Personality and Social Psychology Bulletin, 13,* 123-133.

Westin, A. F. (1978). Privacy and personnel records: A look at employee attitudes. *The Civil Liberties Review, 4*(5), 28-34.

Wexley, K. M., & Gier, J. A. (1989). Ceilings in the reliability and validity of performance ratings: The case of expert raters. *Academy of Management Journal, 32,* 213-222.

Wexley, K. M., Singh, J. P., & Yukl, G. A. (1973). Subordinate personality as a moderator of the effects of participation in three types of appraisal interviews. *Journal of Applied Psychology, 58,* 54-59.

Wigdor, A. K., & Sackett, P. R. (1993). Employment testing and public policy: The case of the General Aptitude Test Battery. In H. Schuler, J. L. Farr, & M. Smith (Eds.), *Personnel selection and assessment: Individual and organizational perspectives* (pp. 183-204). Hillsdale, NJ: Lawrence Erlbaum.

Wilson, E. O. (1978). *On human nature.* Cambridge, MA: Harvard University Press.

Wilson, J. Q. (1993). *The moral sense.* New York: Free Press.

Wittmer, J. M., Carnevale, P. J., & Walker, M. E. (1991). General alignment and over support in biased mediation. *Journal of Conflict Resolution, 35,* 594-610.

Wright, R. (1994). *The moral animal.* New York: Pantheon.

Youngblood, S. A., Trevino, L. K., & Favia, M. (1992). Reactions to unjust dismissal and third-party dispute resolution: A justice framework. *Employee Responsibilities and Rights Journal, 5,* 283-307.

Zajonc, R. B. (1968). Cognitive theories in social psychology. In G. Lindzey & E. Aronson (Eds.), *The handbook of social psychology* (Vol. 1, pp. 320-411). Reading, MA: Addison-Wesley.

Zedeck, S. (1971). Problem with the use of "moderator" variables. *Psychological Bulletin, 76,* 295-310.

Zohar, D. (1995). The justice perspective of job stress. *Journal of Organizational Behavior, 16,* 487-495.

Zwerling, C., Ryan, J., & Orav, E. J. (1990). The efficacy of preemployment drug screening for marijuana and cocaine in predicting employment outcome. *Journal of the American Medical Association, 264,* 2639-2643.

Author Index

Subject Index

About the Authors

Russell Cropanzano is Associate Professor of Industrial/Organizational Psychology at Colorado State University. He received his PhD in I/O Psychology from Purdue University in 1988. He is a member of both the Academy of Management and the Society for Industrial/Organizational Psychology and serves on the editorial board for the *Journal of Applied Psychology*. He has published more than 35 scholarly articles and chapters, which have appeared in such places as the *Journal of Applied Psychology, Journal of Organizational Behavior,* and *Social Justice Research*. In addition, he has edited two books: *Justice in the Workplace* and *Organizational Politics, Justice, and Support*. He is a coauthor of the forthcoming book *Advances in Organizational Justice* and of *Justice in the Workplace (Vol. 2)*. He has lectured widely, delivering more than 25 talks. He has also been active internationally, having presented papers in Australia, Canada, New Zealand, and The Netherlands.

Robert Folger is Freeman Professor of Doctoral Studies and Research, and Professor of Organizational Behavior, at the A. B. Freeman School of Business, Tulane University. He received his PhD at the University of North Carolina, Chapel Hill. His research interests include work motivation, fairness, performance appraisal, compensation, layoffs, workplace aggression, and ethics. His honors and awards include the New Concept Award from the Organizational Behavior Division of the Academy of Management for his work on reactions to perceived unfair treatment. He has also served as a consultant with the U.S. Department of Justice, the U.S. Postal Service, the IRS, and with companies in various industries.

He has authored more than 75 publications, including articles in the *Academy of Management Journal, Organizational Behavior and Human Performance, Journal of Applied Psychology, Research on Negotiations in Organizations,* and *Research in Organizational Behavior.* He edited a book on *The Sense of Injustice* and coauthored a book on *Controversial Issues in Social Research Methods.*